Palgrave Studies in Islamic Banking, Finance, and Economics

The aim of this series is to explore the various disciplines and sub-disciplines of Islamic banking, finance and economics through the lens of theoretical, practical, and empirical research. Monographs and edited collections in this series will focus on key developments in the Islamic financial industry as well as relevant contributions made to moral economy, innovations in instruments, regulatory and supervisory issues, risk management, insurance, and asset management. The scope of these books will set this series apart from the competition by offering in-depth critical analyses of conceptual, institutional, operational, and instrumental aspects of this emerging field. This series is expected to attract focused theoretical studies, in-depth surveys of current practices, trends, and standards, and cutting-edge empirical research.

More information about this series at
http://www.palgrave.com/gp/series/14618

Salman Syed Ali
Editor

Towards a Maqāṣid al-Sharīʿah Index of Socio-Economic Development

Theory and Application

palgrave
macmillan

Editor
Salman Syed Ali
Islamic Development Bank
Jeddah, Saudi Arabia

ISSN 2662-5121 ISSN 2662-513X (electronic)
Palgrave Studies in Islamic Banking, Finance, and Economics
ISBN 978-3-030-12792-3 ISBN 978-3-030-12793-0 (eBook)
https://doi.org/10.1007/978-3-030-12793-0

This Palgrave Macmillan imprint is published by the registered company Springer Nature Switzerland AG
The registered company address is: Gewerbestrasse 11, 6330 Cham, Switzerland

Foreword

Islamic Research and Training Institute (IRTI) is committed to contribute to the socio-economic development of IsDB Member Countries. Among other initiatives, IRTI formed a research cluster to tackle the issues of socio-economic development in the light of *Maqāṣid* al-Sharīʿah, i.e. the objectives of Islamic law. Part of this effort is to devise ways for the measurement of socio-economic development through the lens of *Maqāṣid* al-Sharīʿah. This approach projects socio-economic development into five dimensions: protection of faith, life, progeny, intellect and wealth. Development, therefore, is a multidimensional goal that cannot be judged by a single number or index.

The present book is an attempt to provide alternative and more comprehensive measures of development in two ways: firstly, indexing in terms of achievement level and secondly, indexing in terms of short fall from a threshold, i.e. poverty in the above mentioned five dimensions. It is outcome of one of the first workshops on this topic organized by IRTI in Jeddah, Saudi Arabia.

The book offers a new perspective to scholars and development practitioners. We hope that the proposed *Maqāṣid* al-Sharīʿah based indices of socio-economic development will find acceptance in the practice of economic development, poverty measurement and its reporting. It highlights a part of the broader research agenda of the Islamic Research and Training Institute to break new grounds in theory and practice of economic development and finance with an Islamic perspective.

Sami al-Suwailem
Acting Director General
Islamic Research and Training Institute
Islamic Development Bank
Jeddah, Saudi Arabia

Preface

Having a clear understanding of the objectives of socio-economic development is fundamentally important to measuring the meaningful things for gauging economic development. The Islamic perspective advocates comprehensive human development by considering progress in multiple dimensions beyond GDP, income or standard of living. Not only should socio-economic progress be balanced but it should also have a higher purpose towards achievement of human well being in the short and the long run. It should work to provide benefits and remove harms.

With this view, Islamic Research and Training Institute (IRTI) organized a series of workshops to operationalize the concept of *Maqāṣid* based socio-economic development and its measurement. These workshops attracted considerable participation and intellectual contributions. I consider myself fortunate to lead this initiative in IRTI. The present book, *Towards a Maqāṣid al-Sharī'ah Index of Socio-Economic Development: Theory and Application*, is the outcome of the first workshop held in 2014. It is a book for understanding, learning and experimentation towards creating a comprehensive measure of socio-economic development.

It conveys the concepts and demonstrates the application of two major approaches in constructing such a development measure—the achievement approach and the deprivation approach. I personally prefer the deprivation approach for its ease and clear focus by measuring development in terms of reduction in deprivations in society.

I pray that whatever is useful for others in this book, may Allah make that portion widespread, and if there is anything incorrect herein, may Allah stop that portion just there. I hope that students, economists and policymakers will find the book useful for understanding the underlying theory of *Maqāṣid* al-Sharīʿah based development index, learn a different perspective on how to create and apply it in policy making.

Here, I would like to thank the authors of different chapters; their names appear in the respective chapters. I also want to thank those who helped in various stages of editing and publication process; prominent among them were Mr. Sajjad Qurban from IRTI, Ms. Preetha Kuttiappan, Project Manager (Book Production), and Tula Weis, Senior Editor, both from Palgrave.

Jeddah, Saudi Arabia — Salman Syed Ali

Acknowledgements

We acknowledge with thanks the permission granted by the Islamic Research and Training Institute to reprint five articles that have previously appeared in their journal *Islamic Economic Studies,* Vol. 22, No. 2, Muharram 1436 (Nov 2014) and Vol. 23, No. 1, Rajab 1436 (May 2015). We also thank the *Journal of Economic Cooperation and Development* for permission to reprint one article. These six are listed as follows:

Chapter No	*Reprinted from*
Chapter 2	"*Maqāṣid* al-Sharīʿah: Are We Measuring The Immeasurable?" *Islamic Economic Studies* Vol. 22, No. 2, Muharram 1436 (Nov 2014), pp. 1–32, by *Rafi Amir-Ud-Din.*
Chapter 9	"Socio-Economic Philosophy of Conventional and Islamic Economics: Articulating Hayat-e-Tayyaba Index (HTI) on the Basis of *Maqāṣid* al-Sharīʿah", *Islamic Economic Studies* Vol. 22, No. 2, Muharram 1436 (Nov 2014), pp. 65–98, by *Muhammad Mubashir Mukhtar, et al.*
Chapter 10	"Islamic Inclusive Growth Index for the Organization of Islamic Cooperation (OIC) Member Countries", *Journal of Economic Cooperation and Development* Vol. 37, No. 2., by *Reza Ghazal and Muhamed Zulkhibri.*
Chapter 12	"A Structural Model for Human Development, Does *Maqāṣid* al-Sharīʿah Matter!" *Islamic Economic Studies* Vol. 22, No. 2, Muharram 1436 (Nov 2014), pp. 47–64, by *Medhi Mili.*
Chapter 14	"Non-Monetary Poverty Measurement in Malaysia: A *Maqāṣid* al-Sharīʿah Approach", *Islamic Economic Studies* Vol. 22, No. 2, Muharram 1436 (Nov 2014), pp. 33–46, by *Mohamed Saladin Abdul Rasool & Ariffin Mohd Salleh.*
Chapter 13	"Assessing Socio-Economic Development based on *Maqāṣid* al-Sharīʿah Principles: Normative Frameworks, Methods and Implementation in Indonesia", *Islamic Economic Studies*, Vol. 23, No. 1, Rajab 1436 (May 2015), pp. 73–100, by *Rahmatina Kasri & Habib Ahmed.*

Contents

List of Contributors

Junaidah Abu Seman Faculty of Economics and Muamalat, Universiti Sains Islam Malaysia, Nilai, Malaysia

Habib Ahmed Durham University Business School, Durham, UK

Salman Syed Ali Islamic Research and Training Institute, Islamic Development Bank, Jeddah, Saudi Arabia

Rafi Amir-ud-Din International Institute of Islamic Economics, International Islamic University, Islamabad, Pakistan;
Department of Economics, COMSATS University Islamabad, Lahore, Pakistan

Necati Aydin Department of Finance, College of Business, Alfaisal University, Riyadh, Saudi Arabia

Houssem Eddine Bedoui Islamic Development Bank Group, Jeddah, Saudi Arabia;
Ecole Normale Superieure, Lyon, France

Nazam Dzolkarnaini The Business School, Edinburgh Napier University, Edinburgh, UK

Adem Esen Istanbul University, Istanbul, Turkey

M. Fevzi Esen Istanbul Medeniyet University, Istanbul, Turkey

Fahim M. Khan Professor Emeritus and Director International Centre for Research in Islamic Economic, Minhaj University Lahore, Lahore, Pakistan

Reza Ghazal Islamic Research and Training Institute, Islamic Development Bank, Jeddah, Saudi Arabia;
Business and Management Sciences Department, University of Kurdistan-Hawler, Kurdistan, Iraq

Hamid Hasan King Faisal University, Hufuf, Saudi Arabia;
IIIE, International Islamic University, Islamabad, Pakistan

Rahmatina Kasri Faculty of Economics and Business, Universitas Indonesia, Jakarta, Indonesia

Moussa Larbani School of Mathematics and Statistics, Carleton University, Ottawa, ON, Canada

Mehdi Mili University of Bahrain, College of Business Administration, Zallaq, Bahrain

Muhammad Mubashir Mukhtar Center for Entrepreneurial Development (CED), Institute of Business Administration (IBA), Karachi, Pakistan;
New Zealand Society of Local Government Managers (SOLGM), Wellington, New Zealand

Arif Naveed Faculty of Education, University of Cambridge, Cambridge, UK

Hafiz Muhammad Sarfraz Nihal Department of Economics, University of Karachi, Karachi, Pakistan;
Islamic Banking Division, Bank Al-Habib Ltd, Karachi, Pakistan

Ismail Nizam FTMS College, Cyberjaya, Kuala Lumpur, Malaysia

Muhammad Shahid Qureshi Center for Entrepreneurial Development (CED), Institute of Business Administration (IBA), Karachi, Pakistan

Mohamed Saladin Abdul Rasool Universiti Teknologi MARA, Shah Alam, Malaysia

Hafiz Abdul Rauf Center for Entrepreneurial Development (CED), Institute of Business Administration (IBA), Karachi, Pakistan;
Meezan Bank, Karachi, Pakistan

Atiq ur Rehman Pakistan Institute of Development Economics, Islamabad, Pakistan

Ariffin Mohd Salleh Universiti Teknologi MARA, Shah Alam, Malaysia

Waleed Wasti Center for Entrepreneurial Development (CED), Institute of Business Administration (IBA), Karachi, Pakistan;
Iqra University, Karachi, Pakistan

Asad Zaman Pakistan Institute of Development Economics, Islamabad, Pakistan

Muhamed Zulkhibri Islamic Research and Training Institute, Islamic Development Bank, Jeddah, Saudi Arabia

List of Figures

Chapter 2

Chapter 3

Chapter 5

Chapter 7

Chapter 8

Chapter 9

Chapter 10

Chapter 11

Chapter 12

Chapter 13

Chapter 15

List of Tables

Chapter 4

Chapter 5

Chapter 7

Chapter 9

Chapter 10

Chapter 12

Chapter 13

Chapter 14

Chapter 15

CHAPTER 1

Towards *Maqāṣid* al-Sharīʿah-Based Index of Socio-Economic Development: An Introduction to the Issues and Literature

Salman Syed Ali

1 Why Should Development be Based on Maqāsid al-Sharīʿah?

People like success and well-being. Socio-economic developments that bring us closer to this desire are valued in all societies. In this sense, the study and measurement of economic development are not only useful for the low-income poor countries in determining ways to bring them out of poverty but also important for higher income countries to improve their socio-economic situation. It is important for the industrialized and the non-industrialized, modernized and non-modernized economies alike. At the heart of economic development is building healthy economies and healthy communities. However, healthy communities are not simply the product of high income and modernization of a country. Human societies value development and they understand development as more than just a rise in income and wealth or standard of living. Yet, the discussions of development and its measurement in

S. S. Ali (✉)
Islamic Research and Training Institute,
Islamic Development Bank, Jeddah, Saudi Arabia
e-mail: ssyedali@isdb.org

S. S. Ali (ed.), *Towards a Maqāṣid al-Sharīʿah Index of Socio-Economic Development*, Palgrave Studies in Islamic Banking, Finance, and Economics,
https://doi.org/10.1007/978-3-030-12793-0_1

economics are focused on GDP growth, material progress, various measures of standard of living, and occasionally even some higher notions of well-being as freedom and increased capabilities, but with ill-defined purposes.

In reality, it is our understanding of the purpose of life that determines our goals and helps define the meaningful 'development', its measurement and targets for the individual as well as for the society collectively. It is true that humans are endowed with basic ingredients that keep them continuously motivated and restless. Want for more, impatience, and desire to possess all good and deflect all hardship and pain are part and parcel of human nature. These traits work to ensure continuity of life on earth. However, without a well-defined purpose of life, these endowed ingredients would shape the definition of progress, development and the development targets in very limited ways. Whereby, well-being and happiness become very transitory and directionless. With a well-defined purpose of life, there is an added element in moulding or shaping of the purpose of development and hence in defining and setting of the direction of progress and advancement.

The presently available measures of socio-economic development are mostly based on, and driven by, the impetus of human desire to live a better life in this world; these measures therefore focus on current and future level of income, production and wealth. To the extent, they focus on other aspects such as health and education it is also for attaining higher income, wealth and prosperity in the near future. Some measures go beyond this to encompass happiness, fulfilment, freedom and life satisfaction but still limited in purpose to doing so for the sake of this life only.

2 What Is Socio-Economic Progress and Development?

Quran clearly states that the creation of this world is not purposeless.[1] It defines the purpose of creation of the human beings as (*ibādah*) worship and obedience to Allah.[2] However, humankind's sphere of *ibādah* transcends *tasbeeh* and *taqdees* forms of the worship to include in the worship

[1]And We created not the heavens and the earth, and all that is between them, in play (Quran, 44:38) [Source: http://quran.com/44/38, Pickthal's translation].

[2]I created the jinn and humankind only that they might worship Me (Quran, 51:56) [Source: http://www.theonlyquran.com/quran/Az-Zariyat/English_Mohammed_M_Pickthall/?ayat=56].

the management of his affairs in this world in accordance with the will of Allah. Humankind has thus been appointed as vicegerent of Allah (*khālifah*) on this earth to manage the affairs in conformity to the will of Allah. This agency required bestowment to him a free will, provisions for his sustenance on earth, guidance about his assignment and ability to make decisions. Humans are given all these. They are free to become obedient and grateful or to reject the wilful obedience and remain unthankful and misuse the delegated authority with the respective consequences.[3] The existence of death and life on earth is to provide an opportunity (of time, space and circumstances given to individuals in their life until their death) to perform and pass this test[4] the reward of which will come in the hereafter.[5] Thus, the socio-economic development of human society needs to be geared towards these goals. Any increase in wealth, health, living standards and culture should be to facilitate in our *ibādah* of Allah and increase the likelihood of passing the test. Obedience to Allah calls for carrying out the rights of Allah and the rights of human beings because Allah ordains both these duties.[6] In this way, the purpose of life

Asad: And [tell them that] I have not created the invisible beings and men to any end other than that they may [know and] worship Me.

Malik: We have not created jinns and mankind except to worship Me.

Pickthall: I created the jinn and humankind only that they might worship Me.

Yusuf Ali: I have only created jinns and men that they may serve Me.

(Source: http://www.alim.org/library/quran/ayah/compare/51/56/allah,-who-built-the-heavens-and-spread-out-the-earth,-has-assigned-prophet-muhammad-to-be-a-warner-for-mankind)

[3] Lo! We have shown him the way, whether he be grateful or disbelieving (Quran, 76:3) [Source: http://legacy.quran.com/76/3].

Also see Quran, 90:8–10.

'Have We not made for him a pair of eyes? And a tongue and a pair of lips? And shown him the two ways (good and evil)?' (Quran, 90:8–10) [Source: http://legacy.quran.com/90/8-10, Muhsin Khan's translation].

[4] [He] who created death and life to test you [as to] which of you is best in deed—and He is the Exalted in Might, the Forgiving (Quran, 62:2) [Source: http://quran.com/67].

Who hath created life and death that He may try you which of you is best in conduct; and He is the Mighty, the Forgiving (Quran, 62:2) [Source: http://www.theonlyquran.com/quran/Al-Mulk/english_mohammed_m_pickthall/?pagesize=15].

[5] Add reference to al-Akhirah.

[6] Note that human rights towards self and others are not omnipotent, do not exist by themselves or supreme in themselves but founded on Allah's commandment. These rights

helps define the meaning and purpose of socio-economic development as an associated strategy to achieve the main goals. Any development that is not aligned with these higher objectives would not deserve to be called progress and improvement.

This worldview may be true for Muslims, who adhere to this purpose of life. Nevertheless, we know that not all the world population is Muslim nor we expect them to convert to Islam within a short time. Thus, it is not expected that all individuals would strive to understand and adopt this cognizance of the purpose of life and hence this purpose of socio-economic development. It should also be clear that Muslims are not tasked to forcefully change the beliefs of others.[7] Their responsibility is to convey and disseminate the true information only.[8] Moreover, the realization of the real purpose of life, if it comes, may be asynchronous in time among different individuals and societies. Some people accept the truth right away, some realize it later, some others linger undecided and some reject the above-defined purpose. Therefore, the objectives of socio-economic development have to be all-encompassing and inclusive for humanity, yet targeted for the key purpose of life on earth. This brings us to state that the objective of development is twofold:

- First, to strengthen the development needs to facilitate the achievement of *ibādah* as well as success in the life hereafter for those who accepted Islam and the purpose of life that it describes.
- Second, to gear the development towards providing opportunity to non-believers for making informed choices in attaining the correct belief and gaining the understanding of the purpose.[9] In this way,

are called huqooq ul-ibad, a category of rights that run parallel in importance to the category of rights called huqooq Allah—rights of Allah on humans.

[7] Had Allah willed, they had not been idolatrous. We have not set thee as a keeper over them, nor art thou responsible for them (Quran, 6:107) [Source: http://quran.com/6/107 Pickthal's translation].

[8] But if they turn away, [O Muhammad]—then only upon you is [responsibility for] clear notification (Quran, 16:82) [Source: http://quran.com/16/82, Pickthal's translation].

And our duty is but plain conveyance (of the message) (Quran, 36:17) [Source: http://quran.com/36/17, Pickthal's translation].

[9] Lo! We have shown him the way, whether he be grateful or disbelieving (Quran, 76:3) [Source: http://tanzil.net/#trans/en.pickthall/76:3].

> the benefits of development are made universal without restriction to one's belief.[10] As Allah has created this world for the benefit of believers and non-believers alike.

Islam takes this broad and encompassing view of human development and asserts the centrality of achieving the above objectives in any public policy.

The purpose of law (Sharīʿah) and the purpose of socio-economic development thus complement each other in attaining the higher objectives of *ibādah* and passing the test. While progress and development are open-ended, unbounded from above, both in its quantity and variety of dimensions, the knowledge of the basic protections emphasized in the law sheds light on the key minimum dimensions of protections for socio-economic development. Islamic law emphasizes five key dimensions: (i) protection of faith, (ii) protection of life, (iii) protection of wealth, (iv) protection of mind or rationality, and (v) protection of progeny. Thus, a measurement of a comprehensive concept of development can be made along these five dimensions, though addition of more dimensions can also be possible.

In each of these dimensions, Islam's position is to provide a minimum protection as well as to develop the society with a view as mentioned above to facilitate the achievement of *ibādah* for Muslims (specific protections) and providing opportunity for everyone else to survive, live

Indeed, We guided him to the way, be he grateful or be he ungrateful (Quran, 76:3) [Source: http://quran.com/76/3].

[10]Note the supplication of Prophet Ibrahim (PBUH) for Makkah and its people and the reply of Allah with much broader acceptance to include even the non-believers in providing good livelihood to them.

And (remember) when Ibrahim (Abraham) said, 'My Lord, make this city (Makkah) a place of security and provide its people with fruits, such of them as believe in Allah and the Last Day'. He (Allah) answered: 'As for him who disbelieves, I shall leave him in contentment for a while, then I shall compel him to the torment of the Fire, and worst indeed is that destination!' (Quran, 2:126) [Source: http://www.noblequran.com/translation/index.html].

In a Hadith, it is said that Sahl bin Sa'd narrated that the Messenger of Allah (sal Allahu alaihi wa sallam) said: 'If the world to Allah were equal to a mosquito's wing, then He would not allow the disbeliever to have a sip of water from it' (Hasan) [Chapters on Zuhd: Jami At-Tirmidhi].

and grow to be able to make informed choices without any compulsions (universal protections).

Going further, within each dimension three levels (or three shades) of protection are possible starting from the basic minimum, to a better need fulfilment, and then to perfection and embellishment of development. This is in line with the thinking of legal scholars who see the protections are available in each dimension in three categories: Necessities (*ḍarūriyāt*), Requirements (*ḥajiyāt*) and Embellishments (*taḥsiniyāt*) (Kamali, 2009).

Another important aspect in measuring development along these five dimensions is that a broad consensus already exists in the Muslim societies on the validity of these dimensions as objectives of Sharīʿah, so it is easy to communicate the outcome of the measurement and conceive development policies based on those findings. Ready understanding of the objectives of development policy by the masses is an essential aspect for the successes in implementation of any policy.

3 Approaches to Measurement of Socio-Economic Development

Within the objectives of Sharīʿah-based measurement, there can be two approaches to the measurement of socio-economic progress. One is a welfare achievement approach. The other is deprivations reduction approach.

In the welfare approach, the progress is measured in terms of how high an individual or a society (whichever is the unit of analysis) rose in the fore-mentioned five dimensions. For example, by increase in faith and moral behaviour in society, improvement in the survival and quality of life, growth in the level of income and wealth, increased level of education and intellectual discourse to solve the problems, better chances of survival, improved environment and progress for the future generations. This approach has its own difficulties of measurement. For example, how to perform aggregation across the five very different dimensions. How to handle interpersonal comparison across different countries, societies and individuals. Since there is no limit, how much high a society can go in each dimension, what is the target achievement goal? Moreover, whether cross-dimension substitution is possible.

In the second approach, the deprivation approach, a minimum required level of protection is defined for each dimension and then a counting is made for how many individuals or household fall short of this minimum in each dimension. A second cut-off specifies a threshold minimum number of dimensions a person or unit of analysis should not be deprived in. If a person or household is found deprived in more than this number of dimensions, then he/she/it is classified as multidimensional poor. Lesser the number of deprived units are, the better developed the society is. Advantages of this approach are that it does not require measurement of how high each individual or household reached in their progress, and then it also does not have to deal with interpersonal comparison for aggregation of welfare across these units of analysis. The deprivation approach reduces itself to a counting approach, i.e. counting how many units of analysis fell short of the minimum, whereby not only aggregation across individuals becomes easy but also aggregation across conceptually different dimensions does not pose any problem. However, one has to decide about the minimum thresholds for deprivation count.

A further refinement of this method is possible. For example, within the deprivation approach, specification of three different levels of cut-offs of deprivation in each dimension can capture the different levels of progress towards attainment of Necessities (*ḍarūriyāt*), Requirements (*ḥajiyāt*) and Embellishments (*taḥsiniyāt*).

Both the welfare approach and the deprivation approach are subjective in the sense that they depend on the life perspective of the society. Moreover, the constituent indicators of progress in each of the five dimensions have to be parsimonious, so only few indicators have to be selected. The selection process through informed social consensus is itself subjective in nature.

4 Current Trends in the *Maqāṣid* al-Sharīʿah-Based Development Literature

There is a long history of literature on *Maqāṣid* al-Sharīʿah from legal, moral and social policy perspectives.[11] However, our focus here is on the literature that attempts to create socio-economic development indexes based on *Maqāṣid* al-Sharīʿah. A number of papers have been written

[11] Early scholars approached the subject from the legal perspective and as theory of legal preference (e.g. Juwaini, Shatibi, Abdussalam, etc.). Later scholars writing from legal and social perspectives tried to operationalize the objectives separately at the level of individual, family, society and *ummah* (see, for example, Atiyah) or into philosophy of law and freedom (e.g. Audha, Ramadan, etc.).

from this perspective. Some of these papers only outlined the theory and provided a sketch of proposed indicator variables that can be used to construct such index; Chapra (2008) is an example of such attempt that proposes some indicator variables without attempting to analyse the availability of data or to analyse if such index can be quantified. Some other authors attempted empirical measurement using available data but without creating a full theoretical framework for the index; of which Dar (2004) and Anto (2011) are good examples. In the light of the importance of socio-economic development to be guided by *Maqāṣid* al-Sharīʿah and to create development policies aligned with these objectives, it is vital to debate and create some measurement methods or indexes of *Maqāṣid*-based socio-economic development.

There have been other recent attempts to measure socio-economic development in the light of *Maqāṣid* al-Sharīʿah. Most researchers have used the welfare approach. Ali and Hasan are the only ones to date to try out the deprivation approach in the measurement of *Maqāṣid*-based socio-economic development.

Some of the basic difficulties in these endeavours are: (1) To settle down on key indicators to depict a dimension. The indicators should be few in number to make the index worthwhile for construction and tracking. The selection should be well accepted in the society and among the policymakers to create a buy-in. (2) Ascertaining the availability of data. Data should be available on those indicator variables or the data can be collected with reasonable effort. (3) Creation of some method of aggregation across different indicators and dimensions to create the index. (4) The index should be *flexible, robust and sensitive* in the following sense. That it should be flexible enough for aggregation and disaggregation (decomposable) across the dimensions as well as across space and time. It should be robust enough that adding one more indicator or dropping one indicator from a dimension should not drastically change the index. Yet, it should be sensitive enough that the index should be able to capture the variations over time and space when there is a change in the values of the indicators.

Cognizant to these difficulties, IRTI initiated and organized a series of MSI Workshops with the aim to address these very issues as well as to develop a network of researchers and policymakers who may be interested in creating a *Maqāṣid*-based socio-economic development index. The workshops attracted a number of contributed papers on *Maqāṣid* al-Sharīʿah-based socio-economic development index (MSI).

These workshops were held in Jeddah (Saudi Arabia, 2014), Yogyakarta (Indonesia, 2015) and Kuala Lumpur (Malaysia, 2015). The papers of these workshops are published in three volumes. Volumes 1 and 2 focus on MS index for overall socio-economic development, whereas Volume 3 focuses on MS index for evaluating the Islamic financial sector.

5 Review of Papers in the Present Volume 1

The present volume 1 contains the edited and revised papers from the first workshop. These fifteen papers can be categorized in four groups:

1. Studies that focus explicitly on constructing MSI theoretically and empirically.
2. Studies that suggest a methodology of constructing MSI but do not attempt to empirically create the index.
3. Miscellaneous studies that use MS variables only as part of a broader index or those that clarify some aspects towards creation of MS index without necessarily attempting to create it.
4. Studies that debate the usefulness and theoretical possibility or impossibility of MS-based index.

The first category of studies that focus explicitly on constructing a MSI is that of Amiruddin (2014), Bedoui (2014), Ghazal and Zulkhibri (2014), Mili (2014), Kasri and Ahmed (2014), and Ali and Hasan (2014). All these studies use a welfare approach in construction of the index, except Ali and Hasan (2014) who used deprivation approach and utilized the Alkire Foster technique of multidimensional poverty tailored for the specificities of MS-based socio-economic development index. For brevity of exposition, a comparison of methodologies, indicator variables and data sources across all these studies is presented in Tables 1–3. Table 1 compares the index creation methodologies used by these authors. Table 2 compares the indicators used for each dimension. Table 3 compares the data sources.

As can be seen, these papers have used various methodologies including that of Human Development Index (HDI) albeit with different variables; partial least square (PLS) path modelling methods, a kind of principle components analysis for analysing multiple relationships between blocks of variables representing the latent concepts; multidimensional index, and Alkire and Foster dual cut-off methodology.

Table 1 Comparison of methodologies across studies

Amiruddin	*Bedoui*	*Ghazal and Zulkhibri*	*Mili*	*Kasri and Ahmed*	*Ali and Hasan*
3 sub-indices summed up to MSI with unequal weights. Followed Chakravarty (2003)	Similar to HDI methodology: Indicators are normalized in sub-indices which in turn averaged using arithmetic mean, geometric mean or pentagon-shaped measure	HDI methodology	PLS path modelling	Multidimensional poverty methodology with equal weights for dimensions and indicators	Alkire-Foster dual cut-off methodology

Table 2 A comparison of indicators for MSI across studies

Studies/ Dimensions	*Amiruddin*	*Bedoui*	*Ghazal and Zulkhibri*	*Mili*	*Kasri and Ahmed*	*Ali and Hasan*
Faith	a. Necessity level (faith) b. Complementary level (salat, fasting, hajj, zakat) c. Embellishment level (sadaqa)	Absence of corruption, civil justice, multidimensional poverty, environment	Percentage of total expenditure in religious education, overall ranking in corruption index	Percentage of total expenditure in religious education, governmental favouritism of religious index, government regulation of religious index	Prayers and fasting, Islamic/Quranic studies, charity, Hajj	Attendance in religious services, frequency in prayer, religious, non-religious or atheist person, belief in God
Life	a. Average life expectancy b. Freedom of malnutrition c. Life satisfaction	Dignity and human rights, life security, fundamental rights, mental peace and happiness crime and anomie	Universal human rights index, incidence of crime	Health care, human rights, and crime indices, and poverty gap	Consumption, access to health care, health awareness, sickness frequency	Freedom of choice in life, preferred not to go out at night, victim of crime last year, immediate family victim of crime last year, a war involving my country, a terrorist attack, a civil war, gone without enough food to eat, felt unsafe from crime in your home

(continued)

Table 2 (continued)

Studies/ Dimensions	*Amiruddin*	*Bedoui*	*Ghazal and Zulkhibri*	*Mili*	*Kasri and Ahmed*	*Ali and Hasan*
Lineage	a. Child mortality rate b. Homicide rate c. Environmental safety	Health, education, shelter, family	Divorce rate	Divorce rate, child mortality rate	Better future for family, harmony, un-Islamic or anti-social activities, participation in community activities	Justifiable: homosexuality, prostitution, abortion, divorce, sex before marriage, parents beating children
Intellect	a. Primary education b. Secondary education c. Tertiary education	Freedom of thought and expression, creativity, High quality of education	Primary enrolment rate, secondary enrolment rate	Primary enrolment rate, secondary enrolment rate, public spending on education as a percentage of GDP	Access to school, school attendance, basic knowledge from school, academic/school achievement	Not being able to give my children a good education, highest level of education, alcohol consumption in streets, drug sale in streets
Property	a. $1.25 poverty line b. $2 poverty line c. Property security	Freedom of enterprise, employment and self-employment opportunities, GDP per capita	International property rights index	International property rights index, inclusive wealth index	Skill, employability, income, purchasing power, savings	Satisfaction with financial situation, occurrence of robberies, worry about losing job or not finding a job, which income group you belong to

Table 3 A comparison data sources across studies

Amiruddin	*Bedoui*	*Ghazal and Zulkhibri*	*Mili*	*Kasri and Ahmed*	*Ali and Hasan*
PEW[a] WGI[b] WB[c] UNSTATS[d] WB UNODC[e]	1. WJP Rule of Law Index, MPI, EPI 2. Human Rights Rank Indicator, WJP Rule of Law index, HPI 3. FAO, WHO, WB, UNICEF, UNESCO, Gallup, WFFGSI[f] 4. FEI[g], GCCII[h], WB, Times Higher Education 5. Economic Freedom Index, World Development Index, Global Entrepreneurship Monitor	World Bank database	Number of databases: Universal Human Rights Index Database, World Bank, Ministry of education/finance of respective country, The Association of Religious Data Archives (Thearda), UNESCO, UNEP, UNDP, Euro monitor, International Property Rights Index Organization	Households were randomly selected from households receiving zakah assistance for a *Maqāṣid* al-Sharīʿah-based survey	World Values Survey (WVS)

[a]PEW Research Center
[b]World Giving Index
[c]World Bank
[d]United Nations Statistics
[e]United Nations Office on Drugs and Crime
[f]Walk Free Foundation Global Slavery Index
[g]Freedom Expression Index
[h]GCC Innovation Index

The variables employed also range from traditional HDI type variables to very innovative uses of a variety of objective and subjective variables obtained from various data sources such as World Bank, World Health Organization, World Giving Index, United Nations Statistics, Pew Index, Global Slavery Index, Freedom Expression Index, GCC Innovation Index, and World Values Surveys. In most cases, only the secondary data have been used in new ways or with different interpretation.

Since the papers in this first category attempt to create some indexes, these are introduced below in slightly more detailed manner than other papers in the present volume.

Amir-ud-Din (Chapter 2) compares 57 OIC member countries on an MS-based index that he constructed from a variety of data sources. The study has the limitation that the choice of indicators is not wholly grounded in the theory. The author is cognizant of the fact the data required for MSI-based concepts are not readily available and the existing data are not a good proxy. Nevertheless, the study is a good attempt to developed a *Maqāṣid* al-Sharīʿah Index (MSI) corresponding to three levels of necessities, complementarities and embellishments by giving different weights to these aspects. It employs Chakravarty (2003) methodology in assigning geometric weights (r ϵ [0, 1]) that allows for giving more importance to the deficient aspects in the calculation of the index. The MSI ranking of countries shows high correlation with HDI, which raises the question of what is the gain from this complicated exercise. Nevertheless, some divergence is also visible at the higher levels of achievement. For example, Tunisia ranks 1st in MSI ($r=0.5$) but in HDI it ranks 17th among the countries belonging to OIC. Albania presents a reverse case where it ranks 10th in HDI but 30th in MSI.

Bedoui (Chapter 3) attempts to compare 187 countries in terms of socio-economic development using the objectives of the Islamic Law but finds that data on his chosen variables are available only on 128 countries for all five dimensions of *Maqāṣid* al-Sharīʿah. The ranking of these countries showed similarity with HDI, with many non-Muslim countries ahead of Muslim countries in the MS-based ranking. The paper also provides a comparison between the arithmetic mean and the geometric mean approaches commonly used in creating a summary measure from the respective dimensional scores. It proposes a measure that is calculating the area of a pentagon formed by the levels of normalized achievements among the five dimensions of the objectives of Sharīʿah. This area is also dependent on the sequence in which the five objectives are arranged. The pentagon-shaped area measurement approach represents a middle ground between the two earlier described methods.

Ghazal and Zulkhibri (Chapter 10) attempt to develop an Islamic Inclusive Growth Index (i-IGI) for the member countries of the Islamic Development Bank Group. The index comprises of three sub-pillars to measure the countries' performance based on three building blocks of inclusiveness: (a) Islamic-adjusted economic growth; (b) performance of poverty reduction; and (c) performance of the society inequality and social inclusion. The only adjustment different from conventional Inclusive Growth Index (IGI) is in taking non-*ribā* income growth in the first building block. Nevertheless, the country rankings in i-IGI somewhat change from IGI rankings. The country rankings also become different from those in the existing models in the literature (i.e. Rehman and Askari 2010; Anto 2011; Dar 2004). However, it points to the same general conclusion that majority of the Muslim countries are not conforming to Islamic principles, at least in the realm of economics and development.

Medhi Mili (Chapter 12) tests how *Maqāṣids* al-Sharīʿah contributes to promote human welfare. The objective of this study is not the creation of a new index for human development. Rather, it seeks to test the impact of the Maqāṣid-related variables on Human Development as measured by HDI. The study uses a PLSs Path model that allows identifying the causal relationships between the five *Maqāṣid* al-Sharīʿah components (Hifẓ al-Nafs, Hifẓ al-Din, Hifẓ al-Aqal, Hifẓ al-Mal and Hifẓ al-Nasl) and their impact on human well-being. Using a sample of 30 Islamic countries, the empirical results show that the five dimensions used for Maqāṣid al-Sharīʿah objectives are homogeneous and representative. Maqāṣid al-Sharīʿah contributes significantly to human well-being in Islamic countries with Hifẓ al-Nafs and Hifẓ al-Aqal as the most significant components that affect human well-being when measured by HDI.

Kasri and Ahmed (Chapter 14) propose a framework based on *Maqāṣid* principles to assess socio-economic development of Muslim societies and to use it to formulate policies to resolve development challenges. The study draws insights from the discourses on happiness, quality of life and multidimensional poverty measures that are based on the capability approach pioneered by Amartya Sen. It reviews a number of operational indicators and multidimensional poverty indices. The study then proposes a simple, linear and decomposable multidimensional

Maqāṣid al-Sharīʿah-based poverty index encompassing five dimensions of well-being/poverty consistent with the *Maqāṣid* perspective. The value of study lies in its attempt to apply this indexing method to evaluate the welfare changes among the recipients of *zakāh* in Indonesia by using data collected through a survey of 685 households living in Jakarta, Indonesia. The study found that *zakāh* institutions have the expected positive contribution in reducing poverty among the poor. It also provides a workable example of how *Maqāṣid* al-Sharīʿah principles can be implemented in assessing impacts of socio-economic policies.

Ali and Hasan (Chapter 15) in this study utilize the deprivation counting approach of multidimensional poverty to measure socio-economic development in the reverse manner. Their contribution is that they created a theoretical framework as well as developed the axioms to gauge socio-economic development in line with the five dimensions of *Maqāṣid* al-Sharīʿah. Their proposed measure is granular, open to aggregation and multidimensional that would facilitate policy guidance at various levels of aggregation and disaggregation. Given the limitation that the data that would be most appropriate for MSI-based measure is not currently being actively collected by countries, the study uses the available data from World Values Survey to demonstrate the feasibility and usefulness of MSI-based index. As an example, individual-level data on Pakistan from the WVS wave 2007–2008 were utilized to calculate the proportion of population who are not even able to enjoy the minimum desired levels of protections in the five dimensions of *Maqāṣid* al-Sharīʿah. The analysis shows that the protection of material wealth is below the minimum desired threshold and it is contributing about 50% for keeping people below the multidimensional MS-based poverty. While the lowest contributor to the overall shortfall in achieving *Maqāṣid* al-Sharīʿah-based progress is from posterity protection dimension. Based on the analysis, an immediate policy direction for Pakistan is to focus attention on improving the safety and security of wealth of the poor and weak and improving the law and order situation. Another interesting feature of this MS-based measure is that it is theoretically and empirically different from other measures of poverty and development such as the multidimensional poverty index (MPI) calculated for Pakistan by the OPHI and UNDP, the usual income poverty measure in terms of $1.25 a day, and the HDI.

Among the second category of studies that suggest a methodology of constructing MSI but without an empirical attempt for its construction are papers by Abu Seman and Dzolkarnaini (2014), Aydin (2014), Rasool and Salleh (2014), and Esen and Esen (2014). In this group, Abu Seman and Dzolkarnaini (Chapter 5) advocate the HDI method of UNDP with indicators normalized to unit intervals and then measuring the distance of each indicator from the ideal position, i.e. the value 1. A Cartesian distance over the five dimensions would then represent MS-based index. Aydin (Chapter 11) offers an interesting perspective of requirements of a complete human (insan-e-kamil) and suggests some variables that can be possibly used for creation of index that can compare countries. He suggests the use of various objective and subjective indicators from a variety of publically available databases. However, he does not apply any of these to construct an index on those lines. Rasool and Salleh (Chapter 13) advocate a multidimensional poverty type index with dual cut-offs. Their contribution is in proposing a weighting scheme for the five dimensions and the individual hypothetical indicators they selected. According to them, the weights were selected through expert group consultations. However, they also do not apply their methodology on any actual data to calculate the index. Esen and Esen (Chapter 7) start with a theoretical framework for five-dimensional MS-based concept. They do not identify specific variables but propose that once data on a number of variables representing these dimensions are gathered, which can be subjective and objective measures, and then an exploratory factor analysis can be performed using Bayesian techniques to reduce the number of variables or combine them in key principal components to construct the index.

Among the third category are miscellaneous studies that use MS variables only as a part of a broader index or that clarify some aspects in the creation of or use of MS index without attempting to create an index. We can count Khan (2014), Larbani and Nizam (2014) and Mukhtar et al. (2014) in this category. Khan (Chapter 4) focuses on individual consumption behaviour and shows how a public policy in the light of *Maqāṣid* al-Sharīʿah can be used to influence reduction in non-essential consumption in society. Paper by Larbani and Nizam (Chapter 8) shows how fuzzy logic techniques can be elegantly utilized to handle various types of variables encountered in data for the creation of *Maqāṣid*-based index. We believe that the membership classification method of fuzzy logic can prove to be very useful in refining the deprivation-based approach to MS index. Mukhtar et al. (Chapter 9) used a very different approach and tried to build an index from fundamentals of Islamic values and teachings in Quran and Sunnah which constitute some MS dimensions and some other dimension which they termed outlook to life. They thus proposed a *Hayat-e-Tayyibah* index and used primary data collected through a questionnaire. The index is simple average of the scores taken over the entire group or split by gender and geographical locations.

The fourth category are studies that question the possibility to construct and practical usefulness of MS index. There is only one study in this category. Zaman et al. (Chapter 6) raise the issue that rewards for any Muslim in al-Akhirah depend on his intention and deed. An increase in wealth if it is accompanied with thankfulness to Allah is rewarded. Likewise, a state of poverty if endured with patience is also rewarded. Thus, there is no clear and simple relationship between wealth and welfare. This means that Islamic approaches to constructing an index for welfare must be substantially more complicated than those currently in use. According to the authors, it is worth reconsidering the reasons for undertaking the project of measurement and assessing what needs to be measured, and whether measurement itself is necessary, for achieving these goals.

This assertion shows a possible confusion that can arise in Muslim societies if MS index project is not well-understood. Ali and Hasan's paper in this same volume (Chapter 15) answers the source of confusion by addressing in its very first section a rationalization of why and what to measure for MS-based index. They show the fine difference between (i) objectives of Islam and objectives of Sharīʿah; (ii) the book (law) and *tazkiyah* (purification); and (iii) the test and the preferred state. First, the objectives of Islam are more broader and geared towards success in al-Akhirah than objectives of Sharīʿah that connotes law—the purpose of which is to provide some basic protections both in this world and ensure success in the hereafter. Thus, the progress in attainment of the objectives of Sharīʿah provides the basic minimum for humans. Second, progress in *tazkiyah* attainment provides measurement focused at individualistic level, it is intention based that is in hearts and hence hidden. We cannot measure *tazkiyah* (and *taqwah*) of others and we are not required to do this evaluation. This is also what forms the 'test' for human beings. Thus, this aspect has to be dropped from our measurement. Third, it is also clear from Islam's message that Allah does not want people to put themselves in undue hardships, neither in acts of worship (*ibādah*) nor in their mutual dealings (*muamalat*). He does not recommend inviting tests and difficulties on themselves. Allah would like to provide ease over difficulty and would like his slaves to choose in similar way. Thus, there is a clear preference for ease and lightness over difficulties and burden. Due to this, health is preferable over disease (though there can be test in both situations), sufficiency over poverty, liberty of time over shortage of time, happiness over gloom, etc. The MS-based index project measures the attainment of preferred state for the individuals and the society.

6 Conclusions from the Literature Survey and the Way Forward

The collection of papers in this volume shows the diversity of approaches in MS-based socio-economic development index creation. Research in this area is at exploratory stage as evident from the papers. This implies need for further experimentation and testing robustness of the approaches and data before one or more indexes become useable for evaluation and policy guidance. A few more things are evident.

First, majority of the attempts have been to construct the index at macro-level—i.e. at the level of country or region or city.

Second, the created indexes are based on data that are not frequent enough. Sometimes, various nearest year data are used together to create the index. This means the dearth of data will not allow for yearly or more frequent calculation. Data that are more frequent are needed if the index is to be used for policy direction or evaluation.

Third, many of the MS based indexes created by using the welfare approach are highly correlated with conventional indexes such as HDI or the World Bank index. The question therefore is what one gains by creating an MS based index. One needs to study carefully, are they measuring what they intend to measure through the selected variables. As opposed to this, the MS-based index through deprivation approach creates very different ranking of countries than from HDI, World Bank and the Global MPI. Thus, indicating that the Sharīʿah deprivation dimensions addressed therein are different from those measured by the conventional indexes.

Fourth, but related to the above, most of the MS-based indexes were constructed by using available data which were not collected for the intended purpose. Therefore, many a times it may be measuring something different from the concepts or variables we intend to measure. Similarly, many aspects are left unmeasured due to unavailability of the right kind of data. Therefore, there is an urgent need to start collecting purposeful primary data and institutionalize such data collection efforts.

Fifth, there is a need for creating the index from first principles and based on the decisions and choices made by smallest social unit, i.e. a family of household. Along with this, there is a need for further experimentation and robustness tests. These efforts will make the index more useful for policy-making, targeting and impact evaluation.

References

Anto, Hendrie. (2011). "Introducing an Islamic Human Development Index (I-HDI) to Measure Development in OIC Countries". *Islamic Economic Studies*, vol. 19(2), pp. 69–95.

Chakravarty, S. R. (2003). "A Generalized Human Development Index". *Review of Development Economics*, vol. 7(1), pp. 99–114.

Chapra, M. Umer. (2008). "The Islamic Vision of Development in the Light of *Maqāsid* al-Sharī'ah" (Research Paper). Jeddah: Islamic Research and Training Institute (IRTI).

Dar, Humayon. (2004). "On Making Human Development More Humane". *International Journal of Social Economics*, vol. 31(11–12), pp. 1071–1088.

Kamali, Mohammad Hashim. (2009). "Maqasid al Sharī'ah Made Simple" (Occasional Papers Series 13). London and Washington: The International Institute of Islamic Thought. Available from http://i-epistemology.net/v1/attachments/-01_Maqasid_Shariah%20-%20hashim%20kamali.pdf.

Rehman, Scheherazade S., & Askari, Hossein. (2010). "An Economic Islamicity Index (EI2)". *Global Economy Journal*, vol. 10(3), Article 1. https://doi.org/10.2202/1524-5861.1680.

CHAPTER 2

Maqāṣid al-Sharīʿah: Are We Measuring the Immeasurable?

Rafi Amir-ud-Din

1 Introduction

Islam takes a broad and encompassing view of human development and asserts the centrality of achieving the *Maqāṣid* al-Sharīʿah in any public policy. The existing development indices do not completely conform to the normative judgments of Islam especially because of their disproportionate emphasis on the material aspect of the development and their disregard for the dimensions which are crucial for the world hereafter. This highlights the need for an index which accommodates the dimensions which are consistent with *Maqāṣid* al-Sharīʿah. However, operationalizing the *Maqāṣid* al-Sharīʿah as a measurable concept has been a relatively new discipline and the instruments to scientifically investigate

R. Amir-ud-Din (✉)
International Institute of Islamic Economics, International Islamic University, Islamabad, Pakistan
e-mail: rafi.amiruddin@cuilahore.edu.pk

Department of Economics, COMSATS University Islamabad, Lahore, Pakistan

S. S. Ali (ed.), *Towards a Maqāṣid al-Sharīʿah Index of Socio-Economic Development*, Palgrave Studies in Islamic Banking, Finance, and Economics,
https://doi.org/10.1007/978-3-030-12793-0_2

the religious constructs have so far been not adequate even where they are available. This paper seeks to explore the conception of *Maqāṣid* al-Sharīʿah as a measurable concept, identifies the indicators relevant to these *Maqāṣid* and develops a tentative multidimensional index which makes a cross-country comparison within the OIC region.

Section 2 highlights important features of the Islamic concept of development, while Sect. 3 discusses some of the conceptual and operational problems regarding the measurement of the concepts which are intrinsically problematic because of being unobservable. This section also discusses some of the possibilities with the framework of Sharīʿah and briefly discusses the available methodology to measure such intangible factors as spirituality. Section 4 develops the methodology for constructing a *Maqāṣid* al-Sharīʿah Index (MSI) and discusses some of the methodological issues. Section 5 discusses the issues of data collection within the framework of multidimensional view of development. Section 6 discusses the results.

2 Islamic Concept of Development

A standard definition of economic development is "... removal of poverty, unemployment, inequality, illiteracy, and ill-health, and one of ensuring participation in government... incorporating, in the final result, the technological safeguards for human development and conserving of the biosphere that has been developed" (Adiseshiah 1991). This concept of economic development has its roots in the post-enlightenment period. Islam, however, does not subscribe to this materialistic worldview, nor it considers human life to be determined by material, psychological, instinctive or environmental forces (Chapra 2008).

Islamic approach to development rests on a set of well-defined philosophical foundations (Ahmad 1994; Khurshid 1980). The first foundation is *Tawhid*, which posits the unity and sovereignty of Allah and helps define the nature of the relationship between man and his lord as well as the relationship between man and man. The principle of *Tawhid* entails that there is a unity of purpose in the design of this universe, and any dichotomy is at best a state away from the equilibrium which will be removed over time. In the world hereafter, the angularities in both the human relationships as well as the other dimensions of the universe will be physically removed: "Nothing crooked or curved wilt thou see in their place" (Qur'ān, 20:107). The *Rabubiyya* principle entails that the human beings as well as other creatures are governed by a power who is benevolent, compassionate and merciful. This principle assures the human beings that the resources essential for a good life in this world exist and they do not have to thwart their life in a mad pursuit of necessities of life. Such philosophical constructs as fatalism and determinism stand opposite to the *Rabubiyyah* principle because the former isms see man as a puppet in the hands of forces which are indifferent to his plight and man is totally helpless against these forces.

The *Khilafah* principle provides that human beings are responsible for their deeds and actions, and this principle refutes all such *isms* which take a non-serious or hedonist view of life. *Tazkiyyah*, the fourth principle, means purification and growth. Islamic concept of development directly follows from this principle because "it addresses itself to the problem of human development in all its dimensions: development is concerned with growth towards perfection through purification of attitudes and relationships. The result of *tazkiyah* is *falah* – prosperity in this world and the hereafter" (Ahmad 1994). Chapra (2007) includes another dimension of *Adalah* (justice) that provides for the satisfaction of the needs of everyone and ensures equitable distribution of income and wealth and environmental protection.

At a more abstract level, Islam considers development in terms of a journey along the *sirat* (path), suggesting that Islam has a dynamic concept of development which requires continuous struggle on the part of Muslims. Those who are successful in this journey are referred to as *muflihin* (successful ones) or *muhsinun* (achievers of perfection) (Zaman and Asutay 2009).

The important feature of Islamic concept of development is that it considers development a multidimensional activity and seeks to establish a balance between different factors and forces. The neoclassical economics was mistaken in taking an isolated view of economic activity by excluding many dimensions of real life (Zaman and Asutay 2009). "Islamic concept of development is comprehensive in character and includes moral, spiritual and material dimensions. Development becomes a goal and value-oriented activity, devoted to the optimization of human well-being in all these areas" (Ahmad 1994). Human beings and their basic needs need to be at the center of development effort and not simply the growth rate (El-Ghazali and Series 1994). Tahir and Haque (1995) say that even economic development is contingent on a number of non-economic conditions: the fulfillment of fundamental economic rights; the surety that growth does not lead to the weakening of the moral, social and institutional fabric of the society; the growth of economy does not widen inequalities of society; there is no deviation from the divine mandate; and the society keeps a credible deterrent against the possible external aggression.

3 Measuring the Sharīʿah Concepts: Challenges and Possibilities

The empirical investigation of Sharīʿah concepts is a relatively new discipline in the Islamic scholarship. In the absence of adequate instruments, the measurement of religious constructs is very challenging. I shall discuss here some of the challenges. Some of the challenges arise from the unobservable nature of many facts.

3.1 Observable Dependent on Unobservable: Challenge and Possibility

The first challenge is that deeds, even if they are observable, cannot be judged at their face value because the intentions behind these deeds are supremely important in Islam. Intentions, however, are not observable by their very nature. In the absence of the right intention, great acts of virtue such as martyrdom, generosity and scholarship bring no reward at all. Some individuals will suffer damnation *because* of the undesirable intentions behind these great acts of virtue (Tirmidhi, 2:270). However, if the issue of intention is taken too far, it will not be possible to judge the relative merit of any action because theoretically, any conceivable good deed may be motivated by bad intentions, and vice versa.

Even if Islam emphasizes in no uncertain terms the obligation of truthfulness, it gives due share to the claims of the individuals and considers them sufficient in most circumstances in the absence of an objective evaluation of the *intention*. The Islamic laws related to, inter alia, testimony, *li'aan* and divorce are enforceable only on the basis of the expression, explicit or implicit. The general principal seems to be to analyze the motives with the appropriate means, while leaving the veracity of intention, and their consequences, to be judged by Allah.[1]

Islam guides us toward certain *indicators* which serve as reliable source of knowledge regarding the state of *faith* of an individual. For example, some physical attributes of the hypocrites are mentioned in the Qur'ān: "Indeed, the hypocrites [think to] deceive Allah, but He is deceiving them. And when they stand for prayer, they stand lazily, showing [themselves to] the people and not remembering Allah except a little" (Qur'ān, 4:142). Similarly, offering prayer in the mosque, paying *zakāt* and fearing none other than Allah are presented as the physical manifestation of the faith. Qur'ān says: "Only he shall visit the mosques of Allah who believes in Allah and the latter day, and keeps up prayer and pays the poor-rate and fears none but Allah; so (as for) these, it may be that they are of the followers of the right course" (9:18).

These *indicators* of faith are expounded in greater detail in Hadith literature. Many Aḥādīth of the Prophet SAW take strong exception to certain human attributes and go so far as to exclude the individuals with these attributes from the community of the Muslims. These attributes include: taking up (brandishing) arms against the Muslims (Bukhari, 3:1991), plundering the wealth of others (Sunan Abu Dawood, 3:997), not showing mercy to the younger ones and not respecting the rights of the elders (Abu Dawood, 3:1535), instigating someone against one's spouse (Abu Dawood, 3:1759) and claiming something from someone illegally (Ibn Majah, 2:477).

3.2 *Islam's Unique Normative Judgments*

Dividing the sphere of human activity into permissible and impermissible indeed reflects Islam's unique normative judgments and is based on the principle that only Allah knows what is good and bad for the humanity, and as a logical corollary, only He has the prerogative to declare anything permissible or impermissible. Islam emphasizes the superiority

[1] See, for example, the incident in which Prophet Yaqoob (AS) responded to his sons who had plotted against their brothers (Quran, 12:18). The Hadith about the person who had killed his opponent in a battle even after the latter had pronounced faith, and the Prophet (SAW)'s remark "Did you tear his heart in order to find out whether it had professed or not?" is also very revealing. See Sahih Muslim, Book of Faith: 176.

of knowledge over ignorance, “Are those equal, those who know and those who do not know?” (Qur’ān, 39:9) and goes so far as to urge the Prophet (SAW) to pray for an increase in knowledge. Say, “O my Lord! Advance me in knowledge” (Qur’ān, 20:114). However, Sharīʿah makes a clear demarcation between the useful and useless knowledge. The Messenger of Allah (saw) said: “Ask Allah for beneficial knowledge and seek refuge with Allah from knowledge that is of no benefit” (Sunan Ibn Majah, 3:723).

The Muslim societies under the influence of the Western world have replicated various educational disciples from social and biological sciences and the fine arts without adequately reconciling the assumptions at the basis of Western epistemology with its own unique worldview. The theory of evolution, for example, is totally antithetical to Islam as a philosophical construct because of its negation of any divine role in the creation and sustenance of the universe. However, the theory of evolution has made inroads into the standard academic curricula of the Islamic world. The measurement of the concepts of Sharīʿah, as it is shown here, is value-laden and requires a higher degree of discretion and care.

3.3 *Challenges Unique to Modern Ages*

There are many challenges in measuring the *Maqāṣid* al-Sharīʿah which are of relatively recent origin. Islam takes a clear position on the ethical questions about procreation. In Islam, it is a major sin to permanently destroy the organs of reproduction and is tantamount to the change in the creation of Allah. Infanticide is portrayed as a grave sin which invites the wrath of Allah (Qur’ān, 81:8–9). However, in recent times, family planning (a euphemism for reduced family size) in the Muslim world has been changing into a norm in response to the demographic changes in the Western societies. The biggest challenge in this regard is to disaggregate the causes of the falling fertility rates into two distinct categories: Western influence precipitated by the process of globalization, or some genuine physical necessity. It is critical to distinguish these two causes because of different consequences they entail in the Sharīʿah framework.

3.4 *Possibilities: Empirical Leads from Other Disciplines*

Though it is difficult to measure the concepts which are not observable, a lot of research effort has found workarounds to address the issue of immeasurability. Various scales have been developed to measure subjective non-material subjects which are considered to be accessible only through self-reports such as anomie, attitudes and prejudices. Spirituality is a subject of particular interest and over time it has been recognized that spirituality is no more intangible than many other internalized phenomena that have already been investigated in the disciplines like psychology, epidemiology and sociology. Since the 1960s, many indices and instruments have been developed to measure religious constructs. Gorsuch (1984) claimed that sufficient number of instruments have already been developed to address any conceivable issue related to the psychology of religion. The spirituality research generally uses quantitative methods gathering data based on questionnaires or schedules. The questionnaires define some observable reflector and the data based on these reflectors is assigned some ordinal value. However, these problems also suffer from imprecision, lack of objective interpretation and oversimplifications (Moberg 2010).

4 *Maqāṣid* al-Sharīʿah Index (MSI)

4.1 *Issues in Multidimensional Indices*

Unlike the traditional approaches to the measurement of well-being where income or some alternative indicator is conveniently used as a proxy of well-being, no such space is readily available in the multidimensional approach to the measurement of development. Which aspects of life should be included in the conceptualization of poverty has been at best an arbitrary choice. Aggregation of various dimensions of development in the multidimensional framework is a subject of ongoing controversy. Though by definition, any aggregation is a loss of information, at times it becomes essential to summarize a large amount of data into an easily interpretable form as an input for policy formulation. The moment we compress this information into an index, a whole range of conceptual and methodological issues surface. Ravallion (2012a, b) has summarized some of the issues of multidimensional indices and suggested some ways in which the existing indices can be modified to avert the problems presently found in the literature.

Ravallion (2012a) believes that the composite indices are unwarranted because the components of the index rather than the composite index itself are more informative for the policymakers. He comes down heavy over the issue of weighting in the composite indices. He believes that uncertainty about components and their weights are not adequately acknowledged. For non-market goods (e.g., being able to participate fully in the society), constant weights are assumed for everyone in a given country which is implausible. Conclusion about the country performance over time is not clear when the country-specific context of the performance is missing (e.g., the initial conditions in a country and how much it has progressed). Actual weights used in lieu of prices are not made explicit, even if prices are regarded as unreliable guide to trade-offs. Little guidance to robustness of country rankings is provided.

Ravallion (2012b) finds that even if the weights attached to the scaled varies are made explicit, the weights attached to component parts are not made explicit which may in fact be implausible. As income is one of the components of the Human Development Index (HDI), Ravallion believes that it is possible to monetize all the dimensions using the trade-offs implicit in the HDI. He finds out that a low monetary value is attached to poor countries. In the newer version of HDI since 2010, that value has been lowered still further but the weight on income has increased for most of the countries. For example, if Zimbabwe increases national income by $0.52 while its average life expectancy is reduced by one year, it will still "promote" human development.

Given that the composite indices are the norm rather than the exception now, Ravallion (2012a) suggests that the composite measures should be clear what exactly they are measuring. More attention needs to be given to trade-offs implicitly embodied in the index. They need to be more humble because they often far fewer dimensions of welfare than measures based on consumption at household level. It also must be recognized that important aspects of development cannot be captured in a single index.

4.2 *Methodology*

Unlike other multidimensional indices which generally use the ad hoc assumption of equal importance of all the sub-components of an index, we have a priori information about the relative importance of various dimensions of the objectives of Sharīʿah. I shall follow two-step strategy to construct our index: computing three subindices corresponding to three levels of objectives of Sharīʿah: necessities (*ḍarūriyāt*), complementarities (*ḥajiyāt*), embellishments (*taḥsiniyāt*) and then I shall aggregate these subindices by assigning unequal weights to compute the MSI.

In the subindices, I shall use the Chakravarty methodology which is an extension of HDI because of its suitable properties and because it is relatively free from the problems suffered by HDI (Chakravarty 2003).

Let x_i be the level of achievement of attribute i for a country, and $i=1, 2, \ldots, k$. The lower and upper levels of x_i are m_i and M_i, denoted by x_i subset of $[m_i, M_i]$. A is a real value function of indicator i which associates a value $A\ (x_i, m_i, M_i)$ to each x_i subset of $[m_i, Mi]$. All the indicators considered in the model are assumed to follow the same functional form. In the presence of variables of different types such as literacy rate and longevity, same functional form is useful.

The properties of the single indicator satisfy the properties of normalization (NM), monotonicity (MN), translation invariance (TI), homogeneity (HM) and lower gain in indicators at higher levels of attainment difference (LI). For a detailed exposition of these properties, see Chakravarty (2003).

The normalization (NM) of an indicator i is in fact the transformation of an indicator such that its minimum and maximum values take the value of zero and one, respectively. This is an alternative to the choice of an arbitrary cutoff values. The World Development Index, for example, assumes the 20 and 83.57 as the lower and upper bounds of longevity. For an inter-temporal comparison, the same lower and upper values may be used in the subsequent versions of indices for a valid inter-temporal comparison. The monotonicity (MN) assumes that an increase in the achievement level, *ceteris paribus*, increases the value of index. The translation invariance (TI) means that if there is a same absolute change in the value of indicators as well as its upper and lower bounds, the value of the indicator will remain the same. Homogeneity (HM) means that the index is insensitive to the units of measurement. For example, if the per capita income expressed in dollars is expressed in cents, the indicator value remains the same. The LI means that an increase in the value of an indicator at lower level will result in greater increase as compared to the increase in the indicator value at higher levels. For example, an increase of 1 year of life expectancy in a country where average life expectancy is 50 years will show a greater gain in the index than an addition of one year to average life expectancy of 70 years. This LI postulate is used in

Gender Related Development Index (GDI) by UNDP (Dijkstra and Hanmer 2000).

As we are considering the case where there are five indicators associated with three levels of MS, The general form of the index for k attributes is for an arbitrary index I.

$$I = \frac{\sum_{i=1}^{k}\left(\frac{x_i - m_i}{M_i - m_i}\right)}{k}$$

The above functional form satisfies the following important properties.

Normalization (NOM): For any $z \in [0, 1]$, $I(z, \ldots, z) = z$

Consistency in Aggregation (CIA): For any $\underline{a}, \underline{b} \in [0, 1]^k$,

$$I(a_1 + b_1, a_2 + b_2, \ldots, a_k + b_k) = I(a_1, a_2 \ldots, a_k) + I(b_1, b_2, \ldots, b_k)$$

Symmetry (SYM): For all $\underline{a} \in [0, 1]^k, I(\underline{a}) = I(\underline{a}P)$ where P is any $k \times k$ permutation matrix.

The NOM postulate shows that if all the indicators in the index I take the same value α, the achievement will also be α. This is an alternative way of saying that the achievement is an average of individual indicators. If there is only indicator in the index, then the value of that indicator will be the value of the index.

CIA property says that if an indicator i has multiple components, for example, the *complementary* level of attribute "Faith" which consists of four components (*salāt*, saum, *zakāt* and Hajj) and splitting the indicator is not possible, we can attach zero values to all the components of the indicator except the component of interest. Here the components which have not been assigned zero value become the level of indicator. I is not sensitive to the order in which the components are broken down. CIA requires that The SYM postulate says that I is insensitive to the permutation of the arguments, that is, only the individual indicator level is relevant for measuring achievement. The relevance of this property lies in the fact that there are some indicators such as World Giving Index which are composed of sub-components:

CIA also assumes substitutability among various indicators. If symmetry holds, the marginal rate of substitution between i and j attribute is independent of the level of the other attributes in the index. For example, how many percent of population is to be allowed to suffer from reduced wages as a result of imposing a stricter environmental regime, is independent of the level of charitable spending. It may be noted that the constant marginal rate of substitutability requires the linearity of the functional form.

$$\left(\frac{x_i - m_i}{M_i - m_i}\right)$$

As said earlier, if we want to attach greater weight to the differences in the lower levels of achievements, the achievement index takes a modified form I_r where I_r is a decreasing function of *r*.

$$I_r = \frac{\sum_{i=1}^{k}\left(\frac{x_i - m_i}{M_i - m_i}\right)^r}{k}, 0 < r < 1$$

The parameter *r* can be justified on the ground that the low-contributing attributes require attention from policy point of view for improving their levels in order to reach a higher position in achievement.

This method becomes helpful in calculating the percentage contributions made by individual attributes to overall achievement and hence in isolating attributes according to their degrees of contribution. This is an important policy application of our general index.

Another useful property is that the marginal rate of substitution remains constant as shown by Ravallion (2012b).

Now that I_r will measure the three levels of *Maqāṣid* separately which will be averaged to give MSI.

$$\text{MSI} = \frac{\sum_{i=1}^{k}\alpha_i I_i}{k}$$

As the theory of *maqāṣid* explicitly says that three levels are unequal, necessities being the most important, following by the complementary and embellishment. I shall assign unequal weights to these three subindices 3/6, 2/6 and 1/6. Though these weights are arbitrary, revisable and are open for debate, such a weighting has some theoretical justification as well.

5 Data

The *Maqāṣid* of Sharī'ah have been classified into three levels of interests (*masalih*) in the descending order of importance: necessities (*ḍarūriyāt*), complementarities (*ḥajiyāt*) and embellishments (*taḥsiniyāt*).

Though a sound theoretical work on various dimensions of *Maqāṣid* of the Sharīʿah already exists, the empirical analysis of these dimensions has not reached the same level of maturity. In this section, I shall propose a few indicators relevant for the measurement of *Maqāṣid* provide their justifications and highlight the mismatch between the available and ideal data.

5.1 Preservation of Religion

Islam considers the faith in Oneness of Allah the bare minimum for escaping the eternal damnation.[2] Abu Sa'eed Khudri (RA) reported that the Prophet (SAW) said, "Every person who has faith in his heart so much as the weight of an atom will be taken out of Hell" (Tirmidhi, 2:505). I have therefore chosen faith as the relevant indicator for the *necessary* level of the dimension "preservation of religion."

Given the centrality of monotheism in Islam, the ideal indicator should explicitly reflect the faith in the oneness of Allah. However, the only available data is collected by PEW in its report *The World's Muslims: Unity and Diversity* (2012) which consists only of a set of questions about the importance of the role of religion in life. PEW asks the question: "How important is religion in your life?" and the possible answers are: "very important, somewhat important, not too important and not at all important." I have chosen to include only two categories "very important and somewhat important" to serve as a proxy for the indicator *faith*.

In the *complementary* category of preservation of religion, I have used four indicators considered the "pillars" of Islam: *salāt*, fasting, pilgrimage and *zakāt*. Again, the data is from PEW. The justification for including these important acts of worship, considered the pillars of Islam, in the category of *ḥajiyāt* is that failure to carry out these *ʿibādāt* will not lead to eternal damnation as is warned in case of polytheism.[3] "The person who does not pray five times a day, there is no promise of Allah with him. He may forgive him or punish him" (Abu Dawood, Vol. 1, 1416).

[2] "Allah forgiveth not that partners should be set up with Him; but He forgiveth anything else, to whom He pleased; to set up partners with Allah is to devise a sin Most heinous indeed" (Quran, 4:48).

[3] Various juristic schools interpret the importance of these *ʿibādāt* in different ways.

There are lot of problems with the data collection of PEW with regard to *salāt, saum, hajj* and *zakāt*. The *salāt* indicator, as measured by PEW, can take any one of the four attributes (going to mosque for more than once a weak, once a week for Jumah prayer, once or twice a month, a few times a year especially for Eid). Such a distinction has clearly no basis in Islam. Islam requires total submission and is not content with half-hearted acts of worship. "When they stand up to prayer, they stand without earnestness, to be seen of men, but little do they hold Allah in remembrance" (Qur'ān, 4:142). Theoretically, a more satisfactory approach could have been the introduction of a binary variable stating whether a Muslim offers the five obligatory prayers in a day or not. I chose only one case where the percentage of population attended the mosques for more than once a weak. Other data problems relate to the paying of *zakāt* due and performing *hajj*. PEW measures only the percentage of population performing these duties, while these *'ibādāt* are obligatory for the Muslims satisfying certain monetary standards (they have *Istita'at*). The *saum* obligation is also contingent on the health, age and gender but the PEW data does not make these important distinctions.

The well-known Hadith-i-Jibrail gives us important insights regarding various degrees of faith. When the angel Jibrail asked the Prophet (SAW) regarding Imaan, the Prophet (SAW) replied: "It is to believe in Allah, His angels, His Books, His Messengers (peace be upon them all), in the Last Day and in Predestination of good and evil." He asked, "And what is Islam?" He said, "It is. to testify that there is no God but Allah and that Muhammad is His slave and His Messenger (SAW) to establish the Salah, to pay the *Zakāt*, to perform pilgrimage of the House and to fast in Ramadan." He asked, "And what is *Iḥsān*?" He said, "It is that you worship Allah as though you see Him, for it you cannot see Him, He sees you" (Tirmidhi, 2:518). This Hadith clearly points to the *embellishment* level of faith, but the problem is that the quality of *Iḥsān* is neither measurable nor observable.

Spending in the way of Allah is both emphasized and is often praised in Qur'ān in a highly commendatory terms. On a number of occasions, the virtues of faith are discussed in parallel with the spending in the way of Allah. "So he who gives (in charity) and fears (Allah). And (in all sincerity) testifies to the best. We will indeed make smooth for him the path to Bliss" (Qur'ān, 92:5–7). "But give them preference over themselves, even though poverty was their (own lot)" (Qur'ān, 59:9).

So I have included *infāq fi sabilillah* in the *embellishment* category of the preservation of faith. After the inclusion of *Zakāt* in the *complementary* category, we can avoid the overlapping issue by restricting the spending in the way of Allah to supererogatory spending, which is a special case of the general spending in the path of Allah (*infāq fi sabilillah*).

In the absence of any available data on the supererogatory *ṣadaqāt*, we use the data from World Giving index which is aggregation of three sub-components: percentage of the population helping the stranger, donating money and volunteering time. The problem with this data however is that it does not make explicit the amount of money or time actually devoted. The WGI also does not make explicit the size of the donation relative to the total wealth, which is an important concern in Islamic framework, and is highlighted in the example of Abu Bakr RA in the Battle of Tabuk when he devoted all of his household goods while Umar RA could devote only half of his wealth, though in absolute terms, the wealth of Umar RA far exceeded the share of Abu Bakr.

5.2 *Preservation of Life*

The Prophet SAW has termed this world as a tillage for the next world. Sharīʿah is a concept which is relevant to the life in this world, and the faith or deeds not done in this world will not be of any consequence in the world hereafter. "If only thou couldst see when the guilty ones will bend low their heads before their Lord, (saying:) 'Our Lord! We have seen and we have heard: Now then send us back (to the world): we will work righteousness: for we do indeed (now) believe'" (Qur'ān, 32, 12). So the preservation of life is an important objective of Sharīʿah.

The indicator chosen to measure the *necessary* level of preservation of life is the average life expectancy. The problem with this indicator is that it treats the question of life and death at its face value without looking into the spirit of life and reason behind the death. Islam looks at life and death through a different perspective: Life spent in the earnest service of Allah is considered as meritorious as death in the path of Allah. "Allah hath purchased of the believers their persons and their goods; for theirs (in return) is the garden (of Paradise): they fight in His cause, and slay and are slain…" (Qur'ān, 9:111).

The indicator chosen to represent the *complementary* level of the dimension "preservation of life" is freedom from malnutrition. Adequate nourishment as an important determinant of human well-being is well documented in the development literature (Qizilbash 1996). A closely related indicator relevant in the present context could be health which is expected to be broadly correlated with the indicator of freedom from malnourishment. It means that health is an important mercy of Allah. However, the problem with using health as the relevant indicator is not feasible primarily because of the reason that while it is easy to measure disease, it is not easy to measure health because it can be adversely affected by a range of diseases. Arguably, freedom from all types of diseases could mean a gain in the well-being, freedom from malnutrition is a better reflection of the adequacy of means required for a good life.

The *embellishment* category of life is by definition a life that should inspire other nations and instill confidence in others about the superiority of the Islamic way of life. So I have chosen the life satisfaction as the relevant indicator because it reflects the level of satisfaction with the conditions obtaining in the society. An ideal indicator should make a distinction between a subjective sense of good life (*hayaatan tayyibah*) that is characteristic of and is the consequence of the righteous deeds (Qur'ān, 16:97), and the facile smugness caused by an easy access to power and influence (see Qur'ān, 74:11–16). In order to qualify for the *embellishment* category, we might also like to have an indicator that should measure the life satisfaction above some predefined benchmark but life satisfaction used here is a continuous variable measuring the level of satisfaction from least satisfied to most satisfied for over seventy countries of the world.

5.3 *Preservation of Lineage*

Procreation is a fundamental condition for the continuity of human life on the earth. A Hadith suggests that Prophet SAW would feel proud of the large number of his *Ummah* on the Day of Judgment (Sunan Abu Dawood, 2:285). But this Hadith may only be construed as an exhortation because Islam has not expressly recommend any finite number of children. The number of children in a family being dependent on the age of the parents, their genetic composition, climate and many other factors is of secondary importance and may vary over time. So the survival of the children seems to be a more direct concern of the Sharīʿah. Qur'ān has given a stern warning for killing the children. "And when the seas are set on fire. And when souls are united. And when the female infant buried alive is asked. 'For what sin she was killed?'" (Qur'ān, 81:6–9).

A relevant indicator associated with the *necessary* category of the dimension of preservation of lineage is the survival of children. I have used in the *essential* category the World Bank data on the child mortality rate and transformed it by subtracting it from 100%. The overlap between the life expectancy and child survival can be rectified when more disaggregated data on the life expectancy of the population subgroups becomes available.

The relevant indicator corresponding with *complementary* category of the dimension of preservation of lineage seems not so clear. Some behavioral attributes like obedience and dutifulness on the part of children could be more direct candidate as a proxy of the *complementary* level. Although it can be safely assumed that the absence of these behavioral attributes will bring hardship and distress in the society, analysis of these attributes as a measurable concept is at best not straightforward. The concept of obedience to parents, for example, is dependent on the assumption that the expectations of the parents conform to the Sharīʿah standards. I have therefore chosen the safety of person as a relevant indicator here because it is not only the survival which is important but also sense of security for the children. The available data on the homicide rate collected by UNSTATS (United Nations Statistics Division's Regional Composition) serves as a proxy about the perceived security of person in a given society (Harrendorf et al. 2010). I have again transformed this indicator by subtracting it from 100% to make it reflect safety of person.

Literature on the *Maqāṣid* al-Sharīʿah relates environmental safety to the dimension of preservation of progeny (Amin et al. 2013). I associate environmental safety with the *embellishment* level of the dimension of preservation of lineage because such development paradigms are favored now which balance environment safety with economic growth. Again the environmental safety is of direct concern to the coming generation and this care about the coming generation is highly valued spirit in Islam. In an answer to the question regarding how much of the wealth should be spent, the Prophet SAW recommended that it was better to leave one's inheritors wealthy rather than poor (finding themselves) forced to beg of others (Bukhari, Volume 007, Book 064, Hadith Number 266).

5.4 *Preservation of Intellect*

There are a number of factors which affect human intellect such as drug use (see Ibn-Ashur 2006), mental disorders, accidents and heredity

(Mrazek et al. 1994), arguably, it is the education that affects human intellect most comprehensively (Chickering and Gamson 1987; Child et al. 1946; Lewin 1935; Masten and Coatsworth 1998). So we have used education as the relevant indicator with respect to the preservation of intellect. Some studies use religious education as a contradistinction from the formal education for the Sharīʿah-based indices (Kamali 1999). However, the limited data available on the religious education system in OIC countries and the disagreement about the concept of religious education as a separate academic construct force us to use the formal education and its various levels corresponding to the three levels of *Maqāṣid*. We have used the World Bank data on the three levels of education (primary, secondary and tertiary) corresponding with *necessary*, *complementary* and *embellishment* categories of *Maqāṣid*.

5.5 *Preservation of Property*

The traditional concept of property has undergone many changes over time and has included concepts like intellectual property. The job for the salaried persons could also be considered in a more indirect way as a counterpart of the property. Any conceivable means of living could therefore serve as a proxy for property. Conversely, the lack of the means of living both in the form of tangible or intangible property could be considered as poverty.

The relevant indicator with regard to the *necessary* and *complementary* categories of the dimension of the preservation of property is therefore the freedom from poverty. We have used the two levels of poverty (extreme poverty corresponding with $1.25 poverty line and poverty corresponding with $2 poverty line) computed by the World Bank[4] to correspond to two categories of *Maqāṣid*, *necessary* and *complementary*. We have chosen security of property as the relevant indicator for the *embellishment* level. The available relevant data relates to the crime against property is gathered by UNODC (Harrendorf et al. 2010). We consider four variables about the crime against property (robbery, theft,

[4]The World Bank's income poverty measure is not the ideal measures and suffers from many conceptual and methodological issues. See my PhD thesis "*An Inter-Temporal Comparison of International Poverty as an Achieved Functioning Deprivation*" for a detailed discussion.

motor vehicle theft and burglary) and transform the data to reflect the safety of property in a given country.

5.6 *Tackling Missing Data*

Given the range of indicators used in this study, it must be expected that data should not be available for all the indicators for all the OIC countries in this study, and the available data may not come from the same year. So we have to make to be caution in our interpretation of the results. For missing values, we developed a rule. Unless indicated otherwise, if some observation for a country is missing, we take the simple average of the values of the neighboring countries. WHO has in fact made this fine-grained grouping of different UN regions and subregions (WHO, Iodine status worldwide: WHO Global Database on Iodine Deficiency, 2004). When no data was available for the whole region, though it was very rare, we used the world averages.

6 Paternalism and Arbitrariness in the Choice of Indicators

As regards the issue of paternalism that is essentially embedded in any conceivable choice, ranking and weighting of dimensions of well-being, it may be argued that the concept of well-being may be conceptualized at various levels of generality. Nussbaum's list of valuable capabilities is severely criticized for being paternalistic (see Clark 2002), and she introduces the concept of plural and local specifications to deal with the problem of paternalism. A high level of generality in the conceptualization of well-being corresponds with the plural specification. There are some dimensions such as health and education which are expected to be generally important in almost all cultures of the world. Even if there is a broad consensus among all societies that health and education are desirable in their own right, individual societies might differ with regard to the broad outlines of the education or the best means to ensure health. The concept of local specification specifically accommodates the differences which are culture-specific or are based on some other local dynamic. Local specification thus "leaves a great deal of latitude for citizens to specify each of the components more concretely, and with much variety, in accordance with local traditions, or individual tastes" (Clark 2002, p. 94).

In our analysis, we chose the dimensions of well-being that are quite general in nature and are not much affected by local tastes. There might hardly be any society which does not consider longevity, health and adequate nourishment as important dimensions of human well-being. Political freedom, environmental safety and the freedom to do business are also expected to be valuable across all cultures.

7 Results

We have developed MSI which can be used to measure the objectives of Sharīʿah. This index can also be used to see the percentage share of the individual attributes to the overall achievement.

7.1 Maqāṣid-*al-Sharīʿah Index*

We have divided the 57 countries of the OIC region into four subgroups of roughly the same size in terms of development level within the framework of objectives of Sharīʿah. The development levels corresponding to these four subgroups are "Very High Development," "High Development," "Low Development" and "Very Low Development." The OIC countries are thus divided because MSI values have no cardinal value, and they can at best be used for geographical comparison. We have presented here only three scenarios of the index corresponding to three levels of r. It may be recalled that r, when it is less than 1, attaches greater weight to the differences in the lower levels of achievements (Table 1).

The most developed region in the Muslim world is predominantly Western and Southeastern Asia and Northern Africa, while the least developed area is in Africa. The notable fact is that there is only a narrow range [0.175, 0.259] within which the development spectrum in the Muslim world is exhausted. The regional distribution also reveals certain patterns: Southeast Asia, Asia and Western Asia have almost the same level of development, while the rest of Asia, South America and Southern Europe make another distinct group (highlighted in the Table 2). Africa, especially the western and eastern Africa bear the brunt of underdevelopment both in the framework of MSI as well as HDI.

Table 1 The *Maqāṣid* al-Sharī'ah Index

Country	*Index (r= 0.5)*	*Rank*	*Index (r= 0.25)*	*Rank*	*Index (r= 1)*	*Rank*	*Level of development*
Tunisia	0.279	1	0.261	2	0.276	3	Very high development
Iran	0.279	2	0.259	3	0.281	1	
Saudi Arabia	0.276	3	0.258	5	0.278	2	
Jordan	0.275	4	0.262	1	0.268	6	
Turkey	0.273	5	0.255	7	0.272	4	
Maldives	0.271	6	0.253	10	0.268	7	
Syria	0.270	7	0.256	6	0.263	14	
UAE	0.269	8	0.255	8	0.265	10	
Malaysia	0.268	9	0.253	9	0.267	9	
Algeria	0.267	10	0.252	12	0.264	12	
Lebanon	0.266	11	0.251	13	0.265	11	
Egypt	0.266	12	0.250	14	0.263	13	
Libya	0.266	13	0.247	16	0.272	5	
Brunei	0.264	14	0.252	11	0.267	8	
Qatar	0.261	15	0.249	15	0.260	15	High development
Kuwait	0.260	16	0.245	17	0.258	16	
Turkmenistan	0.255	17	0.259	4	0.240	25	
Morocco	0.254	18	0.237	20	0.251	22	
Bahrain	0.253	19	0.239	19	0.255	19	
Oman	0.253	20	0.234	21	0.257	17	
Gabon	0.248	21	0.231	22	0.252	20	
Palestine	0.248	22	0.228	23	0.255	18	
Azerbaijan	0.248	23	0.243	18	0.234	29	
Indonesia	0.245	24	0.228	24	0.252	21	
Kyrgyzstan	0.240	25	0.223	27	0.242	24	
Guyana	0.239	26	0.223	26	0.242	23	
Uzbekistan	0.238	27	0.223	28	0.237	26	
Iraq	0.235	28	0.220	29	0.235	28	
Kazakhstan	0.234	29	0.224	25	0.229	31	Low development
Albania	0.232	30	0.220	30	0.228	32	
Suriname	0.232	31	0.216	32	0.236	27	
Tajikistan	0.230	32	0.217	31	0.231	30	
Afghanistan	0.215	33	0.205	34	0.219	33	
Bangladesh	0.212	34	0.207	33	0.209	35	
Cameroon	0.209	35	0.202	35	0.209	36	
Sudan	0.207	36	0.198	36	0.212	34	
Djibouti	0.204	37	0.197	37	0.207	37	
Pakistan	0.202	38	0.194	38	0.207	38	
Senegal	0.198	39	0.193	39	0.200	39	
Yemen	0.196	40	0.192	40	0.194	42	
Gambia	0.196	41	0.191	41	0.198	40	
Mauritania	0.191	42	0.186	43	0.195	41	

(continued)

Table 1 (continued)

Country	*Index (r = 0.5)*	*Rank*	*Index (r = 0.25)*	*Rank*	*Index (r = 1)*	*Rank*	*Level of development*
Togo	0.188	43	0.186	42	0.188	43	Very low development
Benin	0.183	44	0.183	45	0.179	44	
Comoros	0.182	45	0.184	44	0.173	46	
Uganda	0.178	46	0.180	48	0.176	45	
Guinea	0.178	47	0.181	47	0.173	47	
Mali	0.177	48	0.183	46	0.164	49	
Nigeria	0.173	49	0.179	49	0.160	51	
Niger	0.170	50	0.172	51	0.165	48	
Guinea-Bissau	0.169	51	0.175	50	0.160	50	
Burkina Faso	0.162	52	0.169	52	0.157	52	
Somalia	0.161	53	0.164	53	0.156	54	
Ivory Coast	0.158	54	0.162	54	0.157	53	
Mozambique	0.149	55	0.159	55	0.138	56	
Sierra Leone	0.148	56	0.149	56	0.144	55	
Chad	0.135	57	0.140	57	0.136	57	

Source Author's calculations

Table 2 MSI: regional comparison

	Index (r = 0.5)	*Index (r = 0.25)*	*Index (r = 1)*
Southeastern Asia	0.259	0.244	0.262
Northern Africa	0.256	0.241	0.256
Western Asia	0.256	0.242	0.254
Central Asia	0.239	0.229	0.236
South America	0.236	0.220	0.239
Southern Asia	0.236	0.224	0.237
Southern Europe	0.232	0.220	0.228
Middle Africa	0.197	0.191	0.199
Western Africa	0.176	0.178	0.172
Eastern Africa	0.175	0.177	0.170

Source Author's calculations

7.2 *Comparison with HDI*

Interestingly, the same scenario holds in other paradigms of development such as human development as measured by UNDP. One might be tempted to assume that this is not a mere coincidence, and in some indirect way it is the empirical evidence of the claim in the Qur'ān that "If the people of the towns had but believed and feared Allah, We should

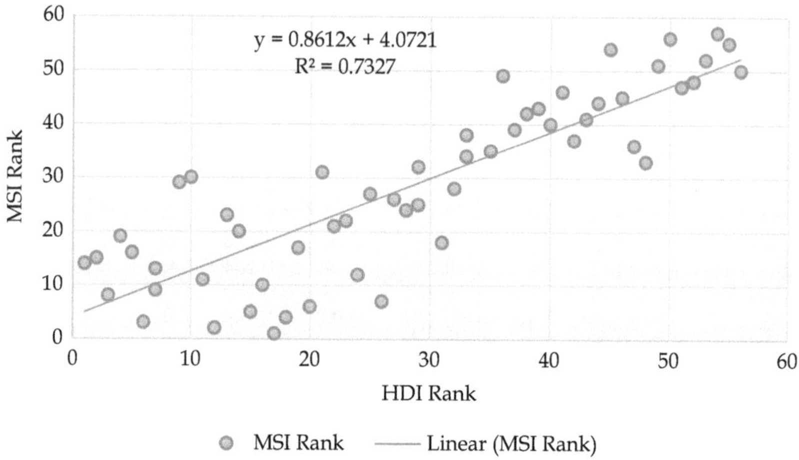

Fig. 1 Rank comparison: MSI vs. HDI (*Source* MSI ranking based on author's calculations. HDI ranking is based on Human Development Index 2012)

indeed have opened out to them (All kinds of) blessings from heaven and earth…" (Qur'ān, 7:96).

Even if MSI is broadly correlated with HDI, much of the divergence is visible at the higher levels of achievement (1st rank represents the highest level of development in MSI). Tunisia ranks 1st in MSI ($r=0.5$) but in HDI it ranks 17th among the countries belonging to OIC. Tunisia has performed extraordinarily well in the indicators which are generally not included in the HDI such as freedom of person and property and adherence to faith and deeds considered important in Islam. Albania presents a reverse case where it ranks 10th in HDI but 30th in MSI. An important reason is that among all the Islamic countries, it is in Albania that the smallest number of people consider religion to be important and its performance on the indicator of faith is also poor (Fig. 1).

7.3 *Individual Contribution of Indicators to Overall Achievement*

MSI is particularly useful when there are an unbalanced achievements in various indicators. Standard deviation being a measure of the distance from the mean, the policymakers can easily trace the indicator in which they are lagging relative to other indicators and may make the intervention. In view of the charge that the multidimensional indices only pack

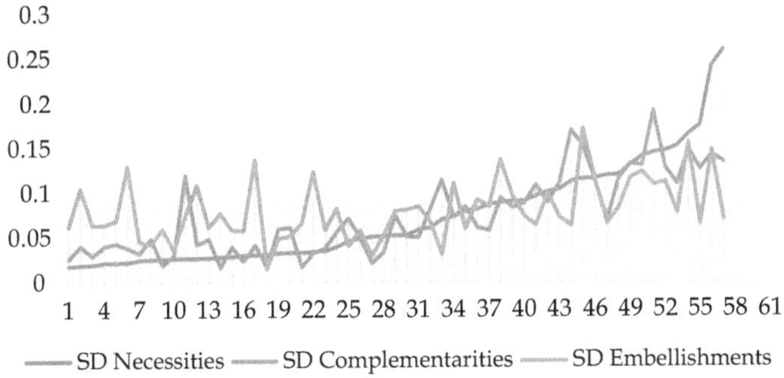

Fig. 2 Standard deviation of the individual contribution of indicators (*Source* Based on author's calculations)

dimensions which have neither theoretical justification nor any intuitive interpretation (Ravallion 2012a, b), this property of MSI to decompose all the indicators to show their individual contribution to overall achievement is extremely important property.

In Fig. 2, one can visually see the countries which have uneven development by their larger standard deviations.

7.4 *Substitutability*

The biggest problem with multidimensional indices is that even if they make explicit the apparent weights, they do not reveal the actual trade-offs for critical scrutiny. We have computed the trade-offs. As there is no monetary variable in our index, we cannot monetize the trade-offs. We chose two indicators from the *necessary* category, Life Expectancy (years) and Primary Completion Rate, and computed their trade-offs.

In Fig. 3, the trade-offs are marginal rates of substitution: An increase of one year in the life expectancy leads to some decrease in the primary completion rate. If we consider the magnitude of the percentage decrease in primary completion rate as a result of one year increase in life expectancy, the results are reassuring. The highest change in the given dataset is that of 2.6% for Saudi Arabia, which is quite negligible as compared to the implausibly small weights attached by HDI to the least developed countries, while astronomically high weight attached to the rich countries (Ravallion 2012b).

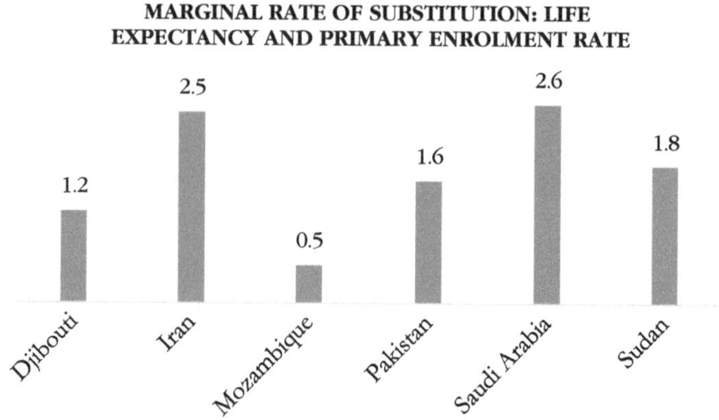

Fig. 3 Percentage decrease in the primary enrollment rate as a result of 1 year increase in life expectancy (*Source* Based on author's calculations)

7.5 *Robustness Check*

The choice of the parameter *r* as well as the indicators is, in essence, arbitrary and therefore it is important to change the assumptions of the model to see how it behaves. I have presented here the MSI ranks of the OIC countries with respect to three cases where *r* equals 0.5, 0.25 and 1.

We see in Fig. 4 that with the exception of two countries which are markedly off the line, the ranks of the countries in the three scenarios do not show any major divergence. Since *r* is a decreasing function of MSI, these two countries (Turkmenistan and Azerbaijan indicated by the circles hold the 4th and the 18th rank) rank higher when the magnitude of *r* is 0.25. However, when *r* equals 0.5, these countries do not show such a drastic difference from the pattern when *r* equals 1. As regards the comparison between the two scenarios when *r* equals 0.5 and 0.25 respectively, the latter parameter makes the divergences from the straight line look more accentuated.

7.6 *Limitations and Future Directions*

The empirical application of the concept of *Maqāṣid* al-Sharīʿah being a relatively new discipline, one should not expect that a consensus on important aspects of the measurement will evolve any time soon. Some of the limitations of this study are that the choice of indicators is not

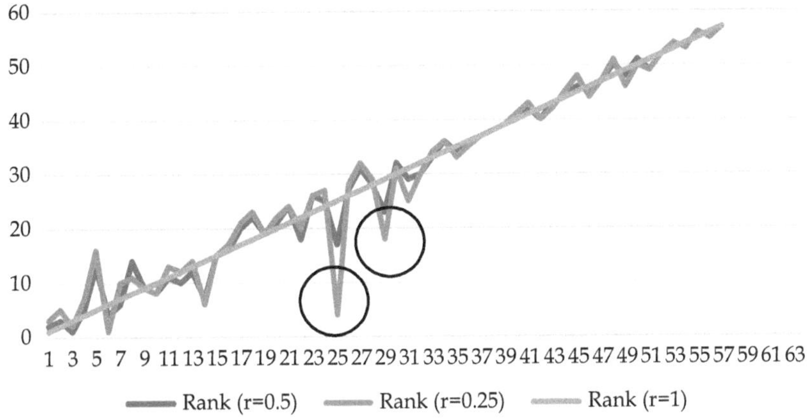

Fig. 4 Rank comparison using various magnitudes of *r* (*Source* Based on author's calculations)

wholly grounded in theory, and a lot of ad hoc and arbitrary assumptions go in the construction of this index. Secondly, the database required for the measurement of unobservable concepts is woefully lacking and whatever is available is not necessarily relevant to the normative framework of Islam. The empirical exercise will therefore require more coordinated efforts on the part of religious scholars and development practitioners.

8 Concluding Remarks

The empirical investigation of the Sharīʿah concepts is intrinsically problematic and the available tools to measure the religious constructs are not satisfactory partly because they have been developed on the basis of value judgments which may not always be admissible in the Sharīʿah. Some of available tools suffer from conceptual and methodological problems. This paper discussed the challenges related with the measurement of *Maqāṣid* al-Sharīʿah and provided some insights as to how to address these issues. We also developed a MSI corresponding to three levels of *necessities, complementarities* and *embellishments.* This measure has tried to overcome the serious conceptual and methodological problems characteristic of many existing indices. It makes explicit the trade-offs which generally remain implicit and create serious bias in the assessment of development. The contribution of individual components to the overall well-being is an additional advantage of this measure. However, the *empiricism* being new to Muslim scholarship, this work is carried out in the spirit of extending the debate further with a view to search for better measurement instruments.

Appendix

See Tables 3, 4, 5 and Fig. 5.

Table 3 Percentage contribution of five indicators of the necessary category

Individual share	*Necessities*				
	Religion	*Life*	*Progeny*	*Intellect*	*Property*
Afghanistan	31.3	20.9	8.8	21.9	17.1
Albania	0.0	29.3	23.3	19.0	28.4
Algeria	23.6	21.1	17.9	17.3	20.2
Azerbaijan	17.5	23.1	16.1	17.9	25.3
Bahrain	21.6	22.8	21.3	16.3	18.1
Bangladesh	31.4	26.9	17.8	17.5	6.4
Benin	37.3	23.9	11.8	19.7	7.3
Brunei	23.9	23.9	22.9	17.5	11.8
Burkina Faso	41.1	22.8	10.9	17.3	7.9
Cameroon	33.6	17.2	9.8	18.1	21.3
Chad	60.4	23.3	5.8	0.0	10.5
Comoros	35.5	24.2	13.3	21.3	5.7
Djibouti	31.1	22.5	11.7	15.9	18.8
Egypt	23.7	20.6	17.3	17.4	21.0
Gabon	24.4	17.6	10.8	24.6	22.7
Gambia	34.6	21.7	13.6	18.2	11.8
Guinea	39.4	22.0	10.6	18.0	10.0
Guinea-Bissau	43.3	21.7	7.1	20.4	7.5
Guyana	25.0	21.4	16.6	18.2	18.8
Indonesia	26.8	23.4	17.3	19.3	13.3
Iran	23.1	21.2	17.7	16.8	21.1
Iraq	26.0	22.4	16.3	13.2	22.2
Ivory Coast	39.8	15.3	9.7	18.0	17.1
Jordan	23.1	21.3	17.3	15.6	22.7
Kazakhstan	17.4	21.2	19.0	18.2	24.1
Kuwait	21.6	22.0	20.5	17.9	18.0
Kyrgyzstan	23.2	22.4	17.7	18.4	18.2
Lebanon	22.0	23.8	21.3	14.9	18.0
Libya	23.5	22.7	19.1	17.0	17.8

(continued)

Table 3 (continued)

Individual share	*Necessities*				
	Religion	*Life*	*Progeny*	*Intellect*	*Property*
Malaysia	24.3	23.0	22.9	17.6	12.1
Maldives	22.2	21.7	19.5	15.3	21.3
Mali	44.0	23.1	7.6	19.1	6.2
Mauritania	33.8	23.4	11.5	17.4	13.9
Morocco	23.3	21.6	15.9	17.7	21.5
Mozambique	47.5	17.3	15.2	17.5	2.5
Niger	42.1	25.8	9.4	14.2	8.6
Nigeria	46.0	20.4	8.5	25.2	0.0
Oman	21.6	22.8	20.2	17.4	18.0
Pakistan	31.0	24.6	10.3	16.7	17.4
Palestine	24.3	22.6	17.7	16.4	19.0
Qatar	20.8	22.6	23.0	16.2	17.4
Saudi Arabia	21.2	22.0	21.6	17.4	17.8
Senegal	33.7	24.6	15.4	15.0	11.3
Sierra Leone	59.8	0.0	0.0	32.4	7.8
Somalia	42.5	22.5	4.5	19.9	10.5
Sudan	30.0	21.6	12.0	21.7	14.7
Suriname	24.2	23.0	19.3	17.0	16.6
Syria	21.0	21.6	18.4	17.3	21.6
Tajikistan	25.4	22.6	13.0	19.6	19.5
Togo	36.3	20.5	10.6	20.0	12.6
Tunisia	23.2	22.0	18.4	15.4	20.9
Turkey	20.7	22.2	19.2	17.3	20.7
Turkmenistan	21.3	20.4	13.1	18.5	26.7
Uganda	36.8	23.0	15.3	14.0	11.0
United Arab Emirates	21.0	22.3	21.5	17.7	17.5
Uzbekistan	19.9	23.1	16.2	18.7	22.1
Yemen	29.2	23.2	14.6	16.7	16.3

Source Author's calculations

Table 4 Percentage contribution of five indicators of the complementary category

Individual share	*Complements*				
	Religion	*Life*	*Progeny*	*Intellect*	*Property*
Afghanistan	26.8	19.8	23.9	18.9	10.6
Albania	8.4	26.4	19.5	22.1	23.6
Algeria	19.2	23.2	21.6	21.3	14.7

(continued)

Table 4 (continued)

Individual share	*Complements*				
	Religion	*Life*	*Progeny*	*Intellect*	*Property*
Azerbaijan	10.3	24.6	20.3	22.8	22.1
Bahrain	18.9	18.1	25.4	23.1	14.6
Bangladesh	28.3	19.9	27.9	22.1	1.7
Benin	32.0	27.1	17.0	21.3	2.5
Brunei	20.7	23.1	22.8	22.4	11.0
Burkina Faso	40.3	18.9	19.4	18.2	3.2
Cameroon	26.9	17.7	24.4	18.9	12.2
Chad	42.6	15.3	21.6	17.1	3.4
Comoros	38.1	0.0	23.4	33.8	4.8
Djibouti	30.6	16.0	23.7	17.9	11.8
Egypt	19.9	24.7	19.3	19.8	16.3
Gabon	24.8	23.8	14.4	14.7	22.4
Gambia	30.6	20.5	19.0	22.7	7.3
Guinea	36.5	22.3	14.8	21.4	4.9
Guinea-Bissau	35.2	28.6	15.4	18.9	1.9
Guyana	20.7	25.7	12.2	25.6	15.7
Indonesia	24.5	20.5	25.8	22.2	7.1
Iran	20.2	23.2	18.3	19.9	18.4
Iraq	22.7	20.1	23.6	18.5	15.2
Ivory Coast	41.1	22.2	0.0	24.5	12.2
Jordan	17.9	22.6	19.2	19.8	20.4
Kazakhstan	0.0	29.8	18.4	27.4	24.4
Kuwait	18.2	24.5	20.3	22.9	14.1
Kyrgyzstan	16.5	24.7	19.5	25.2	14.1
Lebanon	19.7	25.2	20.8	19.9	14.5
Libya	20.0	24.1	19.2	22.9	13.9
Malaysia	20.1	23.0	18.9	17.1	20.9
Maldives	21.0	21.8	20.8	18.8	17.6
Mali	28.9	26.8	21.6	21.6	1.2
Mauritania	32.6	26.2	17.6	15.0	8.7
Morocco	20.8	22.4	21.5	18.7	16.5
Mozambique	35.5	12.0	33.9	18.1	0.4
Niger	33.3	25.0	28.8	10.8	2.2
Nigeria	33.7	26.9	19.0	20.4	0.0
Oman	19.2	18.4	24.4	23.2	14.8
Pakistan	31.5	18.7	23.0	18.8	8.0
Palestine	25.4	10.8	22.1	24.8	16.9
Qatar	18.9	18.1	23.3	25.1	14.6
Saudi Arabia	17.6	23.7	21.4	23.7	13.6
Senegal	31.5	18.7	22.6	20.5	6.8
Sierra Leone	38.6	16.5	20.7	23.0	1.2

(continued)

Table 4 (continued)

Individual share	*Complements*				
	Religion	*Life*	*Progeny*	*Intellect*	*Property*
Somalia	41.0	11.9	40.0	0.0	7.1
Sudan	31.8	10.4	13.5	33.2	11.1
Suriname	21.6	19.2	20.4	23.9	15.0
Syria	18.4	24.7	20.4	19.6	16.9
Tajikistan	21.8	11.3	26.3	27.0	13.6
Togo	31.5	19.7	19.5	22.7	6.6
Tunisia	18.9	22.7	20.3	20.1	18.1
Turkey	17.3	24.1	18.8	21.0	18.9
Turkmenistan	12.4	24.0	17.9	21.6	24.0
Uganda	35.9	14.1	24.7	18.8	6.4
United Arab Emirates	18.1	24.4	22.6	21.0	14.0
Uzbekistan	13.8	23.3	21.1	25.6	16.2
Yemen	27.4	12.9	27.4	22.4	9.9

Source Author's calculations

Table 5 Percentage contribution of five indicators of the embellishment category

Individual share	*Embellishments*				
	Religion	*Life*	*Progeny*	*Intellect*	*Property*
Afghanistan	25.9	21.1	30.1	6.0	16.9
Albania	11.3	15.3	23.6	27.4	22.4
Algeria	16.4	13.8	23.0	22.9	23.9
Azerbaijan	23.0	7.3	21.5	18.3	29.8
Bahrain	30.6	5.8	12.8	30.4	20.5
Bangladesh	15.2	24.4	23.4	11.3	25.7
Benin	16.2	5.3	32.5	15.5	30.5
Brunei	30.8	16.1	8.8	22.1	22.1
Burkina Faso	17.5	10.5	34.3	7.8	29.8
Cameroon	22.6	9.2	28.6	13.0	26.5
Chad	22.4	6.2	36.9	3.4	31.2
Comoros	19.8	16.0	27.4	11.8	25.0
Djibouti	20.4	9.3	31.4	8.3	30.6
Egypt	17.7	15.2	22.4	20.3	24.3
Gabon	23.1	11.8	26.7	10.0	28.3
Gambia	19.9	14.3	30.8	7.2	27.8
Guinea	21.7	12.6	28.2	10.2	27.4
Guinea-Bissau	20.3	14.7	32.4	4.1	28.5

(continued)

Table 5 (continued)

Individual share	*Embellishments*				
	Religion	*Life*	*Progeny*	*Intellect*	*Property*
Guyana	25.6	18.5	24.4	13.8	17.7
Indonesia	27.8	7.2	22.0	18.3	24.8
Iran	26.4	13.6	15.6	26.3	18.2
Iraq	22.1	12.2	24.0	16.9	24.7
Ivory Coast	0.0	9.6	40.2	14.6	35.7
Jordan	18.5	9.1	22.9	26.0	23.5
Kazakhstan	21.1	16.4	14.8	32.6	15.1
Kuwait	32.5	16.0	4.4	22.0	25.0
Kyrgyzstan	17.9	14.5	24.5	24.1	19.0
Lebanon	21.2	10.4	19.3	25.5	23.7
Libya	28.3	13.5	15.4	20.2	22.5
Malaysia	20.6	22.5	16.8	23.1	17.0
Maldives	27.3	22.6	25.7	15.8	8.6
Mali	18.3	17.5	29.8	9.4	25.0
Mauritania	26.1	1.9	32.5	8.8	30.7
Morocco	17.8	13.3	28.0	17.3	23.6
Mozambique	21.6	0.0	36.2	8.7	33.5
Niger	17.5	23.5	31.7	0.0	27.3
Nigeria	22.6	15.1	26.4	11.3	24.6
Oman	36.3	3.8	11.5	19.5	28.9
Pakistan	21.5	22.0	27.7	11.8	16.9
Palestine	14.7	14.1	24.3	24.7	22.2
Qatar	35.9	18.7	0.0	15.9	29.5
Saudi Arabia	18.1	27.5	9.6	25.1	19.7
Senegal	15.7	25.2	25.3	9.0	24.9
Sierra Leone	23.7	20.0	26.7	8.3	21.2
Somalia	27.2	6.7	30.1	9.7	26.3
Sudan	21.5	16.4	24.4	17.7	20.0
Suriname	32.2	23.9	26.6	17.4	0.0
Syria	22.8	9.7	21.8	18.9	26.8
Tajikistan	20.3	15.7	24.5	16.0	23.6
Togo	13.6	11.4	32.5	13.3	29.1
Tunisia	17.2	21.1	20.7	20.7	20.3
Turkey	11.7	26.1	18.0	26.4	17.8
Turkmenistan	28.3	14.6	14.5	20.2	22.4
Uganda	23.1	14.8	27.8	10.2	24.1
United Arab Emirates	27.0	18.9	9.7	22.8	21.6
Uzbekistan	26.8	23.3	20.9	10.4	18.6
Yemen	15.2	17.5	29.1	13.0	25.1

Source Author's calculations

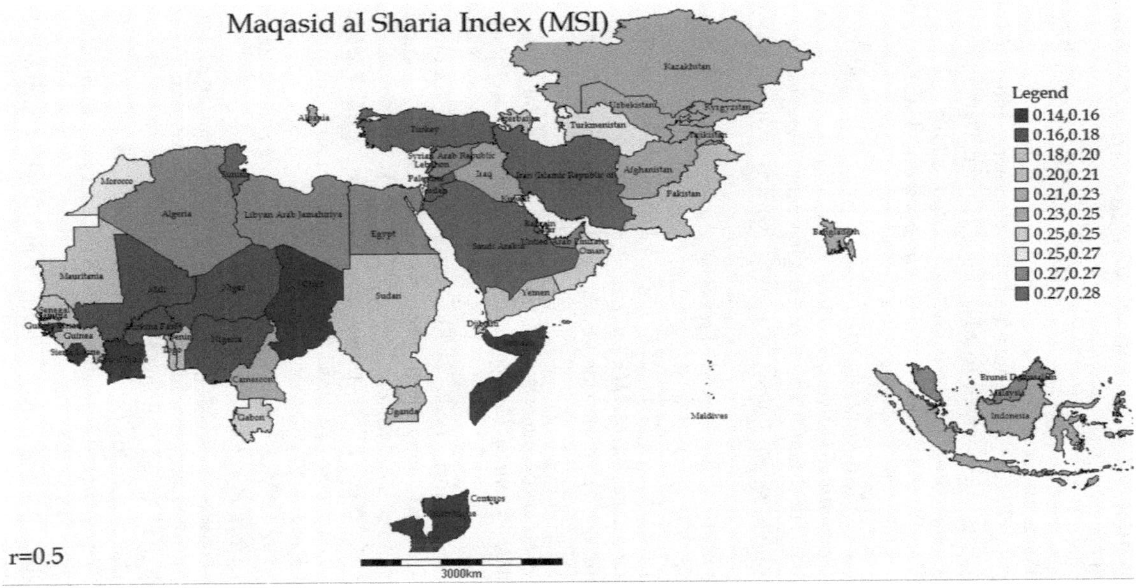

Fig. 5 MSI of the OIC countries (some OIC countries of South America not shown in this map) (*Map Source* Author's generation)

References

Adiseshiah, M.S., 1991. *Sustainable Development: Its Content, Scope, and Prices*, Gower Publishing Company, Limited.

Ahmad, K., 1994. *Islamic Approach to Development: Some Policy Implications*, Institute for Policy Studies.

Amin, R.M. et al., 2013. The Integrated Development Index (I-DEX): A New Comprehensive Approach to Measuring Human Development. In *9th International Conference on Islamic Economics and Finance*.

Bell, J., 2012. *The World's Muslims: Unity and Diversity*, The Pew Forum on Religion and Public Life, Pew Research Center.

Chakravarty, S.R., 2003. A Generalized Human Development Index. *Review of Development Economics*, 7(1), pp. 99–114.

Chapra, M., 2008. The Islamic Vision of Development. *Thoughts on Economics, The Quarterly Journal of Islamic Economics Research Bureau (Bangladesh)*, 18(3), pp. 7–38.

Chapra, M.U., 2007. *Islam and Economic Development: A Strategy for Development with Justice and Stability*, Adam Publishers.

Chickering, A.W. & Gamson, Z.F., 1987. Seven Principles for Good Practice in Undergraduate Education. *AAHE Bulletin*, 3, p. 7.

Child, I.L., Potter, E.H. & Levine, E.M., 1946. Children's Textbooks and Personality Development: An Exploration in the Social Psychology of Education. *Psychological Monographs: General and Applied*, 60(3), pp. i–54.

Clark, D.A., 2002. *Visions of Development: A Study of Human Values*, Edward Elgar Publishing.

Dijkstra, A.G. & Hanmer, L.C., 2000. Measuring Socio-Economic Gender Inequality: Toward an Alternative to the UNDP Gender-Related Development Index. *Feminist Economics*, 6(2), pp. 41–75.

El-Ghazali, A.H. & Series, I.E.T., 1994. *Man Is the Basis of the Islamic Strategy for Economic Development*, Islamic Research and Training Institute, Islamic Development Bank.

Gorsuch, R.L., 1984. Measurement: The Boon and Bane of Investigating Religion. *American Psychologist*, 39(3), p. 228.

Harrendorf, S., Heiskanen, M. & Malby, S., 2010. *International Statistics on Crime and Justice*, European Institute for Crime Prevention and Control, Affiliated with the United Nations (HEUNI).

Ibn-Ashur, Al-Tahir M., 2006. *Treatise on Maqasid al-Shari'ah*.

Kamali, M.H., 1999. Maqasid Al-Shar'ah: The Objectives of Islamic Law. *Islamic Studies*, 38(2), pp. 193–208.

Khurshid, A., 1980. Economic Development in an Islamic Framework. *Studies in Islamic Economics*.

Lewin, K., 1935. *A Dynamic Theory of Personality*.

Masten, A.S. & Coatsworth, J.D., 1998. The Development of Competence in Favorable and Unfavorable Environments: Lessons from Research on Successful Children. *American Psychologist*, 53(2), p. 205.

Moberg, D.O., 2010. Spirituality Research: Measuring the Immeasurable? *Perspectives on Science & Christian Faith*, 62(2), pp. 99–114. https://www.asa3.org/ASA/PSCF/2010/PSCF6-10Moberg.pdf.

Mrazek, P.B., Haggerty, R.J., et al., 1994. *Reducing Risks for Mental Disorders: Frontiers for Preventive Intervention Research*, National Academies Press.

Qizilbash, M., 1996. Capabilities, Well-Being and Human Development: A Survey. *The Journal of Development Studies*, 33(2), pp. 143–162.

Ravallion, M., 2012a. Mashup Indices of Development. *The World Bank Research Observer*, 27(1), pp. 1–32.

Ravallion, M., 2012b. Troubling Tradeoffs in the Human Development Index. *Journal of Development Economics*, 99(2), pp. 201–209.

Tahir, S. & Haque, Z., 1995. Islamic Perspectives on Economic Development [with Comments]. *The Pakistan Development Review*, 34(4), pp. 845–856.

Zaman, N. & Asutay, M., 2009. Divergence Between Aspirations and Realities of Islamic Economics: A Political Economy Approach to Bridging the Divide. *IIUM Journal of Economics and Management*, 17(1), pp. 73–96.

CHAPTER 3

Sharīʿah-Based Ethical Performance Measurement Framework and Relevant Data to Measure Development in Light of *Maqāṣid* al-Sharīʿah

Houssem Eddine Bedoui

1 Introduction

"How Islamic are Islamic countries?", it was the question asked by Rehman and Askari (2010) by developing an index called an "Islamicity index" ranking Muslim and non-Muslim countries based on Islamic values. However, comparing countries in terms of socioeconomic development using the objectives of the Islamic Law faced the issue of availability of data. The current paper presents therefore a socioeconomic development index based on the objectives of Islamic Law. In fact, Socioeconomic development

The views and opinions expressed in this chapter are those of the author and do not necessarily reflect the official policy or position of his institution.

H. E. Bedoui (✉)
Islamic Development Bank Group, Jeddah, Saudi Arabia
e-mail: Hbedoui@isdb.org

Ecole Normale Superieure, Lyon, France

S. S. Ali (ed.), *Towards a Maqāṣid al-Sharīʿah Index of Socio-Economic Development*, Palgrave Studies in Islamic Banking, Finance, and Economics,
https://doi.org/10.1007/978-3-030-12793-0_3

is a process of social and economic development in societies. The index describes how societies behave in the global economy. An important predecessor of modern social indicators research is the Italian statistician and criminologist Alfredo Niceforo works. In his book on "*Les indices numérique de la civilisation et du progress*" (Niceforo 1921), he made an important attempt to identify quantifiable symptoms of living conditions in a broad sense—indicators in our modern terminology—in order to measure and monitor levels and degrees of civilization and social progress across time and space.[1] Moreover since 1990, Human Development Index (HDI) provides a solution that goes beyond GDP; however, three dimensions are seen unsatisfactory. *Maqāṣid* al-Sharīʿah consequently provides a thorough vision of development to assess it. The paper starts with a literature review of socioeconomic development indices, then a methodology of the index. In this methodology section, different approaches are exposed and explained. Finally, by selecting the applicable data with the explained methodology, the results are revealed and revealed in order to assess the socioeconomic development of different countries based on the objectives of the Islamic Law.

2 Literature Review

2.1 Index

Indices are becoming progressively more popular and more widespread tools designed to measure and to inform different stakeholders about the socioeconomic development. According to Alfsen and Sæbø (1993),[2] index user can be classified into 3 main groups:

- The general public
- Politicians, authorities, and decision makers
- Experts and scientists

The major advantage of developing an index is simplifying complexity and reducing the number of measurements and parameters needed to

[1] By treating the topic of "happiness" within the last chapter of his volume and discussing the question whether people subjectively perceive improvements of living conditions and social progress, Niceforo did also touch another essential topic of modern social indicators and quality of life research. This is the correspondence between objective conditions and subjective perceptions and evaluations. In his opinion, people are unlikely to become more happy even if there is social progress and a betterment of living conditions from an objective point of view.

[2] Alfsen, K. H., and Sæbø, H. V. (1993). "Environmental Quality Indicators: Background, Principles and Examples from Norway". *Environmental and Resource Economics* 3: 415–435.

describe the development and to simplify this information for these three users. It is typically accomplished by condensing a wide range of information into a single value. According to Liverman et al. (1988)[3] and Quarrie (1992),[4] an index is a combination of numerous indicators. By summarizing data and information, the index can be valuable and essentially beneficial for establishing inter-country comparisons. Such comparisons engender questions about some countries ranking. Moreover, we can study the individual socioeconomic development dimension of the index and examine why there are inter-country differences.

There is a whole heap of development indices, and the literature is not short of examples. Few of them are presented in Table 1.

2.2 *Indicators*

Indicators are crucial elements in the whole measurement of socioeconomic development. They are indeed important feature of all assessment efforts. They are beneficial because they give relevant information about the state of more complex phenomena. These indicators are aggregated together to measure the index. Actually, it can be done by combining all components into one index through a simple average of the values of separate indicators, but there are openly other calculation alternatives.

Existing definitions of indicators are particularly extensive and confusing (Bakkes et al. 1994) since there is no single, commonly accepted definition of the term "indicator."[5]

In fact, an indicator is defined as *a variable* (Chevalier et al. 1992[6]; Holling 1978[7]); *a measure* (McQueen and Noak 1988[8];

[3] Liverman, D. M., Hanson, M. E., Brown, B. J., and Merideth, R. W. (1988). "Global Sustainability: Toward Measurement". *Environmental Management* 12 (2): 133–143.

[4] Quarrie, J. (1992). *The Earth Summit '92: The United Nations Conference on Environment and Development*. London: Regency Press.

[5] Scrivens, K., and Iasiello, B. (2010). "Indicators of 'Societal Progress': Lessons from International Experiences". OECD Statistics Working Papers, No. 2010/04, OECD Publishing. https://doi.org/10.1787/5km4k7mq49jg-en.

[6] Chevalier, S., Choiniere, R., Bernier, L., et al. (1992). *User Guide to 40 Community Health Indicators*. Ottawa: Community Health Division, Health and Welfare Canada.

[7] Holling, C. S. (1978). *Adaptive Environmental Assessment and Management*. Chichester: Wiley (p. 53).

[8] McQueen, D., and Noak, H. (1988). "Health Promotion Indicators: Current Status, Issues and Problems". *Health Promotion* 3: 117–125 (MWCD).

Table 1 Examples of Socioeconomic development indices

Human Development Index (HDI)
Prosperity Index
Happy Planet Index
Wellbeing Index
Better Life Index
Ecological Footprint
Gross National Happiness
Happy Planet Index
American Human Development Index
Living Planet Index
Green Growth
Gross National Happiness
MAP 2.0
Canadian Index of Wellbeing
National Accounts of Well-Being
Programme for International Student Assessment
Indices of Social Development (ISD)
Gallup-Healthways Well-Being Index
The National Well-Being Project
Wheel of Wellness
Sustainable Society Index

Source Author's own

World Bank 1995[9]; Dever 1979[10]; Holling 1978[11]); *a statistical measure* (Tunstall 1992)[12]; *a proxy for a measure* (McQueen and Noak 1988)[13]; *a meter or measuring instrument* (Adriaanse 1993)[14]; *a value* (OECD 1993; Bakkes et al. 1994); *a parameter* (OECD

[9] World Bank. (1995). *Monitoring Environmental Progress.* Washington, DC: The World Bank (p. 80).

[10] Dever, G. E. A. (1979). *Community Health Analysis.* Germantown, Mary town: Aspen Systems Corporation.

[11] Ibid., 9 (p. 106).

[12] Tunstall, D. (1992). "Developing Environmental Indicators: Definitions, Framework and Issues" (Draft Paper). *Background Materials for the World Resources Institute.* Workshop on Global Environmental Indicators, Washington, DC, December 7–8, 1992. Washington, DC: World Resources Institute.

[13] Ibid., 10.

[14] Adriaanse, A. (1993). *Environmental Policy Performance Indicators.* The Hague: SDV Publishers (p. 7: in his example of the clock and the thermometer as indicators).

1993[15]; Bakkes et al. 1994[16,17]); *an index* (Hammond et al. 1995)[18]; *a subindex or component of an index* (Ott 1978[19]; Adriaanse 1993[20]; Hammond et al. 1995[21]); *a piece of information* (Bakkes et al. 1994)[22]; *an empirical model of reality* (Hammond et al. 1995)[23]; *a sign* (Marcus 1983).[24]

Back to source, the term "*indicator*" dates back to the 1650s and it is derived from Latin "*indicates*," past participle of "*indicare*," which means to announce, point out, or indicate.[25] Chambers Dictionary defines an indicator as "*...something that provides an indication, a pointer...any device for exhibiting conditions for the time being*."[26]

The OECD defines an indicator as "*a parameter, or a value derived from parameters, which points to, provides information about, describes the state of a phenomenon/environment/area, with a significance extending beyond that directly associated with a parameter value*."[27]

[15]OECD [Organization for Economic Cooperation and Development]. (1993). *OECD Core Set of Indicators for Environmental Performance Reviews: A Synthesis Report by the Group on the State of the Environment*. Paris: OECD.

[16]Bakkes, J. A., van den Born, G. J., Helder, J. C., Swart, R. J., Hope, C. W., and Parker, J. D. E. (1994). *An Overview of Environmental Indicators: State of the Art and Perspectives*. UNEP/EATR.94-01; RIVM/402001001. Environmental Assessment Sub-Programme. Nairobi: UNEP.

[17]Ibid., 16.

[18]Hammond, A., Adriaanse, A., Rodenburg, E., Bryant, D., and Woodward, R. (1995). *Environmental Indicators: A Systematic Approach to Measuring and Reporting on Environmental Policy Performance in the Context of Sustainable Development*. Washington, DC: World Resources Institute (p. 8: They considered the WRI's green-house index an indicator).

[19]Ott, W. R. (1978). *Environmental Indices: Theory and Practice*. Ann Arbor, MI: Ann Arbor Science (p. 8).

[20]Ibid., 16.

[21]Ibid., 20 (p. 16).

[22]Ibid., 18.

[23]Ibid., 20.

[24]Marcus, S. (1983). "Towards a Semiotic Approach to Social Indicators". Paper Presented at the International Congress of Logic, *Methodology and Philosophy of Science*, Salzburg, Austria, July 11–16.

[25]Online Etymology Dictionary: http://www.etymonline.com/.

[26]Chambers Online Dictionary: http://www.chambers.co.uk/.

[27]Linster, M. (2003). "OECD Environmental Indicators: Development, Measurement and Use". OECD Reference Paper. http://www.oecd.org/LongAbstract/0,3425,en_2649_34441_24993548_1_1_1_1,00.html.

Hence, "*Indicators are succinct measures that aim to describe as much about a system as possible in as few points as possible…Indicators help us understand a system, compare it and improve it*" (NHS 2008).[28]

Consequently, "Indicators serve to foster understanding of a system and how it can be improved, and to monitor performance against agreed standards or benchmarks."[29]

After outlining general definitions of indicator, the indicators linked to social economic development are called socioeconomic indicators: A socioeconomic indicator can be defined by a measure representing the state and the development of social economics. However, that state cannot be defined by only a single indicator.

Actually, two leading significant definitions arise from the literature. The first one stated by the Australian Bureau of Statistics:

> Social indicators are measures of social well-being which provide a contemporary view of social conditions and monitor trends in a range of areas of social concern over time. (McEwin 1995: 314–315)[30]

The second one from a United Nations document:

> Social indicators can be defined as statistics that usefully reflect important social conditions and that facilitate the process of assessing those conditions and their evolution. Social Indicators are used to identify social problems, that require action, to develop priorities and goals for action and spending, and to assess the effectiveness of programmes and policies. (United Nations 1994)[31]

From both definitions, it is clear that the social indicators focus mainly on living conditions in a variety of social areas. However, the United

[28] Pencheon, D. (2008). "The Good Indicators Guide: Understanding How to Use and Choose Indicators". UK National Health Service Institute for Innovation and Improvement website, www.institute.nhs.uk.

[29] Griffiths, P., et al. (2008). *State of the Art Metrics for Nursing: A Rapid Appraisal.* London: National Nursing Research Unit, King's College London, pp. 1, 2.

[30] McEwin, Marion. (1995). "Social Indicators and Social Statistics in Australia". *Statistical Journal of the United Nations*, Economic Commission for Europe, pp. 314–315.

[31] United Nations. (1994). "Information on Social Development Publications and Indicators in the United Nations System". Working Paper No. 7, United Nations Publications, New York.

Nations definition is much more ambitious than the first one, since it considers the social indicators use not just in trend monitoring and view descriptions, but moreover in identifying problems, developing priorities and the assessment of programs and policies.

Beyond the more general properties of social indicators, Judith Innes (1990) developed criteria making a good indicator effective in public decisions. Conferring to her:

> the measure must be pertinent to questions of concern; the concepts underlying the measures must be clear and agreed upon; the measure must relate to the concept which it is assumed to, and do so in a well understood way; the methods to produce the measure must provide reliable results, measuring what they purport to without hidden or unexpected bias; and the measure must be understandable and understood in its concept and limitations. (Innes 1990: 110)[32]

Finally, McEwin (1995: 315)[33] stated certain features that a social indicator is supposed to pinpoint. Overall, it should reflect a specific social idea and be:

- Valid and meaningful
- Sensitive to the underlying phenomenon
- Summary in nature
- Available as time series
- Able to be disaggregated
- Understandable and easily interpreted
- Relate where appropriate to other indicators

2.3 Human Development Index

The insufficiency of GDP as a single measure of development generated a huge aspiration to endorse a broader vision of human development and a need for an alternative index to the GDP and its family of economic indicators. This alternative index for measuring progress in human development was created and introduced first by *The United Nations Development*

[32] Innes, Judith E. (1990). "Disappointments and Legacies of Social Indicators". *Journal of Public Policy* 9: 429–432.

[33] Ibid., 32 (p. 315).

Programme (UNDP) in *Human Development Report* of 1990. This index is the *Human Development Index* (HDI) and it is yearly since 1990. It is a composite index allowing rating countries based on their overall performance built on three criteria: Education, health, and income. Mahbub al Haq HDI founder insisted on having one single measure but not as blind as GDP regarding social aspects of human life.

The emergence of HDI was generated by Haq works on *basic needs* and Sen's work on the *capabilities* approach. Both remain the main theorist behind the concept of human development who cooperated in the establishment of the index.

Conceptually, Sen identifies two forms integral of the capability approach: Initially, the "*functionings*" that is to say what an individual can do in terms of action, but it can also represent a state. For example, some *functionings* are simple such as eating, reading, writing, and be healthy… While others are more complex like being happy, having a good self-esteem, to be politically active in his community, etc. Then all the specific *functionings* that someone has the freedom to achieve are "capability set" or "capability" for short. Hence, the substantive freedom to pursue different functioning combinations.

> Human development is a process of enlarging people's choices. The most critical ones are to lead a long and healthy life, to be educated and to enjoy a decent standard of living. Additional choices include political freedom, guaranteed human rights and self-respect- what Adam Smith called the ability to mix with others without being "ashamed to appear in public"… Human development has two sides: the formation of human capabilities such as improved health, knowledge and skills - and the use people make of their acquired capabilities - for leisure, productive purposes or being active in cultural, social and political affairs. If the scales of human development do not finely balance the two sides, considerable human frustration may result.
>
> According to this concept of human development, income is clearly only one option that people would like to have, albeit an important one. But it is not the sum total of their lives. Development must, therefore, be more than just the expansion of income and wealth. Its focus must be people.

The HDI was highly criticized particularly in the nineties especially for the aggregation of all the components which is common to several indices. Meaning, HDI assumes that its components are commensurable; for example, an increase in life expectancy would be substitutable for an increase in commodity production (Table 2).

Table 2 List of Human Development Reports[a] (1990–2013)

Year	*Name of the Report*
1990	Concept and Measurement of Human Development
1991	Financing Human Development
1992	Global Dimensions of Human Development
1993	People's Participation
1994	New Dimensions of Human Security
1995	Gender and Human Development
1996	Economic Growth and Human Development
1997	Human Development to Eradicate Poverty
1998	Consumption for Human Development
1999	Globalization with a Human Face
2000	Human Rights and Human Development
2001	Making New Technologies Work for Human Development
2002	Deepening Democracy in a Fragmented World
2003	Millennium Development Goals: A Compact Among Nations to End Human Poverty
2004	Cultural Liberty in Today's Diverse World
2005	International Cooperation at a Crossroads: Aid, Trade and Security in an Unequal World
2006	Beyond Scarcity: Power, Poverty and the Global Water Crisis
2007/2008	Fighting Climate Change: Human Solidarity in a Divided World
2009	Overcoming Barriers: Human Mobility and Development
2010	The Real Wealth of Nations: Pathways to Human Development
2011	Sustainability and Equity: A Better Future for All
2013	The Rise of the South: Human Progress in a Diverse World

Source Author's own
[a]Global Reports Library: http://hdr.undp.org/en/global-reports

Moreover, HDI has also been evaluated as "*redundant*" and a "*reinvention of the wheel*" (McGillivray 1991[34]; Srinivasan 1994[35]). Furthermore, Sagar and Najam (1998)[36] criticized the additivity of the three variables in one measure which do not reflect the level of human development on each dimension.

[34]McGillivray, Mark. (1991). "The Human Development Index: Yet Another Redundant Composite Development Indicator?". *World Development* 19 (10): 1461–1468. https://doi.org/10.1016/0305-750x(91)90088-y.

[35]Srinivasan, T. N. (1994). "Human Development: A New Paradigm or Reinvention of the Wheel?". *American Economic Review* 84 (2): 238–243. JSTOR 2117836.

[36]Sagar, A. D., and Najam, A. (1998, June). "The Human Development Index: A Critical Review". *Ecological Economics* 25: 249–264. https://doi.org/10.1016/S0921-8009(97)00168-7.

In addition, HDI was as well assessed critically by ignoring the magnitude of inequality within a country. Since 2010 Human Development Report, UNDP introduced the inequality-adjusted Human Development Index (IHDI). This index captures the inequality in distribution of the HDI dimensions. Hence, under perfect equality HDI and IHDI are equal. When there is inequality in the distribution (of health, education, and income), the greater the difference between the IHDI and the HDI, the greater the inequality. The USA loosed its 3rd rank in HDI (2012) to become 16th in IHDI (2012), which confirm Stieglitz statements regarding the inequality in the USA:

> The upper 1 percent of Americans are now taking in nearly a quarter of the nation's income every year. In terms of wealth rather than income, the top 1 percent control 40 percent.[37]

2.4 Maqāṣid *al-Sharīʿah*

Sharīʿah is the set of religious law and moral code in Islam.[38] Al-Qurtubi (1240 [2006])[39] describes Sharīʿah as the canonic law of Islam. Containing all Islam's commandments to mankind, it is usually divided into three main subfields, namely *ʿaqidah* (beliefs), *ʿibādah* (worship), and *akhlaq* (moral and ethics).

To understand Sharīʿah, one needs to comprehend its objectives that allow for flexibility, dynamism, and creativity in social policy. *Maqāṣid* al-Sharīʿah is considered as the set of all objectives of Islamic Law. Dusuki (2009)[40] maintains that the scope of *Maqāṣid* al-Sharīʿah covers all aspects of life that are related to social, personal, economic, and

[37] *Vanity Fair*: http://www.vanityfair.com/society/features/2011/05/top-one-percent-201105.

[38] *Fiqh* is the Islamic jurisprudence. The *fiqh* scholars expand the *shari'ah* by studying the two sources of rulings, namely the *Qur'an* (the Muslims' Holy Book) and the *Sunnah* (Prophet Muhammad's practice).

[39] Al-Qurtubi, M. (1240 [2006]). *Al-jamii li-ahkem al-Qur'ān*. Al-Ryadh: Mouassasst Al-Risalah.

[40] Dusuki, A. W. (2009). "Challenges of Realizing Maqāṣid al-Sharīʿah (Objectives of *Sharīʿah*) in Islamic Capital Market: Special Focus on Equity-Based Sukuk". Working Paper, *Sharīʿah* Research Academy for Islamic Finance, Malaysia.

intellectual facets. Ariff and Rosly (2011)[41] claim that the purpose of *Maqāṣid* al-Sharīʿah "*plays a major role in determining the legality of Islamic transactions, as it establishes the relationship between human behavior and its impact on general welfare. It means that once an Islamic product is made available to the public, its impact on bank earnings, consumer welfare, and financial stability should be positive.*"

Moreover, Abu Al-Zahra (1997)[42] considers that *Maqāṣid* al-Sharīʿah cover promotion of welfare, establishing of justice, and enhancing of individuals' behaviors.

Maqāṣid al-Sharīʿah is classified into three descending categories of importance:

- *Ḍarūriyāt* (the essential)
- *Ḥajiyāt* (the complementary)
- *Taḥsiniyāt* (the desirable or the embellishments).

Al-Ghazali (1109 [1937])[43] identified five essentials that are basic from the perspective of Sharīʿah by account of their crucial role for human life. Such essentials are (1) human self (*Nafs*); (2) faith (*Din*); (3) intellect (*ʿAql*); (4) posterity (or procreation) (*Nasl*); and (5) wealth (or property) (*Māl*).

These five are considered absolute necessities to the survival and spiritual well-being of individuals, to the extent that their collapse would engender chaos and the demise of common order in society. The Sharīʿah, seeks, principally, to protect and enrich these vital values, and endorses all needed measures for their preservation and advancement.

2.5 *Development in Light of* Maqāṣid *al-Sharīʿah*

In Islam, the basic goal of development is to create an environment that enables people to enjoy spiritual, moral, and socioeconomic well-being in this world and success in the Hereafter (*falāḥ*).

[41] Ariff, M., and Rosly, S. A. (2011). "Islamic Banking in Malaysia: Unchartered Waters". *Asian Economic Policy Review* 6 (2): 301–319.

[42] Abu Al-Zahra, M. (1997). *Usul al-Fiqh*. Egypt: Dar al-Fikr al-Arabi.

[43] Ibid., 2.

> We did not send you, O Muhammad (s), except as a mercy, that is, to [give] mercy, to all the worlds, [the worlds of] mankind … through you. (Qur'ān, 21[44]:107)

Such an environment can only be built in societies looking for eliminating causes of human deprivation in different scopes. Some scholars of *Maqāṣid* al-Sharīʿah (Chapra 2008[45]; Auda 2008[46]), argue that *Maqāṣid* is the Islamic framework for development.

Maqāṣid al-Sharīʿah definitions above explain that they are the key leitmotif behind the enactment of each of the rulings of the Sharīʿah and wisdom elaborated in these rulings. Indeed, the basic Islamic sources of knowledge (Qur'ān and Sunna), emphasis on the fundamental values that underpin Islamic views on development, poverty alleviation, human rights, and mutual respect…

Chapra (2008) considers that human beings are the target and as well as the means of development. Thus, since they are the end, their well-being (*falāḥ*) must be ensured. Whereas, since they are also the means, they must have the motivation as well as the character and ability to do whatever is necessary for ensuring their well-being. Chapra (2008) as well elaborated in his works different needs that considered as corollaries of the primary five objectives. These needs required to fulfill the principal *Maqāṣid* are exposed below with each objective of the five dimensions:

First Dimension: Enrichment of the Human Self

1.1 Dignity, self-respect, and social equality
1.2 Justice
1.3 Spiritual and moral uplift
1.4 Security of life and property
1.5 Freedom
1.6 Education
1.7 Good governance

[44] Quran- Al Anbiya (21).

[45] Chapra, U. (2008, June). *The Islamic Vision of Development in Light of Maqasid al-Shari'ah*. London: International Institute of Islamic Thought (IIIT).

[46] Auda, J. (2008, March 3). *Maqāṣid al-Sharīʿah as Philosophy of Islamic Law: A Systems Approach*. London: International Institute of Islamic Thought (IIIT), 1st edition.

1.8 Need fulfillment
1.9 Employment and self-employment
1.10 Equitable distribution of income and wealth
1.11 Marriage and proper upbringing of children
1.12 Family and social solidarity
1.13 Mental peace and happiness
1.14 Minimization of crime and anomie

The Second Dimension: Enrichment of Faith

2.1 Religious worldview
2.2 Values
2.3 Proper motivation
2.4 Education
2.5 Justice, freedom, security of life, property and honor, honesty, fulfillment of all socioeconomic and political obligations, patience, thriftiness, prudence, tolerance, mutual care, and trust ...
2.6 Removal of poverty, need fulfillment of all, employment and self-employment opportunities
2.7 Equitable distribution (Human brotherhood)
2.8 Family integrity, social solidarity, and political stability
2.9 Good governance

The Third Dimension: Enrichment of Intellect

3.1 Proper upbringing
3.2 High quality of education at affordable prices
3.3 Library and research facilities
3.4 Freedom of thought and expression
3.5 Reward for creative work
3.6 Finance
3.7 Expansion of knowledge and technological base

The Fourth Dimension: Enrichment of Posterity

4.1 Marriage and family integrity
4.2 Social solidarity
4.3 Intellectual and moral development
4.4 Need fulfillment

4.5 Moral and worldly education
4.6 Healthy environment
4.7 Freedom from conflict and insecurity

The Fifth Dimension: Development of Wealth

5.1 Education, research, and improvement in technology and management.
5.2 Security of life, property, and honor
5.3 Good governance
5.4 Freedom of enterprise
5.5 Employment and self-employment opportunities
5.6 Removal of poverty, need fulfillment, and equitable distribution
5.7 Social solidarity and mutual trust
5.8 Saving and Investment
5.9 Optimum rate of development

3 Calculation Methodology

The socioeconomic development index based on *Maqāṣid* al-Sharīʿah generated in this paper is built on five dimensions of *Maqāṣid* al-Sharīʿah. Accordingly, the calculation method will be described. Initially, the HDI calculation, later two different calculation methods will be explained. Finally, the entire procedure operated is described to measure the index.

3.1 HDI Calculation

The HDI combined three dimensions. The calculation method developed from 1990 to 2009 was the algebraic mean. The HDI then represents the uniformly weighted sum with 1/3 contributed by each factor (dimension).

But from 2010, the calculation changed to the geometric mean:

$$\mathrm{HDI} = \sqrt[3]{\mathrm{LEI} \times \mathrm{EI} \times \mathrm{II}}$$

- LEI: Life Expectancy Index
- EI: Education Index
- II: Income Index

These two formulas were promulgated by the United Nations Development Programme (UNDP). Since all indicators do not share the same unit, HDI used a unit-free one, i.e., One indicator x is transformed into a unit-free ($\in [0, 1]$) with the following formula:

$$x - \text{index} = \frac{x - \min(x)}{\max(x) - \min(x)}$$

- $\min(x)$ is the lowest value the variable x can attain
- $\max(x)$ is highest values the variable x can attain

$$\text{LEI} = \frac{\text{LE} - \min(\text{LE})}{\max(\text{LE}) - \min(\text{LE})} = \frac{\text{LE} - 20}{82.3 - 20}$$

- LE: Life Expectancy at Birth

$$\text{EI} = \frac{\sqrt{\text{MYSI} * \text{EYSI}}}{0.951}$$

- $$\text{MYS Index (MYSI)} = \frac{\text{Mean Years of Schooling (MYS)}}{13.2}$$
- $$\text{EYS Index (EYSI)} = \frac{\text{Expected Years of Schooling (EYS)}}{20.6}$$

  - Mean Years of Schooling (MYS): Years that a 25-year-old person or older has spent in schools (=20 years)
  - Expected Years of Schooling (EYS): Years that a 5-year-old child will spend with his education in his whole life (=20 years)

$$\text{II} = \frac{\ln(\text{GNIpc}) - \ln(100)}{\ln(107{,}721) - \ln(100)}$$

3.2 *Graphical Representation*[47]

In the present paper, Only 5 *Maqāṣid* al-Sharīʿah are considered. Thus, for each one of the five, a score is given to each.

[47]The present calculation method was presented in IFP Harvard Forum 2012 and within Chair for Ethics and financial Norms (Sorbonne University and KAU).

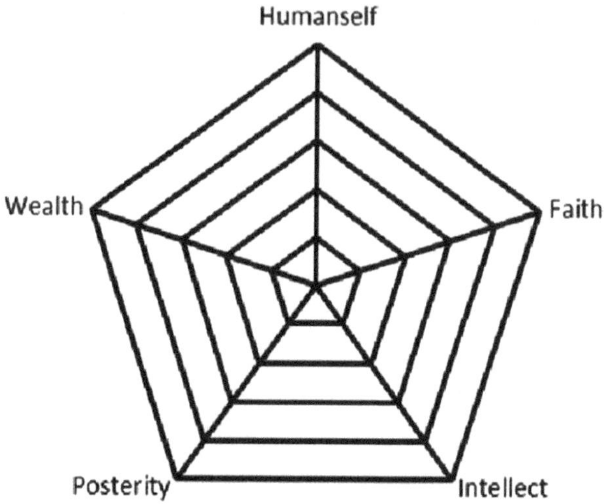

Fig. 1 Five-pillar Pentagon-shaped *Maqāṣid* al-Sharīʿah index (*Source* Author's own)

- Human self (*Nafs*) → the performance measured is p_1
- Faith (*Din*) → the performance measured is p_2
- Intellect (*ʿAql*) → the performance measured is p_3
- Posterity (*Nasl*) → the performance measured is p_4
- Wealth (*Mal*) → the performance measured is p_5

Based on the five *Maqāṣid* al-Sharīʿah, the graphical method objective (*Maqāṣid*[48]) of the five *Maqāṣid* previously defined. The succeeding technique consists of having five axes and assigning a score 'the performance' (p_i) to each axis. Every axis represents one order (and the interdependence of the five *Maqāṣid*), we will have a spider-graph with five axes (a pentagon-shape graph).

Figure 1 shows a regular polygon with five angles. Each of the angles corresponds to one of *Maqāṣid* al-Sharīʿah's objectives. The central point to the pentagon corresponds to zero.

[48] *Maqsid*: singular of *Maqāṣid*.

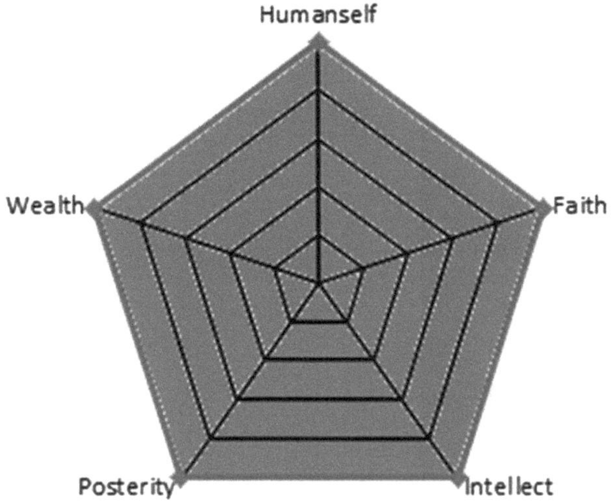

Fig. 2 Balanced, optimal index (*Source* Author's own)

However, Islam endorses balancing between all dimensions more than focus in only one dimension. Thus, the case of a balanced performance corresponds to the case of equal performance regarding all objectives in the five-pillar approach. We could envisage the case of a balanced performance as Fig. 2 shows.

> And thus have we willed you to be a community of the middle way, [118] so that [with your lives] you might bear witness to the truth before all mankind, and that the Apostle might bear witness to it before you. [119] (Qur'ān, 2:118/119)

Geometrically, it takes the form of a regular pentagon. Indeed, this case corresponds to a balanced, optimal performance from *Maqāṣid* al-Sharīʿah's perspective. Indeed, if all objectives are followed equally and fully then this is optimal. Figure 2 shows that the entire pentagon surface is colored, which means that the performance is optima.

As a result, to get logically a balanced performance, the representation should be like a regular pentagon colored. This representation has the advantage to distinguish the favorite axes adopted by each country in case the balance does not exist.

In this regard, the following model is proposed to measure the surface area S that can help in measuring the index

$$S = \frac{\sin\left(\frac{2\pi}{5}\right)}{2}(w_1p_1w_2p_2 + w_2p_2w_3p_3 + w_3p_3w_4p_4 + w_4p_4w_5p_5 + w_1p_1w_5p_5) \quad (1)$$

$$= \frac{\sin\left(\frac{2\pi}{5}\right)}{2}\left(\sum_{i=1}^{i=4} w_ip_iw_{i+1}p_{i+1} + w_1p_1w_5p_5\right)$$

And w_i are the weightage for each axis.

Hence,

$$\text{SEDIBMS} = \sqrt[2]{\frac{1}{5}\left(\sum_{i=1}^{i=4} w_ip_iw_{i+1}p_{i+1} + w_1p_1w_5p_5\right)} \quad (2)$$

In the general case, when we n *Maqāṣid* al-Sharī'ah

$$\text{SEDIBMS} = \sqrt[2]{\frac{1}{n}\left(\sum_{i=1}^{i=n} w_ip_iw_{i+1}p_{i+1} + w_1p_1w_np_n\right)} \quad (3)$$

SEDIBMS: socioeconomic development index based on *Maqāṣid* al-Sharī'ah.

3.3 Vector Representation

Let's have the standard basis in R^n consisting of the coordinate axes.

Let's start with R^2, the standard basis consists of two vectors $e_1=(1, 0)$ and $e_2=(0, 1)$.

Any vector $w=(a, b)$ can be written uniquely as the linear combination $w=ae_1+be_2$.

In our case since we have 5 *Maqāṣid* al-Sharī'ah, we build a space vector and its basis in R^5 with the standard basis:

$e_1=(1, 0, 0, 0, 0)$; $e_2=(0, 1, 0, 0, 0)$; $e_3=(0, 0, 1, 0, 0)$; $e_4=(0, 0, 0, 1, 0)$; $e_5=(0, 0, 0, 0, 1)$

Every measure in each objective can be represented in one vector

Examples: The measure of the development from enrichment of human self= $V_{\text{Humanself}}$:

$V_{Humanself} = (p_1, 0, 0, 0, 0)$

The same thing will be for other dimensions:

$V_{Faith} = (0, p_2, 0, 0, 0)$
$V_{Intelect} = (0, 0, p_3, 0, 0)$
$V_{Posterity} = (0, 0, 0, p_4, 0)$
$V_{Wealth} = (0, 0, 0, 0, p_5)$

The sum vector will be the socioeconomic index vector $= (p_1, p_2, p_3, p_4, p_5)$

The single measure of the index can be expressed in different ways:

- First, it can be measured as the norm of the vector.

$$\text{SEIDBMS} = \sqrt[2]{(p_1)^2 + (p_2)^2 + (p_3)^2 + (p_4)^2 + (p_5)^2} \tag{4}$$

- Moreover, this measure can be considered based on the volume (dimension 5) delimited by these 5 vectors:

$$\text{Hence, the volume(5)} = \text{determinant} \begin{bmatrix} p_1 & \cdots & 0 \\ \vdots & \ddots & \vdots \\ 0 & \cdots & p_5 \end{bmatrix}$$

In this specific case with an orthogonal matrix (5×5), the volume $= p_1 * p_2 * p_3 * p_4 * p_5$

Accordingly:

$$\text{SEDIBMS} = \sqrt[5]{p_1 * p_2 * p_3 * p_4 * p_5} \tag{5}$$

Therefore, we find again the geometric mean in dimension 5

Application (dimension 3):

Given the case of HDI, based on the following three dimensions (Fig. 3):

- LEI: Life Expectancy Index
- EI: Education Index
- II: Income Index

We may have a vector HDI = (LEI, EI, II)

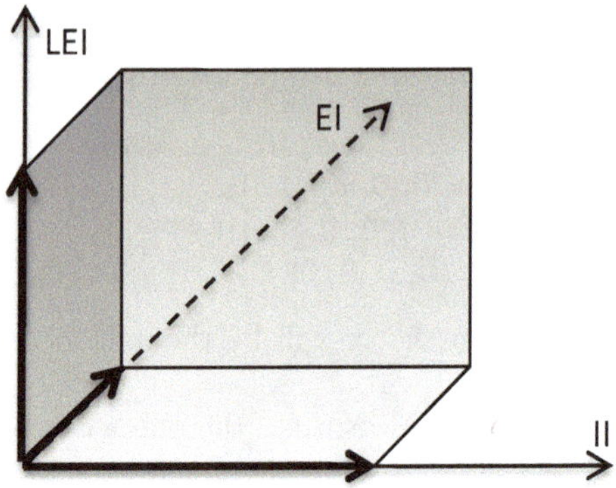

Fig. 3 Vector representation of three HDI vectors and the volume enclosed (*Source* Author's own)

The Matrix formed with each vector of each dimension will have this form

$$\begin{matrix} LEI & 0 & 0 \\ 0 & EI & 0 \\ 0 & 0 & II \end{matrix}$$

$$\text{Hence, The volume} = LEI * EI * II$$

$$\text{And finally: } HDI = \sqrt[3]{LEI \times EI \times II}$$

3.4 *The Methodology*

The socioeconomic development index is based on five *Maqāṣid* al-Sharīʿah:

- Enrichment of human self
- Enrichment of faith
- Enrichment of Intellect
- Enrichment of Posterity
- Development of Wealth

In the coming Sect. 4, data are selected from different available and open databases. Each dimension is measured based on the selected criteria and indicators.

Each dimension is divided on limited subindices. Each subindex is measured based on other indicators.

Each indicator is normalized using the unit-free formula:

$$x - \text{index} = \frac{x - \min(x)}{\max(x) - \min(x)}$$

This formula is used in positive criteria.

To have the unit-free measure in a negative criteria (ex: unemployment), the following formula is used:

$$x - \text{index} = \frac{x - \max(x)}{\min(x) - \max(x)}$$

The result of this first step is to have unit-free indicator (from 0 to 1).

The second step, for a given subindex with n indicators, is to measure the average of the required n indicators to get the subindex.

Once all subindices are measured, their average will give the final result of the selected dimension (*Maqṣid*) what we called p_i.

The final step is to measure the final index using one of the following calculation methods:

- Arithmetic mean
- Geometric mean
- Pentagon-shaped measure explained previously

4 Data Selection

First of all, most indicators are built using data that are readily available. In fact, the objective of this paper is initially to identify practical guidelines which can assist index measurement to select and apply socioeconomic development indicators. Therefore, the assessment of the development toward this goal should be based on:

- A limited number of indicators or indicator combinations to provide a clearer signal.
- Standard measurement wherever possible to permit comparison.
- Availability of more than 70 countries in the database.

4.1 First Dimension: Enrichment of the Human Self

Safeguarding or Enrichment of Human self is one of the five primary objectives of the Sharīʿah. There are four main subjects that are crucial in assessing enrichment of human self.

- Dignity
- Security of life
- Freedom
- Mental peace and happiness
- Minimization of crime and anomie

First, Dignity is the basis of fundamental human rights. Hence, it is inviolable and it must be valued and protected. The dignity of the human person is not only a fundamental right in itself, but constitutes the basis of fundamental rights in international law. The 1948 Universal Declaration of Human Rights enshrined this principle in its preamble: "*recognition of the inherent dignity and of the equal and inalienable rights of all members of the human family is the foundation of freedom, justice and peace in the world.*"[49]

Consequently, the dignity of the humans is part of the substance of any right protected by international human rights. To assess rights within countries, the best solution is to rely on the International Human Rights Rank Indicator (IHRRI)[50] to assess the enrichment of human self as a first subindex. Moreover, all data and rankings available are of 2014.

Second, human security is one of the defining aspects *Maqāṣid* al-Sharīʿah and mainly the first objective: enrichment of human self. Actually, protecting human, mainly guaranteeing the security of persons and property, is a vital function of the state. Under the rule of law, it must effectively prevent crime and violence. The evaluation of this sub-index depends on the factor 5 of the World Justice Project, *Order and Security.*[51] It consists of 17 variables combined to form the following three sub-factors:

- Crime is effectively controlled
- Civil conflict is effectively limited
- People do not resort to violence to redress personal grievances

Which is interesting, in that this subindex is part of the *WJP Rule of Law Index 2014.* It measures how the rule of law is experienced in

[49] The universal declaration of Human Rights: http://www.un.org/en/documents/udhr/.

[50] The International Human Rights Rank Indicator website: http://www.ihrri.com/.

[51] World Justice Project website: http://www.worldjusticeproject.org/factors/order-and-security.

everyday life in 99 countries around the globe, based on over 100,000 household and 2400 expert surveys worldwide.

Hence, from the same index, the evaluation of freedom is based on *factor 4: Fundamental Rights* and the evaluation of minimization of crime and anomie is based on *factor 8: Criminal Justice*. Indeed, as suggested by Chapra (2008), the minimization of crime and anomie should be fulfilled to enrich human self. The subindex criminal justice consists of 97 variables combined to form the following seven sub-factors:

- Criminal investigation system is effective.
- Criminal adjudication system is timely and effective.
- Correctional system is effective in reducing criminal behavior.
- Criminal justice system is impartial.
- Criminal justice system is free of corruption.
- Criminal justice system is free of improper government influence.
- Due process of law and rights of the accused.

Additionally, without a doubt, one of the primary objectives of Prophet Muhammad (pbuh) was to relieve mankind of the burdens and chains that have been imposed on them (al-Qur'ān, 7:157). Hence, freedom is Chapra's (2008) fifth component in enrichment of human self. The *factor 4: Fundamental Rights* in *WJP Rule of Law Index* consists of 115 variables combined to form the following 8 sub-factors:

- Equal treatment and absence of discrimination.
- The right to life and security of the person is effectively guaranteed.
- Due process of law and rights of the accused.
- Freedom of opinion and expression is effectively guaranteed.
- Freedom of belief and religion is effectively guaranteed.
- Freedom from arbitrary interference with privacy is effectively guaranteed.
- Freedom of assembly and association is effectively guaranteed.
- Fundamental labor rights are effectively guaranteed.

Finally, the fourth essential component in assessing the first objective Sharīʿah is mental peace and happiness. The relevant subindex to evaluate that component is the Happy Planet Index (HPI).[52] The HPI is

[52]The Happy Planet Index website: www.happyplanetindex.org.

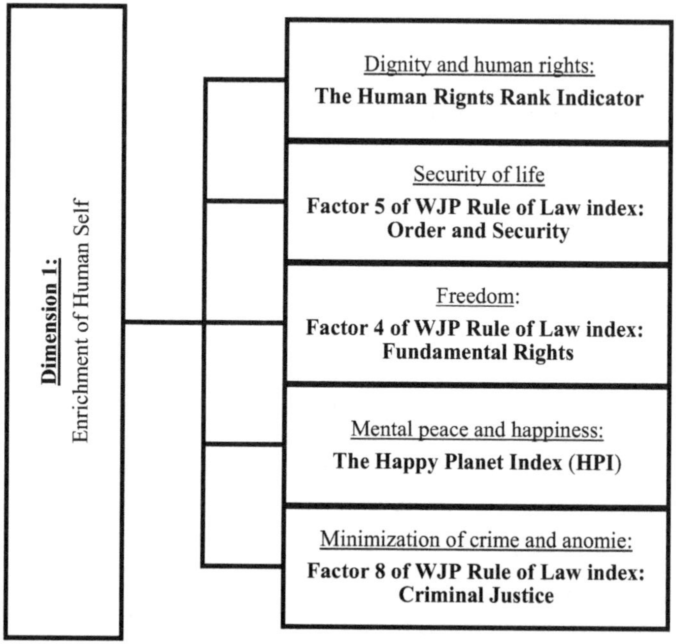

Fig. 4 Enrichment of human self selected indicators (*Source* Author's own)

a global measure of sustainable human well-being. This index is based mainly on what they called "*experienced well-being.*" It is assessed using a question called the "Ladder of Life" from the Gallup World Poll. This asks respondents to imagine a ladder, where 0 represents the worst possible life and 10 the best possible life, and report the step of the ladder they feel they currently stand on (Fig. 4).

4.2 The Second Dimension: Enrichment of Faith

In this dimension, Chapra (2008) identified "the worldview" as a primary factor which unfortunately cannot be assessed. However, the religiosity of a country can be assessed but will not be taken into account in this assessment since the objective of religion is beyond practice even imperative and central. In fact, since the definition of prayer is different from a religion to another, hence from one country to another.

Consequently, the outcome of this practice is evaluated within this exercise. Allah in Qur'ān says: *Recite what is sent of the Book by inspiration to thee, and establish regular Prayer: for Prayer restrains from shameful and unjust deeds; and remembrance of Allah is the greatest (thing in life) without doubt. And Allah knows the (deeds) that ye do* (29:45).

Therefore, the first two subindices measured in assessing enrichment of faith are Justice and Corruption. Moreover, Poverty and Environment are considered as 3rd and 4th components of faith enhancement.

Regarding the freedom of faith, it was considered with freedom in the first dimension. Hence, it will not be measured in the present one.

Primarily, Justice is a fundamental focus in Islam. It is an elementary objective of Islam to the extent that it stands next in order of priority to belief in *Allah's* exclusive right to worship (*Tawhid*) and the truth of Muhammad's Prophethood. "*God commands justice and fair dealing...*" (Qur'ān, 16:90).

> O you, who believe, be upright for God, and (be) bearers of witness with justice! (Qur'ān, 5:8)

Consequently, injustice is forbidden and justice is compulsory in Islam and is one pillar in faith enrichment.

To assess justice within this dimension of faith, *WJP Rule of Law Index 2014* offers the subindex *factor 7: Civil Justice*. This factor consists of 57 variables combined to form the following seven sub-factors:

- People can access and afford civil justice.
- Civil justice is free of discrimination.
- Civil justice is free of corruption.
- Civil justice is free of improper government influence.
- Civil justice is not subject to unreasonable delays.
- Civil justice is effectively enforced.
- ADRs are accessible, impartial, and effective.

In addition, Islam strictly prohibits corruption since it has a devastating impact on the economy and the whole society. Proofs from Sunna and Qur'ān are clear.

Ahmad narrated from *Tawban* who said: "*The Messenger of Allah (SAW) cursed the briber, bribe-taker and the mediator meaning the one who walks between the two*" Ḥadīth narrated by *Ahmad, Abu Dawud, Tirmidhi and ibn Majah*.

Accordingly, absence of corruption is key subindex in measuring the enrichment of faith. It is available through the *factor 2: The Absence of Corruption* of *WJP Rule of Law Index*. There are 3 forms of corruption that are examined with respect to government officers in the executive branch, the judiciary, the legislature, and the police and the military. It consists of 68 variables combined to form the following four sub-factors:

- Government officials in the Executive Branch do not use public office for private gain.
- Government officials in the judicial branch do not use public office for private gain.
- Government officials in the police and the military do not use public office for private gain.
- Government officials in the legislative branch do not use public office for private gain.

Thirdly, poverty is measured in faith enhancement. Islam encourages putting a proportion of wealth aside to purify it. Islam established solutions such as *Waqf* or *zakāt* or Charity (*ṣadaqah*) to alleviate poverty.

These institutions are not available in all countries; hence assessment of their impact is more relevant and straightforward. Moreover, the level of poverty among a nation assesses the mutual care and cooperation which are key components in enriching faith.

Ali ibn Abi Talib, the fourth Islamic caliph once said: "*If Poverty were a man, I'd have killed him*!"

Therefore, measuring poverty within a country can stand for assessing the enrichment of faith. The Multidimensional Poverty Index developed in 2010 by Oxford Poverty & Human Development Initiative and the United Nations Development Programme[53] can be the finest tool to assess the third subindex of this dimension even it is not yet updated to 2014. It is measured using ten indicators.

- Health
  - Child Mortality
  - Nutrition
- Education
  - Years of school
  - Children enrolled

[53] Multidimensional Poverty Index (MPI) website: http://hdr.undp.org/en/statistics/mpi.

- Living Standards
  - Cooking fuel
  - Toilet
  - Water
  - Electricity
  - Floor
  - Assets

This index identifies deprivations across the previous three dimensions, shows the number of people who are poor (suffering deprivations in 33 of weighted indicators) and the number of deprivations with which poor households typically contend.

Finally, in assessing enrichment of faith it is relevant to make clear that in the Islamic worldview, all things belong to God (*Allah*) and they are held by human beings in trust. Moreover, human beings as trustees and vicegerents (*khalifah*) of God (*Allah*) on earth are told to look after the world for Allah and for the future, therefore are responsible of protecting the environment. In fact, from different aḥdīth we understand that

> Allah created earth and has appointed humans as His stewards over it. The whole earth has been created a place of worship, pure and clean. Whoever plants a tree and diligently looks after it until it matures and bears fruit is rewarded. If a Muslim plants a tree or sows a field and humans and beasts and birds eat from it, this is ṣadaqa for him.

Moreover, in Qur'ān human beings are instructed to look after the environment and not to damage it:

> Devote thyself single-mindedly to the Faith, and thus follow the nature designed by Allah, the nature according to which He has fashioned mankind. There is no altering the creation of Allah. (Qur'ān, 30:30)

In view of that, assessing this component as a fourth subindex of this dimension is possible through Environmental Performance Index (EPI).[54] The EPI was preceded by the Environmental Sustainability Index (ESI), published between 1999 and 2005. Both indexes were developed by Yale

[54]Environmental Performance Index website: http://epi.yale.edu/epi.

University (Yale Center for Environmental Law and Policy) and Columbia University (Center for International Earth Science Information Network) in collaboration with the World Economic Forum and the Joint Research Centre of the European Commission. The EPI uses outcome-oriented indicators, then working as a benchmark index that can be more easily used by policymakers, environmental scientists, advocates, and the general public.[55]

The index is constructed based on two objectives that provide the overarching structure of the 2014 EPI:

- Environmental Health: measures the protection of human health from environmental harm.
- Ecosystem Vitality: measures ecosystem protection and resource management.

These two objectives are further divided into nine issue categories that span high-priority environmental policy issues, including: health impacts, air quality, water and sanitation, water resources, agriculture, forests, fisheries, biodiversity and habitat and as well climate and energy. All these issues are covered with the below 25 indicators:

- Environmental Burden of Disease
- Adequate Sanitation
- Drinking Water
- Indoor Air Pollution
- Urban Particulates
- Local Ozone
- Regional Ozone
- Sulfur Dioxide Emissions
- Water Quality Index
- Water Stress
- Conservation Risk Index
- Effective Conservation
- Critical Habitat Protection

[55]Yale Center for Environmental Law & Policy/Center for International Earth Science Information Network at Columbia University. "2008 Environmental Performance Index Report". Retrieved March 18, 2008. See Executive Summary, pp. 32–35 for a detailed comparison between the ESI 2005, the EPI 2006 and the EPI 2008.

- Marine Protected Areas
- Growing Stock
- Marine Trophic Index
- Trawling Intensity
- Irrigation Stress
- Agricultural Subsidies
- Intensive Cropland
- Burnt Land Area
- Pesticide Regulation
- Emissions per capita
- Emissions per electricity generated
- Industrial carbon intensity (Fig. 5)

Others components may be considered in this dimension, such as the quality of roads and the infrastructure. Indeed, *Umar bin al Khattab*, the second Caliph in Islam said "*even if a mule gets stumbled in Iraq, God will ask me why I didn't pave the way for it.*" This component may be considered within the security of life of the first dimension. The available indicators on the World Bank database are regarding this issue are:

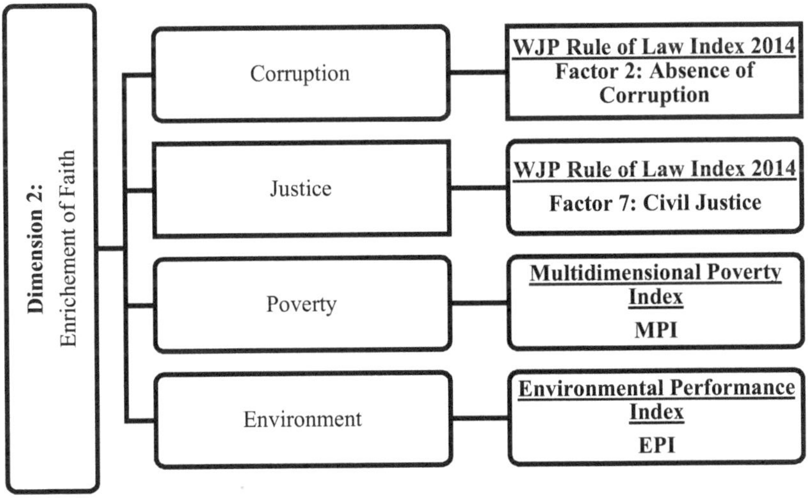

Fig. 5 Enrichment of faith selected indicators (*Source* Author's own)

- Quality of overall infrastructure
- Quality of roads
- Quality of railroad infrastructure
- Quality of port infrastructure
- Quality of air transport infrastructure

4.3 Third Dimension: Enrichment of Intellect

Enrichment of intellect is the third dimension of objectives of Sharīʿah. There are three main subjects that are fundamental in assessing enrichment of intellect.

- Freedom of thought and expression
- Creativity
- High quality of education

To begin with, Intellectual freedom is the right to freedom of thought and of expression of thought. It is a human right as defined by Article 19 of the Universal Declaration of Human Rights states:

> Everyone has the right to freedom of opinion and expression; this right includes freedom to hold opinions without interference and to seek, receive and impart information and ideas through any media and regardless of frontiers.[56]

This freedom is assessed through the Press Freedom Index compiled annually and published by "Reporters without Borders"[57] on January 30, 2013 and reflects events between December 1, 2011 and November 30, 2012.

Secondly, creativity and innovation are considered a key component is assessing intellect enhancement. There are 3 available indices assessing global innovation.

- Global Innovation Index (Boston Consulting Group and National Association of Manufacturers [NAM])
- Global Innovation Index (INSEAD, Cornell University, and WIPO)
- Global Innovation Quotient (Bloomberg)

[56] Article 19 of the Universal Declaration of Human Rights website: www.un.org/en/documents/udhr/index.shtml#a19.

[57] Reporters Without Borders website: www.rsf.org.

The second was chosen in this evaluation. It is compiled annually by Cornell University, INSEAD and WIPO (World Intellectual Property Organization). It is a composite index that ranks countries in terms of their enabling environment to innovation and their innovation outputs. In the latest edition (2013), the Confederation of Indian Industry, Booz and Company, du (Emirates Integrated Telecommunications Company) and Huawei joined as knowledge partners.

Lastly, the quality of education is key component is this dimension more than basic education. The education quality expresses the development of intelligence within a country. Four key indicators are chosen in this subindex:

- Years of tertiary schooling: The average years of tertiary education completed among people over age 25. The source is Barro-Lee Educational Attainment Dataset.[58]
- Number of globally ranked universities (0=none; 5>50): The number of universities ranked in the top 400 on any of the three most widely used international university rankings, measured on a scale from 0 (no ranked universities) to 5 (more than 50 ranked universities). The source of this indicator is: Times Higher Education World University Rankings,[59] QS World University Rankings,[60] and Academic Ranking of World Universities.[61]
- Adult literacy rate (of pop. aged 15+): This indicator determines the percentage of the population aged 15 and above (who can, with understanding, read and write a short, simple statement on their everyday life). Literacy also encompasses numeracy, the ability to make simple arithmetic calculations. The source of this indicator is United Nations Educational, Scientific, and Cultural Organization Institute for Statistics.[62]

[58] World Bank database: http://databank.worldbank.org/Data/Views/VariableSelection/SelectVariables.aspx?source=Education%20Statistics.

[59] Times Higher Education website: http://www.timeshighereducation.co.uk/world-university-rankings/2013-14/world-ranking.

[60] QS World University Rankings website: http://www.topuniversities.com/university-rankings/world-university-rankings/2013.

[61] Website: http://www.shanghairanking.com/ARWU2013.html.

[62] http://data.worldbank.org/indicator/SE.ADT.LITR.ZS.

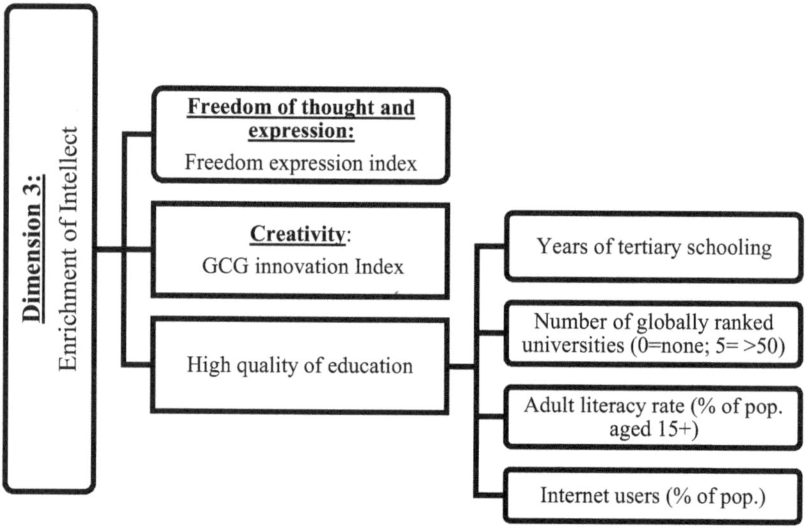

Fig. 6 Enrichment of intellect selected indicators (*Source* Author's own)

- Internet users (of pop.): This indicator is relevant since Internet nowadays is refining education and enhancing its quality. It respresents the estimated number of Internet users out of the total population, using the Internet from any device (including mobile phones) in the last 12 months. This indicator is published by International Telecommunications Union (Fig. 6).[63]

4.4 *Fourth Dimension: Enrichment of Posterity*

Evaluating the enrichment of posterity can be done once the needed elements of future generations are settled. In fact, new generations need a decent a roof over their heads, a healthy environment, good education and mainly an upstanding family.

To assess the healthy environment needed in enriching posterity, I gave emphasis to the following indicators:

[63] International Telecommunications Union website: http://www.itu.int/en/ITU-D/Statistics/Documents/statistics/2013/Individuals_Internet_2000-2012.xls.

- Undernourishment (of pop.): The percentage of the population whose food intake is insufficient to meet dietary energy requirements continuously. The source of this indicator is Food and Agriculture Organization of the United Nations.[64]
- Depth of food deficit (calories/undernourished person): The number of calories needed to lift the undernourished from their status, everything else being constant. The average intensity of food deprivation of the undernourished, estimated as the difference between the average dietary energy requirement and the average dietary energy consumption of the undernourished population (food-deprived), is multiplied by the number of undernourished to provide an estimate of the total food deficit in the country, which is then normalized by the total population. The source as well of this indicator is Food and Agriculture Organization of the United Nations.[65]
- Maternal mortality rate (deaths/100,000 live births): The annual number of female deaths from any cause related to or aggravated by pregnancy or its management (excluding accidental or incidental causes) during pregnancy and childbirth or within 42 days of termination of pregnancy, irrespective of the duration and site of the pregnancy, per 100,000 live births. This indicator is collected by World Health Organization.[66]
- Stillbirth rate (deaths/1000 live births): Third trimester fetal deaths (>1000 grams or >28 weeks), per 1000 live births. This is compiled as well by World Health Organization.[67]
- Child mortality rate (deaths/1000 live births) is the probability of a child born in a specific year dying before reaching the age of five per 1000 live births. The source of this indicator is United Nations Inter-agency Group for Child Mortality Estimation.[68]
- Deaths from infectious diseases (deaths/100,000): This indicator prepared by World Health Organization. It represents the age-standardized mortality rate from deaths caused by tuberculosis, sexually transmitted diseases, HIV/AIDS, diarrhea, pertussis, polio, measles, tetanus, meningitis, hepatitis B, hepatitis C, malaria,

[64] http://databank.worldbank.org/data/views/variableselection/selectvariables.aspx?source=world-development-indicators.

[65] http://data.worldbank.org/indicator/SN.ITK.DFCT.

[66] http://apps.who.int/gho/data/node.main.15?lang=en.

[67] http://apps.who.int/gho/data/node.main.ChildMort-2?lang=en.

[68] http://data.worldbank.org/indicator/SH.DYN.MORT.

trypanosomiasis, Chagas disease, schistosomiasis, leishmaniasis, lymphatic filariasis, onchocerciasis, leprosy, dengue, Japanese encephalitis, trachoma, intestinal infections, and other infectious diseases per 100,000 people.[69]

- Outdoor air pollution attributable deaths (deaths/100,000): It is also arranged by World Health Organization. It is the number of deaths resulting from emissions from industrial activity, households, cars and trucks, expressed as the rate per 100,000 people.
- Indoor air pollution attributable deaths (deaths/100,000): Age-standardized deaths caused from indoor air pollution, including indoor air pollution-derived cases of influenza, pneumococcal pneumonia, H influenzae type B pneumonia, respiratory syncytial virus pneumonia, other lower respiratory infections, trachea, bronchus, and lung cancers, ischemic heart disease, ischemic stroke, hemorrhagic and other non-ischemic stroke, chronic obstructive pulmonary disease, and cataracts per 100,000 people. In the SPI model, data are scaled from 3 (<30 deaths per 100,000 people) to 1 (>100 deaths per 100,000 people). This measure is compiled by Institute for Global Health Metrics and Evaluation.[70]

Secondly, to ensure the enrichment of posterity, shelter is highly recommended. To build this subindex, the subsequent 6 indicators are required:

- Availability of affordable housing (satisfied): it is a measure of Gallup World Poll. It embodies the percentage of respondents answering satisfied to the question, "*In your city or area where you live, are you satisfied or dissatisfied with the availability of good, affordable housing?*"
- Access to electricity (of pop.) is the percentage of the population with access to electricity. It is published by United Nations Sustainable Energy for All Project.[71]
- Quality of electricity supply (1 = low; 7 = high): This measure is produced by World Economic Forum published in the annual Global

[69] http://apps.who.int/gho/data/node.main.18?lang=en.

[70] https://cloud.ihme.washington.edu/public.php?service=files&t=5a680ed82f7be84d10b32052099fb617&download&path=/2010/IHME_GBD_2010_RESULTS_2010_HOUSEHOLD_AIR_POLLUTION_FROM_SOLID_FUELS_Y2013M11D20.zip.

[71] http://www.se4all.org/wp-content/uploads/2013/09/11-gtf_data_annex.pdf.

Competitiveness Report. It is the average response to the question: "*In your country, how would you assess the reliability of the electricity supply (lack of interruptions and lack of voltage fluctuations)?*"[72]

- Access to piped water (of pop.) is the percentage of the population with a water service pipe connected with in-house plumbing to one or more taps or a piped water connection to a tap placed in the yard or plot outside the house. This metric is measured by WHO/UNICEF Joint Monitoring Programme for Water Supply and Sanitation.[73]
- Rural vs. urban access to improved water source (absolute difference between of pop.): This is the absolute value of the difference between rural and urban access to improved drinking water, which is defined as the percentage of the population with piped water into dwelling, piped water to yard/plot, public tap or standpipe, tube well or borehole, protected dug well, protected spring, or rainwater. This is measured by Social Progress Imperative using WHO/UNICEF Joint Monitoring Programme for Water Supply and Sanitation data.[74]
- Access to improved sanitation facilities (of pop.) is a calculation of WHO/UNICEF Joint Monitoring Programme for Water Supply and Sanitation. It is the percentage of the population with improved sanitation, including flush toilets, piped sewer systems, septic tanks, flush/pour flush to pit latrine, ventilated improved pit latrines (VIP), pit latrine with slab, and composting toilets.[75]

In addition, Education is a major component in ensuring an enhanced posterity Subindex. It is one of the priorities of UNESCO (United Nations Educational, Scientific and Cultural Organization). This subindex is measured with the ensuing 5 indicators:

- Adult literacy rate (of pop. aged 15+): This indicator determines the percentage of the population aged 15 and above (who can, with understanding, read and write a short, simple statement on their everyday life). Literacy also encompasses numeracy, the ability to

[72] http://www.weforum.org/issues/competitiveness-0/gci2012-data-platform/.

[73] http://www.wssinfo.org/data-estimates/table/.

[74] http://www.wssinfo.org/data-estimates/tables/.

[75] http://www.wssinfo.org/data-estimates/table/.

make simple arithmetic calculations. This indicator is provided by UNESCO Institute for Statistics.

- Primary school enrollment (of children): It is the ratio of the number of children of the official primary school age who are enrolled in primary school to the total population of official primary school age children. It is delivered too by UNESCO Institute for Statistics.[76]
- Lower secondary school enrollment (of children): It represents the total enrollment in lower secondary education, regardless of age, expressed as a percentage of the total population of official lower secondary education age. The gross enrollment ratio can exceed 100 due to the inclusion of over-aged and under-aged students because of early or late school entrance and grade repetition. In the SPI model, data are capped at 100. UNESCO Institute for Statistics provides this measure.[77]
- Upper secondary school enrollment (of children): Total enrollment in upper secondary education, regardless of age, expressed as a percentage of the total population of official upper secondary education age. UNESCO Institute for Statistics is the source of this metric too.[78]
- Gender parity in secondary enrollment (girls/boys): It is the ratio of girls to boys enrolled at the secondary level in public and private schools. UNESCO Institute for Statistics provides this indicator.[79]

Finally, the foremost component of enrichment of posterity is ensuring the family integrity. This can be completed by guaranteeing a freedom over life choices in order to avoid divorce. Moreover, the good treatment of women guarantees family upstanding and integrity. The following 4 indicators are selected to measure Family integrity subindex:

- Freedom over life choices (satisfied) is Gallup World Poll metric. It is the percentage of respondents answering satisfied to the question, "*Are you satisfied or dissatisfied with your freedom to choose what you do with your life?*"

[76] http://databank.worldbank.org/data/views/variableselection/selectvariables.aspx?source=education-statistics-~-all-indicators.

[77] http://databank.worldbank.org/Data/Views/VariableSelection/SelectVariables.aspx?source=Education%20Statistics#.

[78] http://databank.worldbank.org/Data/Views/VariableSelection/SelectVariables.aspx?source=Education%20Statistics#.

[79] Ibid.

- Suicide rate (deaths/100,000) is the mortality due to self-inflicted injury, per 100,000 people. It is provided by the Institute for Health Metrics and Evaluation.[80]
- Modern slavery, human trafficking and child marriage (1=low; 100=high): It is part of "Walk Free Foundation Global Slavery Index" and is a combined measure of three variables: estimated prevalence of modern slavery in each country (accounting for 95 of the total); a measure of the level of human trafficking to and from each country (accounts for 2.5); and a measure of the level of child and early marriage in each country (accounts for 2.5), scaled from 1 (low slavery) to 100 (high slavery).[81]
- Women treated with respect (0=low; 100=high): It is a Gallup World Poll metric. It is the percentage of female respondents answering yes to the question, "*Do you believe that women in this country are treated with respect and dignity, or not?*" (Fig. 7).

4.5 *Fifth Dimension: Development of Wealth*

Finally, developing wealth is beyond GDP per capita in this paper, four components are considered:

- Freedom of enterprise: this represents the right of humans to control their own labor and property. In an economically free society, individuals are free to work, produce, consume, and invest in any way they please. *The 2014 Economic Freedom Index*[82] is an annual guide published by heritage foundation and Wall Street Journal.
- Employment and self-employment opportunities:
  - Employment opportunities are measurement based on unemployment rate. The former refers to the share of the labor force that is without work but available for and seeking employment. It is a key Indicator of the Labor Market database and is part of World Development Indicators Catalog of the World Bank.[83]

[80] https://cloud.ihme.washington.edu/public.php?service=files&t=d559026958b-38c3f4d12029b36d783da&download&path=/2010/IHME_GBD_2010_RESULTS_2010_SELF-HARM_Y2013M11D15.zip.

[81] http://www.globalslaveryindex.org/report.

[82] The 2014 Economic Freedom Index website: http://www.heritage.org/index/.

[83] http://data.worldbank.org/indicator/SL.UEM.TOTL.ZS.

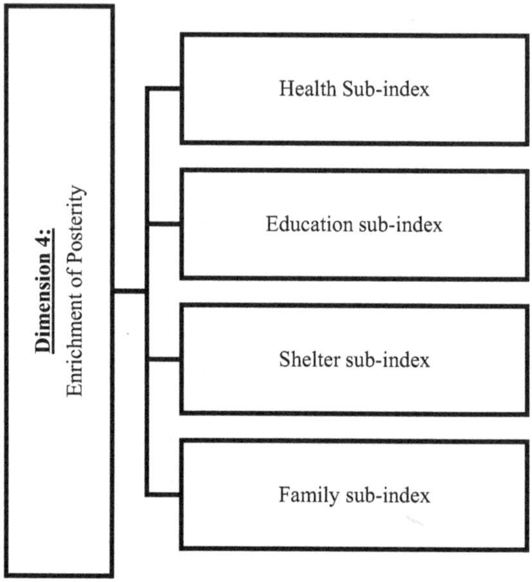

Fig. 7 Enrichment of posterity selected indicators (*Source* Author's own)

- Self-employment opportunities are measured from Global Entrepreneurship Monitor (GEM) consortium.[84] From all indicators available, this measure is compiled based on the following indicators[85]:

  Established Business Ownership Rate: Percentage of 18–64 population who are currently owner-manager of an established business, i.e., owning and managing a running business that has paid salaries, wages, or any other payments to the owners for more than 42 months.

  Fear of Failure Rate: Percentage of 18–64 population with positive perceived opportunities who indicate that fear of failure would prevent them from setting up a business.

  Media Attention for Entrepreneurship: Percentage of 18–64 population who agree with the statement that in their country, you will often see stories in the public media about successful new businesses Perceived Opportunities.

[84]Global Entrepreneurship Monitor website: http://www.gemconsortium.org/.

[85]http://www.gemconsortium.org/docs/download/414.

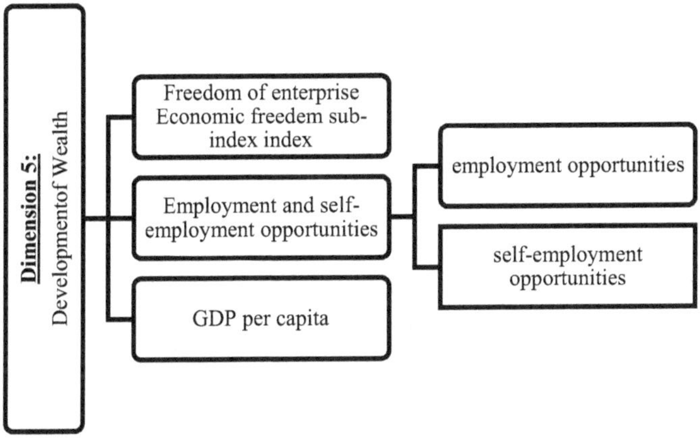

Fig. 8 Development of wealth selected indicators (*Source* Author's own)

Total early-stage Entrepreneurial Activity (TEA): Percentage of 18–64 population who are either a nascent entrepreneur or owner–manager of a new business (as defined above).

- GDP per capita: GDP per capita based on purchasing power parity (PPP). PPP GDP is gross domestic product converted to international dollars using purchasing power parity rates. This indicator is part of World Bank World Development Indicators (Fig. 8).[86]

5 Results

5.1 *The All Countries Ranking*

All indicators are aggregated respecting the described methodology above. The available data are found for a total number of 187 countries. Only 128 are entirely assessed by the indicators and indices hitherto selected. The following table illustrates the ranking and the score of each country from the complete list of 187.

After measuring each score in each dimension (each objective of Sharīʿah), these measures are putting together with an arithmetic mean of the available score. The first columns represent the overall score and

[86] http://data.worldbank.org/indicator/NY.GDP.PCAP.PP.KD.

rank measured. The ten latest columns are basically the score and the rank of each country on each of the five objectives of Islamic Law.

Additionally, this table displays all OIC countries (The Organization of Islamic Cooperation). From this list of 187 countries, there are 59 countries that do have a fully measures in the five objectives of Sharīʿah. The overall score then is calculated with the available data, i.e., for countries with 4 results only from 5, the index score is the arithmetic mean of these four values. For some countries with only one measure (ex. Palestine), the overall score is simply this single available score.

The existing 2014 *Maqāṣid* al-Sharīʿah-based socioeconomic development ranking is topped by European countries. Liechtenstein and Luxembourg head the table.

Only 26% of Muslim countries are ranked in the first 50% of considered countries. In fact, considering 187 countries, there are only 15 are ranked from 1 to 92:

- Qatar (7)
- Brunei (14)
- UAE (22)
- Kuwait (35)
- Suriname (41)
- Malaysia (46)
- Saudi Arabia (54)
- Oman (60)
- Bahrain (62)
- Jordan (64)
- Kazakhstan (68)
- Guyana (71)
- Turkey (77)
- Tunisia (89)
- Albania (92)

In this ranking, two only OIC countries (Qatar [7th] and Brunei [14]) are ranked better than the USA (26), France (29) and Germany (17). Europe has 65% of positions in the top 20 "*Maqāṣid* al-Sharīʿah" countries. OIC countries represent only 10% of these twenty. However, they represent 50% of the twentieth worst ranked of this "Islamic" index. These 10 countries are:

- Sudan (168th)
- Benin (169th)
- Mali (171th)
- Guinea-Bissau (172nd)
- Sierra Leone (176th)
- Guinea (177th)
- Togo (178th)
- Niger (180th)
- Chad (183rd)
- Afghanistan (185th)

5.2 128 Countries Ranking (Arithmetic Mean)

The available indicators defined hitherto are shared by 128 countries. There are only 128 countries that have all the required five scores in the all *Maqāṣid* al-Sharīʿah.

Comparing to Table 3, Table 4 is missing 59 countries. Among them, this table presents only 39 OIC countries. The remaining 17 countries are missing data only some *Maqāṣid* al-Sharīʿah from the selected database.

The current "*Maqāṣid* al-Sharīʿah" index ranking exposed in Table 4 is topped as well by European countries. Norway, Switzerland, and Denmark head the table. Hence, 2 Scandinavian countries are in the top 3 of this "Islamic" index. Moreover, Switzerland is ranked first in four objectives of Sharīʿah out of five. But in terms of Enrichment of Human self, it is ranked 14 out of 128. However Norway ranked first with a score of (78.88%) is ranked first in enriching human self and second in three other Sharīʿah objectives (Enrichment of faith, of Intellect and development of Wealth).

Only 9 (23%) OIC countries out of 39 are in the first half of the ranking.

- UAE (15)
- Kuwait (25)
- Malaysia (33)
- Saudi Arabia (36)
- Jordan (40)
- Kazakhstan (44)

Table 3 All countries *Maqāṣid* al-Sharīʿah index ranking

Countries	*Overall Rank*	*Overall score (%)*	*Humanself*		*Faith*		*Intellect*		*Posterity*		*Wealth*	
			Score (%)	*Rank*	*Score (%)*	*Rank*	*Score (%)*	*Rank*	*Score (%)*	*Rank*	*Score (%)*	*Rank*
Liechtenstein	1	92.39	NA		NA		NA		NA		92.39	2
Luxembourg	2	86.69	83.61	10	93.93	3	84.61	3	NA		84.61	4
Macau	3	84.44	NA		NA		84.44	4	NA		84.44	5
Singapore	4	83.74	74.78	21	89.46	7	85.36	2	NA		85.36	3
Norway	5	78.88	96.43	1	94.54	2	76.23	7	50.99	17	76.23	8
Hong Kong	6	77.55	65.53	31	80.18	20	82.24	5	NA		82.24	6
Qatar	7	77.20	57.42	41	65.87	49	92.75	1	NA		92.75	1
Switzerland	8	77.07	78.62	15	100.00	1	77.19	6	52.34	7	77.19	7
Denmark	9	76.70	94.42	2	92.75	4	70.96	17	54.41	1	70.96	18
Australia	10	75.69	87.69	6	88.31	10	75.63	8	51.22	12	75.63	9
Netherlands	11	75.24	87.34	7	90.54	6	72.55	13	53.25	3	72.55	14
Sweden	12	75.12	94.31	3	89.01	8	70.87	18	50.55	20	70.87	19
Finland	13	74.19	92.42	4	85.57	12	69.51	24	53.94	2	69.51	25
Brunei	14	73.89	NA		70.66	36	75.51	9	NA		75.51	10
Austria	15	73.40	88.75	5	84.09	14	72.26	14	49.62	25	72.26	15
New Zealand	16	72.74	85.32	8	86.20	11	70.50	20	51.16	14	70.50	21
Germany	17	72.57	81.71	12	88.46	9	71.15	16	50.35	21	71.15	17
Canada	18	72.21	84.40	9	78.45	22	74.25	12	49.72	24	74.25	13
Ireland	19	70.90	79.90	14	81.99	17	69.90	23	52.79	5	69.90	24
Iceland	20	70.73	77.57	16	84.53	13	70.73	19	50.06	22	70.73	20
United Kingdom	21	70.64	81.51	13	80.24	19	70.12	22	51.19	13	70.12	23
UAE	22	70.46	76.51	18	77.47	24	74.72	10	48.89	30	74.72	11
Taiwan	23	69.35	NA		64.70	51	71.67	15	NA		71.67	16
Belgium	24	69.09	82.31	11	73.83	31	68.78	27	51.72	10	68.78	28

Countries	*Overall Rank*	*Overall score (%)*	*Humanself*		*Faith*		*Intellect*		*Posterity*		*Wealth*	
			Score (%)	*Rank*	*Score (%)*	*Rank*	*Score (%)*	*Rank*	*Score (%)*	*Rank*	*Score (%)*	*Rank*
Japan	25	68.53	71.46	23	79.92	21	70.24	21	50.76	18	70.24	22
USA	26	68.40	76.92	17	66.98	44	74.56	11	49.01	28	74.56	12
South Korea	27	68.22	NA		66.93	45	68.87	26	NA		68.87	27
Czech Republic	28	66.49	74.79	20	76.00	26	66.27	30	49.11	27	66.27	31
France	29	66.23	76.30	19	74.38	29	64.62	34	51.24	11	64.62	35
Estonia	30	65.54	69.49	25	82.38	16	64.89	33	46.07	47	64.89	34
Cyprus	31	65.11	64.64	32	70.30	37	62.74	39	NA		62.74	40
Israel	32	63.28	68.01	29	69.68	39	66.60	29	45.49	53	66.60	30
Slovenia	33	63.10	68.62	27	72.86	33	62.35	42	49.34	26	62.35	43
Slovakia	34	62.53	55.75	45	90.84	5	60.71	50	44.65	62	60.71	51
Kuwait	35	61.76	57.60	40	67.13	42	68.47	28	47.12	40	68.47	29
Spain	36	61.69	70.92	24	70.15	38	59.21	57	48.95	29	59.21	58
Chile	37	61.38	62.30	33	67.02	43	66.04	31	45.48	54	66.04	32
Poland	38	60.85	68.21	28	64.06	52	61.01	47	49.97	23	61.01	48
Uruguay	39	60.76	56.22	43	75.05	28	61.83	44	48.87	31	61.83	45
Trinidad and Tobago	40	60.51	61.43	34	73.93	30	60.94	48	45.27	57	60.94	49
Suriname	41	60.45	NA		73.35	32	54.00	91	NA		54.00	91
Malta	42	60.33	54.13	50	58.56	67	64.31	35	NA		64.31	36
Costa Rica	43	59.43	72.93	22	59.64	64	59.36	54	45.86	49	59.36	55
Italy	44	59.35	68.98	26	61.21	59	61.76	45	43.02	77	61.76	46
Seychelles	45	59.04	NA		55.53	78	60.80	49	NA		60.80	50
Malaysia	46	59.02	55.55	46	66.02	48	63.35	38	46.85	42	63.35	39
Hungary	47	59.00	59.65	38	66.54	46	60.46	51	47.89	35	60.46	52

(continued)

Table 3 (continued)

Countries	Overall Rank	Overall score (%)	Humanself		Faith		Intellect		Posterity		Wealth	
			Score (%)	Rank	Score (%)	Rank	Score (%)	Rank	Score (%)	Rank	Score (%)	Rank
Portugal	48	58.68	60.19	35	68.09	40	58.73	63	47.72	36	NA	
Latvia	49	58.11	43.34	82	83.18	15	59.25	56	45.55	50	59.25	57
Bahamas	50	57.92	NA		43.09	117	65.33	32	NA		65.33	33
Vanuatu	51	57.73	NA		61.01	60	56.09	73	NA		56.09	73
Bhutan	52	57.56	NA		62.47	56	55.10	82	NA		55.10	82
Belize	53	57.23	54.05	51	72.36	34	51.26	115	NA		51.26	115
Saudi Arabia	54	57.08	43.74	80	70.90	35	62.63	40	45.51	51	62.63	41
Georgia	55	56.84	51.83	57	66.06	47	56.80	67	52.73	6	56.80	67
Montenegro	56	56.70	NA		77.27	25	53.77	95	42.00	88	53.77	95
Lithuania	57	56.70	47.74	71	63.42	54	62.56	41	47.21	39	62.56	42
Saint Lucia	58	56.55	NA		NA		56.55	68	NA		56.55	68
Saint Vincent Grenadines	59	56.47	NA		NA		56.47	70	NA		56.47	70
Oman	60	56.45	NA		44.71	112	62.32	43	NA		62.32	44
Tonga	61	56.33	NA		64.00	53	52.50	104	NA		52.50	104
Bahrain	62	56.12	35.88	108	50.36	96	69.13	25	NA		69.13	26
Croatia	63	55.72	60.06	37	61.71	57	55.98	76	44.87	59	55.98	76
Jordan	64	55.70	55.26	47	65.08	50	56.42	71	45.31	56	56.42	71
Belarus	65	55.60	49.56	63	67.17	41	56.49	69	48.27	33	56.49	69
Thailand	66	54.74	51.86	56	51.93	90	59.66	53	50.59	19	59.66	54
Mauritius	67	54.68	39.85	100	59.03	65	63.74	36	47.05	41	63.74	37
Kazakhstan	68	54.17	48.88	69	52.26	86	59.32	55	51.08	16	59.32	56
Armenia	69	54.03	34.69	115	81.92	18	53.83	93	45.89	48	53.83	93
Botswana	70	54.01	51.64	59	56.41	74	59.04	61	43.92	68	59.04	62
Guyana	71	53.86	54.90	49	63.31	55	52.39	105	46.33	44	52.39	105

Countries	Overall Rank	Overall score (%)	Humanself		Faith		Intellect		Posterity		Wealth	
			Score (%)	Rank	Score (%)	Rank	Score (%)	Rank	Score (%)	Rank	Score (%)	Rank
Brazil	72	53.82	55.80	44	56.42	73	56.06	74	44.73	60	56.06	74
Greece	73	53.62	58.16	39	60.87	61	53.19	101	42.71	81	53.19	101
Fiji	74	53.29	NA		52.09	88	53.89	92	NA		53.89	92
Romania	75	53.00	60.16	36	46.25	108	59.07	60	40.48	99	59.07	61
Kiribati	76	52.90	NA		55.89	76	51.40	113	NA		51.40	113
Turkey	77	52.60	44.16	77	58.91	66	58.77	62	42.39	87	58.77	63
Cuba	78	52.32	42.78	87	54.85	81	63.54	37	36.91	112	63.54	38
Panama	79	52.07	57.21	42	38.76	128	60.17	52	44.01	67	60.17	53
Colombia	80	51.93	45.52	75	52.42	85	59.16	59	43.37	73	59.16	60
Bulgaria	81	51.84	50.59	60	45.49	110	57.74	65	47.63	37	57.74	65
Paraguay	82	51.82	42.12	90	61.48	58	55.98	75	43.52	71	55.98	75
Argentina	83	51.49	52.51	54	56.54	72	52.90	102	42.62	84	52.90	102
Sri Lanka	84	51.36	41.49	95	53.10	83	55.55	79	51.14	15	55.55	79
Honduras	85	51.36	45.11	76	60.75	62	54.15	88	42.66	82	54.15	88
Mexico	86	51.31	42.09	91	47.59	102	61.13	46	44.62	63	61.13	47
Macedonia	87	50.91	50.37	61	58.42	69	50.97	118	43.82	69	50.97	118
Mongolia	88	50 83	51.80	58	48.36	98	54.24	86	45.50	52	54.24	86
Tunisia	89	50.60	48.79	70	60.01	63	50.84	121	42.52	85	50.84	121
Palau	90	50.54	NA		50.54	94	NA		NA		NA	
Russia	91	50.50	43.77	79	52.18	87	55.93	78	44.68	61	55.93	78
Albania	92	50.49	49.17	68	51.36	92	55.22	81	41.48	91	55.22	81
Dominica	93	50.46	NA		43.78	113	53.80	94	NA		53.80	94
Cape Verde	94	50.15	NA		39.61	125	55.42	80	NA		55.42	80
China	95	49.93	43.43	81	46.42	106	54.02	90	51.78	9	54.02	90
Serbia	96	49.69	49.52	64	56.86	71	50.35	124	41.38	94	50.35	124

(continued)

Table 3 (continued)

Countries	*Overall Rank*	*Overall score (%)*	*Humanself*		*Faith*		*Intellect*		*Posterity*		*Wealth*	
			Score (%)	*Rank*	*Score (%)*	*Rank*	*Score (%)*	*Rank*	*Score (%)*	*Rank*	*Score (%)*	*Rank*
Peru	97	49.48	46.86	73	41.89	119	59.20	58	40.27	101	59.20	59
Jamaica	98	49.42	52.65	53	42.04	118	56.22	72	39.95	103	56.22	72
Gabon	99	49.38	NA		43.12	116	52.51	103	NA		52.51	103
Uzbekistan	100	49.37	43.99	78	47.04	103	51.31	114	53.20	4	51.31	114
Ecuador	101	49.35	42.70	88	53.24	82	52.23	106	46.34	43	52.23	106
South Africa	102	49.17	43.30	83	55.89	75	51.08	116	44.51	64	51.08	116
Bosnia and Herzegovina	103	49.16	55.08	48	51.81	91	47.55	131	43.81	70	47.55	131
Moldova	104	49.09	49.31	67	46.39	107	53.45	97	42.85	80	53.45	97
Ukraine	105	49.00	49.98	62	47.97	100	50.86	120	45.33	55	50.86	120
Azerbaijan	106	48.97	30.96	126	55.40	79	57.07	66	44.34	66	57.07	66
El Salvador	107	48.69	52.07	55	34.52	141	58.00	64	40.83	98	58.00	64
Tajikistan	108	48.34	29.52	129	55.69	77	52.12	107	52.24	8	52.12	107
Morocco	109	48.33	41.64	93	52.04	89	53.28	99	41.39	93	53.28	99
Dominican Republic	110	48.27	41.81	92	50.73	93	54.36	84	40.09	102	54.36	84
Philippines	111	48.05	38.87	104	46.52	104	54.29	85	46.30	45	54.29	85
Ghana	112	47.70	49.32	66	45.57	109	54.09	89	35.43	118	54.09	89
Indonesia	113	47.69	43.12	86	43.48	114	54.17	87	43.52	72	54.17	87
Guatemala	114	47.45	42.63	89	39.79	124	55.98	77	42.85	79	55.98	77
Papua	115	47.31	NA		35.48	138	53.23	100	NA		53.23	100
Swaziland	116	47.22	NA		58.45	68	43.58	140	43.27	74	43.58	140
Kyrgyzstan	117	46.94	41.63	94	40.39	123	53.74	96	45.19	58	53.74	96
Sao Tome Principe	118	46.87	NA		NA		46.87	132	NA		46.87	132
Laos	119	46.55	34.72	114	46.45	105	52.08	108	47.41	38	52.08	108

Countries	*Overall Rank*	*Overall score (%)*	*Humanself*		*Faith*		*Intellect*		*Posterity*		*Wealth*	
			Score (%)	*Rank*	*Score (%)*	*Rank*	*Score (%)*	*Rank*	*Score (%)*	*Rank*	*Score (%)*	*Rank*
Micronesia	120	46.16	NA		NA		46.16	133	NA		46.16	133
Equatorial Guinea	121	45.21	NA		35.44	139	50.09	125	NA		50.09	125
Egypt	122	45.18	34.64	116	52.65	84	50.45	123	37.69	110	50.45	123
Maldives	123	45.12	NA		NA		45.12	138	NA		45.12	138
Syria	124	45.04	14.68	146	75.39	27	NA		NA		NA	
Venezuela	125	44.87	40.42	97	43.24	115	48.13	127	44.43	65	48.13	127
Zambia	126	44.69	37.08	106	35.63	137	51.06	117	48.64	32	51.06	117
Vietnam	127	44.56	47.07	72	28.33	155	51.42	112	NA		51.42	112
Bolivia	128	44.55	39.28	102	39.46	126	50.68	122	42.63	83	50.68	122
Nicaragua	129	43.89	43.22	84	28.23	156	53.38	98	41.23	96	53.38	98
Namibia	130	43.87	43.21	85	54.99	80	39.64	149	41.88	89	39.64	149
Algeria	131	43.83	29.83	127	47.94	101	50.91	119	39.54	104	50.91	119
Timor-Leste	132	43.37	NA		38.54	129	45.78	134	NA		45.78	134
Cambodia	133	43.34	33.95	119	29.44	151	55.08	83	43.14	75	55.08	83
India	134	43.05	39.13	103	29.32	152	51.92	110	42.98	78	51.92	110
Iran	135	42.68	29.52	128	45.15	111	47.82	128	43.12	76	47.82	128
Lesotho	136	42.36	NA		41.55	120	43.27	142	41.34	95	43.27	142
Iraq	137	42.05	29.18	130	57.81	70	44.87	139	33.50	122	44.87	139
Bangladesh	138	40.43	36.84	107	22.11	163	51.97	109	39.25	105	51.97	109
Lebanon	139	40.27	49.39	65	33.39	144	40.29	147	37.98	108	40.29	147
Palestine	140	40.07	40.07	99	NA		NA		NA		NA	
Turkmenistan	141	38.88	53.71	52	41.00	121	30.41	165	NA		30.41	165
Gambia	142	38.88	NA		49.53	97	33.55	158	NA		33.55	158
Pakistan	143	38.65	25.54	136	26.95	157	51.71	111	37.35	111	51.71	111
North Korea	144	38.63	65.61	30	77.97	23	0.70	181	48.19	34	0.70	181

(continued)

Table 3 (continued)

Countries	*Overall Rank*	*Overall score (%)*	*Humanself*		*Faith*		*Intellect*		*Posterity*		*Wealth*	
			Score (%)	*Rank*	*Score (%)*	*Rank*	*Score (%)*	*Rank*	*Score (%)*	*Rank*	*Score (%)*	*Rank*
Djibouti	145	38.29	33.97	118	48.21	99	33.92	156	41.44	92	33.92	156
Myanmar	146	37.97	32.31	122	21.00	165	49.29	126	NA		49.29	126
Mozambique	147	37.85	35.09	111	20.17	166	47.81	129	38.36	107	47.81	129
Libya	148	37.71	33.18	120	37.74	132	39.95	148	NA		39.95	148
Nepal	149	37.64	40.89	96	35.22	140	35.88	154	40.33	100	35.88	154
Malawi	150	37.55	46.36	74	40.75	122	30.76	163	39.16	106	30.76	163
Kenya	151	37.08	34.02	117	32.09	146	40.75	146	37.76	109	40.75	146
Senegal	152	36.98	37.33	105	36.99	134	37.38	150	35.83	116	37.38	150
Cameroon	153	36.95	31.86	123	24.93	158	42.77	144	42.45	86	42.77	144
Samoa	154	36.55	NA		NA		36.55	152	NA		36.55	152
Yemen	155	36.46	26.34	135	38.13	130	42.05	145	33.74	121	42.05	145
Central African Republic	156	36.22	10.65	149	38.05	131	47.75	130	36.91	113	47.75	130
Nigeria	157	35.45	21.83	141	31.68	147	45.66	135	32.41	125	45.66	135
Mauritania	158	34.31	35.09	110	16.23	170	42.90	143	34.45	120	42.90	143
Comoros	159	34.16	23.71	138	22.05	164	45.43	136	NA		45.43	136
Cote d'Ivoire	160	33.53	34.76	113	34.41	142	32.48	159	NA		32.48	159
Madagascar	161	33.32	40.35	98	24.15	159	34.36	155	33.37	123	34.36	155
Tanzania	162	33.16	32.34	121	32.78	145	32.42	160	35.82	117	32.42	160
Rwanda	163	33.02	14.21	147	36.55	135	36.25	153	41.83	90	36.25	153
Haiti	164	32.84	27.60	134	29.16	153	37.30	151	NA		37.30	151
Congo	165	32.84	15.27	145	50.40	95	NA		NA		NA	
Uganda	166	32.25	27.81	133	29.75	149	33.56	157	36.55	114	33.56	157
Burkina Faso	167	31.67	39.79	101	31.64	148	28.30	170	30.32	130	28.30	170

Countries	*Overall Rank*	*Overall score (%)*	*Humanself*		*Faith*		*Intellect*		*Posterity*		*Wealth*	
			Score (%)	*Rank*	*Score (%)*	*Rank*	*Score (%)*	*Rank*	*Score (%)*	*Rank*	*Score (%)*	*Rank*
Sudan	168	31.56	22.76	140	12.70	174	45.37	137	31.62	127	45.37	137
Benin	169	30.65	28.17	132	29.65	150	32.09	161	31.26	128	32.09	161
Angola	170	29.62	35.21	109	18.31	168	29.13	167	36.31	115	29.13	167
Mali	171	29.34	16.30	143	8.59	176	43.44	141	34.94	119	43.44	141
Guinea-Bissau	172	28.57	NA		28.41	154	28.66	168	NA		28.66	168
Congo (Democratic Republic of the)	173	28.41	12.45	148	38.94	127	22.22	178	46.22	46	22.22	178
Kosovo	174	27.67	NA		NA		27.67	174	NA		27.67	174
Ethiopia	175	27.67	31.20	125	23.68	160	27.89	172	NA		27.89	172
Sierra Leone	176	26.93	29.00	131	22.21	162	28.26	171	NA		28.26	171
Guinea	177	26.48	25.18	137	19.29	167	29.82	166	28.31	131	29.82	166
Togo	178	26.25	7.19	151	36.50	136	27.79	173	31.97	126	27.79	173
Liberia	179	26.11	34.92	112	17.47	169	22.84	177	32.51	124	22.84	177
Niger	180	25.92	23.55	139	14.41	172	30.55	164	30.51	129	30.55	164
Burundi	181	25.86	15.71	144	15.86	171	28.41	169	40.92	97	28.41	169
Solomon Islands	182	25.32	NA		22.38	161	26.79	175	NA		26.79	175
Chad	183	24.04	9.42	150	33.98	143	25.17	176	26.46	132	25.17	176
Zimbabwe	184	23.67	31.68	124	37.05	133	12.98	180	NA		12.98	180
Afghanistan	185	22.05	21.57	142	2.82	177	31.92	162	NA		31.92	162
Eritrea	186	18.90	NA		14.25	173	21.23	179	NA		21.23	179
Somalia	187	9.97	NA		9.97	175	NA		NA		NA	

Source Author's own

Table 4 128 countries *Maqāṣid* al-Sharīʿah index ranking

Countries	*Overall Rank*	*Overall score (%)*	*Humanself*		*Faith*		*Intellect*		*Posterity*		*Wealth*	
			score (%)	*Rank*	*score (%)*	*Rank*	*score (%)*	*Rank*	*score (%)*	*Rank*	*score (%)*	*Rank*
Norway	1	78.88	96.43	1	94.54	2	76.23	2	50.99	17	76.23	2
Switzerland	2	77.07	78.62	14	100.00	1	77.19	1	52.34	7	77.19	1
Denmark	3	76.70	94.42	2	92.75	3	70.96	10	54.41	1	70.96	10
Australia	4	75.69	87.69	6	88.31	8	75.63	3	51.22	12	75.63	3
Netherlands	5	75.24	87.34	7	90.54	5	72.55	7	53.25	3	72.55	7
Sweden	6	75.12	94.31	3	89.01	6	70.87	11	50.55	20	70.87	11
Finland	7	74.19	92.42	4	85.57	10	69.51	17	53.94	2	69.51	17
Austria	8	73.40	88.75	5	84.09	12	72.26	8	49.62	25	72.26	8
New Zealand	9	72.74	85.32	8	86.20	9	70.50	13	51.16	14	70.50	13
Germany	10	72.57	81.71	11	88.46	7	71.15	9	50.35	21	71.15	9
Canada	11	72.21	84.40	9	78.45	19	74.25	6	49.72	24	74.25	6
Ireland	12	70.90	79.90	13	81.99	15	69.90	16	52.79	5	69.90	16
Iceland	13	70.73	77.57	15	84.53	11	70.73	12	50.06	22	70.73	12
United Kingdom	14	70.64	81.51	12	80.24	17	70.12	15	51.19	13	70.12	15
<u>UAE</u>	<u>15</u>	<u>70.46</u>	<u>76.51</u>	<u>17</u>	<u>77.47</u>	<u>21</u>	<u>74.72</u>	<u>4</u>	<u>48.89</u>	<u>30</u>	<u>74.72</u>	<u>4</u>
Belgium	16	69.09	82.31	10	73.83	26	68.78	18	51.72	10	68.78	18
Japan	17	68.53	71.46	21	79.92	18	70.24	14	50.76	18	70.24	14
USA	18	68.40	76.92	16	66.98	34	74.56	5	49.01	28	74.56	5
Czech Republic	19	66.49	74.79	19	76.00	22	66.27	21	49.11	27	66.27	21
France	20	66.23	76.30	18	74.38	24	64.62	24	51.24	11	64.62	24
Estonia	21	65.54	69.49	23	82.38	14	64.89	23	46.07	46	64.89	23
Israel	22	63.28	68.01	27	69.68	30	66.60	20	45.49	52	66.60	20
Slovenia	23	63.10	68.62	25	72.86	27	62.35	30	49.34	26	62.35	30
Slovakia	24	62.53	55.75	39	90.84	4	60.71	36	44.65	61	60.71	36

Countries	Overall Rank	Overall score (%)	Humanself		Faith		Intellect		Posterity		Wealth	
			score (%)	Rank	score (%)	Rank	score (%)	Rank	score (%)	Rank	score (%)	Rank
Kuwait	25	61.76	57.60	35	67.13	32	68.47	19	47.12	39	68.47	19
Spain	26	61.69	70.92	22	70.15	29	59.21	43	48.95	29	59.21	43
Chile	27	61.38	62.30	29	67.02	33	66.04	22	45.48	53	66.04	22
Poland	28	60.85	68.21	26	64.06	39	61.01	34	49.97	23	61.01	34
Uruguay	29	60.76	56.22	37	75.05	23	61.83	31	48.87	31	61.83	31
Trinidad and Tobago	30	60.51	61.43	30	73.93	25	60.94	35	45.27	56	60.94	35
Costa Rica	31	59.43	72.93	20	59.64	48	59.36	40	45.86	48	59.36	40
Italy	32	59.35	68.98	24	61.21	44	61.76	32	43.02	75	61.76	32
Malaysia	33	59.02	55.55	40	66.02	37	63.35	27	46.85	41	63.35	27
Hungary	34	59.00	59.65	33	66.54	35	60.46	37	47.89	35	60.46	37
Latvia	35	58.11	43.34	72	83.18	13	59.25	42	45.55	49	59.25	42
Saudi Arabia	36	57.08	43.74	70	70.90	28	62.63	28	45.51	50	62.63	28
Georgia	37	56.84	51.83	48	66.06	36	56.80	52	52.73	6	56.80	52
Lithuania	38	56.70	47.74	62	63.42	40	62.56	29	47.21	38	62.56	29
Croatia	39	55.72	60.06	32	61.71	42	55.98	57	44.87	58	55.98	57
Jordan	40	55.70	55.26	41	65.08	38	56.42	54	45.31	55	56.42	54
Belarus	41	55.60	49.56	54	67.17	31	56.49	53	48.27	33	56.49	53
Thailand	42	54.74	51.86	47	51.93	69	59.66	39	50.59	19	59.66	39
Mauritius	43	54.68	39.85	89	59.03	49	63.74	25	47.05	40	63.74	25
Kazakhstan	44	54.17	48.88	60	52.26	66	59.32	41	51.08	16	59.32	41
Armenia	45	54.03	34.69	102	81.92	16	53.83	71	45.89	47	53.83	71
Botswana	46	54.01	51.64	50	56.41	56	59.04	47	43.92	67	59.04	47
Guyana	47	53.86	54.90	43	63.31	41	52.39	78	46.33	43	52.39	78
Brazil	48	53.82	55.80	38	56.42	55	56.06	56	44.73	59	56.06	56
Greece	49	53.62	58.16	34	60.87	45	53.19	76	42.71	79	53.19	76

(continued)

Table 4 (continued)

Countries	Overall Rank	Overall score (%)	Humanself		Faith		Intellect		Posterity		Wealth	
			score (%)	Rank	score (%)	Rank	score (%)	Rank	score (%)	Rank	score (%)	Rank
Romania	50	53.00	60.16	31	46.25	83	59.07	46	40.48	95	59.07	46
Turkey	51	52.60	44.16	67	58.91	50	58.77	48	42.39	85	58.77	48
Cuba	52	52.32	42.78	77	54.85	61	63.54	26	36.91	108	63.54	26
Panama	53	52.07	57.21	36	38.76	96	60.17	38	44.01	66	60.17	38
Colombia	54	51.93	45.52	65	52.42	65	59.16	45	43.37	72	59.16	45
Bulgaria	55	51.84	50.59	51	45.49	85	57.74	50	47.63	36	57.74	50
Paraguay	56	51.82	42.12	80	61.48	43	55.98	58	43.52	70	55.98	58
Argentina	57	51.49	52.51	45	56.54	54	52.90	77	42.62	82	52.90	77
Sri Lanka	58	51.36	41.49	85	53.10	63	55.55	61	51.14	15	55.55	61
Honduras	59	51.36	45.11	66	60.75	46	54.15	68	42.66	80	54.15	68
Mexico	60	51.31	42.09	81	47.59	77	61.13	33	44.62	62	61.13	33
Macedonia	61	50.91	50.37	52	58.42	51	50.97	88	43.82	68	50.97	88
Mongolia	62	50.83	51.80	49	48.36	73	54.24	66	45.50	51	54.24	66
Tunisia	63	50.60	48.79	61	60.01	47	50.84	91	42.52	83	50.84	91
Russia	64	50.50	43.77	69	52.18	67	55.93	60	44.68	60	55.93	60
Albania	65	50.49	49.17	59	51.36	71	55.22	62	41.48	88	55.22	62
China	66	49.93	43.43	71	46.42	81	54.02	70	51.78	9	54.02	70
Serbia	67	49.69	49.52	55	56.86	53	50.35	94	41.38	91	50.35	94
Peru	68	49.48	46.86	63	41.89	90	59.20	44	40.27	97	59.20	44
Jamaica	69	49.42	52.65	44	42.04	89	56.22	55	39.95	99	56.22	55
Uzbekistan	70	49.37	43.99	68	47.04	78	51.31	85	53.20	4	51.31	85
Ecuador	71	49.35	42.70	78	53.24	62	52.23	79	46.34	42	52.23	79
South Africa	72	49.17	43.30	73	55.89	57	51.08	86	44.51	63	51.08	86
Bosnia and Herzegovina	73	49.16	55.08	42	51.81	70	47.55	99	43.81	69	47.55	99

Countries	Overall Rank	Overall score (%)	Humanself		Faith		Intellect		Posterity		Wealth	
			score (%)	Rank	score (%)	Rank	score (%)	Rank	score (%)	Rank	score (%)	Rank
Moldova	74	49.09	49.31	58	46.39	82	53.45	73	42.85	78	53.45	73
Ukraine	75	49.00	49.98	53	47.97	75	50.86	90	45.33	54	50.86	90
Azerbaijan	76	48.97	30.96	109	55.40	59	57.07	51	44.34	65	57.07	51
El Salvador	77	48.69	52.07	46	34.52	104	58.00	49	40.83	94	58.00	49
Tajikistan	78	48.34	29.52	111	55.69	58	52.12	80	52.24	8	52.12	80
Morocco	79	48.33	41.64	83	52.04	68	53.28	75	41.39	90	53.28	75
Dominican Republic	80	48.27	41.81	82	50.73	72	54.36	64	40.09	98	54.36	64
Philippines	81	48.05	38.87	93	46.52	79	54.29	65	46.30	44	54.29	65
Ghana	82	47.70	49.32	57	45.57	84	54.09	69	35.43	114	54.09	69
Indonesia	83	47.69	43.12	76	43.48	87	54.17	67	43.52	71	54.17	67
Guatemala	84	47.45	42.63	79	39.79	93	55.98	59	42.85	77	55.98	59
Kyrgyzstan	85	46.94	41.63	84	40.39	92	53.74	72	45.19	57	53.74	72
Laos	86	46.55	34.72	101	46.45	80	52.08	81	47.41	37	52.08	81
Egypt	87	45.18	34.64	103	52.65	64	50.45	93	37.69	106	50.45	93
Venezuela	88	44.87	40.42	87	43.24	88	48.13	95	44.43	64	48.13	95
Zambia	89	44.69	37.08	95	35.63	102	51.06	87	48.64	32	51.06	87
Bolivia	90	44.55	39.28	91	39.46	94	50.68	92	42.63	81	50.68	92
Nicaragua	91	43.89	43.22	74	28.23	115	53.38	74	41.23	92	53.38	74
Namibia	92	43.87	43.21	75	54.99	60	39.64	109	41.88	86	39.64	109
Algeria	93	43.83	29.83	110	47.94	76	50.91	89	39.54	100	50.91	89
Cambodia	94	43.34	33.95	106	29.44	113	55.08	63	43.14	73	55.08	63
India	95	43.05	39.13	92	29.32	114	51.92	83	42.98	76	51.92	83
Iran	96	42.68	29.52	112	45.15	86	47.82	96	43.12	74	47.82	96
Iraq	97	42.05	29.18	113	57.81	52	44.87	102	33.50	118	44.87	102
Bangladesh	98	40.43	36.84	96	22.11	119	51.97	82	39.25	101	51.97	82

(continued)

Table 4 (continued)

Countries	*Overall Rank*	*Overall score (%)*	*Humanself*		*Faith*		*Intellect*		*Posterity*		*Wealth*	
			score (%)	*Rank*	*score (%)*	*Rank*	*score (%)*	*Rank*	*score (%)*	*Rank*	*score (%)*	*Rank*
Lebanon	99	40.27	49.39	56	33.39	106	40.29	108	37.98	104	40.29	108
Pakistan	100	38.65	25.54	117	26.95	116	51.71	84	37.35	107	51.71	84
North Korea	101	38.63	65.61	28	77.97	20	0.70	128	48.19	34	0.70	128
Djibouti	102	38.29	33.97	105	48.21	74	33.92	114	41.44	89	33.92	114
Mozambique	103	37.85	35.09	98	20.17	120	47.81	97	38.36	103	47.81	97
Nepal	104	37.64	40.89	86	35.22	103	35.88	112	40.33	96	35.88	112
Malawi	105	37.55	46.36	64	40.75	91	30.76	118	39.16	102	30.76	118
Kenya	106	37.08	34.02	104	32.09	108	40.75	107	37.76	105	40.75	107
Senegal	107	36.98	37.33	94	36.99	99	37.38	110	35.83	112	37.38	110
Cameroon	108	36.95	31.86	108	24.93	117	42.77	105	42.45	84	42.77	105
Yemen	109	36.46	26.34	116	38.13	97	42.05	106	33.74	117	42.05	106
Central African Republic	110	36.22	10.65	126	38.05	98	47.75	98	36.91	109	47.75	98
Nigeria	111	35.45	21.83	121	31.68	109	45.66	100	32.41	121	45.66	100
Mauritania	112	34.31	35.09	99	16.23	124	42.90	104	34.45	116	42.90	104
Madagascar	113	33.32	40.35	88	24.15	118	34.36	113	33.37	119	34.36	113
Tanzania	114	33.16	32.34	107	32.78	107	32.42	116	35.82	113	32.42	116
Rwanda	115	33.02	14.21	124	36.55	100	36.25	111	41.83	87	36.25	111
Uganda	116	32.25	27.81	115	29.75	111	33.56	115	36.55	110	33.56	115
Burkina Faso	117	31.67	39.79	90	31.64	110	28.30	123	30.32	126	28.30	123
Sudan	118	31.56	22.76	120	12.70	127	45.37	101	31.62	123	45.37	101
Benin	119	30.65	28.17	114	29.65	112	32.09	117	31.26	124	32.09	117
Angola	120	29.62	35.21	97	18.31	122	29.13	121	36.31	111	29.13	121
Mali	121	29.34	16.30	122	8.59	128	43.44	103	34.94	115	43.44	103

Countries	*Overall Rank*	*Overall score (%)*	*Humanself*		*Faith*		*Intellect*		*Posterity*		*Wealth*	
			score (%)	*Rank*	*score (%)*	*Rank*	*score (%)*	*Rank*	*score (%)*	*Rank*	*score (%)*	*Rank*
Congo (Democratic Republic of the)	122	28.41	12.45	125	38.94	95	22.22	127	46.22	45	22.22	127
Guinea	123	26.48	25.18	118	19.29	121	29.82	120	28.31	127	29.82	120
Togo	124	26.25	7.19	128	36.50	101	27.79	124	31.97	122	27.79	124
Liberia	125	26.11	34.92	100	17.47	123	22.84	126	32.51	120	22.84	126
Niger	126	25.92	23.55	119	14.41	126	30.55	119	30.51	125	30.55	119
Burundi	127	25.86	15.71	123	15.86	125	28.41	122	40.92	93	28.41	122
Chad	128	24.04	9.42	127	33.98	105	25.17	125	26.46	128	25.17	125

Source Author's own

- Guyana (47)
- Turkey (51)
- Tunisia (63)

In top worst countries of this ranking, there are 12 OIC countries (60%).

- Yemen (109)
- Nigeria (111)
- Mauritania (112)
- Uganda (116)
- Burkina Faso (117)
- Sudan (118)
- Benin (119)
- Mali (121)
- Guinea (123)
- Togo (124)
- Niger (126)
- Chad (128)

The OIC countries ranking is topped by UAE (15th overall) with a score of 70.46%. In fact, in terms of development of wealth and enrichment of intellect, it is ranked 4th. However, it is ranked beyond regarding Enrichment of human self (17th, 76.51%), enrichment of faith (21st, 77.47%), and enrichment of posterity (30th, 48.89%). In the next part, the ranking is taking a part regarding each objective of Sharīʿah among the five stated by *Ghazali*.

1. The enrichment of human self-ranking is topped by Norway. UAE is the best country in this regard. The worst ranking belongs to OIC countries (respectively Chad and Togo).
2. The enrichment of faith ranking is topped by Switzerland. UAE (21st), Saudi Arabia (28th), and Malaysia (37th) are the top 3 OIC countries in enriching faith. Paradoxically, the worst ranking belongs as well to OIC countries (respectively Niger, Sudan, and Mali).
3. The enrichment of intellect ranking is topped by Switzerland too. UAE (4th), Kuwait (19th) and Malaysia (27th) are the top 3 OIC countries in enriching intellect. The worst 3 positions in intellect enrichment ranking are respectively for Liberia, Democratic

Republic of the Congo and North Korea. Moreover, Chad (125th) is the worst ranked OIC country in this third dimension.

4. The enrichment of posterity ranking is topped by Denmark. Uzbekistan (4th), Tajikistan (8th), and Kazakhstan (16th) are the top 3 OIC countries in enriching posterity. 8 OIC countries are in the bottom of the ranking. They are respectively Nigeria, Togo, Sudan, Benin, Niger, Burkina Faso, Guinea, and Chad.
5. The development of wealth ranking is topped by Switzerland. UAE (4th), Kuwait (19th), and Malaysia (27th) are the top 3 OIC countries in developing wealth. Paradoxically, the worst ranking belongs as well to OIC countries (respectively Niger, Sudan, and Mali).

5.3 *Comparison of All Calculation Methods (128 Countries Ranking)*

In this coming section, the three calculation methods are compared. The comparison is basically on the ranking and obviously not the score itself (Table 5).

There are 3 calculations methods explained previously:

- arithmetic mean
- vector representation approach: in this singular case, it is equal to the geometric mean
- pentagon-shaped method

Associating the three methods together, there are out of 128 countries, 66 with the same ranking using the 3 calculation methods. However, 62 countries present same differences in the three rankings.

- 24 countries where the ranking changed 1 position only.
- 15 countries where the ranking changed 2 positions.
- The remaining 15 countries (12% of total countries) presents differences in ranking more than 2 positions.

First, comparing the pentagon rank and the geometric ranks, there are 75 differences (59% of all countries). Among them, there 44 changed with only one position, 21 two positions. However, the ranking of Tajikistan, Dominican Republic, Mozambique, Mali, and

Table 5 Calculation method comparison

	AR	*GR*	*PR*	*A-Score*	*G-Score*	*P-Score*
Countries	*Arithmetic Rank*	*Geometric rank*	*Pentagon rank*	*Arithmetic score (%)*	*Geometric score (%)*	*Pentagon score (%)*
Norway	1	2	1	78.88	76.97	31.45
Switzerland	2	1	3	77.07	75.49	29.73
Denmark	3	3	2	76.70	75.17	29.76
Australia	4	4	4	75.69	74.33	28.80
Netherlands	5	5	6	75.24	73.98	28.54
Sweden	6	6	5	75.12	73.41	28.55
Finland	7	7	7	74.19	72.92	27.78
Austria	8	8	8	73.40	71.99	27.12
New Zealand	9	9	9	72.74	71.51	26.66
Germany	10	10	10	72.57	71.30	26.50
Canada	11	11	11	72.21	71.08	26.10
Ireland	12	12	12	70.90	70.07	25.25
Iceland	13	14	13	70.73	69.68	25.10
United Kingdom	14	13	14	70.64	69.71	25.06
UAE	15	15	15	70.46	69.47	24.74
Belgium	16	16	16	69.09	68.31	23.93
Japan	17	17	17	68.53	67.78	23.47
USA	18	18	18	68.40	67.52	23.19
Czech Republic	19	19	19	66.49	65.72	22.19
France	20	20	20	66.23	65.59	22.03
Estonia	21	21	21	65.54	64.43	21.56
Israel	22	23	23	63.28	62.53	19.97
Slovenia	23	22	22	63.10	62.57	19.97
Slovakia	24	26	24	62.53	60.84	19.39

	AR	*GR*	*PR*	*A-Score*	*G-Score*	*P-Score*
Countries	*Arithmetic Rank*	*Geometric rank*	*Pentagon rank*	*Arithmetic score (%)*	*Geometric score (%)*	*Pentagon score (%)*
Kuwait	25	24	26	61.76	61.14	18.86
Spain	26	25	25	61.69	61.13	19.12
Chile	27	27	27	61.38	60.76	18.72
Poland	28	28	28	60.85	60.53	18.54
Uruguay	29	29	29	60.76	60.16	18.38
Trinidad and Tobago	30	30	30	60.51	59.78	18.31
Costa Rica	31	31	31	59.43	58.80	17.66
Italy	32	33	32	59.35	58.63	17.58
Malaysia	33	34	34	59.02	58.58	17.30
Hungary	34	32	33	59.00	58.66	17.39
Latvia	35	36	35	58.11	56.51	16.50
Saudi Arabia	36	38	37	57.08	56.06	15.98
Georgia	37	35	36	56.84	56.63	16.11
Lithuania	38	37	38	56.70	56.18	15.89
Croatia	39	39	39	55.72	55.39	15.55
Jordan	40	40	40	55.70	55.33	15.50
Belarus	41	41	41	55.60	55.21	15.38
Thailand	42	42	42	54.74	54.59	14.92
Mauritius	43	44	43	54.68	53.77	14.65
Kazakhstan	44	43	44	54.17	54.00	14.61
Armenia	45	51	49	54.03	51.94	14.06
Botswana	46	45	46	54.01	53.69	14.48
Guyana	47	47	45	53.86	53.59	14.52
Brazil	48	46	47	53.82	53.60	14.45
Greece	49	48	48	53.62	53.24	14.41

(continued)

Table 5 (continued)

	AR	*GR*	*PR*	*A-Score*	*G-Score*	*P-Score*
Countries	*Arithmetic Rank*	*Geometric rank*	*Pentagon rank*	*Arithmetic score (%)*	*Geometric score (%)*	*Pentagon score (%)*
Romania	50	49	50	53.00	52.35	13.85
Turkey	51	50	51	52.60	52.02	13.64
Cuba	52	57	57	52.32	51.14	13.24
Panama	53	55	54	52.07	51.24	13.29
Colombia	54	53	53	51.93	51.50	13.31
Bulgaria	55	52	52	51.84	51.59	13.35
Paraguay	56	56	55	51.82	51.24	13.26
Argentina	57	54	56	51.49	51.27	13.25
Sri Lanka	58	58	58	51.36	51.08	13.14
Honduras	59	59	59	51.36	50.93	13.09
Mexico	60	62	61	51.31	50.67	12.94
Macedonia	61	61	60	50.91	50.70	12.95
Mongolia	62	60	62	50.83	50.71	12.87
Tunisia	63	63	63	50.60	50.29	12.78
Russia	64	65	65	50.50	50.21	12.65
Albania	65	64	64	50.49	50.22	12.66
China	66	66	66	49.93	49.75	12.46
Serbia	67	67	67	49.69	49.44	12.34
Peru	68	75	74	49.48	48.81	11.98
Jamaica	69	74	72	49.42	48.90	12.03
Uzbekistan	70	68	68	49.37	49.25	12.20
Ecuador	71	69	69	49.35	49.17	12.12
South Africa	72	72	71	49.17	48.95	12.03
Bosnia and Herzegovina	73	70	70	49.16	49.01	12.10

	AR	GR	PR	A-Score	G-Score	P-Score
Countries	*Arithmetic Rank*	*Geometric rank*	*Pentagon rank*	*Arithmetic score (%)*	*Geometric score (%)*	*Pentagon score (%)*
Moldova	74	73	75	49.09	48.91	11.98
Ukraine	75	71	73	49.00	48.95	11.99
Azerbaijan	76	78	76	48.97	47.73	11.70
El Salvador	77	79	78	48.69	47.70	11.56
Tajikistan	78	82	79	48.34	47.16	11.53
Morocco	79	76	77	48.33	47.99	11.57
Dominican Republic	80	77	80	48.27	47.87	11.51
Philippines	81	80	81	48.05	47.69	11.47
Ghana	82	83	83	47.70	47.15	11.21
Indonesia	83	81	82	47.69	47.41	11.28
Guatemala	84	84	84	47.45	46.94	11.11
Kyrgyzstan	85	85	85	46.94	46.59	10.95
Laos	86	86	86	46.55	46.06	10.78
Egypt	87	88	88	45.18	44.52	10.03
Venezuela	88	87	87	44.87	44.77	10.05
Zambia	89	90	89	44.69	44.14	10.00
Bolivia	90	89	90	44.55	44.25	9.86
Nicaragua	91	93	92	43.89	42.78	9.44
Namibia	92	91	91	43.87	43.53	9.59
Algeria	93	92	93	43.83	42.97	9.42
Cambodia	94	96	94	43.34	42.01	9.24
India	95	94	95	43.05	42.14	9.16
Iran	96	95	96	42.68	42.05	9.03
Iraq	97	97	97	42.05	40.85	8.60
Bangladesh	98	99	99	40.43	38.66	7.96

(continued)

Table 5 (continued)

Countries	*AR* Arithmetic Rank	*GR* Geometric rank	*PR* Pentagon rank	*A-Score* Arithmetic score (%)	*G-Score* Geometric score (%)	*P-Score* Pentagon score (%)
Lebanon	99	98	98	40.27	39.94	8.04
Pakistan	100	104	100	38.65	36.94	7.27
North Korea	101	128	115	38.63	10.39	5.28
Djibouti	102	100	101	38.29	37.89	7.24
Mozambique	103	106	103	37.85	36.19	7.02
Nepal	104	101	102	37.64	37.56	7.07
Malawi	105	102	104	37.55	37.07	6.98
Kenya	106	105	105	37.08	36.90	6.86
Senegal	107	103	107	36.98	36.98	6.84
Cameroon	108	107	106	36.95	36.14	6.85
Yemen	109	108	108	36.46	35.93	6.55
Central African Republic	110	113	109	36.22	32.10	6.26
Nigeria	111	109	110	35.45	34.19	6.09
Mauritania	112	112	111	34.31	32.47	5.73
Madagascar	113	111	113	33.32	32.87	5.48
Tanzania	114	110	112	33.16	33.13	5.49
Rwanda	115	116	114	33.02	30.98	5.39
Uganda	116	114	116	32.25	32.10	5.21
Burkina Faso	117	115	117	31.67	31.41	5.00
Sudan	118	119	118	31.56	28.50	4.77
Benin	119	117	119	30.65	30.61	4.70
Angola	120	118	120	29.62	28.81	4.32

	AR	GR	PR	A-Score	G-Score	P-Score
Countries	*Arithmetic Rank*	*Geometric rank*	*Pentagon rank*	*Arithmetic score (%)*	*Geometric score (%)*	*Pentagon score (%)*
Mali	121	124	121	29.34	24.72	4.26
Congo (Democratic Republic of the)	122	121	122	28.41	25.63	3.68
Guinea	123	120	123	26.48	26.15	3.50
Togo	124	126	127	26.25	23.03	3.25
Liberia	125	122	126	26.11	25.29	3.29
Niger	126	123	125	25.92	24.95	3.36
Burundi	127	125	124	25.86	24.16	3.47
Chad	128	127	128	24.04	22.18	2.74

Source Author's own

Guinea changed with 3 positions. Pakistan, Senegal, Central African Republic, and Liberia are ranked differently with 4 four positions using the two methods (pentagon and geometric). The big difference belongs to North Korea (115th in pentagon) and (128th geometric mean).

Second, paralleling the pentagon rank and the arithmetic ranks, there are 61 differences (48% of all countries). Among them, there 44 (72% of the whole changes) changed with only one position, 8 two positions. However, the ranking of Bulgaria, Jamaica, Bosnia Herzegovina, Togo, and Burundi changed with 3 positions, Armenia 4 positions, Cuba 5 positions, Peru 6 positions using the two methods (pentagon and geometric). The big difference belongs as well to North Korea (115th in pentagon) and (101st arithmetic mean).

Finally, comparing the geometric rank and the arithmetic ranks, there are 88 differences (69% of all countries). Among them, there 41 (47% of the whole changes) changed with only one position, 24 two positions. Again, the big difference in ranking using both methods goes to North Korea (128th in geometric mean) and (101st arithmetic mean).

This exception of North Korea can be explained by its 5 scores and ranks in each objective of the 5 *Maqāṣid* al-Sharīʿah: 28th in human self enrichment, 20th in faith enrichment, 128th in intellect enrichment, 34th in posterity enrichment, and 128th in wealth development. Hence, more the standard deviation of the five ranks more the difference between the three methods.

To sum up, the difference between pentagon and geometric methods displayed 97 similarities (76%; with maximum on position difference) and 118 "resemblances" (92%; maximum 2 positions difference) out of 128. Moreover, the difference between pentagon and arithmetic mean methods revealed 111 similarities (87%; maximum on position difference) and 119 "resemblances" (93%; maximum 2 positions difference) out of 128. Finally, the difference between arithmetic mean and geometric mean methods presented only 81 similarities (63%; with maximum on position difference) and 105 "resemblances" (82%; maximum 2 positions difference) out of 128.

To conclude, the pentagon-shaped method showed a compromised a solution regarding the two arithmetic and geometric means methods. There are more similarities between pentagon-shaped and each of the others means.

6 Conclusion

The paper presents a socioeconomic development index based on the objectives of Islamic Law. In fact, Rehman and Askari developed in 2010 an "Islamicity index" classifying all countries based on Islamic values. The paper called "How Islamic are Islamic countries" ranked different countries based on that opinion. However, comparing countries in terms of socioeconomic development using the objectives of the Islamic Law faced data availability respecting all dimensions of *Maqāṣid* al-Sharī'ah. The current paper selected available data of 187 countries and aggregated them within *Maqāṣid* al-Sharī'ah structure to measure socioeconomic development.

Hence, data are selected on each dimension and objective of the Islamic Law. The first dimension of *Maqāṣid* al-Sharī'ah (Safeguarding or Enrichment of Human) was measured based on five major components. In fact, Minimization of crime and anomie and security of life are seen imperative to safeguard human self. Moreover, dignity, Freedom and mental happiness are decisive to enrich human beings. Besides, it was challenging to measure the second dimension of *Maqāṣid* al-Sharī'ah (enrichment of faith) since the availability of religiosity and religious beliefs data are scarce and not common to all countries since the belief change obviously from one religion to another. Hence, the practical aspect was taken into account. Therefore, the outcomes of these religious practices are meant to reflect some behavior toward community. For that reason, justice, absence of corruption, poverty levels, and protection of environment are seen fundamental in assessing the enrichment of faith. Thirdly, three other features are considered to evaluate the enrichment of intellect (third dimension of *Maqāṣid* al-Sharī'ah). Clearly, the quality of education (more than education) is fundamental to enhance human intelligence. Besides, creativity and freedom of intellect (thought and expression) are compulsory in measuring the development of intellect within a country.

Regarding the fourth dimension (enrichment of posterity), new generations need essentially an established family, decent a shelter, a healthy environment, and good education. Accordingly, these four elements are measured to assess posterity enrichment efforts within countries. Finally, since GDP is not more seen as the single measure in evaluating economic efforts to develop wealth; As a result, there are dimensions are added to GDP per capita to calculate economic growth.

Freedom of business and enterprise and unemployment levels are vital in implementing a framework assessing this fifth dimension. In addition, self-employment is judged clear in creating wealth. This measure is based mainly on trend of entrepreneurship, behavior of individuals in the country and primarily media implication in encouraging generating wealth.

The paper presented as well, three calculation approaches. The first two ones are simply the arithmetic and geometric mean. The paper revealed the explanation of the second approach with these specific conditions explained in the paper based on a vector representation of the results. Moreover, it explained as well another graphical method (called pentagon-shaped) since as elucidated by Chapra (2008); the order of *Maqāṣid* is significant and each *Maqsid* is connected to succeeding one. Therefore, the paper presented another approach in measuring the index. The first approach was engaged in the HDI from 1990 to 2010, and then reformed since by the second one. The paper by comparing the three methods in assessing socioeconomic development, displayed the divergence between the arithmetic mean and the geometric mean approaches. It concluded that the pentagon-shaped represent a middle ground between the two first methods.

Finally, the paper ranked 187 countries based on *Maqāṣid* al-Sharīʿah but only 128 of them ensure the packed availability of data in entirely five dimensions. The analysis of the ranking of 187 first, then 128 countries exposed thought-provoking results. In fact, ironically most of Muslim countries (OIC countries) do not fulfill the objectives of the Islamic Law. European countries mostly pleased most of the required objectives of Sharīʿah. The ranking showed similarities in terms of results and ranking with HDI and the "Islamicity Index." For that reason, we may ask again the question of Rehman and Askari "How Islamic are Islamic countries."

To conclude, the paper presents a initial socioeconomic development index based on *Maqāṣid* al-Sharīʿah. Many indicators are selected from various databases. However, the paper is subject to enhancements by adding more indicators that expresses and translates the requirements of different *Maqāṣid* al-Sharīʿah. Likewise, this index is linked to *Ghazali* model of *Maqāṣid* al-Sharīʿah. In the future, the paper is subject to many adjustments by adding more dimensions and objectives of Law.

References

Abu Al-Zahra, M. (1997). *Usul al-Fiqh*. Egypt: Dar al-Fikr al-Arabi.

Adriaanse, A. (1993). *Environmental Policy Performance Indicators*. The Hague: SDV Publishers.

Alfsen, K. H., and Sæbø, H. V. (1993). "Environmental Quality Indicators: Background, Principles and Examples from Norway". *Environmental and Resource Economics* 3: 415–435.

Al-Ghazali, A. (1109 [1937]). *al-Mustasfa*. Cairo: al-Maktabah al-Tijariyyah al-Kubra.

Al-Qurtubi, M. (1240 [2006]). *Al-jamii li-ahkem al-Qur'ān*. Al-Ryadh: Mouassasst Al-Risalah.

Ariff, M., and Rosly, S. A. (2011). "Islamic Banking in Malaysia: Unchartered Waters". *Asian Economic Policy Review* 6 (2): 301–319.

Auda, J. (2008). *Maqāṣid al-Sharīʿah as Philosophy of Islamic Law: A Systems Approach*. London: International Institute of Islamic Thought (IIIT).

Bakkes, J. A., van den Born, G. J., Helder, J. C., Swart, R. J., Hope, C. W., and Parker, J. D. E. (1994). *An Overview of Environmental Indicators: State of the Art and Perspectives*. UNEP/EATR.94-01; RIVM/402001001. Environmental Assessment Sub-Programme. Nairobi: UNEP.

Bedoui, H. (2012). "Islamic Finance Ethical Competitive Advantage: How Islamic Finance Institutions Should Measure Their Performance". Tenth Harvard University Forum on Islamic Finance: *Islamic Finance and Development*, March 24–25.

Chapra, U. (2008). *The Islamic Vision of Development in Light of Maqasid al-Shari'ah*. London: International Institute of Islamic Thought (IIIT).

Chevalier, S., Choiniere, R., Bernier, L., et al. (1992). *User Guide to 40 Community Health Indicators*. Ottawa: Community Health Division, Health and Welfare Canada.

Dever, G. E. A. (1979). *Community Health Analysis*. Germantown, Mary town: Aspen Systems Corporation.

Dusuki, A. W. (2009). "Challenges of Realizing Maqāṣid al-Sharīʿah in Islamic Capital Market: Special Focus on Equity-Based Sukuk". Working Paper, *Sharīʿah* Research Academy for Islamic Finance, Malaysia.

Griffiths, P., et al. (2008). *State of the Art Metrics for Nursing: A Rapid Appraisal*. London: National Nursing Research Unit, King's College London, pp. 1, 2.

Hammond, A., Adriaanse, A., Rodenburg, E., Bryant, D., and Woodward, R. (1995). *Environmental Indicators: A Systematic Approach to Measuring and Reporting on Environmental Policy Performance in the Context of Sustainable Development*. Washington, DC: World Resources Institute.

Holling, C. S. (1978). *Adaptive Environmental Assessment and Management*. Chichester: Wiley.

Innes, Judith E. (1990). "Disappointments and Legacies of Social Indicators". *Journal of Public Policy* 9: 429–432.
Linster, M. (2003). "OECD Environmental Indicators: Development, Measurement and Use". OECD Reference Paper. http://www.oecd.org/LongAbstract/0,3425,en_2649_34441_24993548_1_1_1_1,00.html.
Liverman, D. M., Hanson, M. E., Brown, B. J., and Merideth, R. W. (1988). "Global Sustainability: Toward Measurement". *Environmental Management* 12 (2): 133–143.
Marcus, S. (1983). "Towards a Semiotic Approach to Social Indicators". Paper Presented at the International Congress of Logic, *Methodology and Philosophy of Science*, Salzburg, Austria, July 11–16.
McEwin, Marion. (1995). "Social Indicators and Social Statistics in Australia". *Statistical Journal of the United Nations*, Economic Commission for Europe.
McGillivray, Mark. (1991). "The Human Development Index: Yet Another Redundant Composite Development Indicator?". *World Development* 19 (10): 1461–1468. https://doi.org/10.1016/0305-750x(91)90088-y.
McQueen, D., and Noak, H. (1988). "Health Promotion Indicators: Current Status, Issues and Problems". *Health Promotion* 3: 117–125 (MWCD).
Niceforo, A. (1921). Les indices numériques de la civilisation et du progrès. Flammarion.
OECD [Organization for Economic Cooperation and Development]. (1993). *OECD Core Set of Indicators for Environmental Performance Reviews: A Synthesis Report by the Group on the State of the Environment*. Paris: OECD.
Ott, W. R. (1978). *Environmental Indices: Theory and Practice*. Ann Arbor, MI: Ann Arbor Science.
Pencheon, D. (2008). "The Good Indicators Guide: Understanding How to Use and Choose Indicators". UK National Health Service Institute for Innovation and Improvement website, www.institute.nhs.uk.
Quarrie, J. (1992). *The Earth Summit '92: The United Nations Conference on Environment and Development*. London: Regency Press.
Rehman, S., and Askari, H. (2010). "How Islamic Are Islamic Countries?". *Global Economy Journal* 10 (2), Article 2.
Sagar, A. D., and Najam, A. (1998). "The Human Development Index: A Critical Review". *Ecological Economics* 25: 249–264. https://doi.org/10.1016/S0921-8009(97)00168-7.
Scrivens, K., and Iasiello, B. (2010). "Indicators of 'Societal Progress': Lessons from International Experiences". OECD Statistics Working Papers, No. 2010/04, OECD Publishing. https://doi.org/10.1787/5km4k7mq49jg-en.
Srinivasan, T. N. (1994). "Human Development: A New Paradigm or Reinvention of the Wheel?". *American Economic Review* 84 (2): 238–243. JSTOR 2117836.

Tunstall, D. (1992). "Developing Environmental Indicators: Definitions, Framework and Issues" (Draft Paper). *Background Materials for the World Resources Institute*. Workshop on Global Environmental Indicators, Washington, DC, December 7–8, 1992. Washington, DC: World Resources Institute.

United Nations. (1994). "Information on Social Development Publications and Indicators in the United Nations System". Working Paper No. 7, United Nations Publications, New York.

World Bank. (1995). *Monitoring Environmental Progress*. Washington, DC: The World Bank.

Chambers Online Dictionary website: www.chambers.co.uk.

GEM Global Entrepreneurship Monitor website: www.gemconsortium.org.

Institute for Health Metrics and Evaluation (IHME) website: www.healthmetricsandevaluation.org.

International Telecommunications Union website: www.itu.int/en/ITU-D/Statistics/Documents/statistics/2013/Individuals_Internet_2000-2012.xls.

Online Etymology Dictionary website: www.etymonline.com.

QS World University Rankings website: www.topuniversities.com/university-rankings/world-university-rankings/2013.

Reporters Without Borders website: www.rsf.org.

The 2014 Economic Freedom Index website: www.heritage.org/index/.

The Happy Planet Index website: www.happyplanetindex.org.

The International Human Rights Rank Indicator website: www.ihrri.com.

UN Decade for Sustainable Energy for All (SE4ALL) website: www.se4all.org.

Universal Declaration of Human Rights website: www.un.org/en/documents/udhr/index.shtml.

Walk Free Foundation—Global Slavery Index 2013 website: www.globalslavery-index.org.

WHO/UNICEF Joint Monitoring Programme website: www.wssinfo.org.

World Bank website: www.worldbank.org.

World Economic Forum website: www.weforum.org.

World Health Organization (WHO) website: www.who.int.

CHAPTER 4

Consumer Behaviour, Consumption Planning and Objectives of Sharīʿah

Fahim M. Khan

1 Introduction

The present theory of consumer behaviour despite its robustness and amenability to mathematical manipulations covers a very limited ground as far as understanding the consumer behaviour is concerned. The theory may have contributed substantially to understanding the consumer behaviour in some societies of the West, but it hardly proves its relevance to understand the decision-making process of consumers in majority of the countries in the contemporary world. For example, why consumers prefer to spend on conspicuous luxury goods while their basic needs are unfulfilled. Or what type of consumer choice it is to prefer leisure instead of working for contributing even a small income to the poverty-stricken family. Or how a consumer would objectively identify whether there is waste of resources in his consumption pattern. Or why items like education of children and family health are low-priority items in majority of

F. M. Khan (✉)
Professor Emeritus and Director International Centre for Research in Islamic Economic, Minhaj University Lahore, Lahore, Pakistan

S. S. Ali (ed.), *Towards a Maqāṣid al-Sharīʿah Index of Socio-Economic Development*, Palgrave Studies in Islamic Banking, Finance, and Economics,
https://doi.org/10.1007/978-3-030-12793-0_4

the developing countries. Or why sometimes consumers end up spending on items which otherwise have no attraction to them (do not have utility).

Veblen (1899) showed that patterns of consumption and work broadly conform to the boundaries set by class and culture. Veblen saw that it was impossible to understand individual economic choices without understanding the world in which those choices were made. The economic theory misses this point in its framework of analysis.

The contemporary theory of consumer behaviour is not only limited in scope with respect to the understanding of the consumer choice but it also lacks the ability to understand and explain some of the contemporary economic problems that are directly the result of certain peculiarities in the consumer behaviour. High incidence of poverty has a lot to do with the consumer behaviour, but this is not a subject of the existing theory of consumer behaviour. Economic development also has strong roots in the consumer behaviour, but the existing theory is not geared towards understanding consumer behaviour as a reason for development or under-development. The World Summit on Sustainable Development held in Johannesburg, South Africa, from 26 August to 4 September 2002 recognized that changing consumption pattern is one of the essential requirements for sustainable development. But the theory of consumer behaviour has yet to recognize it. The sustainable development will remain a subject outside the mainstream economics unless there is a theory that identifies endogenous elements in consumer decision-making process that can help keeping consumer behaviour in line with the society's perception of sustainable development. Sustainable development is eventually a matter of observing certain ethics in economic behaviour. A theory of consumer behaviour that ignores the role of ethics in consumer's decision-making is bound to leave out such pressing economic problems like alleviation of poverty and sustainable development outside the mainstream of economics. Is it possible to have an alternative theory of consumer behaviour so that we can have a better perspective on how human beings get into economic problems and how some societies end up being poor and underdeveloped while others continue on the path of development?

These are the type of questions that motivate developing an alternate framework that would prove to be more realistic and more comprehensive in understanding economic behaviour and hence would provide better insight into the contemporary economic problems and their solutions. A framework has already been proposed elsewhere that can help us answering the above questions. Various elements of this proposed framework have been published or are now under print in different outlets (see Khan 2013a, b, n.d.). These publications have explained how the economic problems are created, at micro- and macro-level, when human beings fail to behave rationally (defined in a more realistic context) in making choices for consumption, in general, and how rationality in Islamic context (termed as "*Rushd*") can keep man and society away from facing economic problems. This paper discusses that if man fails to follow "*Rushd*" he may end up ignoring his needs by using resources on non-needs. If this happens then consumption pattern gets distorted and well-being gets ignored. How to correct such situation and how to put the consumers back on their natural and rational track? Here comes the role of public policy. It has been argued that state can play a role in this respect not by directly telling consumer what is their need and what is not but by adopting an appropriate policy framework and institutional arrangements that will promote in the economy a consumption pattern conforming to the objectives of Sharīʿah.

This paper first gives a brief overview of the alternative approach to understand consumer behaviour as mentioned above. The main part of the paper then deals with the public policy aspect of how to rationalize consumer behaviour in an Islamic economy to reduce poverty and to enhance sustainable development as well as to increase well-being at micro-level.

2 Part 1: An Alternate View on Theory of Consumer Behaviour

Consumer's allocation of resources and choice of goods and services to consume is related to the objectives of his life and institutional arrangements in which he lives. For a Muslim living in an Islamic economy, these elements are mainly derived from the understanding and adhering to the objectives of Sharīʿah.

The conventional framework for analysis of consumer does not help us if we want to analyse the behaviour of a Muslim consumer in an Islamic economy when his behaviour is to be related to the objective of Sharīʿah. The focus on objectives of Sharīʿah requires us to focus on "need" rather than utility as the basis of consumer behaviour. This has been discussed in detail in the work cited earlier.

Human beings have a natural urge to know their needs and meet them. This urge may come from inside the body as well as from outside (from family, society, religion, etc.). Consumer, thus, has to decide:

1. What are his needs (and what are not)?
2. How to prioritize the needs (because resources are scarce) to meet all needs?
3. What to do with unfulfilled needs?

The consumer is assumed to be instinctively looking for improving their well-being. It is, accordingly, assumed that sensible[1] consumers are primarily inclined to spend on what they need not on what they want. The analysis of consumers' analysis, therefore, is required to focus on the following:

a. What makes the consumers to remain (or not to remain) on the track? What makes him to succumb (or not to succumb) to spend on his non-need wants, instead of spending on meeting needs?
b. When consumers spend on non-need wants or spend on needs more than needed, they waste resources which otherwise could be used to meet their needs in a better way. What makes him (or does not make) him waste his resources?
c. If consumers in an economy are found to be going off-track, what can make them to get back on the track of meeting needs and to maximize their well-being?

2.1 Rationality or Sound Mindedness of the Consumer

Wants and needs may often coincide. Man, endowed with power of reason to judge what is needed for his well-being and what is not, by and large, will often not want what he does not need. Because of multiplicity of needs and scarcity of resources to meet them, the wants that do not meet the criteria of "needs" will often go unsatisfied despite their attraction for the consumer. This is rational consumer behaviour of man. This is, however, not the concept of "rationality" as discussed in conventional

[1] The word "rational" is avoided here because "rationality" in this paper is being defined differently than it is conventionally defined in economics. This will be explained in detail shortly in this paper.

theory of economics. A consumer living in a social environment makes a choice not merely based on his personal perception of what are his needs but his choice is overwhelmingly influenced by what social environment perceives as his needs. The rational choice of a consumer therefore is based on something more than what conventional term in economics refers to as "rationality". We need to give it a different name. Until we have a suitable term, let us call it "sound mindedness".[2] But the concept of sound mindedness recognizes that social environment influences individuals' choice. Often, the individuals will sacrifice their essential food needs for the sake of the education of their children. The pressure of the social environment and social values influences the individual choice.[3]

The concept of sound mindedness as described above enables the individuals

1. To identify what is their need and what is not
2. To rank their needs with respect to the contribution to their well-being
3. To avoid waste in allocation of resources to maximize well-being.

The distinction between wants and needs is not merely a matter of semantics. Though some needs may also be wants, the reverse may not often be true. Many wants may not necessarily qualify as need. We, therefore, assume that a consumer may instinctively have a list of desires to satisfy. But before going ahead to satisfy these desires, the sound-minded consumer would make judgements of which of his desires "need" to be satisfied and which do not need to be satisfied at all.

2.2 *Consumer Decision-Making*

In this framework, it is natural to assume that the needs will have a clear hierarchy. Topmost needs will be fulfilled first before going to the need

[2] For Muslims, we will go beyond the concept of "Sound mindedness". For Muslims, we will refer to ***Rushd*** or right-mindedness recognizing the influence of values of Islamic system of life on his consumption choices. This will be discussed in detail in this paper.

[3] In some sense this is relevant to the concept of bounded rationality because social environment and social values cover the information deficiency at individual level that led Simon to define bounded rationality. Herbert Simon's concept of 'bounded rationality' is somewhat closer to the 'sound-mindedness' referred above.

next in the list. The consumer will continue on this prioritized list until he exhausts his resources. This will be an equilibrium situation for him and will often be stable too, though not always. He is in equilibrium because this allocation of resources maximizes his well-being. Any other resource allocation would mean lower well-being. The equilibrium is stable in the sense that any external influence or shock may change the resource allocation only temporarily but, as a sound-minded person, he will have an urge to come back to the original allocation to restore the well-being level.

The disequilibrium arises if consumer happens to be distorting his list of needs and the hierarchy within the list. In this situation, he will end up not fulfilling some of his needs despite having capacity to do so and will end up at lower level of well-being than what he could afford from his resources. But he cannot remain in disequilibrium for long. Several pressures from inside or outside will work to put him back to the equilibrium position where he will be spending on consumer goods fulfilling his needs in right priority. This state of equilibrium in consumer choice is better described by a biology term known as "homeostasis". Internal pressures resulting from own concern for his well-being and external pressures from social environment around him (built up by family and friends as well by the institutional framework of the society) are triggered as soon as consumer starts getting off the desired track of meeting his needs.

It is always possible that some consumers may not have capacity to make sound judgement or may not like to follow their sound judgement due to various factors such as education, demonstration effect and invasion of foreign culture and hence may allow some of their wants camouflaged as their "needs". If disequilibrium occurs on this account, then this disequilibrium may not be temporary. This is like a chronic disease, which can possibly be controlled but not cured in short run. Such disequilibrium at micro-level also has macroeconomic implications because of their contagion effect.

2.3 Benefit of Taking This Approach

The above-mentioned framework helps us understand additional aspects of human economic behaviour (not covered by the conventional theory of economics) and can allow us to understand some important implications for consumer's well-being and development of the economy. Some potentially benefits of this approach are as below:

Understanding and Recognizing Waste of Resources: If the need is accepted as a motivation for consumption, then a consumer is said to be indulging in a waste of resources when consumer:

a. Spends more on a commodity than required for his well-being, or
b. Spends on lower order needs by sacrificing higher order needs, or
c. Spends on non-need commodities that do not contribute positively to the consumer's well-being.

The sound-minded consumers are assumed to avoid waste. All societies abhor waste and so do individuals in the society. But still waste may occur. Avoiding sound judgment and/or lack of ability to make sound judgement may occur and may lead some or many consumers to indulge in wastes in the sense described above. This may occur in almost all societies. Several factors can be identified that can lead to such a behaviour.

2.4 Divergence in the Individual and Society Concept of Consumers' Well-Being

Consumer may choose a consumption pattern that in his judgment maximizes his well-being but society may not think so. Consumer may also indulge in conspicuous consumption. Consumers may be influenced by foreign cultures. Consumers may also be influenced by wasteful consumption by certain affluent members[4] of society. Such tendencies are detrimental to the well-being of less affluent and low-income consumers as well as to the sustainable development in the society. Such a tendency in a society may generate a consumption pattern that is at variance from society's economic objectives. Such analysis of consumption pattern is useful for the society not only in the interest of sustainable development and to economize on the use of resources but also for the development of individual consumers so that they remain on the track of improving their well-being and are not put off the track by different influences taking place in the society.

[4]The Quran has used the terms of *Itrāf* (wasteful consumption) and *Mutrifeen* (affluent members of society).

Labour Supply Distortions: There may be a situation of lethargy on the part of individual consumers. It is often observed that a consumer has several of his needs unmet while at the same time he has unutilized capacity to work. Why he does not utilize his capacity to work, make income and meet as many of his needs as possible? This situation is generally observed in underdeveloped or developing world and is generally referred to as disguised unemployment. In the framework described above, this is a situation of disequilibrium in consumer behaviour. This framework can help us better understand this phenomenon and develop policies to correct it.

Interpersonal Comparison: Policy makers and social decision-makers often need to make interpersonal comparison to assess social welfare affect of various policy options and of investment decisions. In practice, such comparisons are made consciously or unconsciously and explicitly or implicitly in almost all policy decisions. All such decisions are made with well-being considerations of the members of society in mind. A framework for analysis of consumer behaviour on the lines described above and generating necessary data in that respect would make public decision-making more objective.

Sustainable Development: A sound-minded consumer who has prioritized his needs to maximize well-being would seek sustainable development of self and society. Since affluent members of society can easily slip away from the track of optimizing the fulfilling their needs minimizing waste of resources and since demonstration effect from the affluent section of society are strong in influencing the consumption pattern in the rest of the society, the sustainable development will be at risk in societies that have highly skewed income distribution. The proposed framework will bring the issue of sustainable development within the study of consumer behaviour.

2.5 *Application of Theory*

Some basic questions need to be answered to complete this theory.

1. One basic question is how to determine that the consumers are on track of meeting their needs in their right priority.
2. This will require determining some benchmarks for various needs with which the consumption pattern at individual level could be compared. What will be the basis of developing such benchmarks?

3. If basis of benchmarks can be decided, how the statistics will be collected to fix the indices to measure the deviations in the economy from these benchmarks?

Many countries already conduct household income–expenditure surveys and those who do not conduct may not find it difficult to start conducting such surveys. These surveys are already designed with the implicit objective of determining needs of the household without any explicit theory of consumer behaviour. These surveys can be specifically oriented towards explicitly determining benchmark to serve the purpose of analysing consumer behaviour in the above-mentioned theory. Some countries use these surveys to prepare consumption plans for various food items. The concept determining benchmark for various needs using household survey is, therefore, not a new concept. The question is how to modify the existing household surveys to provide statistics need for the application of the above-mentioned theory.

No society is void of an ethical base that would leave consumers free to behave or leave market free to allow consumers to satisfy whatever wants they intend to satisfy. On the other hand, not all societies have same set of ethics and norms for the market and for the behaviour of its economic agents. Each society has a set of ethics and norms to define rules for behaviour and also to reflect the objective of life that society members are assumed to be pursuing.

Islamic system of life provides a unique and elaborate set of rules for market as well as for the behaviour of its economic agents. Consumer behaviour is particular focus of the Islamic system of life. There is specific divine guidance in the form of Sharīʿah rules and ethics governing consumer behaviour. These rules and ethics lead to the development of such institutions that enable the individuals and society to continuously improve level of their well-being on a path of sustainable development. In this perspective, the above-mentioned framework to analyse consumer behaviour makes more sense than the framework used by conventional framework.

2.6 *Lessons for Islamic Theory of Consumer Behaviour*

The above discussion leads to the conclusion that we need an Islamic theory of consumer behaviour if we need to understand an individual's behaviour in the light of objectives of Sharīʿah. An Islamic theory would be expected to focus on the following:

1. Consumer may waste resources. His well-being may have room to improve if he avoids waste. Waste will be violation of a religious duty as well, which requires not doing *Isrāf.*
2. Commodity mix and the style of their use in the consumer's basket may not be environment friendly. The consumer may prefer satisfying various wants which are not his needs or may opt for such method of meeting needs which violate the norms of good style or good environment and make things ugly for the community ignoring Islamic teachings in this respect and may leave adverse impact for living conditions for future generations.
3. Consumer's behaviour may put economic growth at stake. Pursuit of some wants may lead the consumer to ignore some needs meant for his own economic uplift or economic uplift of the community. The rate of time preference when consumer's only objective is satisfaction of wants may be higher compared to when the consumer's objective is fulfilment of needs including the future needs. Pressure of wants can easily lead to ignoring some of the future needs and hence sacrificing development. The consumer may overspend on present needs and hence wasting the resources that could be used for future needs. The savings and capital accumulation thus will be sub-optimal. Alternatively, the consumer may spend miserly and may spend less than what is needed to meet his present needs to optimize on his well-being. The resources may be used or hoarded in a way not conducive to optimize on meeting future needs.[5]
4. Consumer behaviour may create class conflicts. An affluent class may indulge into *Isrāf* and *Itrāf,* which may create ill feelings among less privileged classes, and hence, peace and harmony in the community may be adversely affected.

[5] Following verses in Quran identify these two types of behaviour:

Verily thy Lord doth provide
Sustenance in abundance
For whom he pleaseth, and He
Straiten it
For He doth know
And regard all His servants. (17:30)
Those who, when they spend,
Are not extravagant and not
Niggardly, but hold a just (balance)
Between those (extremes); (25:67)

5. Human and social development may be thwarted seriously as the development needs like education, health, etc. are sacrificed for satisfying some mundane wants. Lack of commitment on the part of individuals to social well-being may let the community also lag behind in developing institutions needed for such development.

2.7 Objectives of Sharīʿah Relating to Consumption[6]

It may not be unreasonable to suggest that the starting point for an Islamic theory of consumer behaviour should be objectives of Sharīʿah. Reading texts in the Qur'ān and *Sunnah*, it can be visualized that there are specific objectives that Sharīʿah aims at by giving specific injunctions to believers to keep in mind when taking decisions about consumption. Below is a perception on what Sharīʿah aims at by giving rules for consumptions.

Rushd: Reading texts in the Qur'ān and *Sunnah* and their understanding by Fiqh scholars, it can be visualized that a believer's economic behaviour has not been left totally to the sound judgement of an individual. The behaviour has been specifically guided by something beyond sound judgement. Individual's economic choices in the context of Islamic life would be considered rational only if they make "Islamic sense". This common sense or sound mindedness of a common man may not always make Islamic sense.

We also learn that human beings may deviate from the right behaviour when instinctive strength of certain wants may stop them understanding rationality of right behaviour.

> They said, "O Shu'ayb, does your prayer command you that we should leave what our fathers worship or not do with our wealth what we please? Indeed, you are the forbearing, the discerning (Rasheed)!" (11.87)

As wants may not always be needs, so is the sound mindedness that might not always be right mindedness in the perspective of Islamic teachings. Right mindedness is sound mindedness within the value system that consumer shares with other members in the society. Islamic teachings provide a certain value system for sound behaviour.

[6]The author does not claim to be competent to write on this subject. This is only an economists understanding objectives of Sharīʿah relating to consumer behaviour.

The Qur'ān refers to the concept of "*Rushd*" in the context of human behaviour in general behaviour as well as in the context of economic behaviour. The term *Rushd* can be interpreted as "Right mindedness" or "Sound Mindedness in Islamic sense". Teachings of the Qur'ān and *Sunnah* tell us that right-minded judgement should be the basis of human activities and human economic decision-making. They also tell us that there are situations when human choice cannot be left to mere sound judgement or common sense of man and therefore divine guidance has been provided for right behaviour.[7]

We also learn from the Qur'ān that in some societies, some people sometime may not follow sound judgement in their activities and their judgement. We also get information from the divine sources that why this deviation may happen. Refer to the following divine guidance.

> Those who behave arrogantly on the earth in defiance of right--, them I will turn away from my signs: Even if they see all the signs, they will not believe in them, and if they see the way of right conduct (path of Rushd) they will not adopt it as (their) way. (7:146)

This explains that some instincts may overcome the instinctive urge to make sound judgment.

Sound mind of human beings may not always be able to distinguish good from bad. In some situations, sound judgment may fail to make right judgment. It has been mentioned in the Qur'ān that the people of Prophet Shoaib failed to comprehend how it can be good for them to give away the property they own. The Qur'ān guides the human being that giving away to needy is better for those who give away.

> And let not those who [greedily] withhold what Allah has given them of His bounty ever think that it is better for them. Rather, it is worse for them. Their necks will be encircled by what they withheld on the Day of Resurrection. And to Allah belongs the heritage of the heavens and the earth. And Allah, with what you do, is [fully] Acquainted. (3:180)

[7]The Quran quotes the prophet *Lut*, saying to his people, "is there not among you a single right- minded man (*rasheed*)"? (11:78). Also refer to (11:87). The people of *Lūt* may be acting according to sound judgment in their own sense, but they were definitely not acting with right sense of judgment.

> And whatever you give for interest to increase within the wealth of people will not increase with Allah. But what you give in *zakāh*, desiring the countenance of Allah - those are the multipliers. (30:39)

Though this element may be found in non-Muslim behaviour as well, it is not a part of economic choice. They are non-economic decision taken with no economic value in consideration. For a Muslim consumer, this is an integral part of the consumer choice. There is a reward attached to it, and since the reward is big, there are specific instructions not being carried away with this so that their worldly needs are unduly sacrificed. There are instructions to be moderate while making the choice how much to conserve for one's own needs and how much to spend for caring others. Moderation in spending for the worldly consumption as well for a reward hereinafter is an explicit part of *Rushd* in making economic choices. This element in economic decision-making requires an analytical framework different from the one used by the conventional analysis of consumer behaviour. This element in the sound mindedness in Islamic behaviour will be at work in making a choice between meeting one's needs and meeting the needs of others. It will also affect the choice between spending to meet one's present needs and saving for meeting future needs. The inclusion of the element of moderation with other elements of divine guidance for consumer choice (such as avoiding waste, avoiding *Itrāf* and *Tabzeer)* distinguishes *Rushd* (right mindedness) from the commonly known concept of rationality and sound mindedness.

Right mindedness may be claimed by every society with respect to its own culture and religion. When they analyse the consumer behaviour in their society, they may call it right mindedness in their own right. But that will not be considered as *Rushd* in the context of an Islamic economic analysis because of the differences in the perception on what is right and what is not. The Qur'ān has specifically pointed out this aspect of human behaviour in the context of observing the values of Islamic in human decision-making.

> ....if they see the way of error, they will adopt it as a way. That is because they have denied Our signs and they were heedless of them. (7:146)

> ....they followed the command of Pharaoh, and the command of Pharaoh was not [at all] discerning (rasheed). (11:97)

Pharoah was not right minded. He misguided his followers and led them to an unfortunate destiny.

The right mindedness in Islamic sense therefore will refer to the mindset reflecting Islamic system of values and lifestyle. It will be therefore be referred to as Rushd in our analysis of economic behaviour compared to any the right mindedness that any other value system may claim.

Human Needs: Reading the Qur'ān and *Sunnah*, one reaches an unavoidable conclusion that need would be the base for making the choice under the assumption of *Rushd*. The guidance with respect to *Isrāf*[8] and *Tabzeer*[9] and the concept of *al-afw*[10] with respect to *infāq fi sabeelillah* are clear indicators that need should be the basis for resource allocation. It is the set of such injections that creates a mindset that leads believers to identify their needs relevant to the objective of Islamic system of life and make efforts to meet them. Islamic scholars identify the objective of the Islamic system of life as human well-being.[11] Well-being is comprehensive betterment in all aspects of life. For the sake of brevity in this presentation, we will restrict the well-being to following aspects of life (elaborated by Shatibi) only to develop methodology. More elaboration can be added on the aspects of life without any implications for methodology:

1. Self (نفس): Individuals' life in the household
2. Property (مال): Household's net worth and economic security
3. Reason (عقل): Capacity to reason, ability to judge good from bad
4. Procreation (نسل): Family life
5. Religion (دين): Life hereafter

Islamic scholars define different levels of meeting the needs. First level of needs is critical that reflects the protection of the above aspects of life and saving them from destruction. Second level is necessary level,

[8] "... And be not excessive. Indeed, He likes not those who commit excess" (7:31), (6:141).

[9] "Indeed, the wasteful are brothers of the devils" (17:28).

[10] And they ask you what they should spend (as *infāq*). Say, "The excess [beyond needs]" (2:219).

[11] Al-Shatibi, "al-*Muafiqaat*".

and it relates maintaining reasonable of quality of these aspects of life. The third level is aesthetic level reflecting beautification and amelioration of these aspects of life.[12]

Defining needs for each of the aspect of life at individual level will be job of the individual himself, and no direct intervention is implied in the Islamic system of life. Neither the discussion on the objectives of Sharīʿah nor the discussions in the Fiqh literature specify what are the needs that individuals should meet. It has been left to *Rushd* to make the choice. The state or society or both, however, have the responsibility to guide, direct and facilitate the individuals to act and behave with a right mind in all their activities including economic activities.

2.8 Role of State

The above-mentioned responsibility of state or society is reflected in the Qur'ān as below:

> Those who, if We give them authority in the land, establish prayer and give Zakāh and enjoin what is right and forbid what is wrong. And to Allah belongs the outcome of [all] matters. (22:41)

The above guidance requires state and/or civil society to play their role of enjoining what is right and forbidding what is wrong in the consumer behaviour as well. It is their responsibility to oversee if the objectives of Sharīʿah are being followed in the consumer behaviour and if not then how to bring back the consumer behaviour in the community on Islamic Track fulfilling the objectives of Sharīʿah.

The state will need to work in two directions:

1. Understanding the nature and extent of deviation from the Islamic behaviour and factors underlying the deviant behaviour.
2. Identifying and implementing appropriate policy measures.

The objectives of Sharīʿah can be interpreted to imply that state would watch

[12]Al-Shatibi has termed the needs at these three levels as '*ḍarooryyat*', '*ḥajyyaatt*' and '*tahseenyyat*'.

a. If any section of the population is deprived of the minimum level of needs of any aspect of life
b. If any section of population is going off the track of meeting their needs and are spilling demonstration effect on other sections
c. If there is evidence of *Isrāf* and *Itrāf*.

If such distortions are found to be emerging in the society, then necessary measures should be taken to correct these distortions.

3 Part 2: Consumption Planning and Consumption Policy

The contents in this part are still being developed as a part of an empirical research project. The contents are not yet final. The presentation of this part here aims at receiving feedback to improve the research project.

State will be faced with the following questions in order to play the role mentioned above:

1. How to measure the adherence to right mindedness in the consumers' choices in the economy?
2. What indicators will reflect that consumers in the economy are getting off the track in meeting their needs?
3. What policy measures state can take to contain deviating behaviour of consumers in the economy?
4. What policy measures are needed to minimize the negative influences of deviations from right-minded behaviour?

3.1 Measuring the Adherence to Right Mindedness in Consumers' Behaviour in the Economy

This may require undertaking two exercises.

1. Defining key needs (distinct from the World Bank concept of basic needs).
2. Fixing benchmarks for key needs at the critical level and necessary level as explained earlier.

Key needs: At the outset, it may be clarified that the term "key needs" is not same as the term "Basic Needs", adopted by the ILO/World Bank/

UNDP. Key needs refer the needs required for maintaining all aspects of human life on earth in relation to objectives of Sharīʿah. Our focus is neither "poverty line" (ILO/World Bank approach) nor our focus is "Capabilities" (Amartya Sen approach). Our focus, in the context of objectives of Sharīʿah, is human well-being with dignity as basic human right.

> And We have certainly honored the children of Adam and carried them on the land and sea and provided for them of the good things and preferred them over much of what We have created .... (17:70)

This right is denied if any aspect of life is endangered. This is an approach distinct from the basic needs approach. In consumption planning, the role of state in an Islamic economy will be substantially complemented by voluntary sector.

> Those who spend their wealth in the way of Allah and then do not follow up what they have spent with reminders [of it] or [other] injury will have their reward with their Lord, and there will be no fear concerning them, nor will they grieve. (2:263)

For the purpose of rationalizing consumption pattern in an Islamic economy, state will identify key needs covering all aspects of human life. The civil society and individuals will be motivated to meet these needs for all in the society. The identification of key needs is an exercise that will be done by state through its consultative bodies and institutions. Below, we give a suggestive list of key needs to be defined with respect to different aspects of life.

1. Food and clean water
2. Clothing
3. Shelter
4. Access to medical and health facilities
5. Liquid/fixed assets as means of economic security
6. Means for improving reasoning faculties (basic capacity to perceive, to reason and to communicate
7. Institutions for facilitating marriage and raising family
8. Means to acquire religious knowledge and availability of institutions to practise it.

Fixing Benchmarks: Once the key needs have been identified, then the next step would be to fix benchmarks for these key needs. There can be two levels of benchmarks, one referring to critical level and the other referring to necessary level. Fixing the benchmark for critical level will help determining if any section of the population is deprived of the minimum level of needs of any aspect of life.[13] Fixing the benchmark for necessary level will help determining

i. If any section of population is going off the track of meeting their needs and is spilling demonstration effect on other sections
ii. If there is evidence of *Isrāf* and *Itrāf*.

How to fix these benchmarks? The following suggestions are made.

3.1.1 *Life* (نَفس)

The protection and maintenance of life requires needs such as food, water, clothing, shelter, gas, electricity and medical facilities and provisions. Fixing the benchmarks for these needs is not an unusual or difficult task. Several countries do this exercise. And several research institutions have carried out elaborate studies to determine minimum requirements to meet these needs.[14] The benchmarks at critical level to ensure survival will indicate the minimum requirements of individuals to sustain their physical efficiency. At necessary level, the benchmark will reflect the minimum requirements for maintaining a reasonable level of physical efficiency as well as some reasonable level of comfort and ease in life.

3.1.2 *Property* (مَال)

The benchmark would reflect some perception of minimum economic security that one should have. This benchmark can be fixed in terms of some value of liquid and fixed assets owned by household as a ratio of household's monthly income.

[13] Some Islamic scholars have argued that it is the duty of state to guarantee of minimum needs of the population living in an Islamic state (Siddiqi 1988).

[14] Methodologies, however, are available to make such calculations. The most difficult requirement in this category perhaps is to calculate benchmark for water requirement. International Water Association, for example, has carried elaborate exercises to define water requirements and to explain how to calculate minimum requirements.

3.1.3 Reason (عقل)

1. Benchmark of an invisible asset like this may seem to be a bit difficult to fix. Mere years of schooling will not be a good indicator of this asset. The benchmark should reflect some minimum level of capacity in the household to perceive, comprehend, reason and communicate. Since this benchmark will be reflective of the capacity to perceive, to reason, to associate and to communicate, the access to sources of formal and informal educational facilities and access to electronic and print media include some level of understanding of Qur'ān, *Sunnah* and early history of Islam that can develop this capacity. The quantification of benchmark may be based on
   a. Number of institutions of formal educational, religious schools/madaris per population of children from 5 to 15 years of age.
   b. Proportion of households with education beyond primary school or equivalent or having access to newspapers/books/magazines, or to TV, or to Radio.

3.1.4 Procreation (نسل)

The benchmark may be expressed in terms of

a. Marital status of the adult members in the household
b. Number of couples married for defined period with specified number of children.

3.1.5 Religion (دين)

The benchmark in this respect will reflect the minimum level of opportunities to learn religion and practise it. The benchmark may be fixed in terms of the availability of institutional arrangements for facilitating the population to discharge its religious obligations and acquire religious knowledge. Benchmark may also relate to specifying institutional arrangements to establish prayers, to pay *Zakāh*, to observe fasting in Ramadan, to perform Hajj, to remind the practice of Islamic good, and advising to refrain from vices. A benchmark can be fixed, for example, having at least one mosque with a facility to teach the Qur'ān and *Sunnah* within a specified radius. Some countries in the Middle East have provided other examples of institutional arrangements in facilitating knowledge as well as the practice of religion in the society.

3.2 *Developing Indices to Measure Deviations in the Economy from the Benchmarks*

Once the Benchmarks have been fixed, the next step would be the calculation of values and indices relating to the actual situation in the economy and to compare them with the benchmark. The project intends to suggest of several indices that can be worked out by utilizing the information from already available surveys and/or conducting specially designed household surveys on allocation of time and resources (to be abbreviated as ATR surveys). The project is using the existing questionnaires of household income–expenditure survey, livestock survey and agriculture census, conducted in Pakistan, and is identifying areas for changes in these questionnaires. Some surveys are being freshly designed.

This paper identifies only the following important indices.

1. Index of *Isrāf*
2. Index of *Faqr*
3. Index of *Rushd*
4. Index of human development

3.2.1 Index of Isrāf

If we have a benchmark on different components of life (نَفس) described above, we can use statistical methods to identify normal and abnormal consumption pattern and develop our criteria for identifying *Isrāf* and *Itrāf*. Details of the methodology cannot be given here. This is still a subject of research. As a hint towards our methodology, the following may be mentioned.

Assuming C_i is the actual expenditure on i_{th} component of the expenditure relating to life (نَفس) in a household and B_i the benchmark for i_{th} component, we define a variable $D_i = C_i - B_i$ representing the deviation of the household from the benchmark. We analyse the distribution of all households with positive D_i. If it is a skewed distribution, then this can be taken as a potential indicator of the *Isrāf* and *Itrāf*. Some average of this distribution can help us identifying *Isrāf* and *Itrāf*. Constructing a normal distribution of D_i around its average and superimposing it on the actual distribution will identify the area where *Isrāf* and *Itrāf* are occurring. A weighted average of the consumption beyond upper limit of normal band can become the basis of constructing an index of *Isrāf and Itrāf*.

Following statistics may also serve as indicators of deviating behaviour:

1. Proportion of expenditure on goods harmful to health and environment: The items injurious to health or environment are clearly known in a community. If expenditure on such items in proportion to income is found substantial in the budget of large number of households, then it should be the reflection of marked deviation from Islamic behaviour of consumption. An increasing trend in the use of such expenditure relative to income will be indicator of increasingly moving away from *Rushd*.
2. Presence of goods prohibited in Islamic law in the consumption basket of consumer is obvious indicator of the violation of Islamic teachings on consumption and hence violence of *Rushd*.
3. The proportion of male population in working age waiting for a suitable job opportunity to arise for them is the indicator of waste of time and indicator of *Isrāf*.

Various other indicators can be derived through the normal household income–expenditure surveys and market surveys being currently conducted in different countries. Special surveys can also be conducted with carefully designed questions to assess the commitment to Islamic rules and norms for consumer behaviour.

3.2.2 Index of Faqr

The number of people in the community not being able to meet critical needs in any aspect of their life as a ratio to the total population is considered indicator of *Faqr*.

All those households whose C values fall below B values are to be considered as suffering from Faqr. The value of C for all households below B will form the basis for constructing this index to reflect increase or decrease of *Faqr* in the economy.

There can be several other indicators. Number of children out of school/or religious education arrangements or without home study is a reflection of deprivation from critical level of human needs. Special surveys can be conducted from time to time to assess the proportion of population not having proper shelter, incidence of sick population deprived of opportunity to get treated, average age of unmarried adult population in low-income households, etc.

3.2.3 *Index of* Rushd

This is the most important index for the establishment of an Islamic economy. The index will indicate the direction in which the rightly sound mindedness is moving over time and hence affecting the individuals' well-being in the society and development in the economy. Methodology to construct this index is still being finalized. Briefly, the following is mentioned here.

a. One quick proxy of Rushd can be seen in the ratio of households that fall in the area between normal distribution and the actual distribution of household expenditure to total households having expenditure above B. Thus, the index of *Rushd* may be based on the following variable:
   $R = (1 - H_d / H_b)$
   where
   H_d is the number of households showing deviations from normal, and
   H_b is the number of households showing above benchmark expenditure.
b. Drawing from main household income–expenditure survey, sub-samples stratified by income groups and getting more detailed information on their lifestyle and consumption pattern in order to determine the needs of any aspect of life fulfilled at necessary level and above while needs at critical level in other aspects of life are being ignored, and constructing an index on the basis of this information.
c. Conducting opinion surveys to determine the perception of consumer's own perception on what is rightly guided consumption and what is not and using this information for constructing an index.
d. Analysing the trend in non-critical consumer goods imported as well as domestically produced goods compared with the trends in the growth in per capita household income.

3.2.4 *Index of Human Development*

This will aim at measuring growth or decline in the level of human well-being in the society over time. This will also measure the increase or decrease in the human dignity over time in the society.

The changes in human well-being or human development or human dignity are reflected by the changes in the level at which needs of various aspects of human life are being met in the society. A composite index therefore can be based on the following:

a. Proportion of total number of households falling in the right half of the normal curve described above in the context of index for *Isrāf*.
b. Proportion of total number of households with liquid or fixed asset beyond the benchmark fixed for minimum need for this aspect of life.
c. Proportion of total number of households beyond the benchmark fixed for عقل.
d. Proportion of households meeting the bench requirement for نسل.
e. Proportion of households indicating receiving some level of religious education and practice.

Such index may not possibly be prepared annually. And no significant changes are expected in such index in short run. It may be synchronized with population censuses that are normally conducted once in 10 years.

It may be mentioned here that the above concept of human development is different from the currently popular concept developed under the sponsorship of UNDP. The annexure to this paper briefly explains the UNDP concept of the Index of Human Development. The UN-sponsored HDI does not help the Muslim world know where they stand with respect to their own concept of well-being and how to improve the well-being at national level and at *Ummah* level. (See brief discussion in the Annexure to this paper.)

Human development is objective of Sharīʿah with the ultimate goal of achieving comprehensive human well-being. Though the Mahbub ul Haq terminology of human development and human well-being is the terminology that Islamic scholars have also been using since long, the meaning and substance of human development in the work of Mahbub ul Haq (adopted later on universally by United Nations Development Programme) is not what Islamic scholars refer to as well-being when discussing objectives of Sharīʿah.

The concept of well-being as adopted by UN is vague if not doubtful. The three criteria income, education and life expectancy will indicate well-being even if the prostitution, same-sex marriages, gambling and drugs like Marijuana are being legalized and protected through developing necessary institutions for that purpose. The HDI on these three variables will not be concerned with increasing organized crime, gang rapes, increasing pedophiles, etc. The HDI also has no room for the consideration of adherence of moral and ethical values.

The Human Development Index in the light of objectives of Sharīʿah outlined above is needed not only by individual Islamic countries for designing policies for improving well-being in Islamic sense at national level, but this index is also needed as a reference point for *Ummah*-level organizations like IDB to make investment decisions.

IDB needs to use such index to allocate its resources for improving human well-being and human development in Muslim/OIC countries. The Annexure discusses that the ranking of Muslim countries does not provide any guidance on how to perceive human development in the Muslim world as a whole when using the UNDP index of human development. It is proposed that an IDB_OIC joint committee needs to be assigned a project to formally develop a methodology of IHDI for the benefit of member countries in their investment planning as well as for IDB for allocating its resources for the well-being of member countries.

3.3 Consumption Policy

As already mentioned at the beginning of this part of the paper, state needs to take two types of policy measures to keep the consumption pattern in the economy:

a. Policy measures that state can take to contain deviating behaviour of consumers
b. Policy measures that state can take to minimize the negative influences of deviations from right mindedness in consumer behaviour
c. Policy measures state can take to improve well-being in the society by improving the state of Rushd and human development in the economy.

Containing Isrāf and Faqr: All societies abhor waste and all societies want to eliminate Faqr. But the two phenomena still coexist in almost all societies. And it is absolutely undesirable if it coexists in Muslim economies although elimination of both these vices is religious obligations of individuals as well as of society and state.

There are plenty of examples of public policies in different societies dealing with both these problems. A variety of systems of taxes, incentives, programmes and packages can be seen in different economies to contain these two negative elements in consumption pattern in an economy. State in Islamic economy, however, has an extra leverage from religion to effectively deal with these problems.

Zakāh, *Sadaqāt*, *Infāq fi Sabeelillah* is an important element of Islamic System. Despite weakening practice of religious convictions, in present times, this element remains important in the lives of Muslims. Muslims do want to help wholeheartedly to the needy, irrespective of their economic status. A very large proportion of affluent people have plenty of money to spare to help the needy. Even poor people like to spend *fi-sabeelillah* whenever and whatever they can. This is particularly true when there is the question of help of helping people suffering from *Faqr*. There are, however, several reasons that do not allow this spirit to come into action. This is not the place to go into the details of these reasons. One thing is clear. This potential is sufficient to eliminate *Faqr* in most of the contemporary Muslim economies, and a well-planned institutional framework needs to be designed to exploit this potential to eliminate *Faqr* from the economy on voluntary basis.

States in some Muslim countries are aware of this potential, and they do intend to exploit it for the well-being of less privileged members of the society. But often this effort is focused only on *Zakāh* collection and using it for alleviation of poverty. The states are inclined to use the funds so collected in investing on behalf of the poor to get a sustained financial resource to uplift their future economic status. As a result of this approach, we can find several contemporary Muslim countries, where state has collected huge amounts of *Zakāh* and is waiting to be invested in various projects to contribute to sustainable development while a section of population continues to suffer from starvation, diseases, infant deaths, maternity deaths, child labour, etc. This is apparently not in line with the objectives of Sharīʿah. There is no intention to create a dispute with Sharīʿah scholars on permitting *Zakāh* funds for sustainable development, but following arguments do seem to point to the fact that the priority for use of *Zakāh* funds is to meet urgent needs of extreme poor if they exist in the society, rather than for meeting future needs of poor in general.

a. According to the Qur'ānic verse 9:60, the priority for the use of *Zakāh* is to meet the urgent needs of needy rather than to invest for meeting future needs of poor.
b. A tradition of Prophet (peace be upon) narrates that *Faqr* brings closer to *Kufr* and also implies that top priority be given to *Zakāh* funds to eliminate *Faqr* on spot on immediate basis.
c. Another tradition says that one is not a believer if he sleeps full stomach and his neighbour is starving.

For the purpose of consumption policy, it is proposed that immediate elimination of *Faqr* be made the primary objective of an Islamic economy. If *Faqr* is allowed to stay in a society, it may not only leave an important objective of Sharī'ah unfulfilled but may also generate crimes in the society and may also disturb its peace and harmony. It is now being increasingly witnessed even in Muslim world that people suffering from *Faqr* murder their children or sell them for small amounts of money just to fight *Faqr*.

Objectives of Sharī'ah for an Islamic economy will not be considered fulfilled if *Faqr* is allowed to continue in an Islamic economy. Muslim states currently are more engaged in the following UNDP approach of Millennium Development Goal, which focuses more on putting very poor sections of population on the track of their sustainable higher socio-economic status, which will free them from hunger and extreme poverty and make them stay on their own feet on the long run.

This is indeed a thoughtful strategy, but it is at variance with Islamic approach because under this approach a substantial proportion of population suffering from *Faqr* will continue to remain in *Faqr* for a considerable time until the target of sustainable development is achieved.[15] It may not be wrong to say that there is a zero tolerance in Islamic system for the existence of *Faqr* in an Islamic economy. If it comes into existence, then individuals, society and state have to act to eliminate it on the spot.

Consumption policy can potentially take care of both the deviations from right path in consumption behaviour. An institutional arrangement

[15]MDG target aimed to halve the proportion of people whose income is less than $1 a day during the period between 1990 and 2015. According to UN, roughly 920 million people would still be living under the international poverty line in 2015, even if the target is achieved.

is needed that would not only cut the *Isrāf* but would also make the resources thus saved to go directly to reduce *Faqr* in the economy. One important element in this arrangement will be to develop confidence and transparency in the institutional arrangement developed for this purpose. There is enough evidence that affluent consumers are willing to spare resources to get people out of *Faqr*. If a transparent system ensures the direct and immediate flow of resources from affluent members of society to genuinely reduce their state of *Faqr*, the affluent members of society would not mind being taxed for their excessive consumption or penalized for their lavish spending. With the modern technology, it is not difficult to put such a transparent system in place. The technology may also allow the affluent members of the society to help directly the households faced with *Faqr*.

The other important element is putting confidence in the system that would guarantee that the households identified in *Faqr* are actually *Faqeer* (those suffering from *Faqr*) and the funds received by them are genuinely used to remove their *Faqr* in all aspects of their life. Putting a robust database in place can help achieve this objective.

The institutional framework of Islam encourages voluntary efforts on the part of believers. The institution of *Awqāf* is the obvious example of such voluntary efforts. State's role in this respective would be to provide a legal structure to protect property rights of *Awqāf*. State can develop simple structures on its own in different parts of the country that would be used by devoted Muslims for feeding hungry and providing basic and immediate medical care to needy. Role of state can be simply regulatory and supervisory as central bank is to banking and financial institutions.

Containing negative influences: Consumption pattern may generate several negative influences in the economy. At micro level, the consumption pattern of affluent members in the society (who are few in numbers) creates a demonstration effect on less affluent sections of the population which makes the less affluent sections of society to spend more on the conspicuous items rather than on items that fulfil their needs in different aspects of their life and hence suppressing their well-being. The lifestyle of affluent sections may also create sense of deprivation in the less affluent sections of the population hence creating class conflicts. At macro-level, such tendencies reduce the availability of resources for investments and development.

This is something that cannot be taken care of by state on urgent basis. State would require developing a medium-term plan to provide such public facilities that divert lower and middle class could enjoy and divert their attention from the conspicuous consumption of affluent class. Policies are required to contain such developments in the society that create wide discrimination between rich and poor. Quality of education facilities for affluent section and poor sections of population is an example. Involving civil society at national and local level can be integrated into the consumption policy aiming at mobilizing businesses, consumers and households to pursue Sharīʿah objective in consumption.

A robust database on the impacts of production and consumption patterns on consumer behaviour as well as on environment needs will be required for designing effective policies in this respect.

Streamlining Rushd and Human Development: This is ultimate objective of consumption policy and planning. This objective may not be achievable in a short-term or medium-term plan. It will require a long-term plan. To start with, it may require a perspective plan for 25 years. The plan will require not only launching planned projects but also promoting civil societies to address various aspects of consumer behaviour in the society, re-orienting the syllabi in formal and informal educational institutions to include courses on Islamic economic behaviour in all curricula, training the leaders/imams in religious institutions including mosques to constantly educate the masses visiting these institutions on matters of economic behaviour at individual level and making mass media (print as well as electronic) to increase this focus in their news, discussions and entertainment programmes. Besides, the state will also use fiscal and monetary policies to penalize behaviour not conforming to *Rushd* and giving incentives for *Rasheed* (conforming to *Rushd*) behaviour.

4 Conclusion

Rationalization of consumption and consumer behaviour for the sake of development and growth, and more so, for the sake of what is called sustainable development, is a serious concern of all developing countries, including all Muslim countries. Muslim countries, however, have the advantage that they have very specific guidance in their religion about rationalization of consumption and consumer behaviour that can lead to achieve such goals faster. Since this is divine guidance and integral part of their religious beliefs, the Muslim countries can achieve better results in terms of growth and sustainable development if rationalization of consumption on the lines of Islamic teachings is a specific element of their development strategy.

This paper elaborates on this point in the framework of a theory of consumer behaviour, which is different from the conventional theory but more relevant for developing countries, in general, and Muslim countries, in particular. In the framework of this theory, it has been shown that consumer behaviour rationalized according to Islamic teachings leads to a fast track towards improving human well-being, accelerating sustainable development, reducing class conflicts and promoting peace and harmony in the society.

This paper also negates the claim of some economists (Muslim and others) that we do not need a distinct Islamic theory of economics because conventional theory of economics is general enough to accommodate variations in values and rules of behaviour delineating economic systems. Those who take this view, however, ignore the fact that Islamic teachings refer to a very wide set of concepts and statements about economic values and behaviour of economic agents that the philosophy and methods of conventional economics just cannot capture within its theoretical framework.[16] Islamic teachings on consumption and consumer behaviour refer to several concepts and aspects of human behaviour, which cannot be understood and explained within the theoretical framework and methodology of conventional economics. We need a different theory. This paper outlines the possibility of an alternate theory based on the concept of "needs" rather than on the concept of "wants" not only to appropriately understand consumer behaviour in all its aspects but also to design policies to keep consumption pattern consistent with economic objectives of Sharīʿah requires human being human, human development and human dignity. Using the approach described in this paper, it may be possible to empirically understand the concepts like waste in consumption, conspicuous consumption and so-called irrationalities in consumer behaviour, etc. as well as to show that the norms of consumer behaviour embedded in Islamic teachings can lead to improving well-being and developing man and society on a sustainable track. The paper also

[16]For example, the statement in the Quran (Say: "If ye had control of the Treasures of the Mercy of my Lord, Behold, ye would keep them back, for fear of spending them: for man is (ever) niggardly!" [17:100]) highlights an aspect of human nature, which is obviously outside the assumptions and methodology of conventional economics that fails even to explain why people hold money despite substantial opportunity costs of doing so.

discusses how deviation from these norms can occur and how and who can bring back the consumers on the normal track.

An unwritten moral of the paper is that if "Islamic economists", during the last thirty years, had paid more attention to such aspects of Islamic economic teachings as consumer behaviour instead of theorizing the complex subject of Islamic finance and Islamic financial system, they would have gone a long way to show to the world that Islamic economics is a unique and distinct discipline promising a more peaceful and just economic order for the mankind.

Rationalization of consumption and consumer behaviour is needed not only for improving well-being of individuals in the society but also for the sake of what is called sustainable development which is a serious concern of all developing countries, including all Muslim countries.

Annexure: UNDP Index of Human Development (HDI)

The Human Development Index was developed as numerical measure made up of what most of the Development Economists believe are the very basic ingredients of human well-being: health, education and income. The first Human Development Index was presented in 1990. It has been an annual feature of every Human Development Report since, ranking virtually every country in the world from number one (currently Iceland) to number 177 (currently Sierra Leone).

This composite index has become one of the most widely used indices of well-being around the world and has succeeded in broadening the measurement and discussion of well-being. The following table summarizes the position of Muslim countries according to the UNDP-HDI ranking for 2012.

Table 1 reveals the following:

Low-ranked countries include more OIC countries than non-OIC countries (25:21).

The countries which have not been ranked as low, the ratio OIC and non-OIC countries is 14:33.

There are 92 Countries above the world average of which only 18 countries (19%) are OIC countries.

This does not give as bad a picture as seen with respect to population. Out of the total population living in low-ranked countries, two-thirds (66%) live in OIC countries. Out of the total population of OIC countries, 50% live in the low-ranked countries as defined in the above table.

Table 1 Muslim countries position in 2012

Very high-ranked countries = 47 (Index ranging 0.80–0.96)	Non-OIC members = 44 (Including South Korea, Chile, Seychelles and Croatia)	OIC countries = 3 (Brunei Darussalam, UAE, Qatar)
High-ranked countries = 45 (Index range 0.71–0.80)	Non-OIC countries = 30	OIC countries = 15 Bahrain, Kuwait, Saudi Arabia, Libya, Malaysia, Albania, Lebanon, Iran, Kazakhstan, Mauritius, Azerbaijan, Turkey, Oman, Algeria, Tunisia
Medium-ranked countries = 47 (Index range 0.54–0.71)	Non-OIC countries = 33	OIC countries = 14 Jordan, Turkmenistan, Maldives, Gabon, Guyana, Suriname, Egypt, Uzbekistan, Syria, Indonesia, Kyrgyz Republic, Turkmenistan, Tajikistan, Morocco, Iraq
Low-ranked countries = 46 (Index range 0.34–0.53)	Non-OIC countries = 21	OIC countries = 25 Bangladesh, Pakistan, Cameroon, Tanzania, Nigeria, Senegal, Mauritania, Togo, Yemen, Uganda, Djibouti, Gambia, Comoros, Benin, Cote d'Ivoire, Sudan, Sierra Leone, Afghanistan, Guinea Bissau, Guinea, Mali, Chad, Burkina Faso, Mozambique, Niger
Total = 186 World average HDI = 0.694	Non-OIC countries = 129	Total OIC countries = 57

Source Author's compilation based on data from Wikipedia: http://en.wikipedia.org/wiki/List_of_countries_by_Human_Development_Index

On the other hand, the total population living in non-OIC world, only 7% live in low-ranked countries.

According to Table 1, a total population of 1111 million of the world lives in the high-ranking countries. The total population of OIC countries that lives in the high-ranking world is only 0.1%.

A total population of 1236 million lives in low-ranking countries. The total population of OIC countries that lives in low-ranking countries is 70%.

Is the picture really so bad for Muslim world, or there are some serious problems in the concept and/or measurement?

Speaking globally, how does the information in above table help the world in improving global well-being? If Israel and Norway (where less than two per cent of world population lives) would move up in the above table, how much global well-being would improve?

But if India and China (where 37% of world population lives) move down in rank, it is a disaster for global well-being.

How does the so-called HDI ranking under UN definition help institutions concerned with world development a global well-being?

The same question arises for OIC and IDB. The UN-sponsored HDI does not help these institutions how to improve well-being at Ummah level.

Human development is objective of Sharīʿah with the ultimate goal of comprehensive human well-being. Though the Mahbub ul Haq terminology of human development and human well-being is the terminology that Islamic scholars have also been using since long, the meaning and substance of human development in the work of Mahbub ul Haq (adopted later on universally by United Nations Development Programme) is not what Islamic scholars refer to when discussing the objectives of Sharīʿah.

Their concept of well-being is vague if not doubtful. The three criteria income, education and life expectancy will indicate well-being even if the prostitution, same-sex marriages, gambling and drugs like Marijuana are being legalized and protected through developing necessary institutions for that purpose. The HDI on these three variables will not be concerned with increasing organized crime, gang rapes, increasing pedophiles, etc. The HDI also has no room for the consideration of adherence of moral and ethical values.

References

Khan, Fahim M. (2013a). "An Alternative Approach to Analysis of Consumer Behaviour: Need for Distinguished Islamic Theory". *Journal of Islamic Business Management*, Vol. 3, No. 2, pp. 1–35.

Khan, Fahim M. (2013b). "Theorizing Islamic Economics: Search for a Framework for Islamic Economic Analysis". *Journal of King Abdulaziz University: Islamic Economics*, Vol. 26, No. 1, pp. 209–242.

Khan, Fahim M. (n.d.). "Revising the Fundamental Concepts and Thoughts in Islamic Economics". In *Islamic Economics: Basic Concepts, New Thinking and Future Directions*. Newcastle upon Tyne: Cambridge Scholars Publishing.

Siddiqi, M. N. (1988). "Guarantee of a Minimum Level of Living in an Islamic State". In Munawar Iqbal (Ed.), *Distributive Justice and Need Fulfillment in an Islamic Economy*. Leicester: The Islamic Foundation.

Veblen, Thorstein. (1979, original work 1899). *The Theory of the Leisure Class*. New York: Penguin.

CHAPTER 5

Construction of *Maqāṣid* al-Sharīʿah-Based Index of Socio-Economic Development: Principles and Issues

Junaidah Abu Seman and Nazam Dzolkarnaini

1 Introduction

Maqāṣid al-Sharīʿah is the core of human life. Without the fulfillment of *Maqāṣid* al-Sharīʿah, human's life will be uncertain and aimless. With its observance, human life will be directed objectively (Mohammad and Shahwan 2013). With regard to socio-economic in Islamic perspective, *Maqāṣid* al-Sharīʿah stands as its pillar and base while its development and issues are the manifestation of the pillar. Hence, Islam has taken into account the importance of "purpose" or in Arabic "*maqsud*" and in plural sense "*maqāṣid*," to guide human life.

J. Abu Seman (✉)
Faculty of Economics and Muamalat,
Universiti Sains Islam Malaysia, Nilai, Malaysia
e-mail: junaidah@usim.edu.my

N. Dzolkarnaini
The Business School, Edinburgh Napier University, Edinburgh, UK
e-mail: n.dzolkarnaini@napier.ac.uk

S. S. Ali (ed.), *Towards a Maqāṣid al-Sharīʿah Index of Socio-Economic Development*, Palgrave Studies in Islamic Banking, Finance, and Economics,
https://doi.org/10.1007/978-3-030-12793-0_5

By referring to the Qur'ān and the Sunnah as well as definitions and explanation from a number of scholars, Chapra (2007) concludes that all the *raison d'être* of the Sharī'ah which, as recognized by almost all the jurists, is to serve the interests of all human beings and to save them from harm. Imam Abu Hamid al-Ghazali, an eminent scholar, classified the *Maqāṣid* into five major categories by stating that:

> The very objective of the Sharī'ah is to promote the well-being of the people, which lies in safeguarding their faith (*din*), their self (*nafs*), their intellect (*'aql*), their posterity (*nasl*) and their wealth (*māl*). Whatever ensures the safeguard of these five, serves public interest and is desirable, and whatever hurts them, is against public interest and its removal is desirable. (Chapra 2000)

In the above extract, al-Ghazali has placed great emphasis on the safeguarding of five *Maqāṣid*, i.e., faith (*din*), the human self (*nafs*), intellect (*'aql*), posterity (*nasl*) and wealth (*māl*). Chapra (2007) also added that while these five may be considered as primary, others may be referred to as the corollaries of these. Realization of the corollary *Maqāṣid* is also vital because realization of the primarily *Maqāṣid* may be difficult without this.[1]

It is worth noting that there are increased interests in deliberating the realization of *Maqāṣid* al-Sharī'ah in different areas that range from Islamic banking and Islamic economics (see, e.g., al-Mubarak and Osmani 2010; Eddy Yusof et al. 2010; Mohammad and Shahwan 2013; Rosly 2010), democracy and development (see, e.g., Çizakça 2007), capital market (see, e.g., Dusuki 2009, 2010) to social aspect (see, e.g., Laluddin et al. 2012). However, it can be argued that such studies are rather normative than positive since they are mainly of descriptive and explanatory type of study.

With respect to the study on *Maqāṣid* al-Sharī'ah in socio-economic per se, Chapra (2007) and Mohammad and Shahwan (2013) have made a great contribution in shedding light of connecting these two essential scopes, i.e., *Maqāṣid* al-Sharī'ah and socio-economic. Based on the theory of five *Maqāṣid* that has been mentioned earlier (i.e., primary *Maqāṣid*), Chapra (2007) came out with the corollaries *Maqāṣid* for

[1] The theory of both primary and corollary *Maqāṣid* derived from Chapra (2007) is further discussed in Sect. 3.2.

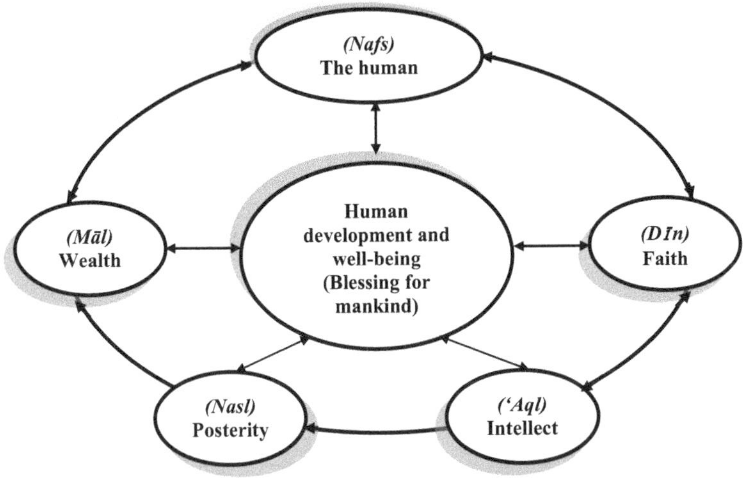

Fig. 1 Realizing Human Development and Well-Being through *Maqāṣid* al-Sharīʿah by Ensuring the Enrichment of the Five Ingredients for Every Individual (*Source* Adopted from Chapra [2007, p. 9])

each of the primary *Maqāṣid*. Figure 1 shows the relationship between the five *Maqāṣid* and human development and well-being, while Figs. 2. 3, 4, 5, and 6 present the corollaries for each of the five primary *Maqāṣid*, namely the human self (*nafs*), faith (*din*), intellect (*ʿaql*), posterity (*nasl*) and wealth (*māl*), respectively.

Mohammad & Shahwan (2013) analyzed critically the conceptual association between the framework of *Maqāṣid* al-Sharīʿah that rooted from both al-Ghazali and al-Zaharah[2] as well as the objectives of Islamic economics and Islamic banking and finance. Adopting content analysis and inductive method, they originated alternative version of the *Maqāṣid* al-Sharīʿah framework as well as the objectives of Islamic banking and finance and Islamic economics. This is shown in Fig. 7. L1, L2, L3 and L4 represent the following title, respectively: the two main types of objective; philosophical-based and operational-based objectives, objective of Islamic Economics, VMO (i.e., vision, mission, objective) of Islamic Bank and the *Maqāṣid* framework.

[2]For further detail, refer Abu Zaharah (1997) and its brief explanation in Mohammad and Shahwan (2013).

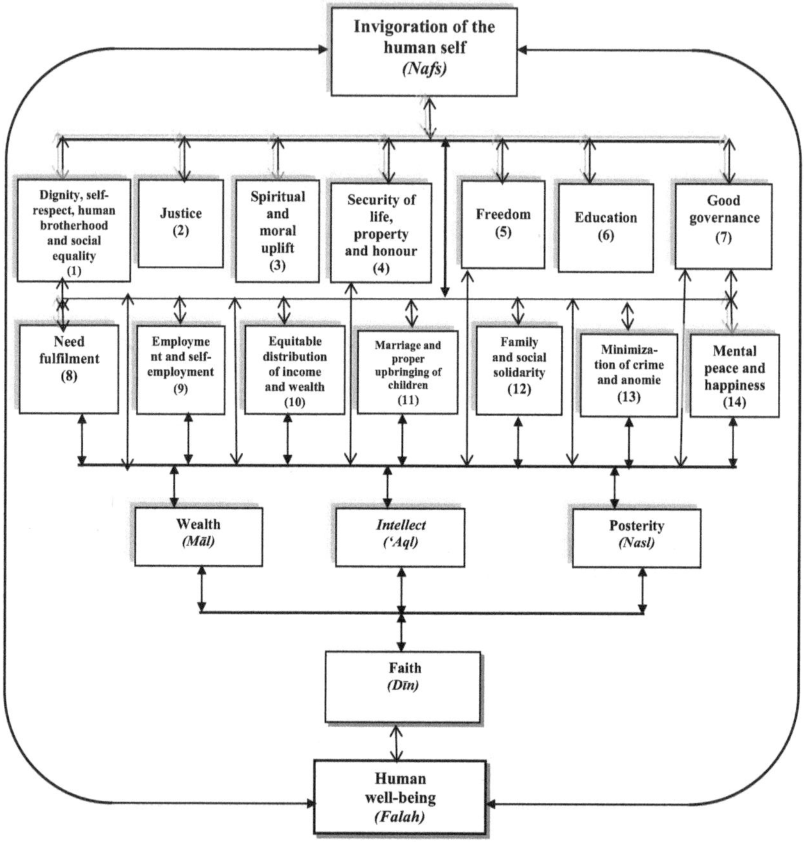

Fig. 2 The Corollaries of Human Self (*Nafs*) *Maqāṣid* (*Source* Adopted from Chapra [2007, p. 11])

However, these two studies are primarily normative than positive. This would suggest that a conceptual association between *Maqāṣid* al-Sharīʿah and socio-economic development as well as a single measurement of socio-economic development in the sphere of *Maqāṣid* al-Sharīʿah that can be applied cross-country does not exist.

The purpose of this study, therefore, is to develop conceptual association between the two concepts and further, to construct a *Maqāṣid* al-Sharīʿah-based index of socio-economic development. This attempt takes into account defining *Maqāṣid* al-Sharīʿah based on socio-economic

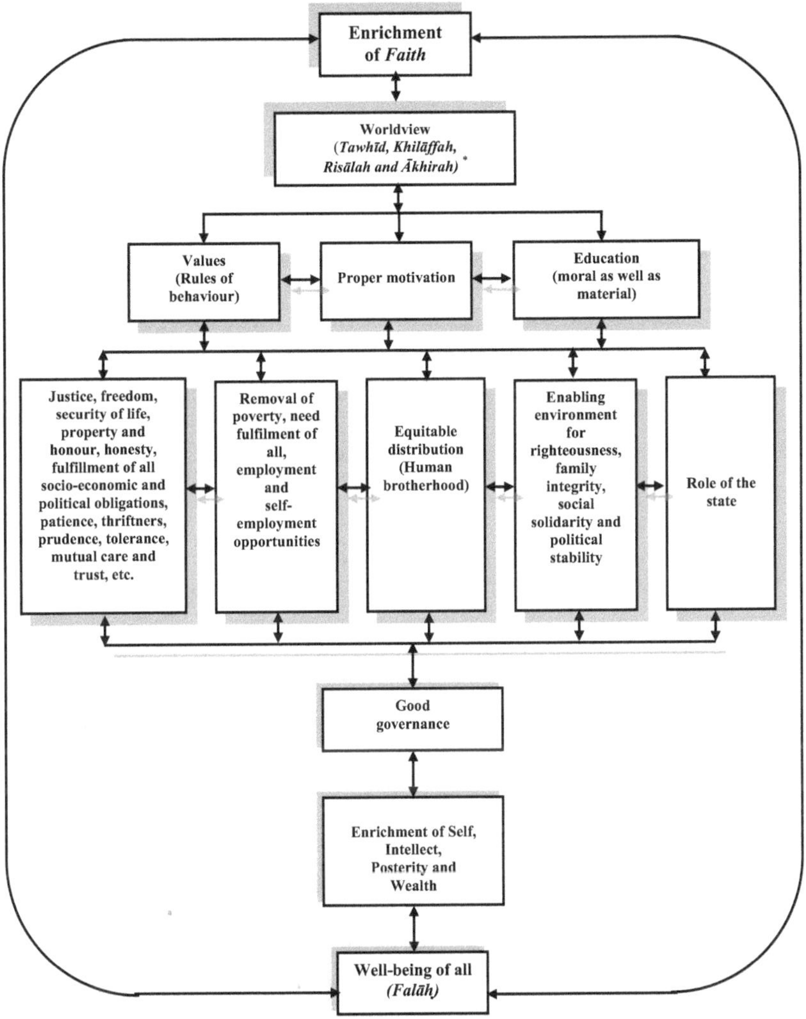

Fig. 3 The Corollaries of Faith (*Din*) *Maqāṣid* (*Source* Adopted from Chapra [2007, p. 32])

development and the process of setting up parameters in determining a multidimensional and multiple indicator aspects to cover a range of dimensions of *Maqāṣid* al-Sharīʿah. Further, it examines the data which

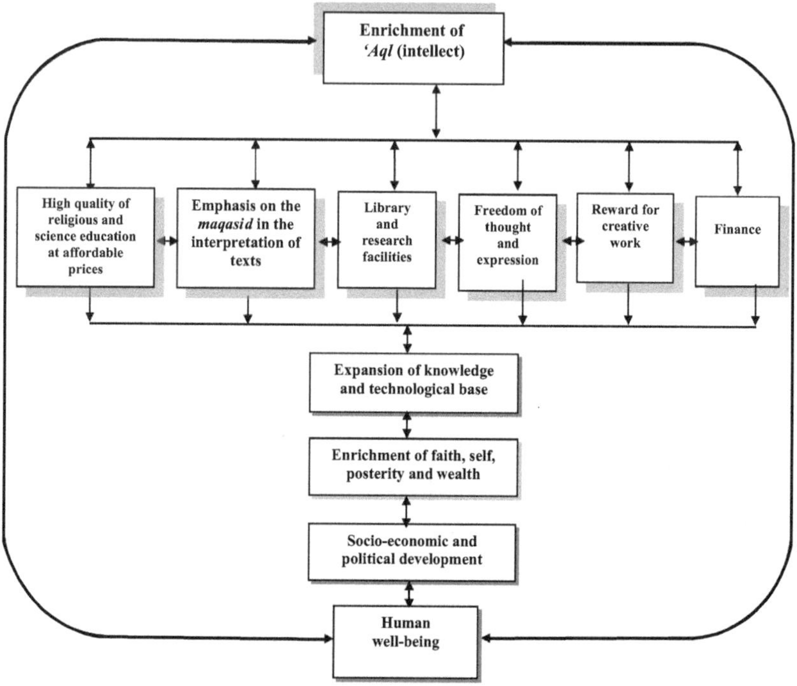

Fig. 4 The Corollaries of Intellectual (*ʿaql*) *Maqāṣid* (*Source* Adopted from Chapra [2007, p. 40])

are compatible in computing the index. Above all, this study recognizes limitation and issues which need further research.

2 Defining *Maqāṣid* al-Sharīʿah-Based of Socio-Economic Development

Acknowledging the meaning between these two components (i.e., *Maqāṣid* al-Sharīʿah and socio-economic development) is essential in shedding the light on the association between them. This connection serves the basis for the construction of *Maqāṣid* al-Sharīʿah-based index of socio-economic development.

Maqāṣid al-Sharīʿah has been defined in previous section as safeguarding of five *Maqāṣid* which are the human self (*nafs*), faith (*din*), intellect

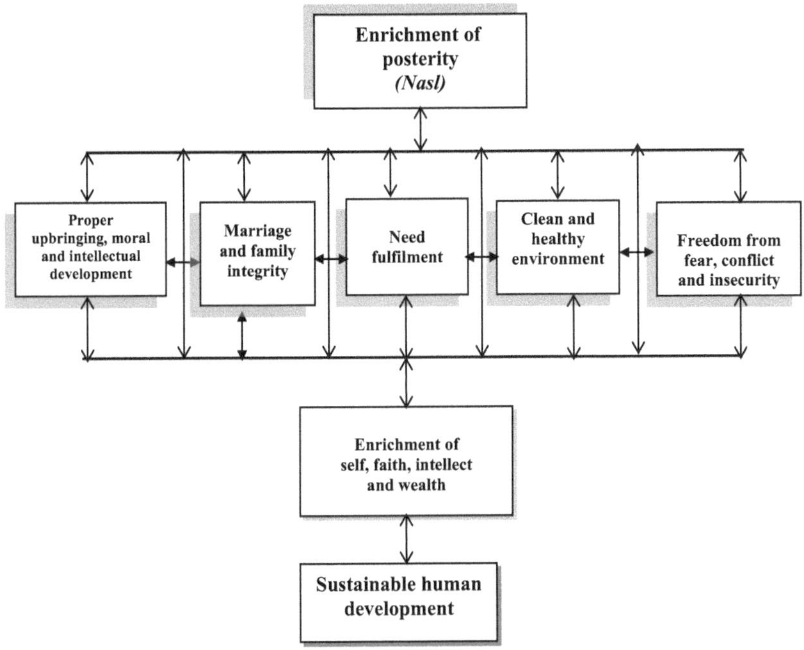

Fig. 5 The Corollaries of Posterity (*Nasl*) *Maqāṣid* (*Source* Adopted from Chapra [2007, p. 45])

(*ʿaql*), posterity (*nasl*) and wealth (*māl*). This term is purely originated from Islamic teaching.

On the other hand, the term development is broadly defined as "progress" (see Fritz (2009) on the definition of socio-economic development[3]). The United Nations Development Programme gives more detailed meaning. According to them, development is "to lead long and healthy lives, to be knowledgeable, to have access to the resources needed for a decent standard of living and to be able to participate in the life of the community" (United Nation Development Programme 2013). This definition is very much related to the manifestation of some other aspects, or in other words, the objectives.

[3]The author defined socio-economic development as the progress in terms of economics and social factor within a geographic unit.

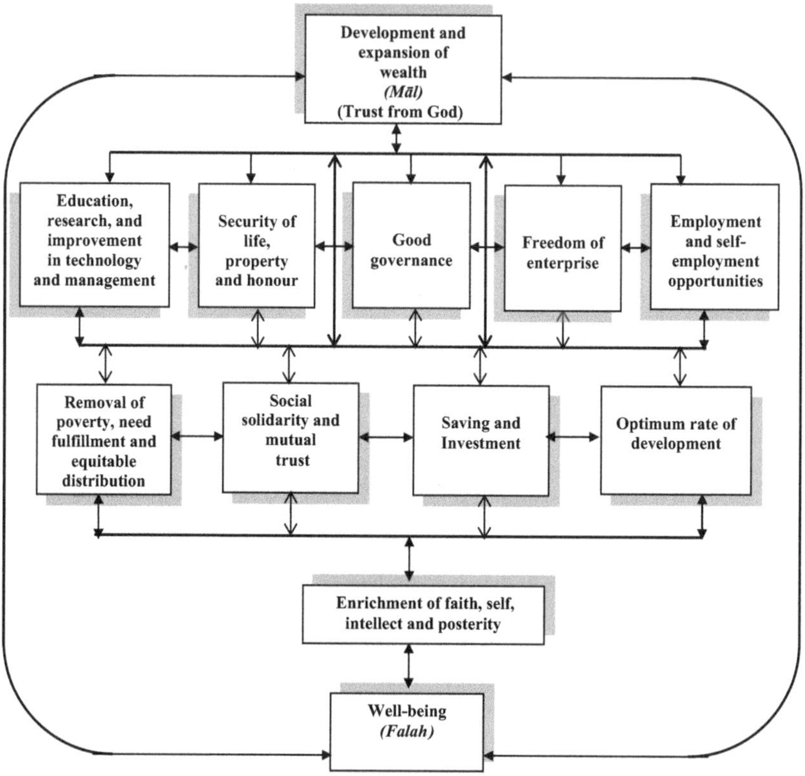

Fig. 6 The Corollaries of Wealth (*Mal*) *Maqāṣid* (*Source* Adopted from Chapra [2007, p. 49])

Specifically, according to Fritz (2009), economic development is the process of raising the level of prosperity through increased production, distribution and consumption of goods and services. Social development refers to the complexity of social dynamics (i.e., interplay of social structures, processed and relationships) and focuses on the following aspects:

i. the social concerns of the people as objectives of development and
ii. people-centered, participatory approaches to development.

The above definitions are in line with the meaning of social development as described by World Bank (2005)[4] which are:

i. the assets and capabilities of individuals to improve their well-being,
ii. the capacity of social groups to exercise agency, transform their relationships with other groups and participate in development processes,
iii. the ability of society to reconcile the interests of its constituent elements, govern itself peacefully and manage change.

Thus, from the above discussion, these two components are very much related in terms of the objectives and scopes. For the purpose of this study, we define *Maqāṣid* al-Sharīʿah-based socio-economic development as *a Maqāṣid approach*[5] *in examining socio-economic development.* This definition emphasizes the five elements/dimensions of *Maqāṣid* al-Sharīʿah, viz., the human self (*nafs*), faith (*din*), intellect (*ʿaql*), posterity (*nasl*) and wealth (*māl*) under the purview of socio-economic development. These dimensions together build a sustainable development.

3 Developing *Maqāṣid* al-Sharīʿah-Based Index of Socio-Economic Development

This section presents the construction of *Maqāṣid* al-Sharīʿah-based index of socio-economic development. It starts by discussing the conceptual association between *Maqāṣid* al-Sharīʿah and socio-economic development. The parameters and methodology are also highlighted. Next, the suggested index, indicators/variables and data collection are further explained, respectively.

3.1 Conceptual Association Between Maqāṣid *al-Sharīʿah and Socio-Economic Development*

In making connection between *Maqāṣid* al-Sharīʿah and socio-economic development, this study adopts the *Maqāṣid* al-Sharīʿah framework

[4]This definition is used in developing conceptual association between *Maqāṣid* al-Sharīʿah and socio-economic development presented in Fig. 8.

[5]This term is also mentioned by Ra'ees (2010) and Laluddin et al. (2012) in their study of *Maqāṣid* al-Sharīʿah.

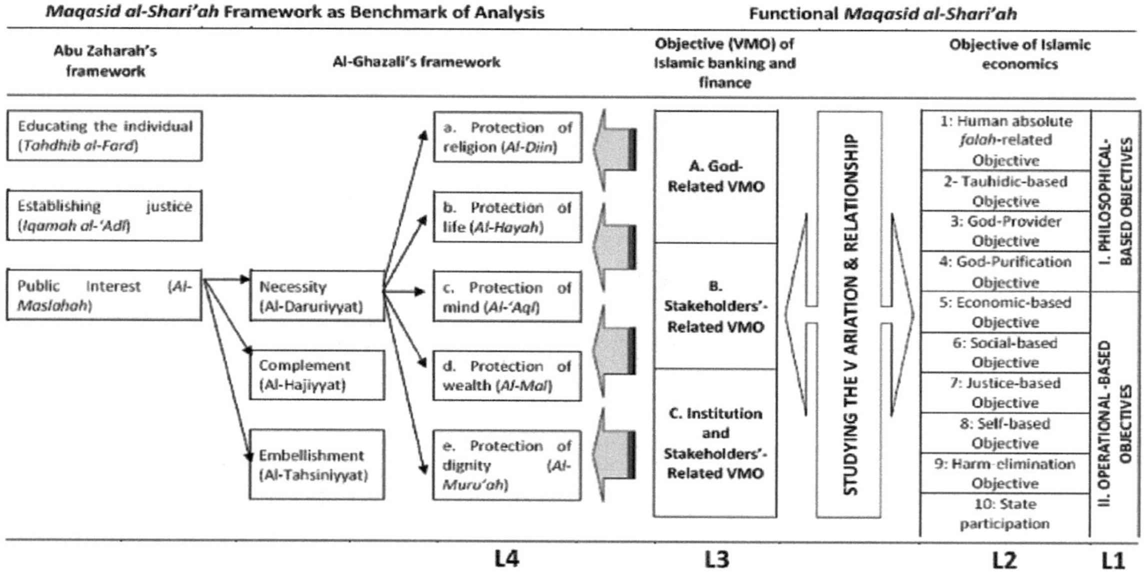

Fig. 7 The Conceptual Association between *Maqāṣid* al-Sharīʿah Framework and the Objectives of Islamic Banks and Islamic Economics (*Source* Adopted from Mohammad and Shahwan [2013, p. 80])

(i.e., using al-Ghazali's framework) by Mohammad and Shahwan (2013) and the objectives of socio-economic development that have been mentioned by previous studies (see, e.g., World Bank 2005; Fritz 2009). This is presented in Fig. 8.

It is worth noting that the five elements of *Maqāṣid* al-Sharīʿah and the objectives of socio-economic development have two basic principles, which are

i. interdependent (Chapra 2007) and
ii. flexible, dynamic and could use creativity[6] (Zuhrah 1958; Mumisa 2002; Hallaq 2004).

In other words, the five *Maqāṣid* elements are connected between each of them and they depend on each other to achieve human development and well-being. The same relationship exists on the objectives of social and economic development.

To conclude this observation, *Maqāṣid* al-Sharīʿah is all about protection of human self, faith, intellectual, posterity and wealth in a comprehensive approach. This core meaning explicitly correlates the current discussion on social and economic development. The elements of *Maqāṣid* al-Sharīʿah are clearly embedded in the aspect of socio-economic development itself.

Hence, for the purpose of computation of *Maqāṣid* al-Sharīʿah-based index of socio-economic development, the current data and information on socio-economic measurement are highly resourceful and relevance.

3.2 Parameters

Some evidences suggest that the measurement of index need to take into consideration as many dimensions as possible that impact the factor studied (see, e.g., Sarma 2008; Kumar and Mishra 2009; Arora 2010; Gupte et al. 2012). Therefore, incorporating as many dimensions as possible will result in a more holistic of socio-economic development index in light of *Maqāṣid* al-Sharīʿah. These dimensions act as the benchmark in looking into the specific area of the study. Therefore, these dimensions

[6]These are the nature of *Maqāṣid* al-Sharīʿah. With respect to socio-economic development, its real situation is also dynamic in nature.

need to be measurable and answerable. To fulfill this aim, indicators of each of the dimension are crucial.

The two parameters are dimensions and indicators. These parameters should be complementary to one another. By doing so, the index is reliable and thus helps to measure socio-economic development using *Maqāṣid* approach. These parameters are grounded from work contributed by Chapra (2007).

With regard to the dimension parameter, this index focuses on the five dimensions as presented in the al-Ghazali's framework (Fig. 8). There are:

i. human self (*nafs*),
ii. faith (*din*),
iii. intellect (*'aql*),
iv. posterity (*nasl*), and
v. wealth (*māl*).

In measuring all the dimensions, the corollaries *Maqāṣid* as listed by Chapra (2007) are referred (Figs. 2, 3, 4, 5, and 6). Those corollaries could provide a pathway in determining the indicators/variables needed in computing the index. Table 1 summarizes the dimensions and corollaries considered by Chapra (2007).

With regard to the second parameter (i.e., indicator), detail discussion on the variables and sources of data is presented in Sect. 3.5.

3.3 Methodology

This section outlines the construction of *Maqāṣid* al-Sharī'ah-based index of socio-economic development or *Maqāṣid*-based index of socio-economic development (hereafter referred to as MISED) with reference to studies done by Sarma (2008), Arora (2010), and Prathap (2011) in constructing financial inclusion index. This study is a gateway to develop the first MISED which focuses on one important aspect, i.e., inclusion of the five dimensions of *Maqāṣid* al-Sharī'ah [i.e., human self (*nafs*), faith (*din*), intellect (*'aql*), posterity (*nasl*) and wealth (*māl*)] that have been used in Chapra (2007).

Since an inclusive measurement of MISED should tackle all the five dimensions, this study suggests a multidimensional approach in constructing the index. Similar to prior studies on financial inclusion computation, this study also employs UNDPs computations of some

Table 1 Dimensions and its Corollaries in Constructing *Maqāṣid* al-Sharī'ah-based Index of Socio-Economic Development

Dimension	*Corollaries*
Human self (*nafs*)	1. Dignity, self-respect, human brotherhood and social equality 2. Justice 3. Spiritual and moral uplift 4. Security of life and property 5. Freedom 6. Education 7. Good governance 8. Need fulfillment 9. Employment and self-employment 10. Equitable distribution of income and wealth 11. Marriage and proper upbringing of children 12. Family and social solidarity 13. Minimization of crime and anomie 14. Mental peace and happiness
Faith (*din*)	1. Values (for example, justice, freedom, honour, honesty, etc.) 2. Removal of poverty, need fulfillment of all, employment and self-employment opportunities 3. Equitable distribution 4. Enabling environment for righteousness, family integrity, social solidarity and political stability 5. Role of state
Intellect (*'aql*)	1. High quality of religious and science education at affordable prices 2. Library and research facilities 3. Freedom of thought and expression 4. Reward for creative work 5. Finance
Posterity (*nasl*)	1. Moral and intellectual development 2. Proper upbringing and family integrity 3. Need fulfillment 4. Healthy environment 5. Freedom from fear, conflict and insecurity
Wealth (*māl*)	1. Education, research and improvement in technology and management 2. Security of life, property and honour 3. Good governance 4. Freedom of enterprise 5. Employment and self-employment opportunities 6. Removal of poverty, need fulfillment and equitable distribution 7. Social solidarity and mutual trust 8. Savings and investment 9. Optimum rate of development

Source Chapra (2007)

well-known development indexes such as the Human Development Index (HDI), the Human Poverty Index (HPI) and the Gender-related Development Index (GDI).[7]

Essentially, this study follows the similar methodology and reasoning (i.e., dynamic concept) as employed by Sarma (2008). Hence, for each dimension, *n* numbers of variables are included:

$$D_i = X_1, X_2, X_3 \ldots X_n \tag{1}$$

where

$D =$ *Maqāṣid* dimension,
$X =$ variable and
$i =$ individual countries.

For each variable, D_i is computed using the Linear Scaling Technique (LST) as follows:

$$D_i = \frac{A_i - m_i}{M_i - m_i} \tag{2}$$

where

$A_i =$ Actual value of dimension i,
$m_i =$ minimum value of dimension i and
$M_i =$ maximum value of dimension i.

Termed as "goalposts" (UNDP 2009), the minimum and maximum values are the minimum and maximum value of each variable in different countries. In arriving at the final index, distance from the ideal point is utilized. The MISED for the *i*th country, then, is measured by the normalized inverse Euclidean distance of the point D_i from the ideal point $I = (1, 1, 1, \ldots.1)$. Thus, the formula is:

$$\text{MISED}_i = 1 - \frac{\sqrt{(1-d_1)^2 + (1-d_2)^2 + \cdots + (1-d_n)^2}}{\sqrt{n}} \tag{3}$$

[7]For more details, see Technical Note in UNDP's Human Development Reports at www.undp.org.

where

d = *Maqāṣid* dimension and
n = number of variable.

In Eq. (3), the numerator of the second component is the Euclidean distance of D_i from the ideal point I, normalizing it by n and subtracting by 1 gives the inverse normalized distance. The normalization is done in order to make the value lie between 0 and 1, and the inverse distance is taken into account so that higher value of the MISED corresponds to higher rate of development.[8] The MISED values lying between 0 and 1, where 0 denotes the complete undeveloped *Maqāṣid*-based socio-economic and 1 indicates the complete *Maqāṣid*-based socio-economic development. This approach is chosen because all the dimensions have equal importance in presenting *Maqāṣid* elements within the purview of socio-economic development. Placing different properties for each dimension as Arora (2010) and Prathap (2011) would not fit the purpose of examining *Maqāṣid*-based socio-economic development as a whole.

3.4 The Suggested Index

In this suggested *Maqāṣid*-based socio-economic development index, five basic dimensions are considered in measuring socio-economic development country: human self, faith, intellect, posterity and wealth. These dimensions, as mentioned earlier, are largely motivated by two factors:

i. the positive association between the al-Ghazali's framework and the current approach of socio-economic development (Fig. 8)
ii. data availability for a large number of countries.

Therefore, considering the five dimensions—human self (hs), faith (f), intellect (i), posterity (p) and wealth (w)—this study can present a country i by a point (hs_i, f_i, i_i, p_i, w_i) within the socio-economic situation,

[8]As noted by Sarma (2008) in her financial inclusion index computation.

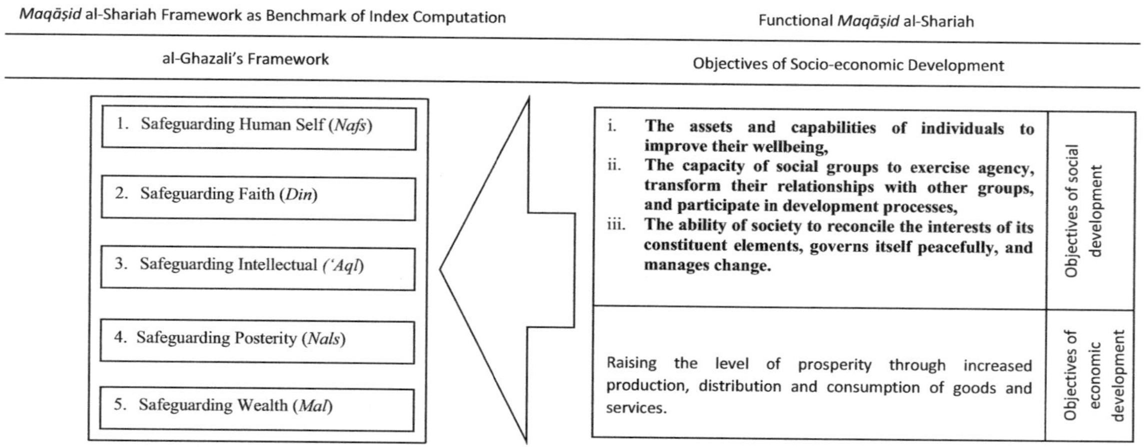

Fig. 8 The Conceptual Association between ***Maqāṣid*** al-Sharīʿah Framework and Objectives of Socio-Economic Development

where data availability is considered. The dimensions lie between 0 and 1, $0 \leq hs_i, f_i, i_i, p_i, w_i \leq 1$, where hs_i, f_i, i_i, p_i, w_i denote the dimension indexes for specific of *Maqāṣid*-based socio-economic development in country i computed using Eq. (2). In the five-dimensional Cartesian space, the point (0, 0, 0, 0 and 0) indicates the worst situation (complete undeveloped *Maqāṣid*-based socio-economic situation), and the point (1, 1, 1, 1 and 1) signifies the best or ideal situation (complete developed *Maqāṣid*-based on socio-economic situation).

Thus, the MISED for the country i is measured by the normalized inverse Euclidean distance of the point (hs_i, f_i, i_i, p_i, w_i) from the ideal point (1, 1, 1, 1, 1). Algebraically,

$$\text{MISED}_i = 1 - \sqrt{\frac{(1-hs_i)^2 + (1-f_i)^2 + (1-i_i)^2 + (1-p_i)^2 + (1-w_i)^2}{5}} \quad (4)$$

where

hs_i = development of human self,
f_i = development of faith,
i_i = development of intellectual,
p_i = development of posterity,
w_i = development of wealth and
i = individual countries.

Apart from that, depending on the value of MISED, countries are classified into three categories, namely:

i. $0.5 < \text{MISED} \leq 1$: high *Maqāṣid*-based socio-economic development
ii. $0.3 \leq \text{MISED} < 0.5$: medium *Maqāṣid*-based socio-economic development
iii. $0 \leq \text{MISED} < 0.3$: low *Maqāṣid*-based socio-economic development

It is worth noting that although the MISED proposed here follows a multidimensional approach of index construction similar to the UNDP approach, there are some methodological differences between the two approaches. These have been highlighted by Sarma (2008) as follows:

i. This index is based on a measure of the distance from the ideal[9] as opposed to the UNDP's methodology of using an average (a simple arithmetic average, for example in the case of HDI, GDI and GEM). Nathan et al. (2008) have shown that this distance-based approach satisfies several interesting and intuitive properties of a development index, viz. normalization, symmetry (or anonymity), monotonicity, proximity, uniformity and signaling (collectively termed as NAMPUS). Desai (1991) also agreed on this by stating that as all dimensions are assumed to be equally important for the overall index value and the perfect substitutability can hardly be appropriate. The distance-based approach does not suffer from this limitation.
ii. In terms of the choice of minimum and maximum values for the dimensions, the UNDP methodology uses prefixed values for the minimum and maximum for each dimension to compute the dimensional index. Whereas this study uses empirically observed minimum and maximum for each dimension. Thus, the index is a dynamic one.

3.5 *Indicators/Variables*

This subsection justifies and describes the variables for each *Maqāṣid* dimension of socio-economic development. Table 2 provides a summary of descriptions, indicators and explanations of each aspect related to the index construction. Based on the basic dimensions, the variables that can explain the *Maqāṣid* dimension of socio-economic development are included.

3.6 *Data Collection*

Ideally, one should take into consideration all the dimensions to arrive at a comprehensive picture on the *Maqāṣid* approach of socio-economic development across the countries. Currently, the World Bank provides richness of data pertaining to the indicator of socio-economic development. As far as al-Ghazali's framework and Chapra's (2007) corollaries

[9] Sarma (2008) was introduced to this methodology that dates back to Zeleny (1974) by her colleague.

Table 2 General Description toward Examining the Indicators/Variables for *Maqāṣid* al-Sharīʿah-based Index of Socio-Economic Development

Description	*Dimension*	*Features*	*Explanation*	*Indicators*	*Source*[a]
Social development	1. Human self (*hs*) 2. Faith (*f*) 3. Intellectual (*i*) 4. Posterity (*p*)	Aid effectiveness	It is the impact that aid has in reducing poverty and inequality, increasing growth, building capacity and accelerating achievement of the millennium Development Goals set by the international community	See Appendix	World Development Indicators, World Bank
		Education	The most powerful instruments for reducing poverty and inequality and lays a foundation for sustained economic growth		
		Environment	Natural and man-made environmental resources		
		Health	Improving health is central to the Millennium Development Goals, and the public sector is the main provider of health care in developing countries		
		Infrastructure	Investments in water, sanitation, energy, housing and transport improve lives and help reduce poverty		
		Labour and Social protection	It includes people who are employed, those who are unemployed but seeking work, first time job-seekers, unpaid workers, family workers, students		
		Poverty	Assess the extent and causes of poverty and inequality as well as examine the impact of growth and public policy		
		Private sector	Private markets drive economic growth. Tapping initiative and investment to create productive jobs and raise incomes		
		Public sector	Effective governments improve people's standard of living by ensuring access to essential services and the opportunity to live and work in peace and security		
		Science and technology	Technological innovation often fuelled by governments, drives industrial growth and helps raise living standards		
		Social development	Covers many areas for example child labour, school enrolment and unemployment		
		Urban development	The effects of urbanisation on meeting basic needs, environment and natural resources		
Economic development	5. Wealth (*w*)	Economy and Growth	It is the central to economic development. When national income grows, real people benefit		
		Financial sector	Strong financial systems provide reliable and accessible information that lowers transaction costs, which in turn bolsters resource allocation and economic growth		

Source Authors
[a]For details see the World Bank Data available at http://data.worldbank.org/

Maqāṣid are concerned, the measurable indicators of the socio-economic development data provided by the World Bank are explicitly interconnected. As one of the important body in providing reliable and latest socio-economic-related information in today's world, the World Bank is deemed as the best source for data collection in this index construction. The World Bank has provided a wide range of indicators for the computation of MISED (see Appendix), for both cross countries and time series analyses.

4 Limitations and Suggestions for Further Research

This study has some limitations. Although the methodology of index computation has been presented, a working example of MISED computation is not presented due to too much data available and relevant for the index construction (see Appendix). This will require further careful data selection and separate research effort. The actual MISED computation is also beyond the scope of this paper.

The interdependence nature of the *Maqāṣid* dimensions, as well as the socio-economic elements, is an area of concern. These are two broad areas which provide various possibilities in the index development hence allowing different interpretations. Therefore, for each dimension of *Maqāṣid* al-Sharī'ah, it is important that only the most relevant data should be included in setting up the parameters.

5 Conclusion

This paper is an attempt to make an association between two disciplines, i.e., socio-economic development and *Maqāṣid* al-Sharī'ah. The inner objective of the authors is to provide a better picture on the status and co-integration between those two. The observation of the previous studies concluded that the five elements (i.e., dimensions) of *Maqāṣid* al-Sharī'ah were fully observed in the objectives of socio-economic development. In addition, this study endeavors the construction of the *Maqāṣid* al-Sharī'ah-based index of socio-economic development. In the next step, a systematic effort on data selections and parameters' setting needs to be in place in order to efficiently computing the index.

Appendix: List of Indicators for Each Feature of *Maqāṣid* Dimension for the Computation of *Maqāṣid* al-Sharīʿah-Based Index of Socio-Economic Development

Agriculture and Rural Development

Agricultural irrigated land (% of total agricultural land)	Forest area (% of land area)
Agricultural land (% of land area)	Forest area (km^2)
Agricultural machinery, tractors per 100 km^2 of arable land	Improved water source, rural (% of rural population with access)
Agriculture, value added (% of GDP)	Land area (km^2)
Agriculture value added per worker (constant 2005 US$)	Land under cereal production (hectares)
Arable land (hectares per person)	Livestock production index (2004–2006 = 100)
Arable land (% of land area)	Permanent cropland (% of land area)
Cereal yield (kg per hectare)	Poverty gap at rural poverty line (%)
Crop production index (2004–2006 = 100)	Poverty headcount ratio at rural poverty line (% of rural population)
Employment in agriculture (% of total employment)	Rural population
Fertilizer consumption (kilograms per hectare of arable land)	Rural population (% of total population)
Food production index (2004–2006 = 100)	

Aid Effectiveness

CO_2 emissions (metric tons per capita)	Net ODA received per capita (current US$)
Contraceptive prevalence (% of women ages 15–49)	Net official development assistance and official aid received (current US$)
Improved sanitation facilities (% of population with access)	Net official development assistance received (current US$)
Incidence of tuberculosis (per 100,000 people)	Population, female (% of total)
Income share held by lowest 20%	Pregnant women receiving prenatal care (%)
Life expectancy at birth, female (years)	Prevalence of HIV, total (% of population ages 15–49)
Life expectancy at birth, male (years)	Primary completion rate, total (% of relevant age group)
Malnutrition prevalence, weight for age (% of children under 5)	Proportion of seats held by women in national parliaments (%)
Maternal mortality ratio (modeled estimate, per 100,000 live births)	Ratio of girls to boys in primary and secondary education (%)
Mobile cellular subscriptions (per 100 people)	Share of women employed in the nonagricultural sector (% of total nonagricultural employment)
Mortality rate, under-5 (per 1000 live births)	Teenage mothers (% of women ages 15–19 who have had children or are currently pregnant)
Net migration	Vulnerable employment, total (% of total employment)
Net ODA received (% of GNI)	

Economy and Growth

Agriculture, value added (% of GDP)
Cash surplus/deficit (% of GDP)
Central government debt, total (% of GDP)
Charges for the use of intellectual property, payments (BoP, current US$)
Charges for the use of intellectual property, receipts (BoP, current US$)
Current account balance (BoP, current US$)
Exports of goods and services (% of GDP)
External debt stocks, total (DOD, current US$)
Foreign direct investment, net inflows (BoP, current US$)
GDP (current US$)
GDP growth (annual %)
GDP per capita (current US$)
GNI, Atlas method (current US$)
GNI per capita, Atlas method (current US$)
GNI per capita, PPP (current international $)
GNI, PPP (current international $)
Gross capital formation (% of GDP)
Gross savings (% of GDP)
Imports of goods and services (% of GDP)
Industry, value added (% of GDP)
Inflation, consumer prices (annual %)
Inflation, GDP deflator (annual %)
Net ODA received (% of GNI)
Net ODA received per capita (current US$)
Net official development assistance received (current US$)
Personal remittances, received (current US$)
Portfolio equity, net inflows (BoP, current US$)
Revenue, excluding grants (% of GDP)
Secondary income, other sectors, payments (BoP, current US$)
Services, etc., value added (% of GDP)
Total debt service (% of exports of goods, services and primary income)
Total reserves (includes gold, current US$)
Trade in services (% of GDP)

Education

Children out of school, primary, female
Children out of school, primary, male
Expenditure per student, primary (% of GDP per capita)
Expenditure per student, secondary (% of GDP per capita)
Expenditure per student, tertiary (% of GDP per capita)
Gross intake ratio in first grade of primary education, female (% of relevant age group)
Gross intake ratio in first grade of primary education, male (% of relevant age group)
Labor force, total
Literacy rate, adult total (% of people ages 15 and above)
Literacy rate, youth female (% of females ages 15–24)
Progression to secondary school, female (%)
Progression to secondary school, male (%)
Public spending on education, total (% of GDP)
Public spending on education, total (% of government expenditure)
Pupil-teacher ratio, primary
Ratio of female to male primary enrollment (%)
Ratio of female to male secondary enrollment (%)
Ratio of female to male tertiary enrollment (%)
Ratio of girls to boys in primary and secondary education (%)
Repeaters, primary, female (% of female enrollment)

Literacy rate, youth male (% of males ages 15–24)	Repeaters, primary, male (% of male enrollment)
Literacy rate, youth total (% of people ages 15–24)	School enrollment, preprimary (% gross)
Mortality rate, under-5 (per 1000 live births)	School enrollment, primary (% gross)
Persistence to last grade of primary, female (% of cohort)	School enrollment, primary (% net)
Persistence to last grade of primary, male (% of cohort)	School enrollment, secondary (% gross)
Population ages 0–14 (% of total)	School enrollment, secondary (% net)
Population ages 15–64 (% of total)	School enrollment, tertiary (% gross)
Prevalence of HIV, total (% of population ages 15–49)	Trained teachers in primary education (% of total teachers)
Primary completion rate, female (% of relevant age group)	Unemployment, female (% of female labor force)
Primary completion rate, male (% of relevant age group)	Unemployment, male (% of male labor force)
Primary completion rate, total (% of relevant age group)	Unemployment, total (% of total labor force)

Environment

Access to electricity (% of population)	Organic water pollutant (BOD) emissions (kg per day)
Agricultural methane emissions (% of total)	Organic water pollutant (BOD) emissions (kg per day per worker)
Agricultural nitrous oxide emissions (% of total)	Other greenhouse gas emissions, HFC, PFC and SF6 (thousand metric tons of CO_2 equivalent)
CO_2 emissions (kt)	Plant species (higher), threatened
CO_2 emissions (metric tons per capita)	Population living in areas where elevation is below 5 meters (% of total population)
Fish species, threatened	Water pollution, chemical industry (% of total BOD emissions)
Forest area (% of land area)	Water pollution, clay and glass industry (% of total BOD emissions)
Forest area (km^2)	Water pollution, food industry (% of total BOD emissions)
GEF benefits index for biodiversity (0 = no biodiversity potential to 100 = maximum)	Water pollution, metal industry (% of total BOD emissions)
Land area where elevation is below 5 meters (% of total land area)	Water pollution, other industry (% of total BOD emissions)
Mammal species, threatened	Water pollution, paper and pulp industry (% of total BOD emissions)
Marine protected areas (% of territorial waters)	Water pollution, textile industry (% of total BOD emissions)
Methane emissions (kt of CO_2 equivalent)	Water pollution, wood industry (% of total BOD emissions)
Nitrous oxide emissions (thousand metric tons of CO_2 equivalent)	

Health

Adolescent fertility rate (births per 1000 women ages 15–19)	Malnutrition prevalence, weight for age (% of children under 5)
Birth rate, crude (per 1000 people)	Maternal mortality ratio (modeled estimate, per 100,000 live births)
Births attended by skilled health staff (% of total)	Mortality rate, infant (per 1000 live births)
Contraceptive prevalence (% of women ages 15–49)	Mortality rate, under-5 (per 1000 live births)
Death rate, crude (per 1000 people)	Out-of-pocket health expenditure (% of private expenditure on health)
Fertility rate, total (births per woman)	Population ages 0–14 (% of total)
Health expenditure per capita (current US$)	Population ages 15–64 (% of total)
Health expenditure, public (% of total health expenditure)	Population ages 65 and above (% of total)
Health expenditure, total (% of GDP)	Population, female (% of total)
Immunization, DPT (% of children ages 12–23 months)	Population growth (annual %)
Immunization, measles (% of children ages 12–23 months)	Population (total)
Improved sanitation facilities (% of population with access)	Pregnant women receiving prenatal care (%)
Improved sanitation facilities, urban (% of urban population with access)	Prevalence of HIV, female (% ages 15–24)
Incidence of tuberculosis (per 100,000 people)	Prevalence of HIV, male (% ages 15–24)
Life expectancy at birth, female (years)	Prevalence of HIV, total (% of population ages 15–49)
Life expectancy at birth, male (years)	Teenage mothers (% of women ages 15–19 who have had children or are currently pregnant)
Life expectancy at birth, total (years)	Unmet need for contraception (% of married women ages 15–49)
Malnutrition prevalence, height for age (% of children under 5)	

Infrastructure

Air transport, registered carrier departures worldwide	Internet users (per 100 people)
Annual freshwater withdrawals, agriculture (% of total freshwater withdrawal)	Mobile cellular subscriptions (per 100 people)
Annual freshwater withdrawals, domestic (% of total freshwater withdrawal)	Motor vehicles (per 1000 people)
Annual freshwater withdrawals, industry (% of total freshwater withdrawal)	Passenger cars (per 1000 people)
Annual freshwater withdrawals, total (billion cubic meters)	Rail lines (total route-km)
Container port traffic (TEU: 20 foot equivalent units)	Renewable internal freshwater resources per capita (cubic meters)
Electric power consumption (kWh per capita)	Renewable internal freshwater resources, total (billion cubic meters)

Fixed broadband Internet subscribers (per 100 people)	Road sector diesel fuel consumption per capita (kg of oil equivalent)
ICT goods exports (% of total goods exports)	Road sector energy consumption (% of total energy consumption)
ICT goods imports (% total goods imports)	Road sector gasoline fuel consumption per capita (kg of oil equivalent)
ICT service exports (% of service exports, BoP)	Roads, paved (% of total roads)
Improved water source, rural (% of rural population with access)	Secure Internet servers (per 1 million people)
Improved water source, urban (% of urban population with access)	Vehicles (per km of road)

Labor and Social Protection

Employees, agriculture, female (% of female employment)	Labor participation rate, total (% of total population ages 15+)
Employees, agriculture, male (% of male employment)	Long-term unemployment, female (% of female unemployment)
Employees, industry, female (% of female employment)	Long-term unemployment, male (% of male unemployment)
Employees, industry, male (% of male employment)	Long-term unemployment (% of total unemployment)
Employees, services, female (% of female employment)	Unemployment, female (% of female labor force)
Employees, services, male (% of male employment)	Unemployment, male (% of male labor force)
Employment in agriculture (% of total employment)	Unemployment, total (% of total labor force)
Employment to population ratio, 15+, total (%)	Unemployment, youth female (% of female labor force ages 15–24)
GDP per person employed (constant 1990 PPP $)	Unemployment, youth male (% of male labor force ages 15–24)
Labor force, total	Vulnerable employment, female (% of female employment)
Labor participation rate, female (% of female population ages 15+)	Vulnerable employment, male (% of male employment)
Labor participation rate, male (% of male population ages 15+)	Vulnerable employment, total (% of total employment)

Poverty

Income share held by fourth 20%	Poverty gap at national poverty line (%)
Income share held by highest 10%	Poverty gap at rural poverty line (%)
Income share held by highest 20%	Poverty gap at urban poverty line (%)
Income share held by lowest 10%	Poverty headcount ratio at $1.25 a day (PPP) (% of population)
Income share held by lowest 20%	Poverty headcount ratio at $2 a day (PPP) (% of population)

Income share held by second 20%	Poverty headcount ratio at national poverty line (% of population)
Income share held by third 20%	Poverty headcount ratio at rural poverty line (% of rural population)
Poverty gap at $1.25 a day (PPP) (%)	Poverty headcount ratio at urban poverty line (% of urban population)
Poverty gap at $2 a day (PPP) (%)	

Private Sector

Average number of times firms spent in meetings with tax officials	ISO certification ownership (% of firms)
Documents to export (number)	Lead time to export, median case (days)
Documents to import (number)	Lead time to import, median case (days)
Domestic credit to private sector (% of GDP)	Logistics performance index: Overall (1 = low to 5 = high)
Ease of doing business index (1 = most business-friendly regulations)	Merchandise trade (% of GDP)
Export value index (2000 = 100)	Net barter terms of trade index (2000 = 100)
Export volume index (2000 = 100)	New businesses registered (number)
Firms using banks to finance investment (% of firms)	Start-up procedures to register a business (number)
Import value index (2000 = 100)	Tax payments (number)
Import volume index (2000 = 100)	Time required to start a business (days)
Informal payments to public officials (% of firms)	Time to prepare and pay taxes (hours)
Investment in energy with private participation (current US$)	Time to resolve insolvency (years)
Investment in telecoms with private participation (current US$)	Total tax rate (% of commercial profits)
Investment in transport with private participation (current US$)	Trade in services (% of GDP)
Investment in water and sanitation with private participation (current US$)	Value lost due to electrical outages (% of sales)

Public Sector

Cash surplus/deficit (% of GDP)	Military expenditure (% of central government expenditure)
Central government debt, total (% of GDP)	Military expenditure (% of GDP)
CPIA economic management cluster average (1 = low to 6 = high)	Proportion of seats held by women in national parliaments (%)
CPIA policies for social inclusion/equity cluster average (1 = low to 6 = high)	Revenue, excluding grants (% of GDP)
CPIA public sector management and institutions cluster average (1 = low to 6 = high)	Tax payments (number)
CPIA structural policies cluster average (1 = low to 6 = high)	Tax revenue (% of GDP)
Expense (% of GDP)	Time to prepare and pay taxes (hours)
IDA resource allocation index (1 = low to 6 = high)	Total tax rate (% of commercial profits)

Science and Technology

Charges for the use of intellectual property, payments (BoP, current US$)	Research and development expenditure (% of GDP)
Charges for the use of intellectual property, receipts (BoP, current US$)	Researchers in R&D (per million people)
High-technology exports (current US$)	Scientific and technical journal articles
High-technology exports (% of manufactured exports)	Technicians in R&D (per million people)
Patent applications, nonresidents	Trademark applications, direct nonresident
Patent applications, residents	Trademark applications, direct resident

Social Development

Adolescent fertility rate (births per 1000 women ages 15–19)	Prevalence of HIV, male (% ages 15–24)
Children in employment, female (% of female children ages 7–14)	Proportion of seats held by women in national parliaments (%)
Children in employment, male (% of male children ages 7–14)	Ratio of female to male primary enrollment (%)
Children in employment, study and work, female (% of female children in employment, ages 7–14)	Ratio of female to male secondary enrollment (%)
Children in employment, study and work, male (% of male children in employment, ages 7–14)	Ratio of female to male tertiary enrollment (%)
Children in employment, total (% of children ages 7–14)	Ratio of girls to boys in primary and secondary education (%)
Children in employment, work only, female (% of female children in employment, ages 7–14)	Refugee population by country or territory of asylum
Children in employment, work only, male (% of male children in employment, ages 7–14)	Refugee population by country or territory of origin
Labor participation rate, female (% of female population ages 15+)	Share of women employed in the nonagricultural sector (% of total nonagricultural employment)
Labor participation rate, male (% of male population ages 15+)	Unemployment, female (% of female labor force)
Life expectancy at birth, female (years)	Unemployment, male (% of male labor force)
Life expectancy at birth, male (years)	Vulnerable employment, female (% of female employment)
Prevalence of HIV, female (% ages 15–24)	Vulnerable employment, male (% of male employment)

Urban Development

Improved sanitation facilities, urban (% of urban population with access)	Pump price for diesel fuel (US$ per liter)
Improved water source, urban (% of urban population with access)	Pump price for gasoline (US$ per liter)
Motor vehicles (per 1000 people)	Road sector diesel fuel consumption per capita (kg of oil equivalent)
Passenger cars (per 1000 people)	Road sector energy consumption (% of total energy consumption)
PM10, country level (micrograms per cubic meter)	Road sector gasoline fuel consumption per capita (kg of oil equivalent)
Population in the largest city (% of urban population)	Urban population
Population in urban agglomerations of more than 1 million (% of total population)	Urban population (% of total)
Poverty gap at urban poverty line (%)	Vehicles (per km of road)
Poverty headcount ratio at urban poverty line (% of urban population)	

Financial Sector

Bank capital to assets ratio (%)	Money and quasi money growth (annual %)
Bank nonperforming loans to total gross loans (%)	Net migration
Claims on central government (annual growth as % of broad money)	Personal remittances, received (current US$)
Claims on other sectors of the domestic economy (annual growth as % of broad money)	Portfolio equity, net inflows (BoP, current US$)
Credit depth of information index (0 = low to 6 = high)	Private credit bureau coverage (% of adults)
Deposit interest rate (%)	Public credit registry coverage (% of adults)
Domestic credit provided by banking sector (% of GDP)	Real interest rate (%)
Foreign direct investment, net inflows (BoP, current US$)	Risk premium on lending (lending rate minus treasury bill rate, %)
Interest rate spread (lending rate minus deposit rate, %)	S&P Global Equity Indices (annual % change)
International migrant stock, total	Stocks traded, total value (% of GDP)
Lending interest rate (%)	Stocks traded, turnover ratio (%)
Listed domestic companies, total	Strength of legal rights index (0 = weak to 10 = strong)
Market capitalization of listed companies (current US$)	Total reserves (includes gold, current US$)
Market capitalization of listed companies (% of GDP)	

References

Abu Zaharah, M. (1997). *Usul al-Fiqh*. Cairo: Dar al-Fikr al-'Arabi.

Al-Mubarak, T., & Osmani, N. M. (2010). *Applications of Maqāṣid al-Shari'ah and Maslahah in Islamic Banking practices: An analysis*. Paper presented at International Conference on Islamic Finance in Kochi, India, organized by the Islamic Research and Training Institute (IRTI).

Arora, R. U. (2010). *Measuring Financial Access* (Discussion Paper in Economics No 7). Australia: Griffith Business School.

Chapra, M. U. (2000). *The Future of Economics: An Islamic Perspective*. Leicester: The Islamic Foundation.

Chapra, M. U. (2007). *The Islamic Vision of Development in the Light of Maqāsid Al-Sharī'ah* (Research Paper). Jeddah: Islamic Research and Training Institute (IRTI).

Çizakça, M. (2007). "Democracy, Economic Development and *Maqāṣid* Al-Shari'ah." *Review of Islamic Economics* 11(1), pp. 101–118.

Desai, M. (1991). "Human Development: Concepts and Measurement." *European Economic Review* 35, pp. 350–357.

Dusuki, A. W. (2009). "Sharīʿah Parameters on Islamic Foreign Exchange Swap as Hedging Mechanism in Islamic Finance." *ISRA International Journal of Islamic Finance* (July), pp. 1–25.

Dusuki, A. W. (2010). "Do Equity-Based Sukuk Structures in Islamic Capital Markets Manifest the Objectives of Sharīʿah?" *Journal of Financial Services Marketing* 15(3), pp. 203–214.

Eddy Yusof, E. F., Kashoogie, J., & Kamal, A. A. (2010). "Islamic Finance: Debt Versus Equity Financing in the Light of *Maqāṣid* al-Shari'ah" (Research Paper). Germany: University Library of Munich.

Fritz, J. M. (2009). *Socio Economic Developmental Social Work* (Research paper). Cincinnati, OH, USA: University of Cincinnati.

Gupte, R., Venkataramani, B., & Gupta, D. (2012). "Computation of Financial Inclusion Index for India." *Procedia Social and Behavioral Sciences* 37, pp. 133–149.

Hallaq, W. (2004). "Can the shari'a be Restored?" In H. Y. Yvonne & S. F. Barbara, eds. *In Islamic Law and the Challenges of Modernity*. Walnut Creek, CA: AltaMira Press, pp. 21–53.

Kumar, C. & Mishra, S. (2009). *Banking Outreach and Household Level Access: Analyzing Financial Inclusion in India*. Paper Presented at 13th Annual Conference on Money and Finance in the Indian Economy, Mumbai, India.

Laluddin, H., Mohd. Nor, A. H., El-Seoudi, A. W. M. M., Ibrahim, I. A., Husni, A. M., Omar, A. F., Samsudin, M. A., Alias, M. N., Mohamad, A. B. B. (2012). "The Relationship between Islamic Human Rights and the *Maqāṣid* Approach." *The Social Sciences* 7(1), pp. 111–116.

Mohammad, M. O., & Shahwan, S. (2013). "The Objective of Islamic Economic and Islamic Banking in Light of *Maqāṣid* al-Sharī'ah: A Critical Review." *Middle-East Journal of Scientific Research 13 (Research in Contemporary Islamic Finance and Wealth Management)* 13, pp. 75–84.
Mumisa, M. (2002). *Islamic Law: Theory & Interpretation*. Amana Publications.
Nathan, H. S. K., Mishra, S., & Reddy, B. S. (2008). *An Alternative Approach to Measure HDI* (Working Paper No.WP-2008-001). India: Indira Gandhi Institute of Development Research (IGIDR).
Prathap, S. K. (2011). *Financial Inclusion of Fisher Households in Coastel Kerala-Role of Microfinance*. Unpublished postgraduate thesis, Cochin University of Science and Technology.
Ra'ees, W. (2010). "The Relationship Between The *Maqāṣid* (Higher Purposes of Shari'ah) Approach and Siyar (Foreign Policy of the Islamic State)." *The Journal of Rotterdam Islamic and Social Sciences* 1(1), pp. 1–9.
Rosly, S. A. (2010). "Sharī'ah Parameters Reconsidered." *International Journal of Islamic and Middle Eastern Finance and Management* 3(2), pp. 132–146.
Sarma, M. (2008). *Index of Financial Inclusion* (Working paper No. 215). New Delhi, India: Indian Council for Research on International Economics Relations.
UNDP. (2009). "Human Development Report 2009: Overcoming Barriers: Human Mobility and Development." New York.
United Nation Development Programme. (2013). *What Is Development?* Retrived March 3, 2014 from http://www.undp.org/content/undp/en/home.html.
World Bank. (2005). *New Frontiers of Social Policy: Development in a Globalizing World*. Concept Note for World Summit for Social Development Conference on 5–12 March 1995 at Copenhagen.
Zeleny, M. (1974). "A Concept of Compromise Solutions and the Method of the Displaced Ideal." *Computers and Operations Research* 1, pp. 479–496.
Zuhrah, M. (1958). *Usul al-Fiqh*. Beirut: Dar al-Fikr al-'Arabi.

CHAPTER 6

Wealth as an Indicator of Socio-Economic Welfare: Islamic Views

Asad Zaman, Arif Naveed and Atiq ur Rehman

1 Measuring Wealth and Welfare

There is now substantial dissatisfaction with wealth (or GNP per capita) as the sole measure of progress. Two Nobel Laureates have listed numerous shortcoming of this measure in the Stiglitz-Sen-Fitoussi (2009) report. Substantial effort is being made to find suitable replacements. In this paper, we consider the Islamic point of view regarding the relationship between wealth and human welfare.

A. Zaman (✉) · A. ur Rehman
Pakistan Institute of Development Economics, Islamabad, Pakistan
e-mail: asad.zaman@alumni.stanford.edu

A. ur Rehman
e-mail: atiq@pide.org.pk

A. Naveed
Faculty of Education, University of Cambridge, Cambridge, UK

S. S. Ali (ed.), *Towards a Maqāṣid al-Sharī'ah Index of Socio-Economic Development*, Palgrave Studies in Islamic Banking, Finance, and Economics,
https://doi.org/10.1007/978-3-030-12793-0_6

At the outset, Islamic scholars are agreed that increase in wealth cannot be equated with development. The prohibition of purposeless accumulation of wealth is definite and clear in this regard:

> Q(9:34) They who hoard up gold and silver and spend it not in the way of Allah, unto them give tidings (O Muhammad) of a painful doom.

It immediately follows that GDP per capita, which is the dominant criterion for measure of wealth, prosperity and welfare of nations, is unacceptable from an Islamic point of view. Before turning to consider what can and should be measured, we offer some general comments on the idea of quantification and measurement. The idea that science is the only source of knowledge, and that science is concerned solely with the observable, quantifiable and measurable, became widely established in the west over the course of the twentieth century. However, as shown in Zaman (2013, 2015), this idea is fundamentally flawed. In this introductory section, we consider three problems with the attempt to quantify all aspects of Islamic concerns about human welfare.

Some of the key Islamic imperatives are qualitative and cannot be measured. For example, the purity of intention is required for charity. Someone who does it for fame will be condemned. This contrasts with standard current approaches to Social Corporate Responsibility, which emphasize social spending as a means to build reputation and goodwill, and ultimately increase profits (see Bashir [2014] for references to the literature). While charitable contributions can be measured, the intentions behind them are substantially harder to evaluate and quantify.

1. Some fundamental concepts of central importance (like faith, trust, generosity, purity of intention) cannot be measured by us, due to limitations of human knowledge.

The "quantitative imperative" of Lord Kelvin suggests that measurement and quantification are essential to the progress of knowledge. This idea was widely believed throughout the twentieth century. Recent failures and deficiencies of this idea have led to the development of qualitative and non-measurable concepts in research, but quantification remains the dominant paradigm; see Rahim and Zaman (2009). From the Islamic point of view, we must seek a careful balance. The Quran is clear that the blessings of Allah are not countable, that His bounty is limitless, and that He provides for humans in ways beyond the possibility of our calculation. Without rejecting the possibility of quantification, we must be clear that there will be bounds, limitations and imperfection in any numerical measure.

Perhaps the most critical feature of an Islamic perspective on development distinguishing it from the competing ones is the worldview which privileges the life after death over the worldly life, even in the matters of economic progress. The purpose of human struggle in this world is to earn rewards in the hereafter rather than in this life. According to Hadith:

> When a non-believer does good, he is made to taste its reward in this world. And so far as the believer is concerned, Allah stores (the reward) of his virtues for the Hereafter and provides him sustenance in accordance with his obedience to Him. (Muslim, 11:7, Hadith No. 6740, by Anas b. Malik)

This has the implication that worldly outcomes may not be in proportion to our efforts, if the rewards are stored for the hereafter. Furthermore, as the example of charity with impure intention illustrates, what can be measured may not correspond to what is desirable to measure. This leads to the second cautionary note in the construction of an index.

2. The outcomes we are able to measure may not be a good match to what Islam teaches us as being desirable. Focusing on the measurable may lead to neglect of what really matters, but is not measurable.

Sometimes, there are things which should be concealed, rather than revealed. Quantifying and attempting to measure such things could actually create problems, rather than solve them. Islam teaches us to look at the virtues of our fellow human beings and to try and conceal their defects. In confirmation of the benefits of this principle, there is substantial evidence that publicizing immoral activities leads to their spread. Publishing statistics showing widespread corruption helps to create an atmosphere in which corruption become an acceptable mode of behaviour. Publicizing good and honest behaviour leads others to try and emulate this.

3. Trying to measure certain types of things, especially evil activities, may actually be harmful to society.

Rahim and Zaman (2009) provide a detailed discussion of certain aspects of this idea. With these three major qualifications on our search for knowledge via quantification and measurement, we proceed to study the Islamic views on the relation between wealth and human welfare.

2 Wealth and Poverty as Trials

According to dominant western conception, wealth is always a good thing and more is always better. Furthermore, all good things can be purchased with wealth, so wealth provides a means to achieve all possible social goals. This leads to a simplistic equation of wealth with welfare and the current dominant methodology for measuring wealth by aggregating it over the society as a whole.

Islamic conceptions of wealth are substantially more realistic, complex and sophisticated.[1] While measuring wealth is easy, the relation between wealth and human welfare is complex. If we want to use wealth as an indicator of welfare, we cannot do so via the naive idea that the more the better. First, we lay out the central issues regarding the Islamic theory, and then, we consider whether it is possible to create an index taking these considerations into account.

2.1 *Sufficiency as the Ideal*

The best amount of wealth for a person is the amount that is exactly according to his needs—neither more, nor less. The following four Aḥādīths in this regard are sufficient, though a lot more material is available.

> That which is little yet sufficient is better than that which is much but distracts. (Abu Ya'la, Ibn Adi and al-Albani authenticated it in al-Sahihah)

> O son of Adam, it is better for you if you spend your surplus (wealth), but if you withhold it, it is evil for you. There is (however) no reproach

[1]For a more complete discussion of the many dimensions of contrast and opposition between Islam and conventional economics, see Zaman (2015).

> for you (if you withhold means necessary) for a living. And begin (charity) with your dependents; and the upper hand is better than the lower hand. (Muslim, 11:16, Hadith No. 2256)

> He is indeed successful who has been guided to Islam, and his sustenance was sufficient for him, and he was content with it. (Saheeh Muslim, 3:102)

> The best sustenance that you are given is that which is sufficient. (Ibn Hibban in al-Silsilah al-Sahihah)

There are clear directions on the optimum level of wealth to be earned, which is the one that meets one's immediate needs.

> The son of Adam has no right except to the following: a house in which he lives, a garment with which he conceals his private parts, dry bread and water. (Tirmidhi, 7:4, Hadith No. 5186)

> He is successful who accepted Islam, who has been provided with sufficient for his want and has been made content by Allah with what He has given him. (Muslim, 12:22, Hadith No. 2291)

As is clearly stated in Surah Al-Fajr, both excess wealth and insufficient wealth are trials:

> Q(89:15–16) Now, as for man, when his Lord trieth him, giving him honour and gifts, then saith he, (puffed up), "My Lord hath honoured me". But when He trieth him, restricting his subsistence for him, then saith he (in despair), "My Lord hath humiliated me!"

As stated in the Ayat, it is common for human beings to mis-interpret these conditions. Excess wealth is interpreted as a sign of the favour of Allah, while poverty is viewed as a sign of His displeasure. In fact, both conditions are trials from Allah. In both cases, success can lead to great rewards, and failure carries severe penalties. This is the sense in which sufficiency is good—there is no trial, and correspondingly, no risk of failure. At the same time, we forsake the potential for great success. The nature of these trials is different, and this is discussed in the next two sections.

3 The Trial by Wealth

As explicitly stated in the following Ayah, wealth and worldly possessions are a trial for us. If we succeed in this trial, we can earn a tremendous reward:

> Q(8:28) and know that your worldly goods and your children are but a trial and a temptation, and that with God there is a tremendous reward.

One of the questions on the day of judgement is about how we earned wealth and how we spent it. The Prophet (saw) stated,

> The two feet of the son of Adam will not move on the Day of Judgement in front of his Lord until he is asked about five things: about his life, and how he spent it? And about his youth, what did he consume it in? And about his money, how did he earn it? And what did he spend it on? And how much did he act upon what he knew? (Tirmidhi, 2:76)

The purpose of wealth is to struggle with it in the path of Allah, as is clarified in many Ayats

> Q(8:72) BEHOLD, as for those who have attained to faith, and who have forsaken the domain of evil and are striving hard, with their possessions and their lives, in God's cause, as well as those who shelter and succour [them]

Wealth beyond our needs is to be spent in the path of Allah; for example:

> Q(2:219) They ask thee how much they are to spend (in the path of Allah); Say: "What is beyond your needs".

Those who accumulate wealth, but do not spend the excess in the way of Allah are warned of a painful doom:

> Q(9:34) They who hoard up gold and silver and spend it not in the way of Allah, unto them give tidings (O Muhammad) of a painful doom.

To summarize, we are supposed to struggle and strive in the path of Allah with our lives and possessions:

> Q(9:111) BEHOLD, God has bought of the believers their lives and their possessions, promising them paradise in return

Those who succeed in this trial by wealth will earn a tremendous reward. Those who fail are subject to a painful doom. Success in this trial requires that the acquisition of wealth be legal (*ḥalāl*), and also the use must be for purposes sanctioned by the Sharīʿah. Details of these issues have been covered in lengthy volumes in the Islamic literature. Below we extract a few details of relevance and importance to the topic under discussion, namely the relation between wealth and human welfare.

3.1 Success in Trial by Wealth

Success in the trial by wealth leads to tremendous rewards. Those who use their wealth to struggle for the sake of Allah are praised in the Quran:

> Q(9:88) The Apostle, however, and all who share his faith strive hard [in God's cause] with, their possessions and their lives: and it is they whom the most excellent things await [in the life to come], and it is they, they who shall attain to a happy state!

Similarly, a Hadith states that:

> O, Amr, good (lawful) wealth for a virtuous man is an excellent thing. (Muslim, 11:6)

For the virtuous man will of course spend his wealth for the sake of Allah and thereby earn great rewards, which are not easily available to the poor. Because of the virtues of wealth for those who spend it appropriately, some commentators have been deceived into considering wealth as an absolute good, in the manner of the west. In fact, there are two conditions attached, indicated in the Hadith above—wealth must be acquired in a lawful way and must be spent virtuously. When both conditions are fulfilled, then wealth is indeed an excellent thing.

Acquisition of wealth must be done in a *ḥalāl* way. In particular, most earning has to be tied to production of value. Deception and gambling are not allowed, since they generate profits for some (and losses for others) which is not tied to any productive or socially beneficial activity.

There are very clear instructions on how to use one's wealth. Wealth has to be spent, to take care of one's dependent and others in need in the community and society at large.

> Q(2:215) They ask you (O Muhammad, PBUH) what they should spend. Say: Whatever you spend of good must be for parents and kindred and orphans and Al-Masakin (the poor) and the wayfarer; and whatever you do of good deeds, truly, Allah knows it well.

> O son of Adam, it is better for you if you spend your surplus (wealth), but if you withhold it, it is evil for you. There is (however) no reproach for you (if you withhold means necessary) for a living. And begin (charity) with your dependents; and the upper hand is better than the lower hand. (Muslim, 11:16, Hadith No. 2256)

At the same time, people who fail to obey the commands with regard to acquisition and disposition of wealth will fail this trial and be subject to severe penalties. This is discussed in the next subsection.

3.2 *Failure in Trial by Excess Wealth*

Anyone who accumulates wealth or spends it without regard to the orders of Allah is subject to a painful doom. For these people, wealth is a curse:

> Q(9:85) And let not their worldly goods and [the happiness which they may derive from] their children excite thy admiration: God but wants to chastise them by these means in [the life of] this world, and [to cause] their souls to depart while they are [still] denying the truth.

Ayats of the Quran show that wealth is a distraction, a trial and a temptation, an illusion, for those who do not obey the orders of Allah in this regard. If excess wealth is wasted, instead of being spent in the path of Allah, this will lead to the displeasure of Allah:

> Q(17:26) And render to the kindred their due rights, as (also) to those in want, and to the wayfarer: But squander not (your wealth) in the manner of a spendthrift.

> Q(17:27) Verily spendthrifts are brothers of the Evil Ones; and the Evil One is to his Lord (himself) ungrateful.

> Verily, Allah likes three things for you and He disapproves three things for you. He is pleased with you that you worship Him and associate not anything with Him, that you hold fast the rope of Allah, and be not scattered; and He disapproves for you irrelevant talk, persistent questioning and the wasting of wealth. (Muslim Hadith, 11:10)

3.3 *Love of Allah Above Wealth*

To succeed in the trial by excess wealth, we must use our wealth for spiritual pursuits, instead of material gain. As the Quran advised Qaroon, one of the wealthiest men:

> Q(28:77) But seek, with the (wealth) which Allah has bestowed on thee, the Home of the Hereafter.

It is not enough to spend in the path of Allah. Rather the spending must also be done with the pure intention of pleasing Allah. Feeding the poor must be done purely for the sake of the love of Allah.

> Q(76:8) And they feed, for the love of Allah, the indigent, the orphan, and the captive,- [saying, in their hearts,] "We feed you for the sake of God alone: we desire no recompense from you, nor thanks".

One cannot seek fame, or other worldly rewards, such as the gratitude of those on whom he spends, in return for charity. If these worldly returns are sought, then this spending no longer qualifies as a blessing. This is why Umar R.A. referred to excess wealth as being a very difficult trial.

> Q(2:264) O you who believe! Do not render in vain your charity by reminders of your generosity or by injury, like him who spends his wealth to be seen of men, and he does not believe in Allah, nor in the Last Day.

As made explicit in the following Ayat, our love of Allah, and His Prophet, and the struggle for the cause of Islam must be greater than our love of all our worldly possessions:

> Q(9:24) Say: If your fathers and your sons and your brothers and your spouses and your clan, and the worldly goods which you have acquired, and the commerce whereof you fear a decline, and the dwellings in which you take pleasure - [if all these] are dearer to you than God and His Apostle and the struggle in His cause, then wait until God makes manifest His will; and [know that] God does not grace iniquitous folk with His guidance.

This makes the trial by wealth difficult, because the love of wealth has been implanted in the hearts of men:

> Q(3:14) ALLURING unto man is the enjoyment of worldly desires through women, and children, and heaped-up treasures of gold and silver, and horses of high mark, and cattle, and lands. All this may be enjoyed in the life of this world - but the most beauteous of all goals is with God.

It requires effort to overcome this and replace it with the love of Allah. This is exactly the process of purification of the heart which is referred to in the Holy Quran:

> Q(92:18) he that spends his possessions [on others] so that he might grow in purity

Spending that which we love is a method to purify the heart of the love of worldly things:

> Q(3:92) Ye will not attain unto piety until ye spend of that which ye love. And whatsoever ye spend, Allah is aware thereof.

Note this is the opposite of the idea of utility maximization. Instead of consuming that which we love, if we give it away, that will weaken the love of material goods and create the love of Allah in our hearts. Purification of the heart occurs when the love of Allah comes to dominate the love of material possessions.

Both external and internal rules relating to acquisition and use of wealth are too detailed and comprehensive to be covered within a brief article (for more details and discussion, see Zaman (2018)). We should be content with whatever has been given to us, and we should not envy others who have been given greater material wealth. Following these rules will lead to purification of the heart, which is the goal of our efforts and struggle:

> Q(87:14) But those will prosper who purify themselves,

In the next section, we consider the opposite of the trial by wealth, and that is the trial by poverty.

4 The Trial by Poverty

Just as wealth is a trial, so poverty is also a trial from Allah. Just as success in the trial brings great rewards, so success in the trial by poverty brings great rewards from Allah. Also, failure in the trial can lead to great loss, just as failures in the trial by wealth lead to great loss. Because poverty can create great difficulties in obedience to Allah, it even has the potential to lead to the loss of faith, which is the greatest possible catastrophe:

> Poverty can lead to *Kufr* – loss of faith (AlShub ul Eeman Lil Bahhaqi, 486)

Because of the severity of this trial, the Prophet taught us prayers to protect the *Ummah* from these difficulties. For instance, these are reported as Masnoon Dua's:

> Allah, I seek Thy refuge from hunger for it is the evil bed-fellow; and I seek Thy refuge from treachery, for it is an evil hidden trait. (Reported by Abu Huraira, cited in Khan [1989])

> Allah, I seek Thy refuge from infidelity and destitution. (Reported by Sa 'id Khudri, cited in Khan [1989])

> Allah, I seek Thy refuge against poverty; and I seek Thy refuge from paucity and humiliation; and I seek Thy refuge that I do wrong or wrong is done to me. (Reported by Abu Huraira, cited in Khan [1989])

However, just as wealth has a dual nature—it can be extremely beneficial for some and extremely harmful for others—poverty also has a dual nature. For those who can bear it with patience, it can lead to tremendous rewards. Our Prophet (saw) chose poverty for himself, as indicated in the following Hadith:

The Prophet (*Sallallaho alaihe wasallam*) said: "My Lord offered to turn the mounts of Mecca into gold for me. But my supplication to Him was; 'O,Allah! I like to eat one day and feel hungry the next, so that I may cry before Thee and remember Thee when I am hungry; and be grateful to Thee and glorify Thee when my hunger is gone!" (Tirmidhi).

Similarly, the Quran (Q[3:196]) warns us not to be covetous of the riches of those who do not believe, and states that Allah T'aala would have provided them with houses of gold and silver:

> Q(43:33) And were it not that [with the prospect of boundless riches before them] all people would become one [evil] community, We might indeed have provided for those who [now] deny the Most Gracious roofs of silver for their houses, and [silver] stairways whereon to ascend,

In another Hadith, our Prophet (saw) chides Umar R.A. for asking for the riches enjoyed by Persian and Roman kings, stating that "Ease and comfort in the Hereafter are much better than ease and comfort in this world" (see Fazail-e-'Amal, Stories of the Sahaba, Chapter III, Story 2). In another Hadith, it is stated that "Indeed, true luxury is the luxury of the *ākhirah*".

It seems clear that the riches of this world would be sought after by the non-believers, while the believers will seek their rewards in the *ākhirah*:

> When a non-believer does good, he is made to taste its reward in this world. And so far as the believer is concerned, Allah stores (the reward) of his virtues for the Hereafter and provides him sustenance in accordance with his obedience to Him. (Reported by Anas b. Malik, cited in Khan [1989])

4.1 *Success in Trial by Poverty*

To succeed in the trial by poverty, we must refrain from begging from others and seek help only from Allah.

> Whoever suffers from destitution and presented it before others, his destitution will not be removed. And whoever suffers destitution but entrusts it to Allah, Allah will provide sustenance to him sooner or later. (Reported by Abdullah b. Malik, cited in Khan [1989])

We must make active efforts to feed ourselves and our family, to fulfil our religious responsibilities towards our own self (*nafs*) and our dependants:

> Anyone of you who gathers a bundle of fuel wood (and carries it to bazar) on his back, is better than one who begs from anyone and he grants him or refuses (to grant) him. (Reported by Abu 'Ubaid, cited in Khan [1989])

There is a great deal of emphasis on developing the quality of contentedness, trust in Allah for the solution of all our problems and acceptance of the will of Allah in all matters.

> Richness is not in the quantity of possessions (that one has); rather, true richness is the richness of one's self (or contentment). (Sahih Al-Bukhari)

Similarly, Allah T'aala has praised those who give to others while they are themselves in need. This is one of the ways to achieve great success in the trial by poverty, by adopting generosity towards others, especially because it is extremely difficult.

Developing these qualities of the heart would lead to success in the trial by poverty.

4.2 *Failure in the Trial by Poverty*

Just as poverty can be a blessing for those who act in accordance with the commandments of Allah, so it can be a curse for those who disobey. One way to fail in the trial by poverty is to beg from others and forget that we are solely dependent on Allah for the provision of Rizq. The following three Aḥādīths are sufficient evidence in this regard.

> When a man is always begging from people, he would meet Allah (in a state) that there would be no flesh on his face. (Saheeh Muslim, 2263)

> He who begs the riches of others to increase his own is asking only for live coals, so let him as a little or much. (Saheeh Muslim, 2266)

> He who begs when has sufficiency will come on the Day of Resurrection with his face scratched, marked or injured. (Reported by Abdullah, cited in Khan [1989])

Similarly, a feeling that I deserve better, and that Q(89:16) "Allah has humiliated me," by putting me in financial difficulty is disliked by Allah. Envying those with greater fortune is also not permissible according to the laws of Islam (Q[4:32]). Those who cannot bear the hardships and trials associated with poverty may be driven to *Kufr*. It is the responsibility of the Islamic society as a whole to make sure that all members have enough for their needs, so as to protect them from this extremity.

4.3 *Required Attitudes Towards Poverty*

The striking feature of Islamic teachings is that the ability to meet the basic necessities is considered equal to owning the entire world. Such an assessment of the worth of material wealth creates a great sense of equality between the haves and the have nots.

> If anyone among you is secure in mind in the morning, healthy in body, possessed of food for the day, it is as if the whole world had been brought into his possession. (Tirmidhi, 7:3, Hadith No. 5001)

The worth of material goods is further elaborated in the Hadith below. Muslims are advised on lowering down their material ambitions for whatever is decreed for them, has to reach them. Tremendous literature on happiness and subjective well-being suggests that most of our dissatisfaction and unhappiness results from the gap between our aspirations and achievements.

> O people, fear God and cut your ambitions of livelihood, for a man will not court death unless he is provided full sustenance (decreed) for him even if he restrains from it. So, fear Allah and cut your ambitions in search of livelihood. Take whatever is lawful and leave whatever is unlawful. (Reported by Jabir b. Abdullah, cited in Khan [1989])

The striking aspect of these teachings is the recommendation to lower standards of living, which stands in stark contrast to the opposite recommendation of conventional economic theory. Obviously, this would have a strong impact on any methodology for constructing an index of welfare.

5 Constructing a Measure of Wealth

The believers are supposed to strive with their lives and wealth in the cause of Allah. This means that the purpose of wealth is not the purchase of the luxuries of this world, which are the objective of the non-believers. A radical difference between other spiritual traditions is that Islam does not ask us to withdraw from worldly pursuits in order to pursue the *ākhirah*:

> Q(57:27) … But as for monastic asceticism, We did not enjoin it upon them: they invented it themselves out of a desire for God's goodly acceptance.

Allah requires us to struggle with the world with the intention of achieving spiritual progress. In particular, wealth is a means towards achieving spiritual progress:

Q(92:18) he that spends his possessions [on others] so that he might grow in purity

There are several traditions of the Prophet which make explicit the idea that engaging with the world is a superior route to spiritual progress over worship, meditation or retirement from the world. It is narrated in Sahih Muslim and Bukhari that according to Abu Huraira R.A., the Prophet (saw) said that the one who strives to help a widow or a needy person earns reward like one who goes for Jihad, or one who stays up all night in worship and fasts all day.

Human welfare lies in obedience to Allah. Given the complex nature of the commands relating to wealth, which we have only briefly summarized above, using wealth as a measure of welfare is quite complex. In the first place, we should count the number of people who have sufficient wealth for their needs (neither more nor less). The idea of sufficiency is a flexible one and should be a range of numbers. Furthermore, if society provides for certain needs, people can achieve sufficiency with less wealth. For example, if education and food are guaranteed (either by government, or by private charity), then less wealth would be required. The larger this class is, the better the score. Then, we need to count the poor and also the wealthy separately. Within the class of both the poor and wealthy, we need to differentiate between those who are obedient to the orders of Allah within their condition, or whether they fail to obey. Welfare cannot be calculated without making this distinction.

As far as the poor are concerned, there is an important caution. The government and those with wealth are supposed to take steps to feed the poor and also use their wealth to care for the needs of the poor. The wealthy are not supposed to counsel patience to the poor, while denying them their rights in the wealth. The poor are supposed to look only to Allah (and not to the government or the wealthy) for help. They are supposed to bear their poverty with patience and seek help of Allah with prayer. The government and the *Ummah* as whole do have responsibility for *Amr bil Ma'rūf*, so they are supposed to preach virtues to both the poor and rich. The poor must be taught the Islamic attitudes towards poverty, while the rich must be taught the Islamic attitudes towards wealth. The extent to which these attitudes are prevalent in society can be measured to some extent. Note that the wealthy are supposed to conceal their charity, and if they do so, then this will become hard to measure. Similarly, the poor are supposed to conceal their poverty and seek help only from Allah. If they do so, it might become difficult to assess the extent of poverty in society.

6 Conclusions

The project of creating Islamic indices for human welfare faces severe conceptual difficulties. In the first place, Islamic conception of welfare relates very strongly to the *ākhirah*. Worldly gains and rewards do not figure prominently. Measuring worldly outcomes may not correlate well with qualities prized by Islam. In the second place, even when there are clear orders of Allah, assessing the degree of compliance with these orders is not at all easy. This is the task that Allah T'aala Himself will do on the day of judgement, and it is not possible for mere mortals. And yet, human welfare lies in obedience to the orders of Allah. As the Quran states, we human beings have only been given a little knowledge. It may be worth questioning the "quantitative imperative"—that we must measure things in order to know them. Even when it comes to something rather simple like wealth, measuring it according to Islamic principles is quite complex. Measuring other intangibles required for the Islamic approach may be even more complicated. We need to look more carefully at the goals of our project of measurement and to assess whether these goals may be achievable by other means not requiring measurements.

To illustrate the import of these comments, it may be worth considering the example of Finland. Several decades ago, the educational system of Finland was in bad shape, and high-level meetings were held for reforming the system. It was decided that a core component of the reforms would be equity—all children would have equal access to the educational system. Other features of the reform were extremely unorthodox. There was no emphasis on measuring capabilities—no quizzes, no performance evaluations and none of the ingredients considered essential in conventional theories of education. Yet, after a few decades, the Finnish educational system has produced tremendously good results. This is surprising to the Finns themselves, since they did not target for excellence; they only targeted for equity.

Contrary to conventional maxims and precepts, measuring outcomes may actually hinder progress towards desirable goals. Good outcomes may require struggle along qualitative dimensions which are not measurable. Focussing on the measurable outcomes may distract attention from achievement of the desirable goals—for example, spiritual progress is inherently unmeasurable and yet clearly desirable. All of these considerations suggest that the project of constructing an Islamic Index for welfare requires considerable caution. We should not construct an index just because it is the popular thing to do in the west. We should consider whether it serves Islamic objectives of *Amr bil Ma'rūf* ordained for us in the Sharī'ah.

These considerations seem important and relevant to the authors, but Allah T'aala knows best.

References

Bashir, Uzma. (February 2014). "*Determinants of Corporate Philanthropy: A Case of Karachi Stock Exchange*," M Phil thesis at IIIE, International Islamic University.

Khan, M. A. (1989). *Economic Teachings of Prophet Muhammad: A Selected Anthology of Hadith Literature on Economics*. Islamabad: International Institute of Islamic Economics and Institute of Policy Studies.

Rahim, Faizur, & Zaman, Asad. (June 2009). "Corruption: Measuring the Unmeasurable," *Humanomics*, Vol. 25, No. 2, pp. 117–126.

Stiglitz, J. E., Sen, A., & Fitoussi, J.-P. (2009). *Report by the Commission on the Measurement of Economic Performance and Social Progress*. Paris. http://www.stiglitzsen-fitoussi.fr/en/index.htm.

Zaman, Asad. (December 2013). "Logical Positivism and Islamic Economics," *International Journal of Economics, Management and Accounting (IJEMA)*, Vol. 21, No. 2, pp. 1–18.

Zaman, Asad. (2015). "Islam Versus Economics," Chapter 2 in *Handbook on Islam and Economic Life*, edited by Kabir Hassan and Mervyn Lewis, Edward Elgar Press.

Zaman, Asad. (2018). "An Islamic Approach to Inequality and Poverty," *Journal of King Abdul Aziz University: Islamic Economics*, Vol. 31, No. 1, pp. 69–92.

CHAPTER 7

Maqāṣid al-Sharīʿah for Socioeconomic Development Index: A Statistical Approach

M. Fevzi Esen and Adem Esen

1 Introduction to Theoretical Study

All rulings of worldly and religious affair have been built on the *maṣlaḥah* (interests).[1] Allah hasn't completely given the legislative authority to human beings. If this authority was left out just for people, it would be a great chaos.[2] Because they will not know the right about themselves Allah has put the main and basic interests (Cessâs 1992).

[1] This article mainly took advantage of Pekcan, Ali. (2013) Makasıd Teorisine Giriş (Fıkhi Hükümlerin Ğai Arka Planı) (Introduction to the Theory Makâsid [fiqh Terms of Gaia Background] Hikmetevi yayınları, İstanbul). Thanks to him.

[2] Surah Yunus verse no 15: "And when Our clear revelations are recited unto them, they who look not for the meeting with Us say: Bring a Lecture other than this, or change it.

M. F. Esen
Istanbul Medeniyet University, Istanbul, Turkey
e-mail: fevzi.esen@medeniyet.edu.tr

A. Esen (✉)
Istanbul University, Istanbul, Turkey
e-mail: adem.esen@istanbul.edu.tr

S. S. Ali (ed.), *Towards a Maqāṣid al-Sharīʿah Index of Socio-Economic Development*, Palgrave Studies in Islamic Banking, Finance, and Economics,
https://doi.org/10.1007/978-3-030-12793-0_7

However, most of the affairs, in essence, are variable. Therefore, as the situation and the time are bound to change, behaviors may also vary with the change in the format. Indeed in the Majallah al-Ahkam al-Adliyah, the Article 39 refers to this situation.[3]

Islam, for the good of the human beings in this world and the hereafter, has put various rules. While putting them, it has observed certain aims and objectives for the benefit of people, and it has no provision unjustified and pointless. Thus, Allah's commandments and prohibitions include some interests for all human beings. These interests are *maṣlaḥah*, for Allah's purpose are *maqāṣid*u's-shari' (the goals of the legislator), and for both sides are the legislative wisdoms (*hikmat tashri'*).[4]

As called, *maqāṣid* may be taken into three categories: those are essentials or necessities (*ḍarūriyāt*), the complementary (*ḥajiyāt*), and embellishments (*taḥsiniyāt*). The Conventional Islamic jurists pointed out that it is necessary to be aware of their meanings for judging.[5] Contemporary Islamic jurists are of the same opinion.[6]

Muslim societies would need to redefine and reshape their own needs and goals in accordance with their religious beliefs. Modernity thus becomes human empowerment because it concerns the needs and ambitions of a people seeking their advancement and progress (Deina 2003).

Say (O Muhammad): It is not for me to change it of my own accord. I only follow that which is inspired in me. Lo! if I disobey my Lord I fear the retribution of an awful Day."

[3] Majallah al-Ahkam al-`Adliyah, the Article 39: "It is an accepted fact that the terms of law vary with the change in the times."

[4] In the Holy Qur'an, and the Prophet Muhammad hadiths, and the other Holy Books (Torah and Bible), there are some goals of Shari'ah. When we look at Mumtahına surah, 60/12, in this verse on the "bey'at," it is seen four essential principles of the five basic excepts of the principle of mind protection (hıfz'ul-*aql*).

Most maqasid issues (the protection of the faith, the intellect, the self, the posperity, and the wealth) were counted in the Moses (pbuh)s' ten commandments. In the Bible, Prophet Jesus (pbuh) mentioned some Moses's commandments. So, they are universal.

[5] See for some conventional opinions: Muhammad ibn Idris al-Shafi'i. (204 hijri) Kitab al-Risala fi Usul al-Fiqh.

[6] Some contemporary writers are: al-Kardawi (2002) and Abû Zahra (1989).

1.1 *Some Terms Related to* Maqāṣid *al-Sharīʿah*

Besides *maqāṣid* some terms have been used in the same or similar meanings. These are: the pleasure (*husün*) and the outrageous (*kubüh*) mean that something is beautiful or ugly. Indeed, intellect is one of Allah Almighty's evidences. Those the intellect considers nice and beautiful are nice and beautiful, and those it counts bad and ugly are bad and ugly. Something may be beautiful or ugly (*li ʿaynihi*) in its essence, or owing to something else (*li ghayrihi*). Again, in Islam, aimlessness and improper behaviors are counted ugly. Religious rules established upon the basics are the wisdom which absolutely contains a benefit. Thus, canonical provisions do contain wisdom.

The intellect (mind) is one of the evidences of Allah too. There are mainly two lights: the Holy Qur'an and the intellect. However, light of the Holy Qur'an is quite outstanding and valuable. While the intellect guides the way (*nur hadi*), the other is a light source that illuminates the way (*ziyaun kafi*). Therefore, both of them do not contradict because these are Allah's evidences. However, the top and front of intellect is Islam.

Islamic jurists have taken jurisprudence (*ijtihad*) and interests (*maslaha*) into account for protection of law in the affair. *Maslaha* is the general considerations of securing benefits or preventing harms. *Ijtihad* is a kind of decision-making process through the knowledge of theology and legal theory within Islamic law by qualified jurists (*mujtahid*). One of them, Imam Abû Yusuf is the second largest representative of Hanafi Fiqh School. According to Abû Yûsuf, the Imam (head of state) prefers the high ideals of Islam and the Muslims should spend their lives based on the current affair (Abû Yûsuf 1302).

Scholars have highlighted the necessity of *ijtihad*. They have adopted an objectives-based approach in their practice of *ijtihad*. Scholars have agreed that *ijtihad* is a collective obligation on Muslim communities and it must consider the needs and differences of communities. While determining primary or secondary objectives of *maqāṣid*, the adaptability and rigidity of the doctrines of Islamic scholars on *ijtihad* should be taken into account (Ibn Ashur 2006). Besides, *maslaha* that embracing the genuine interest of community which are not contradictory to the main idea of Shari'ah needs to be clarified toward *ijtihad* for describing *Maqāṣid* al-Sharīʿah variables. Shatibi introduced the *Maqāṣid* al-Sharīʿah into the *ijtihad* and introduced the *ijtihad* into the term of *Maqāṣid* al-Sharīʿah.

Comparison of Hanafi which is commonly used in order to eliminate the rigidity of the method *istiḥsān*, especially the essentials, interests, and common usages, *istiḥsān*-based varieties, is ultimately based on mursal (forwarded) interests.[7]

1.2 *According to Some of the Scholars:* Maqāṣid

One of the first systematic studies started in *maqāṣid* is Ghazzali's (A.D. 1111). He studied on the life, wisdom, chastity, and goods protection that are required by law. After mentioning four of these purposes, he added the fifth as the protection of religion considering it essential. Reducing his mentor Cuveynî's five divisions to three, he named them *ḍarūriyāt* (the essentials), *ḥajiyāt* (the complementary), and *taḥsiniyāt* (the embellishments) (Ghazzali 1971).

According to Ghazzali, for the analysis to be valid three conditions are sought: to be essential (five mandatory elements protection), to be precise (the exact realization), and to be holistic (comprehensive all Muslims, not part of them).

Ibn Taymiyyah (A.D. 1328) joined in the same division of *maqāṣid*. Besides, in addition to five essential principles, he mentioned a number of elements and said: "… the world and in the Hereafter, for the affairs are some of the contractual commitment to, relatives maintain relationships, the state-public and the neighbors' rights to regard the Muslims each other's rights to comply" (Ibn Taymiyyah 1398).

Shatibi (A.D. 1388), as did the previous method, divided the interests into three: the essential, the complementary, and the embellishment. According to him, canonical obligations are divided into two groups: the obligations that need to be ensured by positive (charged) and preventive protection (*ibqā*) methods. Within the group of positive methods are worship, practices, and transactions, while the murders (penalties) are located in the preventive group. He believes that complementary "*ḥājyyāt*" has been enforced to expand the boundaries of *maqāṣid* and to facilitate the realization of the essential legislative affair. Embellishment consists of things to provide superior morality to behave in accordance with the common sense and to welcome moving away from the negative cases (Raysuni 2005).

[7] Zerkâ, Mustafa Ahmed. (1998). el-Istıslâh ve'l-Mesâlihi'l-Mürsele fi'ş-Şerîati'l-İslamiyye ve Usûli Fıkhihâ, Damascus.

According to Shatibi, three interests are closely tied to each other. This connection is bidirectional. Each interest is complementary and integrative. They are tightly related to each other in order. So embellishment completes the complementary, and complementary completes the essentials. So, each of them is an integral part of the case (Raysuni 2005).

Shatibi said that the essentials are the basis, and a number of these categories relate to each other draw conclusions. Some of these results are:

1. Essential, complementary, and embellishment constitute the principal.
2. Essential when it was a violation, it should not be in violation of both complementary and revenue embellishment.
3. Complementary and not in violation of embellishment from the breach of essential not concerned.
4. Essential for the protection of complementary and embellishment affair which is mandatory.

Shatibi emphasizes that all the mental and intellectual activities are used in the inductive method and applied frequently the five elements in the foundation of the application of this method. He responded to the question of how five essential principles are fixed: Islamic societies and other communities agreed on the five principles essential for the protection. These are religion, self, posterity, wealth, and intellect. According to all communities, religion is one of those known as mandatory. Neither these have been fixed with certain evidence, nor a concrete reality that we can testify as a witness. However, their relevance to religion is known to be the sum of the evidence, more than to be fit in a single issue (Raysuni 2005).

Each affair, that is including the protection of the five elements, is the interest (*maṣlaḥah*). And each affair, that is eliminating them, is the bight (*mafsadah*), wherein the relief of *mafsadah* is the interest.

This five elements (*kulliyyāt-khamsa*) have been completed by adding the sixth: the protection of honor (*hıfzu'l ırḍ*). Islam has banned slander and gossip, and such bad behaviors, especially about adultery libel. Therefore, the protection of honor is the sixth of the set value, may be added as a factor of five.

One of the contemporary Islamic jurists Ashur b. Tahir after mentioning their importance and necessity separates the affairs into different sections in three aspects. According to this, affairs are:

1. In terms of Islamic society, there are three parts: (a) essential, (b) complementary, and (c) embellishment.
2. In terms of the whole of the Muslim community, interest groups and individuals, it is divided into two parts: (a) holistic and (b) partial.
3. In terms of standing society and the survival of individuals, there are three parts: (a) certain, (b) accusative, and (c) notional.

Ibn Ashur (2006) describes the essentials as the beneficiaries which individuals or society can be damaged if they are violated. The state of the nation faces amount of deterioration and disintegration unless the violation of the beneficiaries is abolished. Therefore, economic interests are very important for both community and individuals. So, *Maqāṣid* al-Sharī'ah should be utilized by determining the economic interests.

Essentials of human beings, the sheer aspect of being human, mean necessity to protect the natural needs. Accordingly, *hâciyyât* and *tahsin-iyyat* are regarded as the protectors of essential affairs. In the words of Ibn Ashur, tahsînî affair is the top level and it is an indicator of Islamic civilization and its mature, and it has been set as an ideal level for individuals and community (Pekcan 2013).

2 Benefits of Knowing the Goals of Islam

Knowing the purpose of the religious goals provides some theoretical and practical benefits. They can be listed briefly as follows (Pekcan 2013):

1. Religious terms are understood and interpreted correctly.
2. Religious purposes are a method for the solution of new problems encountered. Indeed, some of the events encountered which do not participate in religious terms, the scope of the phrases and their comparison to the provision cannot be determined. For example, reclamation (*ıstıslah*) is a method to solve problems that has no clear answer in religious texts. So, when there is no clear law that carries the spirit of the general objectives of Islamic law, provisions must be taken into the consideration. Knowing the goals of Islam provides the heart tranquility (*tuma'niyatu'l-qalb*) and complacency (*sharḥu's-sadr*).

3. Today, many studies have been done on the main objectives of the religion in Islamic law. If they are to be brought into the socioeconomic index, they will be a significant contribution to the field of Islamic economics.

In this context, it is possible to benefit from historical study of Islamic economics.[8]

The five objectives of al-Sharīʿah are discussed briefly below.

2.1 *The Protection of the Faith (al-Dīn)*

Whether in the narrow sense of faith-worship, whether generally faith, worship, and legislation, the religion and al-Sharīʿah are phenomena that are indispensable for human life.

God inspired religion in accordance with the creation of humankind and has facilitated its application. Principles of belief consist of Allah, the prophets, the books, the angels, the Last Day, and believing in fate. Faith in God is the foundation of religion. Tawhid (monotheism) is the essence of the Islamic faith. Shatibi included the worship, prayer, fasting, charity, and pilgrimage in the essential part of the religion. Islam primarily comes out against superstitious beliefs, lust and desires to be subject to counterfeiting, superstitions of the human mind dulled, and intelligence extinguishing astrology and augury unfounded pursuit of, ignorance, bigotry opposed these sorts of things faith and reason have maintained.

The faith preserves religion through some principals and worship. In order to provide a better, meaningful life and individual accountability, the importance of protection of the faith has been also underlined by western scholars. Toynbee (1958) states that moral and social refreshment cannot be progressed without moral sanctions of religion. T.S. Eliot remarks on the importance of religion by stating "*without religion the whole human race would die*" (Lukacs 1971). Williams (1985) underlines that the morality is not a product of philosophers but religion.

In "the Islamic Vision of Development in the light of *Maqāṣid* al-Sharīʿah," M. U. Chapra (2008) emphasizes the values, motivation,

[8]For example, see: al-Omar, Fuad Abdullah. (2003). Mukaddima fi Tarihi'l-İqtisadi'l-Islami ve Tatavvruhu. Jeddah, Publication No. 62.

and physical and moral education in the protection of religion (faith). In the scope of values, he puts justice, freedom, dignity, and the like. Also equity allocation is based on brotherhood. Family, social responsibility, provides answers to issues such as employment opportunities. In this context, he adds emphasis on the role of the state (Chapra 2008).

2.2 *The Protection of the Self (an-nafs)*

For the protection of the life or the self (*an-nafs*) purpose is to protect people and humanity. In this context, all people are equal in rights because of a person's obligatory aspect of being human. These rights include the right to life, the right to health protection, the right to make legal transaction, the right to liberty, the right to equality, and the right to freely search and selection. Other rights of the people called vested rights, are the rights acquired by his own efforts outside the natural rights.

Abû Zahra said the following about the preservation of life: the protection of the human self (life) to guarantee people's honorable life. Into the concept of self-defense and protection, all human bodies are also involved in the protection. Indeed, the protection of the dignity of the same clutch of people, tarnishing the honor, spiritual qualities, such as suppression of freedom are also included in the same concept. The human freedoms such as freedoms of work, thought, and residence without being attacked by anyone in the community are essentials of maintaining a virtuous life, and other freedoms supporting virtuous human life are included in these spiritual elements (Abû Zahra 1989).

For the protection of life, its losses should be corrected. These losses are expected from the removal of the target; the existence of life, spirit, and body is to protect the integrity. For example, Islam has prohibited blood feuds completely. Again ordered protection from all kinds of diseases, in particular, has recommended protection from epidemics like the plague.[9]

[9] Bukhari, Kitab al-Tıbb, Ch 30 at https://sunnah.com/bukhari/76; See also Sahih al-Bukhari 5728.

Chapra (2008), in the above-mentioned book, counts the self-protection as the first of five goals, separated into fourteen subtitles.[10]

2.3 *The Protection of the Intellect (al-ʿaql)*

Only to people who own spirit, soul, heart, and mind, the name is also given. Indeed, it is the mind that makes people responsible to have the rights and duties he is supplying. Two important results in the protection of the mind stand out:

1. Protect mind through physically and intellectually. The elements regarding biological needs such as eating, drinking, exercising as well as reading, thinking, criticizing need to be provided. From this point of view, the preservation of life will be covered by mind-body unity with the spirit.
2. Mind the real purpose of the protection, preservation rather than biologically based thinking in terms of function, which is to protect and improve. A mind that lost the ability to think has lost its essential functions and would not have any legal obligation, because the addressee is the mind of the religious proposals and orders.

According to Çizakça (2007), the *Maqāṣid* al-Sharīʿah actually advises Muslim governments of the future whether to undertake or to reject a policy. Of the five components, intellect protection (hıfz al-ʿ*aql*) has been traditionally interpreted as the duty of the state to protect the reason or mind of its citizens and has taken the form of alcohol and drugs prohibition. This author prefers to interpret intellect protection as the duty of the state to protect freedom of thought.

Chapra (2008) has listed the following items on the protection of the mind.[11]

[10]These subtitles are: 1—dignity, self-respect, human brotherhood, and social equality; 2—justice; 3—spiritual and moral uplift; 4—security of life, property, and honor; 5—freedom; 6—education; 7—good governance; 8—need fulfillment; 9—employment and self-employment; 10—equitable distribution of income and wealth; 11—marriage and proper upbringing of children; 12—family and social solidarity; 13—minimization of crim and anomie; 14—mental peace and happiness.

[11]Intellect protection is: high quality of religous and science education at affordable prices, emphasis on the maqasid in the interpretation of texts, library and research facilities, freedom of thought and expression, reward for creative work and finance.

2.4 The Protection of the Posterity (an-nasl)

The purpose of the posterity protection (*an-nasl*) is reproduction of the human species. If healthy and legal growth of human generations is meant by this term, it basically goes into the preservation of life. Because regarding the preservation of life, all people get into it. If the *nasl* is stopped or interrupted, this causes an impairment or decline of the species. In order to provide a continuous improvement in generations, some factors must be assured. One of these is abstaining from the actions that destroy *nasl*, one's progeny, which is one of the essentials under the law. For example, unless otherwise specified in terms of health factors, the males must be prevented from demasculinization and the females from the celibacy. Similarly, unless otherwise specified, females must be prevented from hysterectomy which deprives them of the organs necessary for birth and from abortion (Ibn Ashur 2006).

The second factor is progeny (*al-nasab*). According to Islamic laws, *nasab* ensures the determination of inheritance and contracting of marriages. It concerns the relationship by affinity, alimony, and procuration in *fiqh*. For example, vagueness about the offspring's relationship to their parents may destroy the inclination to protect and educate the children through physically and mentally. Similarly, a lack of family integration that concerns the protection of children's rights may abolish the objectives of a family system. Discouraging divorce, strong abomination of secret marriages, or forbidding the marriage without witnesses also helps to protect the posterity and to have a clean and noble generation.[12]

2.5 The Protection of the Wealth (al-Māl)

Islam has put many rules for the property and wealth preservation and development.[13]

According to Çizakça, the wealth protection has been traditionally interpreted as the right of a Muslim to protect his property. This can be interpreted alternatively as the duty of the state to protect property rights, an absolutely important condition for democracy and economic

[12] Protection of generation states five subtitles. These are: proper upbringing, moral and intellectual development; marriage and family integrity; need fulfillment; clean and healthy envirronment; freedom from fear, conflict, and insecurity.

[13] For this, see: Esen (2007).

development. Moreover, without effective property rights, accumulated capital of the Muslims would be hidden under the mattress, a condition frequently and strongly condemned by the Holy Qur'an (Çizakça 2007).

How the essential values should be sorted is viewed in various ways. By a group of lawyers, if such matters (*maṣlaḥah*) conflict with each other, principle of faith protection is preferred. Respectively afterlife, lineage, intellect, and property are protected (Ibn Humâm 2003). The owners of this opinion say that the protection of religion is more important than the protection of life. In other words, they argue that jihad is a religious duty for the protection of the religion (Ibn Emîri'l-Hâc 1996; Bûtî 1992).

3 *MAQĀṢID* AL-SHARĪʿAH INDEX

Basically, an index is a statistical measure of changes in a given set of individual data points. It helps to clarify the specifics of variables in a particular context. There are two main objectives of statistical indexes:

1. Description by summarizing information.
2. Induction, which involves either generalization from samples or the formulation of the laws based on repeated observation.

The classification of indexes can be based on some criteria of contents and objectives toward socioeconomic processes. Direct objective indexes are generally based on single series or more or less collections. Sometimes they should be standardized by single weights or a fixed concept. Direct objective concepts can be built up from heterogeneous components that are summed up by number or value. On the other hand, dynamic concepts include an iterative learning process exercise a heuristic function in determining the epistemology of socioeconomic concerns. Besides, indirect-derived indexes can emerge from proxy series that are related to main series (Horn 1993).

The conceptual literature of socioeconomic indexes is divided into two groups. Objective indexes are usually applied to the mode of assessment that is based on external evidence. Subjective indexes are often in mode and in concept. They reflect opinions by those close to the issue in question.

The relation of subjectivity to social facts has been discussed in the sociology as has been the link between cardinal and ordinal scaling.

We must avoid confusion between what is being measured and how it is being measured. All objective-type indicators carry a subjective value load inherent in the process of the collection, selection and presentation of statistics, and subjective-type indicators borrow objective modes of grouping, ranking, and partitioning the data.

Linking the interrelations of data within the statistical base and between components is important for establishing correlations within and between indicator elements (the connection between production and trade via high technology, auto-correlation between infant mortality and life expectancy, etc.). In addition, considering the choice between ordinal and cardinal measures for needs is vitally essential.

The methodology of creating indexes depends on placing each variable in an *n*-dimensional space. In the literature, there are kinds of ways for displaying distances of variables to each other but generally the procedure will be (Horn 1993):

1. Formulating the problem—What variables do you want to compare? How many variables do you want to compare?
2. Obtaining input data.
3. Deciding the number of dimensions—It is needed to decide on the number of dimensions they want the computer to create. The more the dimensions, the better the statistical fit, but the more difficult it is to interpret the results.
4. Mapping the results and defining the dimensions—The statistical program (or a related module) maps the results. The map plots each product (usually in two-dimensional space).
5. Testing the results for reliability and validity.
6. Reporting the results comprehensively—Along with the mapping, at least distance measures (e.g., Sorenson index, Jaccard index) and reliability scores (e.g., stress value) should be provided.

3.1 *Variables of* Maqāṣid *al-Sharīʿah in a Statistical Context*

Many variables with fixed scales are familiar in daily life. Since many of the variables can be based on different criteria of contents, there has to be a fair selection and presentation process. What is being measured and how it is being measured must be considered. (As presented in Fig. 1, *Maqāṣid* al-Sharīʿah has five main variables including subvariables. Depending upon various contents, they have different level of measurement.)

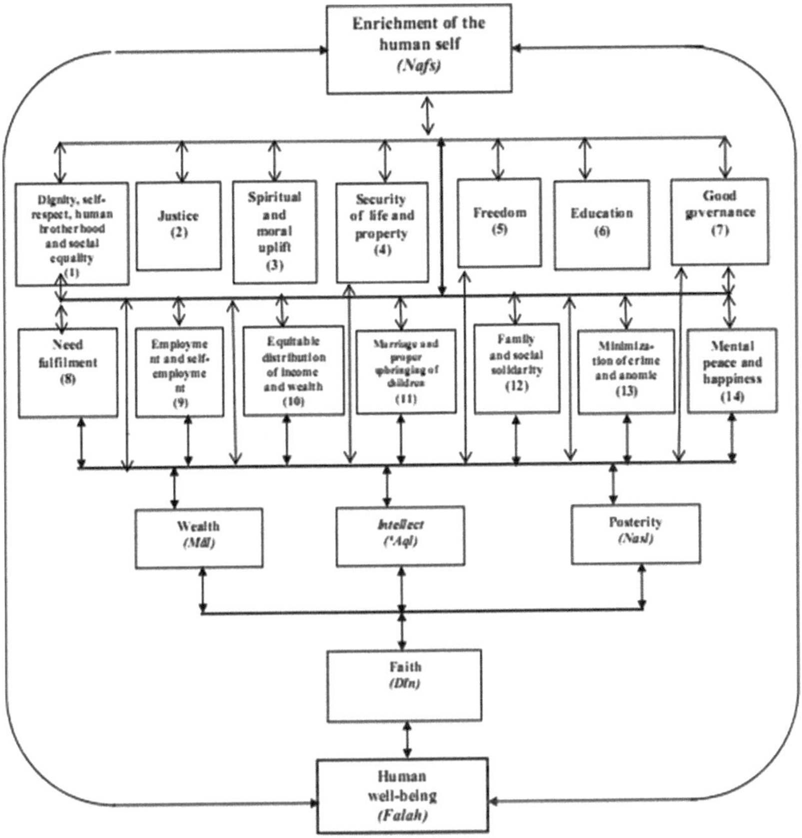

Fig. 1 One of the important variables of *Maqāṣid* al-Sharīʿah variables: *Nafs* (*Source* Chapra 2007, p. 11)

Since being hidden by the parties of study or purely defined nature, obtaining and measuring of objective data are difficult for empirical studies (Olken 2009). Rather than working with objective data, subjective measures like corruption, happiness, intellect, and protection of al-din are being used.

Latent concepts play important roles in the theoretical work of all subfields of statistical indexes. In terms of *Maqāṣid* al-Sharīʿah, there are latent relations between the sub-variables. For instance, security, justice, and freedom are the mutual needs to sustain faith (*al-din*), to protect posterity (*an-nasl*), and to provide freedom of thought which is a sub-variable of intellect (*al-ʿaql*). A comprehensive action of the variables as stated above will induce mutual affection, compliance with norms, growth of economy and wealth. Furthermore, high quality of education which is the need of human personality will enable community to not only strengthen the knowledge and wisdom for society but also perform their engagements by consciously. For this reason, most of the sub-variables of *Maqāṣid* al-Sharīʿah are expected to have direct, indirect, and reverse causality. In this concept, the variables must be clearly defined, understood, and interpreted in the same way by all participants. Reliability, sensitivity, equally weighted, aggregation, and validity are key issues of systematic biases related to scale and also cognitive biases like halo effects as a source of measurement error to be avoided.

Although there are many sub-variables explaining *Maqāṣid* al-Sharīʿah in Islamic context, we used the variables that are measured and evaluated periodically by various organizations. Due to not having a convenient sample and lack of data, the most appropriate indexes and variables related to *maqāṣid* literature are proposed as variables in Table 1, as shown below.

3.2 *Exploratory Factor Analysis*

Multivariate analysis takes multifaceted indicators for social and economic concerns into account and analyses more than one statistical outcome at a time. One approach applied to indicator analysis is so-called factor analysis.

Factor analysis is a popular method in the social sciences for studying the relationships between variables. For a given data set, the factor analysis model assumes that each observed variable arises from a relatively small number of unobservable variables. Some of the unobservable variables, termed common factors, have an effect on many of the observed variables. Other unobservable variables, termed unique factors, have an effect on only one observed variable. An observed variable is consequently assumed to arise from a single unique factor and a combination of common factors. The common factors are assumed to entirely account for the correlations between observed variables. Thus, based on correlations between observed variables, factor analysis can yield insight into the nature of the unobserved, underlying common factors.

Factor analysis attempts to bring intercorrelated variables together under more general, underlying variables. More specifically, the goal

Table 1 *Maqāṣid* al-Sharīʿah related variables for socio-economic index

Maqāṣid *Al-Sharīʿah Variable*	*Explanatory Sub-Variables*	*Measurement Scales*
The protection of the faith (al-dīn)	– Peace index – Values index	Nominal, ordinal, continuous
The protection of the intellect (al-ʿaql)	– Articles published (numbers) – Education expenditure (% of GDP) – Patent grants by filing office (numbers) – Total researchers (numbers) – Internet users (per 100 persons)	Continuous
The protection of the posterity (*an-nasl*)	– Health expenditures (% of GDP) – Prevalence rate of tobacco consumption (%) – Life expectancy at birth (ages) – Fertility rate (births per woman)	Continuous
The protection of the wealth (al-māl)	– GDP, per capita (current prices) – Gross domestic savings (% of GDP) – Household consumption, share in total consumption (percentages)	Continuous
The protection of the self (*an-nafs*)	– Labour participation rate (% of total population ages 15+) – Freedom index – Safety index – Political stability and absence of violence index	Nominal, ordinal, continuous

Source Table is formed by authors

of factor analysis is to reduce "the dimensionality of the original space and to give an interpretation to the new space, spanned by a reduced number of new dimensions which are supposed to underlie the old ones" (Rietveld and Van Hout 1993) or to explain "the variance in the observed variables in terms of underlying latent factors" (Habing 2003). Thus, factor analysis offers not only the possibility of gaining a clear view of the data, but also the possibility of using the output in subsequent analyses (Rietveld and Van Hout 1993).

Examples are studies in which questionnaires are used that consist of a lot of questions (variables), and studies in which social, economic, psychological, spiritual, or medical state is tested via several subtests, like objective and subjective measurements. Because of these big numbers of variables that are into play, the study can become rather complicated. Exploratory factor analysis (EFA) is a statistical method used to uncover the underlying structure of a relatively large set of variables. This technique is within the factor analysis whose overarching goal is to identify the underlying relationships between measured variables. It is commonly used by researchers when developing a scale or economic indexes and serves to identify a set of latent constructs underlying a battery of measured variables. It should be used when the researcher has no a priori hypothesis about factors or patterns of measured variables (Fabrigar et al. 1999).

There are several steps in conducting EFA research (Suhr 2009):

1. Reduce the number of variables.
2. Examine the structure or relationship between variables.
3. Detection and assessment of unidimensionality of a theoretical construct.
4. Evaluate the construct validity of a scale, test, or instrument.
5. Development of parsimonious (simple) analysis and interpretation.
6. Address multicollinearity (two or more variables that are correlated).
7. Used to develop theoretical constructs/used to prove/disprove proposed theories.

3.3 Bayesian Approach to Factor Analysis

The factor analysis model is usually estimated by maximum likelihood methods under the assumption that the observations are normally distributed. In practice, however, the maximum likelihood estimates of unique variances can often turn out to be zero or negative. Such estimates are known as improper solutions, and many authors have studied these inappropriate estimates both from a theoretical point of view and also by means of numerical examples (Kano 1998; Krijnen et al. 1998).

In terms of the explanation of *Maqāṣid* al-Sharīʿah variables within factor analysis framework, one of the sub-variables of protection of al-din, *ʿibādāt*, may be a subjective variable that looks into faith and *īmān* based on ordinal scale. It has a different weight on factor loading. However, *Jinayat* may be presented as an objective variable like number of the laws, based on interval-ratio scale, against apostasy to protect religion that may have a different effect on factor loading. To measure the latent concepts of variables, two complementary approaches have been discussed in the literature. The first approach is about the collection of proxy variables and using quantitative models to focus on data collection. The approaches also include how to take the effects of expert opinions, debates, and simulations into account for the use of measurement models. The second approach is to measure the latent concepts that the responses are either continuous or ordinal. In this situation, most of the studies prefer the analytic procedure as the following (Quinn 2004):

1. Transform the ordinal variables to continuous,
2. Discretize the continuous variables,
3. Use only continuous or ordinal variables,
4. Do not follow a model-based measurement strategy.

In order to prevent the occurrence of improper solutions in factor analysis model and the nature of variables of *Maqāṣid* al-Sharīʿah, the selection of the number of factors and hyper-parameters in prior distribution is determined by using Bayesian approach to factor analysis. Bayesian approach is introduced by specifying a prior distribution for the variances of unique factors. In this analysis, the choice of a prior distribution is a fundamental issue.

According to literature, Press (1982) and Akaike (1987) have introduced a prior distribution for the elements of unique variances and factor loadings. Then, West (2004) used Markov Chain Monte Carlo algorithms and received attention on Bayesian factor analysis. The important advantage of using Bayesian approach is the capability in utilizing useful prior information for accurate solution.

Let $X = (X_1, \ldots, X_p)'$ be a p-dimensional observable random vector with mean vector μ and variance–covariance matrix Σ. The factor analysis model is

$$X = \mu + \Lambda F + \varepsilon,$$

where $\Lambda = (\lambda_{ij})$ is a $p \times k$ matrix of factor loadings, and $F = (F_1, \ldots, F_k)'$ and $\varepsilon = (\varepsilon_1, \ldots, \varepsilon_p)'$ are unobservable random vectors. The elements of F and ε are called common factors and unique factors, respectively. It is assumed that $E(F) = 0$, $E(\varepsilon) = 0$, $E(FF') = I_k$, $E(\varepsilon\varepsilon') = \Psi$ and $E(F\varepsilon') = 0$, where I_k is the identity matrix of order k and Ψ is a $p \times p$ diagonal matrix with i-th diagonal element ψ_i which is called unique variance. Under these assumptions, the variance–covariance matrix of X can be expressed as

$$\Sigma = \Lambda\Lambda' + \Psi.$$

The i-th diagonal element of $\Lambda\Lambda'$ is called communality, which measures the percent of variance in x_i explained by all the factors. It is well known that factor loadings have a rotational indeterminacy since both Λ and ΛT generate the same covariance matrix Σ, where T is an arbitrary orthogonal matrix.

Suppose that we have a random sample of N observations $x_1, \ldots, x_N$ from the p-dimensional normal population $N_p(\mu, \Sigma)$ *with* $\Sigma = \Lambda\Lambda' + \Psi$. Then, the log-likelihood function is given by

$$\log f(X_N|\Lambda, \Psi) = -\frac{N}{2}\{p \log(2\pi) + \log|\Sigma| + \mathrm{tr}(\Sigma S)\},$$

where $X_N = (x_1, \ldots, x_N)'$, $f(X_N|\Lambda, \Psi)$ is the likelihood function and $S = (s_{ij})$ is the sample variance–covariance matrix

$$S = \frac{1}{N}(x_n - \bar{x})(x_n - \bar{x})',$$

with $\bar{x}$ being the sample mean vector. For convenience, let us consider the discrepancy function given by

$$q(\Lambda, \Psi) = \log|\Sigma| + \mathrm{tr}\left(\Sigma^{-1}S\right) - \log|S| - p.$$

The maximum likelihood estimates of Λ and Ψ are given as the solutions of $\partial q(\Lambda, \Psi)/\partial\Lambda = 0$ and $\partial q(\Lambda, \Psi)/\partial\Psi = 0$. Since the solutions cannot be expressed in a closed form, some iterative procedures are required to obtain the maximum likelihood estimates $\hat{\Lambda}$ML and $\hat{\Psi}$ML. Hirose and Kawano (2011) give the maximum likelihood factor analysis and its related problems. They show how to prevent the occurrence of improper solutions. The focus estimating the parameters included in the factor analysis model with the help of Bayesian procedure. In order to compute Bayesian factors, the prior distributions on the parameters of each model must be specified.

We propose that, in practice, Bayesian factor analysis is a powerful method to select a number of factors for exploring the covariance structure of *Maqāṣid* al-Sharīʿah index. Model selection and criterion are based on a Bayesian point of view, and generalized Bayesian information criterion can be applied to choose adjusted parameters that include the hyper-parameter for the proposed prior distribution and the number of factors.

3.4 Bayesian Structural Equation Modeling

Structural equation modeling (SEM) is a methodology for representing, estimating, and testing a network of relationships between variables (measured variables and latent constructs). The goals of SEM are understanding the patterns of correlation/covariance among a set of variables and explaining as much of their variance as possible with the model specified (Kline 1998).

Although the majority of the literature on SEM is frequentist in nature, Bayesian approaches have been proposed by a number of authors. Due to not having linearity assumption, mixed scales of variables, and missing data, Bayesian approach can be easily applied to a very broad class of SEM applications. This method utilizes prior information that may have some advantages over frequentist approaches. For example, while constructing a peace or freedom index that involves latent variables regarding number of political parties or intensity of internal conflict, some prior information about the relationship between latent variables or factor loadings may be available. This information also emerges as knowledge of experts or historical data. Bayesian SEM allows to utilize prior information in inferring properties of an underlying distribution.

Requirement of indication of prior distributions for model unknowns including parameters and latent variables is a difference between Bayesian and classical approaches. Most of the studies generally assume Gaussian distributions for latent variables (Palomo et al. 2007). Also, computational ascendancy of Bayesian approaches has appropriate solutions on simulations from posterior distribution of parameters and hidden variables. Since estimations of posterior distributions for any functional of the model unknowns are applicable, relying on large sample assumptions are not required. As mentioned in Bayesian SEM literature, the sampling-based Bayesian methods depend less on asymptotic theory

(Ansari and Jedidi 2000; Lee and Song 2004). In order to provide the estimates of posterior distribution of latent variables, Bayesian approach can be conveniently used with its some advantages (Lee 2007):

1. To obtain point and interval estimates for the factor scores of each individual,
2. To compare the factor scores for different subjects,
3. To assess whether a particular subject's factor score has changed over time,
4. To identify outlying subjects in the tails of the latent variable distribution,
5. To define the relationships that may not be fully captured by the basic modeling structure.

4 Conclusion

The goals of Islam have a universal nature and are classified by the protection of faith, self, intellect, posterity, and wealth within *Maqāṣid* al-Sharīʿah context. The first result of this study is, what the higher objectives of the law are exactly, and how are they to be systematized by taking early and contemporary scholar's (experts) contributions into account. *Maqāṣid* al-Sharīʿah variables should be sorted by defining some authoritative reference points in *ijtihad* and *maslaha*.

In terms of social context of study, the results can be sorted as follows:

1. *Maqāṣid* al-Sharīʿah concept has been discussed in the science of *fiqh* and jurisprudence procedure. *Fiqh* and Islamic economics are areas that are associated with each other. But both are different methods and work areas. For this reason, the methodology of construction of *Maqāṣid* al-Sharīʿah index should be designed towards both Islamic economics and statistics disciplines.[14]

[14] "The methods of reasoning in *fiqh* and Islamic economics are not necessarily the same. While *fiqh* is well served by its methodology and methods set out in *usul al-fiqh*, Islamic economics should rely on a methodology and methods that suit its social and descriptive nature. Researchers' choice of methods and methodology is influenced by the basic unit of analysis in their discipline. By 'unit of analysis' is meant the object of the particular research—natural phenomena, legal rules, markets behaviors of an individual or a group. The kind of units of analysis in a field influences the choice of methods for the investigation

2. The objectives of Islam in matters covered by the induction method can be applied to an index.
3. The essentials (*ḍarūriyāt*), the complementary (*ḥājyyāt*), and embellishments (*tahsiniyāt-tekmilāt*) can be made into separate indexes.
4. The issue can be discussed in terms of *maṣlaḥah* and *mafsadah.*
5. According to the socioeconomic and political structure, Muslim societies should be categorized.[15]
6. Socioeconomic index in preparing existing national and/or international in nature can benefit from formal or informal index. However, they determine whether the targets must be compatible with Islam. Yet here next objective indicators can be included in the subjective elements.
7. Public and private sector activities can be addressed separately or together.[16]

of the truth in that discipline. Natural phenomena, for example, comprise entities that have no volition of their own; i.e. they do not choose how they behave; rather, how they behave is governed so-called 'natural laws'. For such phenomena, the appropriate methods are those that can discover such laws – they include observation, experimentation, induction, deduction and other scientific methods which are mostly aimed at producing descriptive analyses" (Saleem 2010).

"Economics as we know it is not built on observing the behavior of Muslim people. Despite its claims to universality, it is built on observation of, and imagining of, the behavior of people in the British Isles and western Europe in the 17th century onwards and, lately, in North America. Microeconomic analysis in Islamic perspective has to make up for this deficiency. Our method of doing so is to imagine a people working under the influence of Islamic teachings. We shall also supplement this by historical evidence of Muslim behavior. Also current data on Muslim behavior will be utilized" (Siddiqi 2005).

[15] Some authors indicate in their work like this: "In terms of sustainable development indicators, most of the modern rationales for the use of such indicators are very much ethical in nature despite their not originating from the Islamic worldview. Hence, Islam endorses these indicators, although efforts should be made to meet the need for a distinctively Islamic framework in the near future. It is worth reiterating that we do not wish to replace the existing conventional indicators of sustainability, but merely to supplement them with justifications from Shariah principles" (Duasa and Izyani 2008).

[16] "The Maqasid al- Shari`ah (the Shari`ah's goals/objectives) and the principles of maslahah (the interests) corporate social responsibility mean a set of standards of behavior to which a corporation subscribes in order to have a positive and productive impact on society" (Dusuki et al. 2007).

In the preparation of these indexes, some difficulties and shortcomings may be faced. One of them is the difficulty of measuring variables that are spiritual. In addition, the shortage of providing data may occur in Muslim societies. This study should be carried out by the IRTI, because it is appropriate for the organization's mission.

In this paper, we also propose two statistical approaches to create a high explanatory powered index for *Maqāṣid* al-Sharīʿah. The methods explained above require fewer assumptions and computational easiness. Bayesian approach to both analyses provides the latent variables to have free intercepts and variances and they prevent occurrence of improper solutions. Moreover, it has an advantage that allows for uncertainty in different aspects of the model in performing inferences.

Before creating a statistical index, obtaining, cleaning, inspecting, and transforming data are essential. The quality of data with the quality of measurement instruments should be checked out. Also, it is especially important to exactly determine the structure of the variables before the analysis. For this reason, the process of gathering and measuring information on variables of *Maqāṣid* al-Sharīʿah needs to be performed carefully. In addition, deciding how to get information—whether by direct observation, interviews, surveys, experiments and testing, or other methods—is essential to maintaining the integrity of index.

References

Abû Yûsuf. (1302 Hijri). Kitab al-Khiraj, Beirut

Abû Zahra, Muhammed. (1989). Târîkh al-Mezâhib al-Islamiyah, Beirut.

Akaike, H. (1987). Factor Analysis and AIC. *Psychometrika* 52, 317–332.

al-Kardawi, Yusuf. (2002). Devru'l-Kıyem wa'l-Akhlaq fi al-Iqtisad al-İslami. Beirut.

al-Omar, Fuad Abdullah. (2003). Muqaddima fi Tarikh al-Iqtisad al-Islami wa Tatawwruhu. Jeddah. Publication No. 62.

Ansari, A., and K. Jedidi. (2000). Bayesian Factor Analysis for Multilevel Binary Observations. *Psychometrika* 65(4), 475–496.

Bukhari, Sahih al-Bukhari. Kitab al-Tıbb, Ch 30 at https://sunnah.com/bukhari/76.

Buti, Said Ramadan. (1992). Ḍawābiṭ al-maṣlaḥah fī al-Sharīʿah al-Islāmīyah, Beirut.

Cessâs, Ahmed b. Ali Ebu Bekr er-Razî. (1992). Ahkâm Ul Qur'ân, Beirut.

Chapra, M. Umer. (2007). *The Islamic Vision of Development in the Light of Maqāṣid Al-Shari'ah*. Islamic Training and Research Institute, Islamic Development Bank.

Chapra, M. Umer. (2008). *The Islamic Vision of Development in the Light of Maqāṣid al-Sharī'ah.* Jeddah. IRTI Publication. (Turkish translation: Çakır, M.: Esen, A. *İslam'ın Hedefleri Işığında İslami Kalkınma Vizyonu.* İstanbul Sabahattin Zaim University publication. İstanbul-2013).
Çizakça, Murat. (2007). Democracy, Economic Development and Maqāṣid al-Sharī'ah. *Review of Islamic Economics* 1(1).
Deina, Abdelkader. (2003). Modernity, the Principles of Public Welfare (*maṣlaḥah*) and the End Goals of Sharia (maqa ̄sid) in Muslim Legal Thought. *Islam and Christian-Muslim Relations* 14(2), 163–174.
Dönmez, İbrahim Kâfi. (1981). İslâm Hukukunda Kaynak Kavramı, İstanbul (not published PhD thesis).
Duasa, Jarita, and Izyani Zulkifli. (2008). Sustainable Development in Islamic Economics: An Empirical Study on Muslim Countries. *Review of Islamic Economics* 12(1), 103–123.
Dunson, D., J. Palomo, and K. Bollen. (2005). Bayesian Structural Equation Modeling. SAMSI Technical Report.
Dusuki, Asyraf Wajdi, and A. Nurdianawati Irwani. (2007). Maqasid al-Shari`ah, *Maṣlaḥah*, and Corporate Social Responsibility. *The American Journal of Islamic Social Sciences* 24(1), 25–45.
Esen, Adem. (2007). Mal, Mülkiyet ve Piyasa (Goods, Property, and Market), IDB-IRTI, Jeddah.
Fabrigar, Leandre R., Duane T. Wegener, Robert C. MacCallum, and Erin J. Strahan. (1999). Evaluating the Use of Exploratory Factor Analysis in Psychological Research. *Psychological Methods* 4(3), 272–299.
Ghazzali, Ebû Hâmid Muhammed. (1971). Shifa al-ghalil fi bayan al-shabah wa-al-mukhil wa-masalik al-talil. ed. Hâmid Abîd el-Kubeysî, Bagdad.
Habing, B. (2003). Exploratory Factor Analysis. Website: http://www.stat.sc.edu/~habing/courses/530EFA.pdf.
Hirose, K., and S. Kawano. (2011). Bayesian Information Criterion and Selection of the Number of Factors in Factor Analysis Models. *Journal of Data Science* 9, 243–259.
Horn, R. V. (1993). *Statistical Indicators for the Economic & Social Sciences.* Cambridge University Press.
Ibn Ashur, Muhammad al-Tahir. (2006). *Treatise on Maqasid Al-Shariah.* USA: The International Institute of Islamic Thought.
Ibn Emîri'l-Hâc. (1996). et-Takrîr ve't-Tahbîr fi Ilmi'l-Usûl, Beirut.
Ibn Humâm, Kemâluddîn Muhammed b. Abdulvâhid. (2003). Sharhul Fathul Qadeer. Beirut.
Ibn Taymiyya, Ahmed b. Abdulhalîm. (1398 Hijri). Majmûu Fatâvâ, ed. A. b. Muhammed, Beirut.
Kano, Y. (1998). Improper Solutions in Exploratory Factor Analysis: Causes and Treatments. In A. Rizzi, M. Vichi, and H. Bock (Eds.), *Advances in Data Sciences and Classification.* Berlin: Springer.

Karaman, Hayrettin. (1985). İslam Hukukunda İctihat, Ankara.
Kline, R. B. (1998). *Principles and Practice of Structural Equation Modeling*. New York: The Guilford Press.
Krijnen, W. P., T. K. Dijkstra, and R. D. Gill. (1998). Conditions for Factor (in) Determinacy in Factor Analysis. *Psychometrika* 63, 359–367.
Lee, S. Y. (2007). *Handbook of Latent Variable and Related Models*. North-Holland: Oxford.
Lee, S., and X. Y. Song. (2004). Bayesian Model Comparison of Nonlinear Structural Equation Models with Missing Continuous and Ordinal Categorical Data. *British Journal of Mathematical and Statistical Psychology* 57(1), 131–150.
Lukacs, G. (1971). *Theory of the Novel*. trans. A. Bostock. London: Merlin Press.
Majallah al-Ahkam al-`Adliyah. (1293 Hijri). The Ottoman Courts Manual.
Olken, B. (2009). Corruption Perceptions vs. Corruption Reality. *Journal of Public Economics* 93(7–8), 950–964.
Palomo, J., D. Dunson, and K. Bollen. (2007). Bayesian Structural Equation Modeling. *Handbook of Computing and Statistics with Applications* 1, 163–188.
Pekcan, Ali. (2013). Makasıd Teorisine Giriş: Fıkhi Hükümlerin Gai Arka Planı. İstanbul: Hikmetevi Yayınları.
Press, S. J. (1982). *Applied Multivariate Analysis: Using Bayesian and Frequentist Methods of Inference*. New York: Krieger.
Quinn, K. M. (2004). Bayesian Factor Analysis for Mixed Ordinal and Continuous Responses. *Political Analysis* 12(04), 338–353.
Raysuni, A. (2005). *Imam al-Shatibi's Theory of the Higher Objectives and Intents of Islamic Law*. Herndon, Virginia: The International Institute of Islamic Thought.
Rietveld, T., and R. Van Hout. (1993). *Statistical Techniques for the Study of Language and Language Behaviour*. Berlin and New York: Mouton de Gruyter.
Saleem, Muhammad Yusuf. (2010). Methods and Methodologies in Fiqh and Islamic Economics. *Review of Islamic Economics* 14(1), 103–123.
Siddiqi, Muhammad Nejatullah. (2005). *Teaching Islamic Economics*. King Abdulaziz University Islamic Economics Research Centre.
Suhr, Diane. (2009). Principal Component Analysis vs. Exploratory Factor Analysis. *SUGI 30 Proceedings*. Retrieved 5 April 2012.
Toynbee, A. J. (1958). *A Study of History by D. J. Somervell*. Oxford.
West, M. (2004). Bayesian Model Assessment in Factor Analysis. *Statistica Sinica* 14, 41–67.
Williams, B. (1985). *Ethics and the Limits of Philosophy*. Cambridge, UK.
Zerkâ, Mustafa Ahmed. (1998). el-Istıslâh ve'l-Mesâlihi'l-Mürsele fi'ş-Şerîati'l-İslamiyye ve Usûli Fıkhihâ, Damascus.

CHAPTER 8

An Index of Well-Being Based on *Maqāṣid* al-Sharīʿah and Fuzzy Set Theory

Moussa Larbani and Ismail Nizam

1 Introduction

The idea of expressing the objectives of Islamic, Law (al-Sharīʿah), the *Maqāṣid* al-Sharīʿah, goes back to works of early prominent Muslim scholars Al-Juwayni (1979), Al-Ghazali (1970) and Al-Shatibi (1302H). However, in the time of these scholars and later, no research was undertaken to explore the potential of *Maqāṣid* as a tool for the measurement of well-being of a society, while in the West, with the introduction of quantitative methods into human sciences, many indexes were developed to measure the well-being of a society such as the gross domestic production (GDP), Human Development Index (HDI), etc. See OCDE (1982) for more details. Most of these indexes are not comprehensive and do not include the social and psychological dimensions

M. Larbani (✉)
School of Mathematics and Statistics,
Carleton University, Ottawa, ON, Canada

I. Nizam
FTMS College, Cyberjaya, Kuala Lumpur, Malaysia

S. S. Ali (ed.), *Towards a Maqāṣid al-Sharīʿah Index of Socio-Economic Development*, Palgrave Studies in Islamic Banking, Finance, and Economics,
https://doi.org/10.1007/978-3-030-12793-0_8

of human life. Moreover, they could not predict the devastating financial and economic crises that occurred in the last decade and before. Therefore, they came under severe critics Stiglitz (2009). In the last decade, Chapra (2009), referring to the work of Ibn Khaldun, pointed out that *Maqāṣid* al-Sharīʿah could be used as the components of a socio-economic system. This work revived the interest of Muslim scholars to explore the theoretical and practical potential of *Maqāṣid* al-Sharīʿah in social sciences. However, Chapra did not go beyond the theoretical formulation. Rusita et al. (2013) extended the work of Chapra by Sekaran's operationalization method to include elements and dimensions, but did not reach the measurement stage, which is the essence of operationalization. In 2009, Larbani and Mustafa formulated an operational model for decision making based on *Maqāṣid* Al-Sharīʿah for resource allocation. This work opened a new direction of research called, the *quantitative operationalization of Maqāṣid* al-Sharīʿah. Recently, Bachelor (2013) has introduced an Islamic rating index of well-being for Muslim countries, and Anto (2011) has formulated an Islamic Human Development Index (I-HDI). Both indexes are based on *Maqāṣid* al-Sharīʿah and are measurable. Bachelor's index lacks comprehensiveness For instance, he has omitted financial indicators that are essential for financial and economic crisis prevention. Moreover, he did not purify some indexes as the GDP from non-Islamic content. As for the Anto's index, it is also not comprehensive and relies more on conventional indexes and suffers the same drawbacks as Bachelor's.

As *Maqāṣid* al-Sharīʿah are related to all aspects of human life, including material and non-material or intangible, the construction of an overall index for socio-economic well-being would involve two difficulties: The first is the measurement of different variables or indicators that are used to explain or evaluate each of the five *Maqāṣid*. The second difficulty is the aggregation of the different measurements of each *Maqsad* into one value than the aggregation of the resulting individual measurements of all the five *Maqāṣid* into a unique value, that is, the overall index. As for the first difficulty, many indicators are measurable as the GDP, the birth rate, public debt, etc. However, there are also many indicators, especially, those related to the *Maqāṣid* of *Dīn* and *Nafs* as behavior, happiness, *imān*, etc. that are very difficult to measure. As for the second difficulty, even if one succeeds to measure all the parameters, he/she has to face another problem, the aggregation of measurement made at different scales and dimensions, including material and immaterial ones, into a unique meaningful value that would reflect the aggregated values.

This paper is a further contribution to the operationalization of *Maqāṣid* direction of research initiated in Larbani and Mustafa (2009). Indeed, we introduce an index of well-being of a nation based on *Maqāṣid* al-Sharīʿah and fuzzy sets. The use of fuzzy sets considerably reduces the difficulty of measuring immaterial indicators, eliminates the problem of aggregation of measurement of different scales and dimensions, and easy to compute.

The rest of the paper is organized as follows: Section 2 presents the *Maqāṣid* al-Sharīʿah used in this work. Section 3 presents briefly the fuzzy sets. Section 4 introduces the overall well-being index. Section 5 concludes the paper.

2 *MAQĀṢID* AL-SHARĪʿAH

Many definitions of *Maqāṣid* al-Sharīʿah have been introduced by prominent early Muslim Scholars as Al-Ghazali (1970), Al-Shatibi (1302), and Al-Juwayni (1979). Some contemporary scholars have also made a contribution to the theory of *Maqāṣid* al-Sharīʿah as Ibn Ashur (1998), Atya (2003), Al-Raysuni (2006) and Najjar (2006), including the introduction of new *Maqāṣid* as freedom, environmental protection, etc. Although the scholars differ on a set of *Maqāṣid* to be considered and on their ordering, they all agree that the ultimate goal of Sharīʿah is serving the interests of all human beings (*al-masālih*) and protecting them from harm (*al-mafāsid*).

Al-Ghazali (d. 1111 CE) definition of *Maqāṣid* emphasizes the sharī'ah concern for safeguarding the five objectives as follows (cited in Dusuki and Bouheraoua 2011):

> The very objective of the Sharīʿah is to promote the well-being of the people, which lies in safeguarding their faith (dīn), their lives (Nafs), their intellect (ʻaql), their posterity (nasl) and their wealth (māl). Whatever ensures the safeguarding of these five serves public interest and is desirable, and whatever hurts them is against public interest and its removal is desirable.

For the sake of simplicity of presentation, in this paper, we stick to the basic five *Maqāṣid* introduced by Al-Ghazali. However, the developed index can be adapted to any number of *Maqāṣid*. Another reason for the use of Al-Ghazali's five *Maqāṣid* is to keep the mathematical model as simple as possible. Moreover, almost all the aspects of human life can be related directly or indirectly to the five *Maqāṣid*. For instance, justice can be related to the *Maqsad* of *Dīn*. Environmental protection can be related to *Nafs* because deterioration of the environment ultimately leads to deterioration of *Nafs*. It can also be related to the *Maqsad* of *Māl* because the resources necessary to develop wealth through production come from the natural environment. In this paper, we do not use the ordering of *Maqāṣid* as given above by Al-Ghazali; rather, we consider all the *Maqāṣid* as having the same importance or weights. Indeed, the importance of a *Maqsad* at some point in time depends on the current situation and attention allocation which generate a prioritization of *Maqāṣid* and actions. The priority will be given to the *Maqsad* that is most affected or threatened.

3 Fuzzy Sets

In this section, we give a brief introduction to fuzzy sets. Fuzzy sets will be used in the next section to measure the indicators related to each *Maqsad* and the overall well-being index. We shall first give the formal definition of a fuzzy set.

Definition 3.1. Let X be a universal set. A fuzzy set A in X is characterized by a membership function $\mu_A(x)$ which associates with each point in X a real number in the interval $[0, 1]$, with the value $\mu_A(x)$ at x representing the "grade of membership" of x in A.

The nearer the value of $\mu_A(x)$ is to 1, the higher is the grade of membership of x in A. When $\mu_A(x) = 1$, we say that x belongs fully or completely to A and when $\mu_A(x) = 0$, we say that x is not in A. When A is a set in ordinary sense of the term, its membership function $\mu_A(x)$ can take only two values 0 or 1, with $\mu_A(x) = 1$ or 0 according as x does or does not belong to A.

The set $\{x \in X/\mu_A(x) > 0\}$ is called the support of the fuzzy set A. The set Kernel $(A) = \{x \in X/\mu_A(x) = 1\}$ is the core of the fuzzy set A.

Fuzzy sets have been introduced by Zadeh (1965). In the last two decades, they have been applied extensively and successfully in almost all areas of human activity as industry, medicine, management, economics, etc. For more details about fuzzy sets, we refer the reader to Zimmermann (2001).

Example 3.1 Let us consider the set of "young people." This set is not a set in the ordinary sense as its shape is not precisely known. For instance, a 20-year-old person is definitely young, a 70-year-old person is definitely old, but it is difficult to classify a 38-year-old person as young or not young. The fuzzy set "young people" can be characterized by the following membership function (Fig. 1).

A 30-year-old person has a membership grade or degree of 0.8 to the fuzzy set "young people," while a 70-year-old person has a very small membership grade of 0.1. This reflects the imprecision in human judgment and the power of fuzzy sets to express it.

A fuzzy set can also express imprecise values. For instance, the body temperature of a healthy person should be around 37. Being

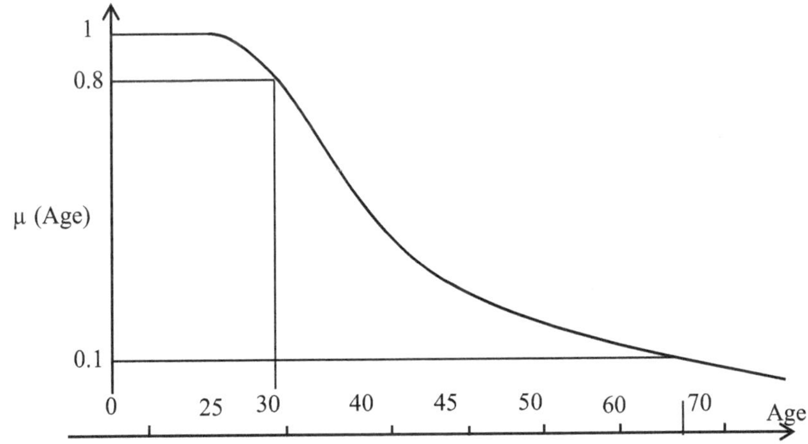

Fig. 1 Membership function of the fuzzy set "young people" (*Source* Authors)

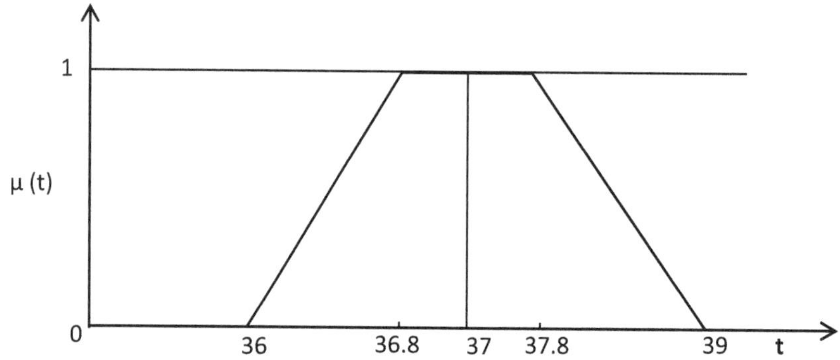

Fig. 2 Membership function of the fuzzy set "around 37" (*Source* Authors)

"around 37" can be represented by a fuzzy set, the membership of which is (Fig. 2).

When temperature, *t*, of a person is between [36.8, 37.8], the membership is $\mu_{\text{Around 37}}(x) = 1$. When the temperature is below 36.8 or above 37.8, the membership declines sharply. When a person's temperature is below 36 or above 39, the membership grade is 0, meaning that the person may be sick. The membership function is

$$\mu_{\text{Around 37}}(x) = \begin{cases} 0 & \textit{if} \quad 0 \leq t \leq 1.2 \\ \frac{t-36}{36.8-36} & \textit{if} \quad 36 < t < 36.8 \\ 1 & \textit{if} \quad 36.8 < t < 37.8 \\ \frac{39-t}{39-37.8} & \textit{if} \quad 37.8 \leq t < 39 \\ 0 & \textit{if} \quad 39 \leq t \end{cases} \tag{1}$$

Similarly, an economic or social indicator that should remain around some target value like the birth rate or inflation can be represented by a fuzzy set. In the next section, we will see how fuzzy sets can be used to construct a comprehensive well-being index based on *Maqāṣid* al-Sharīʿah.

Definition 3.2 Zadeh (1975) A linguistic variable is a variable whose values are words or sentences of a natural or artificial language.

For example, age is a linguistic variable if its values are linguistic rather than numerical, e.g. young, not young, very young, quite young, old, not old, very old, etc. rather than 20, 21, 23, etc. A fuzzy set is used to express the compatibility of numerical values with linguistic values. This is illustrated in Example 4.1. We will use a special linguistic variable to evaluate states of *Maqāṣid* in the next section.

4 *Maqāṣid* al-Sharīʿah and Fuzzy Sets Based Index of Well-Being

In this section, we introduce a *Maqāṣid* and fuzzy set-based index of well-being. The index uses the five *Maqāṣid* as defined by Al-Ghazali as the main indicators of the well-being. As the *Maqāṣid* are too general to be measured or estimated or evaluated, each *Maqsad* will be considered as a dependent variable of some independent variables related to it. For instance, public debt and poverty levels may be considered as independent variables related to the *Maqsad* of *Māl* (Fig. 3).

For the ease of presentation, denote the five *Maqāṣid*, *Dīn*, *Nafs*, *ʿAql*, *Posterity*, and *Māl* by $M_1, M_2, M_3, M_4,$ and M_5 respectively. For each *Maqsad* $\boldsymbol{M_i}$, $i = 1, 2, \ldots 5$, let $x_{i,j}\, j = 1, 2, \ldots n_i$, be the related independent variables, where n_i is their number. Graphically, this can be represented by the following figure (Fig. 4).

To each independent variable $x_{i,j}\, j = 1, 2, .., n_i$, and *Maqsad* $\boldsymbol{M_i}, i = 1, 2, \ldots, 5$, we associate a fuzzy set $\check{x}_{i,j}$ defined on the possible states of the variable. Here, we have five cases:

Case 1 The independent variable $x_{i,j}$ is numerically measurable and the more the better, then one can easily construct the membership function of the fuzzy set $\check{x}_{i,j}$. For instance, if $x_{i,j}$ is the GDP of the country,

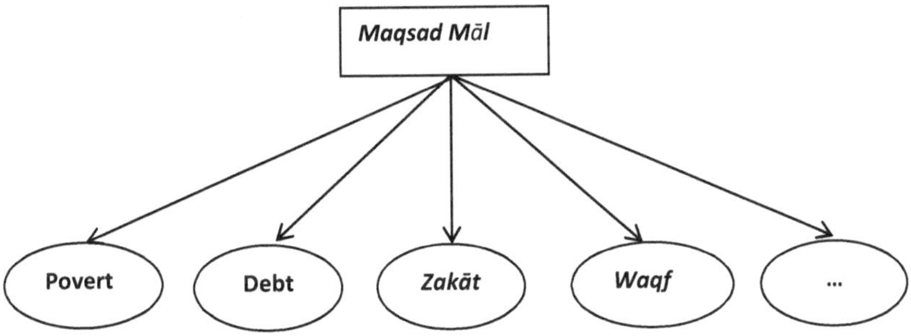

Fig. 3 Structure of *Māl* Index (*Source* Authors)

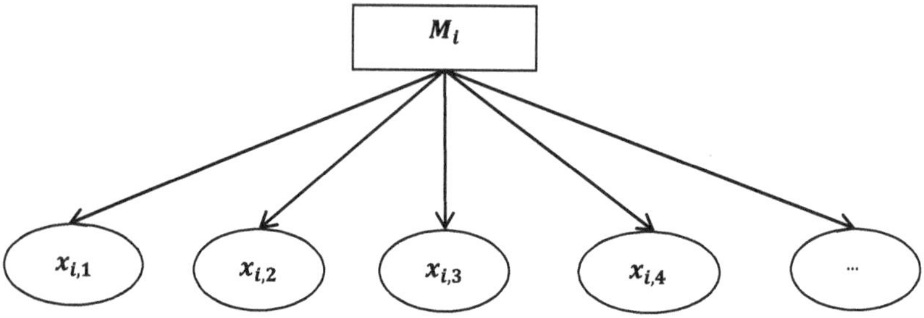

Fig. 4 *Maqsad* M_i and its independent variables (*Source* Authors)

the support of the fuzzy set $\check{x}_{i,j}$ is the interval [0, MaxGDP], where MaxGDP is a maximum or target value for GDP. Then the membership function $\mu_{i,j}(x)$ is defined by

$$\mu_{i,j}(x) = \frac{x}{\text{MaxGDP}}$$

where x is the observed GDP value. The form of this membership function is as follows.

Case 2 The variable $x_{i,j}$ is measurable, but it is such that the lesser the better like public debt, one may use a different formula for the membership function of the fuzzy set $\check{x}_{i,j}$ as follows:

$$\mu_{i,j}(x) = 1 - \frac{x}{\text{MaxDebt}}$$

The support of the fuzzy set $\check{x}_{i,j}$ is [0, MaxDebt], where Maxdebt is the maximum possible for the debt beyond which the collapse of the government is almost a certainty.

Case 3 The variable $x_{i,j}$ is measurable, but it is such that it should be around some desirable value. For instance, the birth rate should be around some value, let say 2.5%, for a high birth rate may be unsustainable, while a low birth rate many lead to population aging. Then a fuzzy set $\check{x}_{i,j}$, being around 2.5% with a membership function of trapezoidal type as depicted in Fig. 2, is the most appropriate. The corresponding membership function is similar to (1) with appropriate thresholds.

Case 4 When it is not possible to numerically measure the variable $x_{i,j}$, one may use a linguistic variable to express its state as the variable taking the following values Extremely Bad (EB), Very Bad (VB), Bad (B), Moderate (M), Good (G), Very Good (VG), and Excellent (E). For ease of presentation, we denote the states by $S_1, S_2, \ldots, S_7$ respectively. Then a fuzzy set has to be constructed based on these states as follows. For each state, we associate a membership value with the interval [0,1], $\mu_{i,j}(S_p)$, $p = 1, 2, \ldots, 7$. Then for any state S in between two states S_p and S_{p+1}, $p \leq 6$, $\mu_{i,j}(S)$ is defined by $\mu_{i,j}(S) = \frac{\mu_{i,j}(S_{p+1}) + \mu_{i,j}(S_p)}{2}$, for any state S in beyond or better than the state S_7, $\mu_{i,j}(S)$ is defined by $\mu_{i,j}(S) = \frac{1+\mu_{i,j}(S_7)}{2}$ and for any state S below the state S_1, $\mu_{i,j}(S)$ is defined by $\mu_{i,j}(S) = \mu_{i,j}(S_1)/2$.

The function $\mu_{i,j}(S)$ can assume any other types of non-decreasing function between the states $S_1, S_2, \ldots, S_6$. For illustration, assume that $\mu_{i,j}(S_p) = 0.1p$, $p = 1, 2, \ldots, 6$ and $\mu_{i,j}(S_7) = 0.8$.

The membership function will look as follows.

Case 5 The decision maker wants to evaluate some numerically measurable independent variable or indicator $x_{i,j}$, by a linguistic variable. For example, the decision maker wants to evaluate the health care system by the ratio of the number of doctors per 1000 citizens. He/she may set the highest ratio in the world as a benchmark, then evaluate the ratio of his/her country using the linguistic variable of the Case 4. Then use the membership function of the form presented in Fig. 5 to incorporate this health care evaluation in the *Maqsad Nafs* evaluation.

Assume now that the fuzzy sets $\check{x}_{i,j}$,$j = 1, 2, .., n_i$ of all the independent variables $x_{i,j}, j = 1, 2, \ldots, n_i$, related to *Maqsad* $\boldsymbol{M_i}$, then the overall individual index of the *Maqsad* $\boldsymbol{M_i}$ is defined by

$$\pi_i\left(\left(z_{i,j}\right)_{\boldsymbol{i,j=1,2,\ldots n_i}}\right) = \prod_{j=1}^{n_i} \mu_{i,j}\left(z_{i,j}\right) \tag{2}$$

where $z_{i,j}$ is a numerical value if the independent variable $x_{i,j}$ is measurable or a state S if the variable $x_{i,j}$ is not measurable. That is the index π_i of the *Maqsad* M_i is the product of all the membership functions of the fuzzy sets of its independent variables.

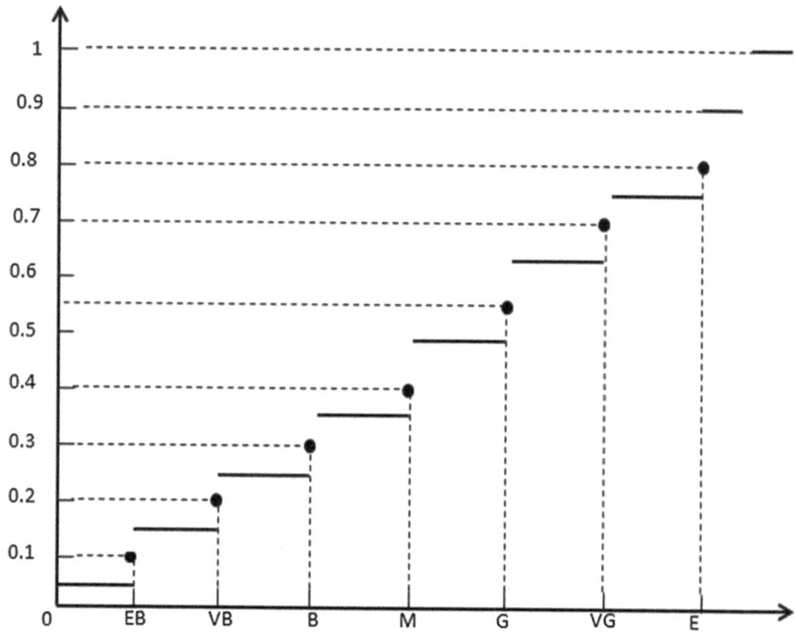

Fig. 5 Membership function for a linguistic variable (*Source* Authors)

Now we are able to formulate an overall index for the well-being of a society by aggregating the individual indexes of the five *Maqāṣid*, $\pi_i, i = 1, 2, \ldots, 5$ as follows:

$$\pi(\pi_1, \pi_2, \ldots, \pi_5) = \frac{\sum_{i=1}^{5} \pi_i\left(\left(z_{i,j}\right)_{i,j=1,2,\ldots n_i}\right)}{5} \tag{3}$$

In other words, the overall index of well-being is the average of the indexes $\pi_i, i = 1, 2, \ldots, 5$ of the five *Maqāṣid*, $M_i, i = 1, 2, \ldots, 5$. As the index π is a number in the interval [0, 1], one can use the fuzzy membership function in Fig. 5 of the linguistic variable introduced in the Case 4 to give a linguistic evaluation of it. This value would help decision makers have an idea about how good is the obtained value π. One needs to locate the index value in the vertical axis then find the corresponding linguistic evaluation in the horizontal axis. Other forms of aggregation may be used. One of them is the product of the five *Maqāṣid* indexes

$\pi_i, i = 1, 2, \ldots, 5$, but the index π will be small as a result of multiplication of numbers smaller than 1.

Let us now explain the computation process of the introduced overall well-being index in steps.

Step 1. Identify the independent variables $x_{i,j}, j = 1, 2, \ldots, n_i$ of each *Maqsad* $M_i, i = 1, 2, \ldots, 5$.

Step 2. Construct the fuzzy sets $\check{x}_{i,j}$ of each of the independent variable $x_{i,j}, j = 1, 2, \ldots, n_i$, associated with each *Maqsad* $\boldsymbol{M}_i, i = 1, 2, \ldots, 5$. The membership function can be constructed according to the Cases 1–5 presented above.

Step 3. Measure the variables that are measurable and determine or assign values to linguistic variables, and as a result we get the values $\left(z_{i,j}\right)_{i=1,2,\ldots 5, j=1,2,\ldots n_i}$.

Step 4. Compute the value of the membership functions $\mu_{i,j}\left(z_{i,j}\right)$ of the fuzzy set $\check{x}_{i,j}$ of each of the independent variable $x_{i,j}, j = 1, 2, \ldots, n_i$, associated with each *Maqsad* $\boldsymbol{M}_i, i = 1, 2, \ldots, 5$. As a result we get the values $\mu_{i,j}\left(z_{i,j}\right), i = 1, 2, \ldots, 5, j = 1, 2, \ldots, n_i$.

Step 5. Compute the individual index π_i of each *Maqsad* $\boldsymbol{M}_i, i = 1, 2, \ldots, 5$ by Formula (2). As a result we get the five indexes $\pi_i, i = 1, 2, \ldots, 5$.

Step 6. Compute the overall well-being index π using Formula (3).

Example 4.1. For illustration purpose, we give the following hypothetical example. Assume that for some country C the following data are available.

- For *Dīn Maqsad*
  $x_{1,1}$– The ratio of people who went to Hajj to the quota allowed is 0.7 in the current year.
  $x_{1,2}$– The result of a survey on the religiosity of Imaams indicating that the level of religiosity is moderate among people on an ordinal scale such as Extremely Bad (EB), Very Bad (VB), Bad (B), Moderate (M), Good (G), Very Good (VG), and Excellent (E).

- For *Nafs Maqsad*
  $x_{2,1}$– The ratio of number of doctors to 1000 citizens is $1.5/1000 = 0.0015$.
- For *Maqsad ʿAql*
  $x_{3,1}$– The proportion of students who left school before university level in the current year is 10%.
  $x_{3,2}$– The literacy level is 90%.
- For *Maqsad Nasl*
  $x_{4,1}$– Birth rate is 1.8%.
  $x_{4,2}$– Mortality rate at birth per 100 is 7% (a ratio of 0.07).
- For *Māl Maqsad*
  $x_{5,1}$– The growth rate is 3.7%.
  $x_{5,2}$– The ratio of public debt to GDP is 0.7.

Step 1. It is straightforward.

Steps 2 and 3. Construction of the fuzzy sets corresponding to the indicators. First, we categorize the indicators into (i) the more the better and not requiring benchmark value, which includes $x_{1,1}$, $x_{3,2}$ (ii) the more the better and requiring a benchmark value, which includes $x_{2,1}$ and $x_{5,1}$ (iii) the lesser the better requiring benchmark or tolerance level, which includes $x_{3,1}, x_{4,2}$ and $x_{3,2}$, (iv) required to be around some target value, which includes $x_{4,1}$, and (v) linguistic indictor, which includes $x_{1,2}$.

i. For the indicators $x_{1,1}$, $x_{3,2}$, the membership function of the corresponding fuzzy sets can be constructed by using the formulas

$$\mu_{1,1}(x_{1,1}) = x_{1,1} \text{ and } \mu_{3,2}(x_{3,2}) = x_{3,2}, \text{ respectively.} \tag{4}$$

ii. The indicators $x_{2,1}$ and $x_{5,1}$ require some benchmark value for 100% does not make any practical sense. Let us assume that $6/1000 = 0.006$ is the benchmark value for $x_{2,1}$ and 12% for $x_{5,1}$, then the membership functions of the corresponding fuzzy sets are

$$\mu_{2,1}(x_{2,1}) = \frac{x_{2,1}}{0.006} \text{ and } \mu_{5,1}(x_{5,1}) = \frac{x_{5,1}}{0.12}, \text{ respectively} \tag{5}$$

For example, the membership function $\mu_{5,1}(x_{5,1})$ has the following shape

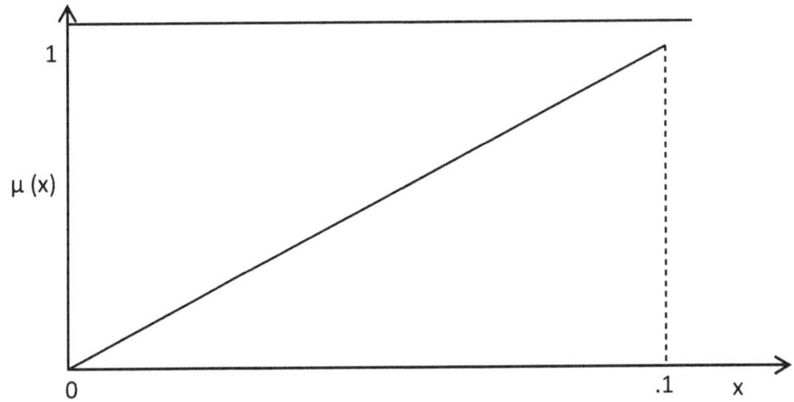

Fig. 6 Membership functions of the corresponding fuzzy sets (*Source* Authors)

iii. The indicators $x_{3,1}$, $x_{4,2}$, and $x_{5,2}$ are of the type: the lesser the better. They all require some tolerance level or maximum value because 100% or more does not make practical sense. Let us assume that for $x_{3,1}$, 40% is the tolerance level; for $x_{4,2}$ the tolerance level is 15%; and for $x_{5,2}$ the tolerance level or ceiling is 120%. Therefore, the membership functions of the corresponding fuzzy sets are (Fig. 6).

$$\mu_{3,1}(x_{3,1}) = 1 - \frac{x_{3,1}}{0.4}, \mu_{4,2}(x_{4,2}) = 1 - \frac{x_{4,2}}{0.15} \quad \text{and} \\ \mu_{5,2}(x_{5,2}) = 1 - \frac{x_{5,2}}{1.2}, \tag{6}$$

respectively. For example, the membership function $\mu_{5,2}(x_{5,2})$ has the shape (Fig. 7).

iv. The indicator $x_{4,1}$ is desired to be around some target value. Let us assume that the birth rate is desired to be around 2.5% to avoid both the aging of the population and its unsustainable increase. We define the membership function of the associated fuzzy set "around 25" similarly to the membership of the fuzzy set "around 37 degrees" in Fig. 7, (Fig. 8).

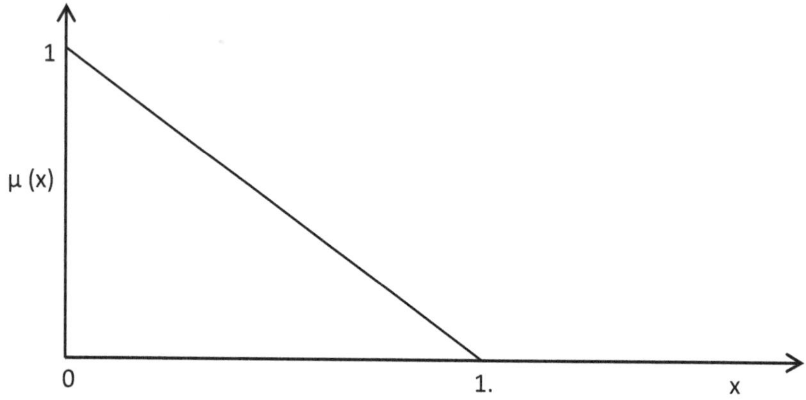

Fig. 7 Membership function shape (*Source* Authors)

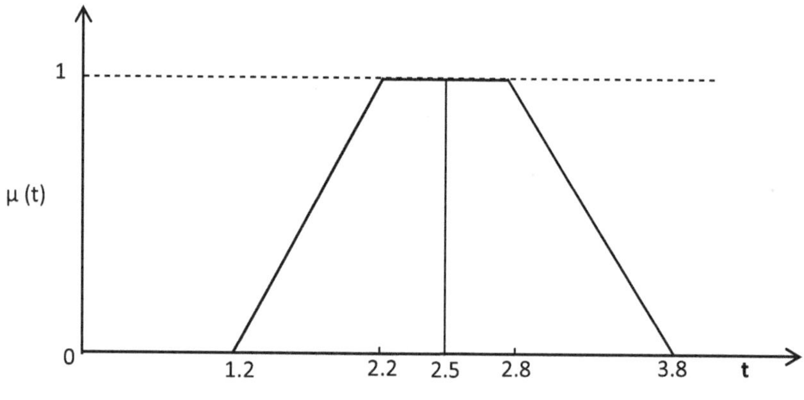

Fig. 8 Membership function of the associated fuzzy set "around 25" (*Source* Authors)

The decision maker has to specify the meaning of "being around 2.5." For instance, a birth rate of 3.8 and above or 1.2 and below are not accepted. Any rate between 2.2 and 2.8 implies that the objective of being around 2.5 is reached. The analytical form of the membership function is as follows:

$$\mu_{4,1}(x) = \mu_{\text{Around2.5}}(x) = \begin{cases} 0 & \text{if} \quad 0 \le x \le 1.2 \\ \frac{x-1.2}{2.2-1.2} & \text{if} \quad 1.2 < x < 2.2 \\ 1 & \text{if} \quad 2.2 < x < 2.8 \\ \frac{3.8-x}{3.8-2.8} & \text{if} \quad 2.8 \le x < 3.8 \\ 0 & \text{if} \quad 3.8 \le x \end{cases} \tag{7}$$

v. The indicator $x_{1,2}$ is linguistic and takes values in the ordinal scale Extremely Bad (EB), Very Bad (VB), Bad (B), Moderate (M), Good (G), Very Good (VG), and Excellent (E). The decision maker may choose the membership function $\mu_{1,2}(x_{1,2})$ of the corresponding fuzzy set as described in Case 4 above and depicted in Fig. 5.

Step 4. Now we are able to compute the values of all the nine membership function for all the indicators based on the given data:

For *Maqsad Dīn*
$\mu_{1,1}(0.7) = 0.7$, see Formula (4), $\mu_{1,2}(\text{Moderate}) = 0.4$ (based on Fig. 4).

For *Maqsad Nafs*
$\mu_{2,1}(0.0015) = \frac{0.0015}{0.006} = 0.25$, see Formula (5).

For *Maqsad 'Aql*
$\mu_{3,1}(0.1) = 1 - \frac{0.1}{0.4} = 0.75$, see Formula (6), $\mu_{3,2}(0.9) = 0.9$, see Formula (4).

For *Maqsad Nasl*
$\mu_{4,1}(1.8) = 0.6$, see Formula (7), $\mu_{4,2}(0.07) = 1 - \frac{0.07}{0.15} = 0.41$, see Formula (6).

For *Maqsad Māl*
$\mu_{5,1}(0.037) = \frac{0.037}{0.12} = 0.308$, see Formula (5), $\mu_{5,2}(0.7) = 1 - \frac{0.7}{1.2} = 0.58$, see Formula (6).

Step 5. Computation of indexes of individual *Maqāṣid*

For *Maqsad Dīn*

$$\pi_1 = 0.7 \times 0.4 = 0.28$$

For *Maqsad Nafs*

$$\pi_2 = 0.25$$

For *Maqsad ʿAql*

$$\pi_3 = 0.75 \times 0.9 = 0.675$$

For *Maqsad Nasl*

$$\pi_4 = 0.6 \times 0.41 = 0.246$$

For *Maqsad Māl*

$$\pi_5 = 0.308 \times 0.58 = 0.178$$

Step 6. Computation of the overall well-being index.

$$\pi = (0.28 + 0.35 + 0.675 + 0.246 + 0.178)/5 = 0.346$$

Evaluating the overall well-being index using the fuzzy set with the membership function in Fig. 5 that is associated with the linguistic variable whose values are Extremely Bad (EB), Very Bad (VB), Bad (B), Moderate (M), Good (G), Very Good (VG), and Excellent (E), we obtain that the considered country is between Bad and Moderate statuses. One can also notice that individually, *Maqāṣid Dīn* and *Nafs* are at bad status. This means that the country has to develop a strategy to improve all the *Maqāṣid* with more resource allocation to *Maqāṣid Dīn* and *Nafs*.

Remark 4.1 The introduced overall well-being index has the following unique features.

1. It can incorporate variables or indicators that are not measurable when it is possible to use a linguistic variable to express them. Therefore, it can operationally incorporate more indicators or variables than the existing indexes.
2. It can incorporate indicators that are assumed to be around some target value (limited excess and/or slack are allowed) and indicators that should remain in some fuzzy range.
3. It can aggregate indicators that are measured in different scales or dimensions via fuzzy sets.
4. It computes individual index for each *Maqsad*, which allows a decision maker to analyze the status of each *Maqsad* individually.

5. It is operational in the sense that it is easy to compute once real data are available and can incorporate as many variables or indicators as one wants.

5 Conclusion

In this paper, we have introduced an overall well-being index of a nation based on *Maqāṣid* al-Sharīʿah. Its unique feature is that it uses fuzzy sets for aggregating variables of different dimensions or scales and allows the incorporation of non-measurable indicators when they can be expressed by linguistic variables. We have shown how to construct a fuzzy set associated with each independent variable or indicator to make the index operational and easy to compute. We intend to use this index to evaluate the overall well-being of Malaysia in the nearer future; we are at the stage of data collection. Later, we apply the index to OIC countries.

References

Al-Ghazali, I. (1970). *Al-Mustasfaa min ʿilm al-usul. Vol 1.* Baghdad: Muthannaa.

Al-Juwayni, Abu al-Maalis. (1979). *Al-burhan fi usul al-fiqh.* (Ed.). Abdul Azim al-Dib. Dar al-Ansar, Cairo.

Al-Raysuni, A. (2006). *Imam Al-Shatibi's Theory of the Higher Objectives and Intents of Islamic Law.* Petailing Jaya: Islamic Book Trust.

Al-Shatibi. (1302H). *Al-Muwafaqaat fi Usool al-Shari'a.* Tunisia: Dawlat Al-Tunisia.

Anto, M. H. (2011). Introducing an Islamic Human Development Index (I-HDI) to Measure Development in OIC Countries. *Islamic Economics Studies, 19*(2), 69–95.

Atya, D. D. (2003). *Nahwa Taf'il al-Maqāṣid al-Shari'ah.* Damascus, Syria. International Institute of Islamic Thought, Dar Al-Fikr.

Batchelor, D. A.-F. (2013). A New Islamic Rating Index of Well-Being for Muslim Countries. *Islam and Civilisational Renewal, 274*(1705), 1–27.

Chapra, M. U. (2009). *The Islamic Vision of Development in the Light of Maqaasid Al-Shari'ah.* Jeddah: IRTI.

Dusuki, A. W., & Bouheraoua, S. (2011). *The Framework of Maqasid Al-shariah (objectives of the Shari'ah) and Its Implications for Islamic Banking.* International Shari'ah Research Academy for Islamic Finance (ISRA).

Ibn 'Ashur, M. al-Tahir. (1998). *Maqāṣid al-Shari'ah al-Islamiyyah*, ed., al-Misawi, Muhammad al-Tahir, Kuala Lumpur, al-Basa'ir.

Ibn Khaldun, Al Mukadima,

Larbani, M., Mustafa, O. M. A. (2009). *Decision Making Tools for the Allocation of Investible Resources Based on Al-Maqāṣid Al-Sharī'ah Framework.* International Conference of Islamic Economics (ICEI2009), 28–29 April 2009, Kuala Lumpur, Malaysia.
Najjar, A. M. (2006). *Maqaasid al-Shari'ah bi-Ab'aad Jadeedah.* Beirut: Daarul Al-Gharb Al-Islaamee.
OECD. (1982). *The OECD List of Social Indicators.* Washington, DC: OECD Social Indicator Development Programme.
Rusita, M. A., Selama, A. Y., Mohamed Aslam, H., Mustafa O. M., & Oziev, G. (2013). *The Integrated Development Index (i-dex): A New Comprehensive Approach to Measuring Human Development.* 9th International conference on Islamic Economics and Finance, 9–10 September 2013, Istanbul, Turkey.
Stiglitz, J. E., Sen, A., & Fitoussi, J.-P. (2009). *Report by the Commission on the Measurement of Economic Performance and Social Progress.* Paris, France: www.stiglitz-sen-fitoussi.fr.
Zadeh, L. A. (1965). Fuzzy Sets. *Information and Control, 8*, 338–353.
Zadeh, L. A. (1975). The Concept of Linguistic Variable and Its Application to Approximate Reasoning. *Information Science, 8*(3), 199–249.
Zimmermann, H. J. (2001). *Fuzzy Set Theory and Its Application.* Norwell, MA: Kluwer Academic Publisher. 199–249.

CHAPTER 9

Socioeconomic Philosophy of Conventional and Islamic Economics: Articulating *Hayat-e-Tayyaba* Index (HTI) on the Basis of *Maqāṣid* al-Sharīʿah

Muhammad Mubashir Mukhtar, Hafiz Muhammad Sarfraz Nihal, Hafiz Abdul Rauf, Waleed Wasti and Muhammad Shahid Qureshi

1 Tracing the Foundations of Conventional Economics[1]

The shape of economics that we currently see in front of us has been powerfully influenced by an eighteenth-century modern philosopher, Immanuel Kant.[2] His pioneering work Critique of Pure Reason (1781)

[1]We seek forgiveness from Allah (*swt*) for the blasphemous statements in this chapter.

[2]In this paper, we will focus more on the works of Immanuel Kant. His workings are a combination of great thinkers, such as, Gottfried Wilhelm von Leibniz, Christian von

M. M. Mukhtar (✉) · H. A. Rauf · W. Wasti · M. S. Qureshi
Center for Entrepreneurial Development (CED), Institute of Business Administration (IBA), Karachi, Pakistan

S. S. Ali (ed.), *Towards a Maqāṣid al-Sharīʿah Index of Socio-Economic Development*, Palgrave Studies in Islamic Banking, Finance, and Economics,
https://doi.org/10.1007/978-3-030-12793-0_9

and his final working notes published as Opus Postumum made the foundations for the current socioeconomic discourse, while embossing the superiority of human reason over the divine commandments. His philosophy has been accepted and implemented by international development agencies, such as, International Covenant on Economic, Social and Cultural Rights (1966), enforce by United Nations UNESCO—based on Kant's practical ideas published in Categorical Imperative and its Implications (1785) (Schönfeld 2012: 40).

Kant's major contribution is on transcendental idealism, in which he argues that "the highest standpoint of transcendental philosophy is that which unites God and the world synthetically, under one principle. Nature and freedom" (Kant 1993: 226, 21:23). Here, the "one principle" indicates toward the human autonomy or full freedom, in which there is no role of God or any supreme authority. This phenomenon can

Wolfius, David Hume, and further taken up by Georg Wilhelm Friedrich Hegel. And to sum up the importance of Kant in contemporary times: "It is hardly necessary at the present day to produce any arguments in support of such a view. The number of books on Kant's philosophy, published during the last century in almost every language of the world, speaks for itself. There is no single philosopher of any note, even among those who are decidedly opposed to Kant, who has not acknowledged his pre-eminence among modern philosophers. The great systems of Fichte, Schelling, Hegel, Herbart, and Schopenhauer branched off from Kant, and now, after a century has passed away, people begin to see that those systems were indeed mighty branches, but that the leading shoot of philosophy was and is still — Kant," Muller (1922; Translation of Kant's Critique of Pure Reason).

M. M. Mukhtar
New Zealand Society of Local Government Managers (SOLGM), Wellington, New Zealand

H. M. S. Nihal
Department of Economics, University of Karachi, Karachi, Pakistan

Islamic Banking Division, Bank Al-Habib Ltd, Karachi, Pakistan

H. A. Rauf
Meezan Bank, Karachi, Pakistan

W. Wasti
Iqra University, Karachi, Pakistan

be further explained under the types of transcendental theology which Kant in his Critique of Pure Reason (1781) developed, i.e., cosmotheology and ontotheology. Cosmotheology is the inference of existence of supreme being through some experience in general, and ontotheology is seeking of supreme being through concepts only (Jones 1996). But this cosmotheological proposition is further understood as by it "must be honored and obeyed in the moral-practical relation, just as much as if it were to be expressed by the highest being, although no proof of it takes place in technical-practical respect, and to believe would be an enthusiastic delusion – taking ideas as perception" (Kant 1993: 227, 21–21). According to Kant, God and the world are "not substances outside my thought, but rather the thought through which we ourselves make these objects," the world is our experience, organized by categories and laws of our own making, and God is the representation of our own capacity to give ourselves the moral law through reason (Kant 1993: 228, 21:21). Here the moral law "emerges from freedom…which the subject prescribes to himself, and yet as if another and higher person had made it a rule for him. The subject feels himself necessitated through his own reason…" (Kant 1993: 208, 22–129). This is a fitting conclusion to Kant's philosophy of human autonomy (Guyer 1998 [2004]: Section 14).

Kant was the philosopher of human autonomy, advocating that the humans can use their reason to discover the knowledge and actions to live, without any divine support or intervention (Guyer 1998 [2004]). The human being "creates the elements of knowledge of the world himself, a priori, from which he, as, at the same time, an inhabitant of the world, constructs a world-vision in the idea" (Kant 1993: 235, 21–31). In this context, human being is a self-determining autonomous being. Further on "the human being, and in general every rational being, exists as end in itself, not merely as means to the discretionary use of this or that will, but in all its actions, those directed toward itself as well as those directed toward other rational beings, it must always at the same time be considered as an end" (Kant 2002: 47). The human actions are subjected to the individual will and must fulfill the universality condition, i.e., categorical imperative; which is defined as, "act only in accordance with that maxim through which you can, at the same time, will that it become a universal law" (Kant 2002: 37). All these actions will fall under the umbrella of freedom, not under reason, as reason is merely a means, not an end. “In other words, freedom implies that practical reason can be pure (non-instrumental, unconditional), and hence that we are subject to the demands of the categorical imperative; and our subjection to morality implies that we must be free” (Williams 2013).

This categorical imperative enforces the notion of freedom and equality for all human beings across the board, giving rise to the discourse of human rights. “Such Enlightenment ideas stimulated the great modern social movements and revolutions, and were taken up in modern constitutions and declarations of human rights” (Gosepath 2011). John Rawls also held the same belief that “the parties arrive at their choice together as free and equal rational persons” (Sterba 1980: 65–66). On the note of Kantian equality, John Rawls put forth two principles and a general conception for a well-ordered society (Sterba 1980: 64):

1. First Principle: Each person is to have an equal right to the most extensive total system of equal basic liberties compatible with a similar system of liberty for all.
2. Second Principle: Social and economic inequalities are to be arranged so that they are both:
    a. To the greatest benefit of the least advantaged, consistent with the just savings principle, and
    b. Attached to offices and positions open to all under conditions of fair equality of opportunity.
3. General Conception: All social primary goods—liberty and opportunity, income and wealth, and the bases of self-respect—are to be distributed equally unless an unequal distribution of any or all of these goods is to the advantage of the least favored.

These principles and general conception based on equality are derived from Kant’s own formula: “every member of the commonwealth must be entitled to reach any degree of rank which a subject can earn through his talent, his industry and his good fortune. And his fellow-subjects may not stand in his way by hereditary prerogatives or privileges of rank and thereby hold him and his descendants back infinitely” (Sterba 1980: 44). Rawls (1999: 79) clearly mentions that a rational man will prefer more of social primary goods—income and wealth, liberty, right and opportunities—rather than less, where the rational man is that who is free from all kinds of external constraints—God, the Angles, another world with heavens and hellfire—as it is beyond the scope of philosophical theory.

2 Requirements of Rational Philosophy in Real World[3]

This rationale philosophy requires a specific theme of life for its progression in this world, getting out of the underdeveloped phobia.[4] Rostow (1961), a market-oriented theorist, put forth five stages of growth cycle which is based on free will of individuals and no governmental constraints, perhaps the current neoliberal economic thought (Giddens 2009: 548–550). These five stages of growth cycle are proposed for the low-income societies to economically develop them; and this economic growth is possible only when they give up their cultural values, bring strong work ethic, reduce family size, reject fatalism,[5] and emphasize on savings and investment (Giddens 2009: 549).[6] Grondona (2000) argues that the developmental values play a vital role in economic revolution, as it occurs when the individuals keep on competing, investing, innovating, and working even when the country has achieved development. For this, the necessary condition is the continuation of developmental values, and thus, these values must be intrinsic regardless of their benefit or costs attached with it (Grondona 2000: 45). He lists down twenty contrasting cultural factors which act as resistant to economic development, this is where the intervention is required in values for long-term economic growth[7]:

1. Religion: From a Christianity point of view, the Catholics have a preference of poor over rich, whereas the Protestant have a vice versa preference. It was the Protestantism—Calvinist—which gave boost to economic development, as to them the rich (God's

[3]We seek forgiveness from Allah (*swt*) for the blasphemous statements in this chapter.

[4]85% of the world population live outside high-income countries (Giddens 2009: 548).

[5]By fatalism we intend for "Logical fatalism," "Metaphysical fatalism," or "Theological fatalism" (Rice 2013).

[6]Giddens (2009: 554–556) further explains the state-centered theories, which give alternative to prevailing market-oriented theories and dependency theories. State-centered theories stress on the role of government for economic development, as successfully seen in recent period within East Asian countries, especially in Hong Kong and Singapore. We argue that still the main objective of the system remains the same, with no difference in conventional ontological, cosmological, and epistemological views.

[7]In this paper, we will discuss few of them which are directly relevant to Islam's standpoint.

blessing) in this world are winners of the world hereafter and the poor (God's condemnation) of this world are losers of hereafter. This view results in a strong incentive for rich and poor, both, to improve their condition through accumulation and investment. Thus, the Catholic values are resistant to economic development and Protestant values are favorable.

2. Trust in the Individual: Work and creativity are the principal engines of economic development. Individual must have faith in himself, they must not feel that others are responsible for them, they should be willing to take on risk contrary to the desires of government, and they must turn themselves into a unique being, to live and think as he wish, to be who he is. If not done, then the development doesn't occur, what takes place then is either obedience or uprising.
3. The Value of Work: The Reformation—Calvinist interpretation—inverted the work ethic scale; the prestige was withheld by religious leaders, intellectuals, military leader, politician, and the artist. But afterward, it was the entrepreneur who was given the crown. It is same inverted value system which gave rise to development in Western Europe, North America and East Asia, and it is the same reason for the poverty of Latin America and other Third World countries.
4. Time Focus: The advanced societies focus on the immediate future, for it is the only one which can be planned or controlled. The traditional societies either glorify their past or see into distant, eschatological (death, judgment, heaven, and hellfire) future.
5. Rationality: The rational person derives his satisfaction from the achievements which he gains, and by the end of the day, it's the progress—sum of small achievements in monetary terms.
6. Authority: Supremacy of law has been established in rational societies, which is based on the cosmological view perceived by the philosophers of modernity, whereas in the economically underdeveloped societies it is on the basis of a prince or an irascible, unpredictable God.

By recommending that cultural values and attitudes as major obstacles to progress, Montaner (2000) discusses the behavior of six elite groups, the politician, businessmen, the military, intellectual, clergy, and leftist.[8]

[8] We will discuss on two groups only in this paper.

According to him, the clergy preach attitudes that are against the very notion of success; they condemn profit motive, competition, and consumerism (Montaner 2000: 62), whereas the intellectuals stress the danger of multinational companies, globalization, and the economic models that emphasize on market forces (Montaner 2000: 63).

We can conclude in the words of Reisman (1998: 19): "it is no accident that the greatest era of capitalist development – the last two centuries – has taken place under the ongoing cultural influence of the philosophy of the Enlightenment," based on the prosecular, proreason trends in religion. There is a need for objectively demonstrable human needs which shows no limit to man's need for wealth; if so done, then there is space for continuous economic growth, else the position held by religious thinkers regarding pursuit of spiritual values solely in this earthly life makes economics a science of secondary importance (Reisman 1998: 42).

3 Islamic Philosophy of Economics

Islamic scholars in twentieth century addressed the issue of rational economic system. They presented the standpoint of Islam on philosophy of economics, in light of the Holy Qur'ān and Aḥādīth. Within this period, one renowned Islamic scholar Shaykh Abdul Bari Nadvi (Professor and Head of Department of Philosophy, Osmania University) extensively wrote on the conventional philosophy and prevailing economic thought. He also compared it with the Islamic spirit, identifying the incoherencies and a way out.[9]

وَمَا خَلَقْتُ الْجِنَّ وَالْاِنْسَ اِلَّا لِيَعْبُدُوْنِ ○ مَآ اُرِيْدُ مِنْهُمْ مِّنْ رِّزْقٍ وَّمَآ اُرِيْدُ اَنْ يُّطْعِمُوْنِ ○ اِنَّ
اللّٰهَ هُوَ الرَّزَّاقُ ذُو الْقُوَّةِ الْمَتِيْنُ58○

> And I did not create the jinn and mankind except to worship Me. I do not want from them any provision, nor do I want them to feed Me. Indeed, it is Allah who is the [continual] Provider, the firm possessor of strength. (Al-Qur'ān: 51:56–58)

[9] In this paper, we will focus more on the writings of Shaykh Abdul Bari Nadvi. His writings are a combination of great Islamic scholars, such as, Allama Shibli Naumani, Syed Sulaiman Nadvi, Maulana Abdul Salam Nadvi, Maulana Abdul Majid Daryabadi, Maulana Manazir Ahsan Gilani, Maulana Ashraf Ali Thanvi, and Maulana Hussain Ahmad Madani.

مَنْ كَانَ يُرِيْدُ حَرْثَ الْاٰخِرَةِ نَزِدْ لَهٗ فِيْ حَرْثِهٖ ۚ وَمَنْ كَانَ يُرِيْدُ حَرْثَ الدُّنْيَا نُؤْتِهٖ مِنْهَا وَمَا لَهٗ فِي الْاٰخِرَةِ مِنْ نَّصِيْبٍ 20

Whoever desires the harvest of the Hereafter - We increase for him in his harvest. And whoever desires the harvest of this world - We give him thereof, but there is not for him in the Hereafter any share. (Al-Qur'ān: 42:20)

Allah (*swt*)[10] have created man as the best of his creations and made him as his vicegerent. All the worldly things have been created for man, whereas the man has been created for life hereafter—*ākhirah*. All these blessings demand that the man must fulfill all the commandments of Allah (*swt*)—without any hesitation—in each and every aspect of his life, so that he could gain pleasure of Allah (*swt*) and eternal welfare and salvation (Nadvi 2005: 39, 58, 71).

On the objective of Islamic knowledge, Nadvi (2005: 22) argues that the real purpose of Islam and the Holy Qur'ān is not to indulge in intellectual or technical, research or comparative theories' dialogues, but to solely provide guidance and directions in this context. Accordingly, only that economic knowledge is fruitful that helps at each and every step in practical process of economic activity, and provides peace of mind in situation of prosperity and poverty.

"If I had a shop near the door of the Masjid, so that I would not miss any *Ṣalāh* with the congregation. Then I shall sell and buy, and make a modest profit every day. Allah, Great and Majestic, has not prohibited trade, but I want to be among those, 'whom neither trade nor does selling distract from the remembrance of Allah' (Al-Qur'ān: 24:37)" (Al-Jezairi: 1/422). This narration is of Hazrat Abu Darda ra,[11] companion of Holy Prophet Muhammad (*saaws*),[12] in which he directs us that man has not been created for wealth accumulation or to over-cogitate upon his sustenance but, he is created only to worship his Creator (*swt*) and fulfill His (*swt*) commandments (Nadvi 2005: 25).

The basic underlying concept (ultimate vision) of economics or its sub-branch politics is on meeting the requirement for human sustenance with convenience and comfort. Their sole objective is focused on bodily/worldly/physical life of human; conclusively, these are necessary means of life but surely not the purpose of life. It is a tragedy though

[10] *Subhanahu wa ta'ala*, Glorified and Exalted be He.

[11] *Razi Allah Tala Anhu; Allah (swt) is well pleased with them.*

[12] *Sallallahu Alaihi Wasallam*, Peace be upon Him.

that they have increased the ranking of means to the purpose. In the eyes of Islam, this world and its life is in its own self, is not a purpose, but a means to unlimited world and unlimited life; then, how can we or should we treat the road with the same affection as of destination, and this is the essential parting point between the Islamic economics and proreason or human self-autonomous economics (Nadvi 2005: 26).

For example, if a Muslim individual or group gets full control over economic and political aspects, and derives all kind of comfort, but he or they are not practically acting upon Islamic principles and *sunnah* of Prophet Muhammad (*saaws*), only discussing it theoretically, nor they offer prayer and fast, nor their financial dealings are according to Islam, nor their moral values are of like Muslims and on the other hand, a Muslim individual or group those are subordinated to some other political party and are not well-off financially but are not negligent from the infinite coming life, their life is in accordance with Qur'ān and practically shining with *Sunnah*, then you decide yourself that who is better-off and preferable? (Nadvi 2005: 28). There is no doubt that economic and political superiority if gained with the combination of *īmān* and piousness, then it will result in much better results—within this context there is no denial of the secondary importance of economic and political arena. Therefore, to be a good Muslim is primary task and to gain economic and political position, in individual or group capacity, is secondary; again, the primary task is to become "*Momin Sualeh*"[13] (Nadvi 2005: 28).

يٰٓاَيُّهَا الَّذِيْنَ اٰمَنُوا ادْخُلُوْا فِي السِّلْمِ كَاۗفَّةً وَّلَا تَتَّبِعُوْا خُطُوٰتِ الشَّيْطٰنِ ۭ اِنَّهٗ لَكُمْ عَدُوٌّ مُّبِيْنٌ
۝208

O you who have believed, enter into Islam completely [and perfectly] and do not follow the footsteps of Satan. Indeed, he is to you a clear enemy. (Al-Qur'ān: 2:208)

The beauty of Islam lies in the code of life which it demands from the man, that is, best of the best in *ākhirah*. This gives an equal opportunity to the rich and poor to gain that stratum.[14] In contrast to it if the religion would have made the worldly possessions or worldly status in lowest of the lowest rank as an ultimate purpose (as an end in itself), then it would have made the man captive and would have given a unequal

[13] A practical practicing Muslim.

[14] Love of Allah (*swt*) and best of best place in Jannah.

opportunity to the rich and poor, because these things are beyond man's grip (Nadvi 2005: 29).

مَنْ كَانَ يُرِيْدُ الْعَاجِلَةَ عَجَّلْنَا لَهٗ فِيْهَا مَا نَشَاۗءُ لِمَنْ نُّرِيْدُ ثُمَّ جَعَلْنَا لَهٗ جَهَنَّمَ ۚ يَصْلٰىهَا مَذْمُوْمًا
مَّدْحُوْرًا 18 ۝ وَمَنْ اَرَادَ الْاٰخِرَةَ وَسَعٰى لَهَا سَعْيَهَا وَهُوَ مُؤْمِنٌ فَاُولٰۗىِٕكَ كَانَ سَعْيُهُمْ مَّشْكُوْرًا
۝ 19

Whoever should desire the immediate - We hasten for him from it what We will to whom We intend. Then We have made for him Hell, which he will [enter to] burn, censured and banished. But whoever desires the Hereafter and exerts the effort due to it while he is a believer - it is those whose effort is ever appreciated [by Allah]. (Al-Qur'ān: 17:18–19)

Apparently it seems that the major tasks of the Prophets of Allah (*swt*) and especially Prophet Muhammad (*saaws*) were on teaching the economic and political aspects of human life, but in reality the directions of Prophetic teachings are toward the achievements of and in, eternal life. All the guiding principles regarding economic and political issues are under the umbrella of eternal successes and just means to achieve them. Though the road of *ākhirah* passes through this world, it was necessary to give directions of this world, so that the man would not lose his sight due to the amusing and detracting views, and with ease could continue his journey toward the ultimate destination (Nadvi 2005: 31–32).

اَلْحَمْدُ لِلّٰهِ الَّذِيْٓ اَنْزَلَ عَلٰي عَبْدِهِ الْكِتٰبَ وَلَمْ يَجْعَلْ لَّهٗ عِوَجًا 1 ۝ قَيِّمًا لِّيُنْذِرَ بَاْسًا شَدِيْدًا مِّنْ لَّدُنْهُ
وَيُبَشِّرَ الْمُؤْمِنِيْنَ الَّذِيْنَ يَعْمَلُوْنَ الصّٰلِحٰتِ اَنَّ لَهُمْ اَجْرًا حَسَـنًا 2 ۝ مَّاكِثِيْنَ فِيْهِ اَبَدًا 3 ۝

[All] praise is [due] to Allah, who has sent down upon His Servant the Book and has not made therein any deviance. [He has made it] straight, to warn of severe punishment from Him and to give good tidings to the believers who do righteous deeds that they will have a good reward. In which they will remain forever. (Al-Qur'ān: 18:1–3)

As far as the economic activity of man is considered, it is a mean for gaining welfare in *ākhirah*. In this context, Allah (*swt*) have explicitly taken care of man's sustenance and thus not demanded any kind of overwhelmed activity for solving the economic problems, which would result in diverting the attention from the real objective of life. Man is only responsible for taking practical steps for his livelihood so that he doesn't become dependent on others and raise barriers in his stratum of *ākhirah*

(Nadvi 2005: 40). The man starts to think that the income which he is gaining is due to his own hardship and struggle, Allah (*swt*) warns that, what so ever man generates economically, it is all due to the blessing of Him (*swt*) solely, and He (*swt*) gives in any quantity to anyone according to His (*swt*) will. *And Allah gives provision to whom He wills without account (Al-Qur'ān*: 24:38*)* (Nadvi 2005: 105). *It should also be noted that the increase and reduction in income, prosperity, and poverty are not related to any economic model and not due to any human intervention or planning, but it is directly from the will of Allah (swt)* (Nadvi 2005: 53). *Again*, man is only responsible for taking practical steps, whereas the results are in the total control of Allah (*swt*).

اَهُمْ يَقْسِمُوْنَ رَحْمَتَ رَبِّكَ ۭ نَحْنُ قَسَمْنَا بَيْنَهُمْ مَّعِيْشَتَهُمْ فِي الْحَيٰوةِ الدُّنْيَا وَرَفَعْنَا بَعْضَهُمْ فَوْقَ بَعْضٍ
دَرَجٰتٍ لِّيَتَّخِذَ بَعْضُهُمْ بَعْضًا سُخْرِيًّا ۭ وَرَحْمَتُ رَبِّكَ خَيْرٌ مِّمَّا يَجْمَعُوْنَ 32 ◯ وَلَوْلَآ اَنْ يَّكُوْنَ النَّاسُ
اُمَّةً وَّاحِدَةً لَّجَعَلْنَا لِمَنْ يَّكْفُرُ بِالرَّحْمٰنِ لِبُيُوْتِهِمْ سُقُفًا مِّنْ فِضَّةٍ وَّمَعَارِجَ عَلَيْهَا يَظْهَرُوْنَ 33 ◯ وَلِبُيُوْتِهِمْ
اَبْوَابًا وَّسُرُرًا عَلَيْهَا يَتَّكِـــُٔوْنَ 34 ◯ وَزُخْرُفًا ۭ وَاِنْ كُلُّ ذٰلِكَ لَمَّا مَتَاعُ الْحَيٰوةِ الدُّنْيَا ۭ وَالْاٰخِرَةُ عِنْدَ رَبِّكَ
لِلْمُتَّقِيْنَ 35 ◯

Is it they who allocate the mercy of your Lord? We have allocated among them their livelihood in the worldly life, and have raised some of them over others in ranks, so that some of them may put some others to work. And the mercy of your Lord is much better than what they accumulate. Were it not that all people would become of a single creed (i.e. disbelief), We would have caused, for those who disbelieve in Rahman, roofs of their houses to be made of silver, and the stairs as well, on which they would climb. And doors of their homes, and the coaches on which they would recline. And (would have made some of these things) of gold-ornaments. And all this is nothing but an enjoyment of the worldly life. And the Hereafter, with your Lord, is (destined) for the God-fearing. (Al-Qur'ān: 43:32–35)

وَمَآ اَمْوَالُكُمْ وَلَآ اَوْلَادُكُمْ بِالَّتِيْ تُقَرِّبُكُمْ عِنْدَنَا زُلْفٰٓي اِلَّا مَنْ اٰمَنَ وَعَمِلَ صَالِحًا ۡ فَاُولٰۗىِٕكَ لَهُمْ
جَزَاۗءُ الضِّعْفِ بِمَا عَمِلُوْا وَهُمْ فِي الْغُرُفٰتِ اٰمِنُوْنَ 37 ◯ وَالَّذِيْنَ يَسْعَوْنَ فِيْٓ اٰيٰتِنَا مُعٰجِزِيْنَ
اُولٰۗىِٕكَ فِي الْعَذَابِ مُحْضَرُوْنَ 38 ◯ قُلْ اِنَّ رَبِّيْ يَبْسُطُ الرِّزْقَ لِمَنْ يَّشَاۗءُ مِنْ عِبَادِهٖ وَيَقْدِرُ لَهٗ ۭ
وَمَآ اَنْفَقْتُمْ مِّنْ شَيْءٍ فَهُوَ يُخْلِفُهٗ ۚ وَهُوَ خَيْرُ الرّٰزِقِيْنَ 39 ◯

And it is not your wealth or your children that bring you nearer to Us in position, but it is [by being] one who has believed and done righteousness. For them there will be the double reward for what they did, and they will be in the upper chambers [of Paradise], safe [and secure]. And the ones who strive against Our verses to cause [them] failure - those will be brought into the punishment [to remain]. Say, "Indeed, my Lord extends

> provision for whom He wills of His servants and restricts [it] for him. But whatever thing you spend [in His cause] - He will compensate it; and He is the best of providers." (Al-Qur'ān: 34:37–39)

In contrast to economics, the study of wealth, Islam propagates on the dangers and drawbacks of it; rather than inducing and commending on the wealth, Islam emphasizes on acquiring the ultimate and unlimited welfare. The end result of conventional economics is to break apart the relation of man from his Creator (*swt*) and from eternal life, thus making him an avarice proliferating one (Nadvi 2005: 98).

لَا يَغُرَّنَّكَ تَقَلُّبُ الَّذِيْنَ كَفَرُوْا فِي الْبِلَادِ ۝196 مَتَاعٌ قَلِيْلٌ ثُمَّ مَاْوٰىهُمْ جَهَنَّمُ وَبِئْسَ الْمِهَاد
۝197

> The arrogance of the disbelievers about the land should not deceive you. It is just a little enjoyment. After that, their resort is Hell; and it is an evil abode. (Al-Qur'ān: 3:196–197).

> Hazrat Abu Zar (ra) narrated that,[15] one day Prophet Muhammad (saaws) was sitting in the shade of Holy Kaba, when I reached there, He (saaws) saw me and said "By the Lord of Kaba, those people are in the most heavy losses, those people are in the most heavy losses…" I asked Him (saaws), "who are those people?," He (saaws) replied, "those who have great wealth, but the man who keeps on spending it from right left front back, to all sides, but such type of people are very few". (Tirmizi: Kitab ul Aimaan wal Al Nuzoor: Bab Kaifa Kanat Yameenu Al Nabi: 2:63, Bukhari: 6638)

The problems faced within the economic system are in reality just two: acquisition of wealth and utilization of it—these two problems make the definition of conventional economics. The terminology used for wealth in Qur'ān and Hadith is "*Māl*." And the word *māl* is used in the context of earning (*kasb*) and spending (*infāq*), whereas when we see the Holy Qur'ān, not a single verse could be found which uses term *māl* in absolute sense of *kasb*, i.e., earning without any differentiation between right and wrong—*ḥalāl* or *ḥarām*. Further on, there is no direct obligation on man to earn of any kind—only for the sake of earning. Wherever it is, it's only forcing to earn in the rightful manner—*ḥalāl*

[15] Meaning of the Hadith, not exact translation.

way and for eternal purpose. The context of *kasb* (earning) and *infāq* (spending) used in Holy Qur'ān and Aḥādīth is in accordance with construction or destruction of life hereafter—*ākhirah. To search lawful earning is obligatory after the compulsory things (like prayer, fasting, belief in God)* (Baghawi, 1405H: 2/128). Accordingly – *And you love wealth with immense love* (Al-Qur'ān: 89:20). *And indeed he is, in love of wealth, intense* (Al-Qur'ān: 100:8) – *the man is already obsessed with the concept of kasb intrinsically, that there is no more need to emphasize directly on it or push towards it. Rather the necessary condition is to bound him and his earning methodology within the taqwá (piousness) and ākhirah context* (Nadvi 2005: 82).

مَا أَفَاءَ اللَّهُ عَلَى رَسُولِهِ مِنْ أَهْلِ الْقُرَى فَلِلَّهِ وَلِلرَّسُولِ وَلِذِي الْقُرْبَى وَالْيَتَامَى وَالْمَسَاكِينِ
وَابْنِ السَّبِيلِ كَيْ لَا يَكُونَ دُولَةً بَيْنَ الْأَغْنِيَاءِ مِنْكُمْ 7

Whatever Fai'Allah has passed on to His Messenger from the people of the towns is for Allah and for the Messenger, and for the kinsmen and the orphans and the needy and the wayfarer, so that it may not circulate only between the rich among you. (Al-Qur'ān: 59:7)

By fanning the notion of *kasb*, the results would be like the social chaos that we are witnessing now, in the shape of increase in sexual desires, by increasing its means: cinema and theater, novel, drama, dances and clubs, pornography, naked or half naked dresses, unveiled, mixed gathering, etc. For the sake of survival of mankind, Allah (*swt*) have already planted the optimal level of desires between both sexes; any kind of external force for enhancing it will result in disaster. The requirement in here is to bring it back within the moderate levels by advocating and promoting for *hijab* (veil).

The same case in here is with *kasb*; it is required to be within moderate levels, need of time is to press it down rather induce it further. But the proreason economic system brought the philosophy with it that the human being and human life are made for progress and growth, it denied the whole history of mankind, culture, civilization, religion, spirituality, morality, and social values and made it the slogan for not only its own nation, but expanded it internationally to the arena of politics and culture along with economics. Raising the slogan of increase in the standard of living, as if it is the ultimate vision and sole problem of life (Nadvi 2005: 85).

In around 75 places in the Holy Qur'ān, there is discussion on *māl* but within it in not a single place it is taken as a demandable; rather the accent is on its condemnable aspect and its recommendation for *infāq* (Nadvi 2005: 89).

In contrast to this, to uphold the slogan of proreason economics of increase in the worldly standard of living, the teachings for individuals, communities, and nations internationally would have to (and are) emphasize(ing) on selfishness, taking more than giving, more on generating than spending; rather than cultivating the benevolent or sacrificing attitude, it is seeding an avarice attitude; because in this path of materialistic economic system, the standard of living can only be increased by generating more income and wealth. On the other hand, the real spirit of Islamic economic system is on *infāq* (spending) and sacrificing for others. *Infāq* doesn't mean spending money only on others, but it also includes the intellect or physical power, leisure time anything which Allah (*swt*) have granted. And from this *infāq* we mean only that which fits perfectly within the framework of Islam, in which the fundamental purpose is not to increase the economic level but to substantially increase the eternal level—higher and higher rank or level in *ākhirah* (Nadvi 2005: 103–104, 107). The significance of this point is discussed over the straight thirteen verses of the Holy Qur'ān (2:261–274), apart from all other places as well.

يٰٓاَيُّهَا الَّذِيْنَ اٰمَنُوْٓا اَنْفِقُوْا مِنْ طَيِّبٰتِ مَا كَسَبْتُمْ وَمِمَّآ اَخْرَجْنَا لَكُمْ مِّنَ الْاَرْضِ ۠ وَلَا تَيَمَّمُوا
الْخَبِيْثَ مِنْهُ تُنْفِقُوْنَ وَلَسْتُمْ بِاٰخِذِيْهِ اِلَّآ اَنْ تُغْمِضُوْا فِيْهِ ۭ وَاعْلَمُوْٓا اَنَّ اللّٰهَ غَنِىٌّ حَمِيْدٌ 267
اَلشَّيْطٰنُ يَعِدُكُمُ الْفَقْرَ وَيَاْمُرُكُمْ بِالْفَحْشَاۗءِ ۚ وَاللّٰهُ يَعِدُكُمْ مَّغْفِرَةً مِّنْهُ وَفَضْلًا ۭ وَاللّٰهُ وَاسِعٌ عَلِيْمٌ
268

> O you who have believed, spend from the good things which you have earned and from that which We have produced for you from the earth. And do not aim toward the defective therefrom, spending [from that] while you would not take it [yourself] except with closed eyes. And know that Allah is Free of need and Praiseworthy. Satan threatens you with poverty and orders you to immorality, while Allah promises you forgiveness from Him and bounty. And Allah is all-Encompassing and Knowing. (Al-Qur'ān: 2:267–268)

The foundation of Islam is not on economic growth (accumulation of wealth) but it is on spending of wealth, without any doubt it is the only Qur'ānic Islamic solution to all the economic problems

(Nadvi 2005: 21). One other mistake we make is that we unconsciously assume the income or wealth which we gained through the blessings of Allah (*swt*), as our own property. But in reality our income and our wealth are in the ownership of Allah (*swt*), our status in this regard is of trustee (*ameen*) and we are bound to spend it according to the will of Allah (*swt*), neither to be thrifty nor to be extravagant (Nadvi 2005: 286–267, 300). *Believe in Allah and His Messenger and spend out of that in which He has made you successors. For those who have believed among you and spent, there will be a great reward* (Al-Qur'ān: 57:7). *And those who, when they spend, are neither extravagant nor miserly and it (i.e. their spending) is moderate in between (the two extremes)* (Al-Qur'ān: 25:67). The purpose of this infāq within Islamic Economics is definitely not to solve the economic problems, in fact it is for gaining the pleasure and loyalty of Allah (*swt*), and this is the fundamental difference between the proreason humanistic approach and Islam's divine approach (Nadvi 2005: 301).

Islamic economics tends to transfer the wealth from the rich to poor with their willingness and happiness, due to which not only the few days of this worldly life of the poor constitutes but more over the eternal and religious life of the rich organizes, which in reality is the essence of Islamic teachings. In connection with the order for spending in the path of Allah (*swt*), it has also been warned that, *and spend in the way of Allah and do not throw [yourselves] with your [own] hands into destruction [by refraining]. And do good; indeed, Allah loves the doers of good* (Al-Qur'ān: 2:195). If the poor safeguard his wealth of *īmān* (faith) with his poverty, then the spiritual and moral doors of patience and pleasure, contentment and trust are opened for him. But the proreason economics have indulged the poor with the slogans of income, poverty, growth, and equality, which have slaughtered the world as well as the poor's peace and inner satisfaction. Compared to this jeopardy, if the economics is tied up with eternal welfare then the poor in their tartly stringency will find their heart full of peace and prosperous (Nadvi 2005: 379).

Although the hatred from māl or calling upon the poverty and misery is not desired in its own self, the path on which the Holy Prophets and especially our Prophet Muhammad (*saaws*) walked on was of poverty and frugality, not of wealth or status (Nadvi 2005: 100). Also the earliest companions of Prophet Muhammad *(saaws)* were poor but they were the most successful among the mankind, *and when it is said to them,*

"Believe as the people have believed," they say, "Should we believe as the foolish have believed?" Unquestionably, it is they who are the foolish, but they know [it] not (Al-Qur'ān: 2:13).

4 Impact of Sins on Worldly Life

The current condition of us (Muslims) in shape of laziness in obedience and extra courage in sins is due to our false thinking that its impact would be on the Day of Judgment only, we are simply not aware that its impact is also on this worldly life (Thanvi 2012: 31). We find a lot of discussion in the Holy Qur'ān regarding the sinful acts of civilization and the punishment from Allah (*swt*) which they faced due to it: *satan* (*iblees*), the people of Prophet Nuh (as), Prophet Aad (as), Prophet Samood (as), Prophet Shoaib (as), firoon, qaroon and bne israel[16] (Thanvi 2012: 37).

وَمَا ظَلَمُوْنَا وَلٰكِنْ كَانُوْٓا اَنْفُسَهُمْ يَظْلِمُوْنَ ۝57

> And they (by their ingratitude) did Us no harm, but were harming only themselves. (Al-Qur'ān: 2:57)

Following are the few direct impacts on life due to sins (Thanvi 2012):

1. Impact on livelihood: *Narrated by Thawban ra, "The Messenger of Allah (saw) said: 'Nothing extends one's life span but righteousness, nothing averts the Divine Decree but supplication, and nothing deprives a man of provision but the sin he commits'"*(Abdullah: Kitab al Fitan/Bab al Uqoobat/4022).
2. Difficulty in acquiring desired objectives: *Whoever fears Allah, He brings forth a way out for him* (Al-Qur'ān: 65:2). One who commits sins faces problems in acquiring desired objectives.
3. Devalued in the eyes of the Creator (*swt*): *And the one whom Allah puts to disgrace, there is none to give him respect* (Al-Qur'ān: 22:18). He is devalued in the eyes of Allah (*swt*) and simultaneously among the whole creations.

[16] Though the damages or disadvantages are to such an extent that we can't encompass it, shall discuss it shortly and in context of economics.

4. Chaos on land and sea: *Calamities have appeared on land and sea because of what the hands of the people have earned, so that He (Allah) makes them taste some of what they did* (Al-Qur'ān: 30:41).
5. Confiscation of blessing and descent of troubles: *All this is because Allah is not the one who may change a favour He has conferred on a people unless they change their own condition* (Al-Qur'ān: 8:53).
6. Contraction in livelihood and contentment: *As for the one who turns away from My message, he shall have a straitened life, and We shall raise him blind on the Day of Judgment* (Al-Qur'ān: 20:124).

The bounty of Allah (*swt*) is showered on those who follow his doable instructions, not only in the life hereafter but also in this worldly life.

1. Expansion in livelihood: *If they had upheld the Torah and the Injil and what had been sent down to them from their Lord, they would surely have had plenty to eat from above them and from beneath them* (Al-Qur'ān: 5:66). If one follows the instructions of Prophet Muhammad (*saaws*) he will be blessed immensely.
2. Descent of unlimited resources *(barakat): If the people of the towns believed and feared Allah, We would have opened for them blessings from the heavens and the earth* (Al-Qur'ān: 7:96).
3. Ease in acquiring desired objectives: *And whoever fears Allah, He brings about ease for him in his affair* (Al-Qur'ān: 65:4).
4. Purified life: *Whoever, male or female, has acted righteously, while being a believer, We shall certainly make him live a good life, and shall give such people their reward for the best of what they used to do* (Al-Qur'ān: 16:97).
5. Increase in wealth and timely rain: *Pray to your Lord for your forgiveness, - Indeed He is Very- Forgiving. And He will cause the heavens to rain upon you in abundance. And will help you with riches and sons, and will cause gardens to grow for you, and cause rivers to flow for you* (Al-Qur'ān: 71:10–12).
6. Blessing of respect and status: *and Allah will raise those, in ranks, who have believed and are given knowledge. Allah is well aware of what you do* (Al-Qur'ān: 58:11).
7. Unlimited increase (*barakat*) in wealth: *and whatever zakāh you give, seeking Allah's pleasure with it (it is multiplied by Allah, and) it is such people who multiply (their wealth in real terms)* (Al-Qur'ān: 30:39).

8. Promises of vicegerent and peace: *Allah has promised those of you who believe and do good deeds that He will certainly make them (His) vicegerents in the land, as He made those before them, and will certainly establish for them their religion which He has chosen for them, and will certainly give them peace in place of fear in which they were before* (Al-Qur'ān: 24:55).

5 Toward *Maqāṣid* al-Sharīʿah and *Hayat-e-Tayyaba* Index

The wisdom and ultimate vision of Sharīʿah as postulated by Allah (*swt*) is to help the mankind in reaping benefits in both the worlds—here and hereafter. In this order, exploring the objectives of Sharīʿah—*Maqāṣid* al-Sharīʿah—could be beneficial for us in understanding the foundations of provisions and wisdom behind the maxims. Accordingly, the *maqāṣid* has been divided into five categories: Religion, Life, Intellect, Lineage, and Property (Shatibi 1388). If we are able to protect all these five foundations, then we (all creations) will be able to prosper in this world and hereafter.

Encyclopedia on Islamic Jurisprudence (2012)[17] compiled a list of variables which works in background supplementing each *maqṣad*, highlighting the fact that positive fulfillment of these variables ensures a complete coherence in *Maqāṣid* al-Sharīʿah. These variables are listed in Table 1:

For each variable, there are few more qualities which comprehensively construct the respective variable. All the qualities are derived from the Holy Qur'ān and Aḥādīth.[18] These qualities are listed in Table 2[19]:

All these *maqāṣids*, variables, and qualities will be helpful in developing an index. Where each *maqṣad* is further divided into micro- and

[17] مجلس أمناء مؤسسة زايد بن سلطان آل نهيان ,معلمة زايد للقواعد الفقهية والأصولية.

[18] In this paper, we have mentioned the verses of the Holy Quran only.

[19] All these qualities are taken from Encyclopedia on Islamic Jurisprudence (2012) معلمة زايد للقواعد- الفقهية والأصولية.

Table 1 Variables

#	*Transliteration*	*Translation*	*Arabic*
1.	*Ar-Rahma*	Mercy	الرحمة
2.	*Al-Istiqama*	Integrity	الاستقامة
3.	*Al-Taqwá*	Piety	التقوى
4.	*Al-Shukur*	Thankfulness	الشكر
5.	*As-Sabar*	Patience	الصبر
6.	*Al-Sidq*	Honesty	الصدق
7.	*Al-ʿAdl*	Justice	العدل
8.	*Al-Iffah*	Chastity	العفة
9.	*Al-Wafah*	Fulfillment	الوفاء
10.	*Al-Samaha*	Tolerance	السماحة

Source Authors

macro-perspective, micro-level perspective will deal with the individual and macro-perspective will deal with government-level policies. Thus, the index will be able to cover variables from individual's perspective, society's perspective, countries perspective, and *ummah* perspective. The combination of *maqāṣid* and qualities is intended to make a comprehensive index which would not only cover the quantitative aspect (as in *Maqāṣid* al-Sharīʿah) but also cover the qualitative aspect, thus taking us toward a broader concept of *Hayat-e-Tayyaba.*

Connecting *Hayat-e-Tayyaba* with *Maqāṣid* al-Sharīʿah.

We now turn toward introducing a unified terminology which could comprehensively cover the essence—in words and spirit—of *Maqāṣid* al-Sharīʿah. At the same time, it could be a referral point, upon which we could gauge the notion of prosperity—according to the philosophy of Islamic economics.

مَنْ عَمِلَ صَالِحًا مِّنْ ذَكَرٍ اَوْ اُنْثٰى وَهُوَ مُؤْمِنٌ فَلَنُحْيِيَنَّهٗ حَيٰوةً طَيِّبَةً ۚ وَلَنَجْزِيَنَّهُمْ اَجْرَهُمْ بِاَحْسَنِ
مَا كَانُوْا يَعْمَلُوْنَ 97

Whoever, male or female, has acted righteously, while being a believer, We shall certainly make him live a good life, and shall give such people their reward for the best of what they used to do. (Al-Qur'ān: 16:97)

The Qur'ānic terminology of *Hayat-e-Tayyaba* captures the philosophy of Islamic economics, and at the same time, it engulfs the crux of *Maqāṣid* al-Sharīʿah within it. Contrastingly, in contemporary economics, everything boils down to the notion of growth and development,

Table 2 Qualities

#	*Variable*	*Qualities (Translation)*	*Qualities (Arabic)*
1.	*Ar-Rahma*	Mercy, pity, kindness, compassion, charity, help Opposite qualities: Harshness, hardship, cruelty, suffering, torture	الرأفة، الشفقة، العطف، الحنان، الاحسان، النجدة صفات متنافية معه: القسوة، الشدة، الغلظة، العذاب، الظلم
	قُلْ لِّمَنْ مَّا فِي السَّمٰوٰتِ وَالْأَرْضِ قُلْ لِّلّٰهِ كَتَبَ عَلٰى نَفْسِهِ الرَّحْمَةَ *Say,.To whom belongs all that is in the heavens and on the earth?. Say,.To Allah. He has prescribed Mercy for Himself.* (Al-Qur'ān: 6:12)		
2.	*Al-Istiqama*	Righteousness, moderation, justice Opposite qualities: Corruption, deviation, libertinism	الصلاح، الاعتدال، العدالة صفات متنافية معه: الفساد، الاعوجاج، الفسق
	إِنَّ الَّذِينَ قَالُوا رَبُّنَا اللَّهُ ثُمَّ اسْتَقَامُوا فَلَا خَوْفٌ عَلَيْهِمْ وَلَا هُمْ يَحْزَنُونَ ○ *Surely, those who say,.Our Lord is Allah. and then stay firm, they will have no fear, nor shall they grieve.* (Al-Qur'ān: 6:12)		
3.	*Al-Taqwá*	Meditation of god, fear of god, devout Opposite qualities: Immorality, inattentive, careless	مراقبة الله تعالى، خشية الله تعالى، الورع صفات متنافية معه: الفجور، الغفلة، اللامبالاة
	يَا أَيُّهَا الَّذِينَ آمَنُوا اتَّقُوا اللَّهَ وَكُونُوا مَعَ الصَّادِقِينَ ○ *O you who believe, fear Allah, and be in the company of the truthful.* (Al-Qur'ān: 3:102) يٰأَيُّهَا الَّذِيْنَ اٰمَنُوا اتَّقُوا اللّٰهَ حَقَّ تُقٰتِهٖ وَلَا تَمُوْتُنَّ اِلَّا وَاَنْتُمْ مُّسْلِمُوْنَ *O you who believe, fear Allah, as He should be feared, and let not yourself die save as Muslims. O you who believe, fear Allah, as He should be feared, and let not yourself die save as Muslims.* (Al-Qur'ān: 3:102)		

(continued)

Table 2 (continued)

#	Variable	Qualities (Translation)	Qualities (Arabic)
4.	*Al-Shukur*	Praise, recognition of blessings, fulfilling Opposite qualities: Non recognition of blessings, ingratitude, disobedience	الحمد، الاعتراف بالنعمة، الوفاء صفات متنافية معه: كفر النعمة، الجحود، العقوق
		وَإِذْ تَأَذَّنَ رَبُّكُمْ لَئِنْ شَكَرْتُمْ لَأَزِيدَنَّكُمْ وَلَئِنْ كَفَرْتُمْ إِنَّ عَذَابِي لَشَدِيدٌ *(Recall the time) when your Lord declared,.If you express gratitude, I shall certainly give you more, and if you are ungrateful, then My punishment is severe.* (Al-Qur'ān: 14:7)	
5.	*As-Sabar*	Deliberate, gentleness, tolerance Opposite qualities: Anxiety, despondent, hasty	التأني، الرفق، الحلم صفات متنافية معه: الجزع، القنوط، العجلة
		إِلَّا الَّذِينَ آمَنُوا وَعَمِلُوا الصَّالِحَاتِ وَتَوَاصَوْا بِالْحَقِّ وَتَوَاصَوْا بِالصَّبْرِ *Except those who believed and did righteous deeds, and exhorted each other to follow truth, and exhorted each other to observe patience.* (Al-Qur'ān: 103:3)	
6.	*Al-Sidq*	Truthfulness, sincerity, qualities Opposite qualities: Lying, hypocrisy, show-off	قول الحق، الإخلاص صفات متنافية معه: الكذب، النفاق، الرياء
		مِنَ الْمُؤْمِنِينَ رِجَالٌ صَدَقُوا مَا عَاهَدُوا اللَّهَ عَلَيْهِ فَمِنْهُمْ مَنْ قَضَىٰ نَحْبَهُ وَمِنْهُمْ مَنْ يَنْتَظِرُ وَمَا بَدَّلُوا تَبْدِيلًا لِيَجْزِيَ اللَّهُ الصَّادِقِينَ بِصِدْقِهِمْ وَيُعَذِّبَ الْمُنَافِقِينَ إِنْ شَاءَ أَوْ يَتُوبَ عَلَيْهِمْ إِنَّ اللَّهَ كَانَ غَفُورًا رَحِيمًا *Among the believers, there are men who came true to the covenant they had with Allah. So, some of them have fulfilled their vows (by sacrificing their lives in the way of Allah), and some of them are (still) waiting, and they did not change (their commitment) in the least. (All this happened) so that Allah may give reward to the truthful ones for their truthfulness, and punish the hypocrites, if He so wills, or accept their repentance. Surely, Allah is Most-Forgiving, Very- Merciful.* (Al-Qur'ān: 33:23–24)	

(continued)

Table 2 (continued)

#	*Variable*	*Qualities (Translation)*	*Qualities (Arabic)*
7.	*Al-'Adl*	Fairness, settlement, wisdom Opposite qualities: Injustice (unfair), oppression, aggression, nepotism, excessive	الإنصاف، التسوية، الحكمة صفات متنافية معه: الظلم (الجور)، البغي، العدوان، المحاباة، الإفراط
		إِنَّ اللَّهَ يَأْمُرُكُمْ أَنْ تُؤَدُّوا الْأَمَانَاتِ إِلَىٰ أَهْلِهَا وَإِذَا حَكَمْتُمْ بَيْنَ النَّاسِ أَنْ تَحْكُمُوا بِالْعَدْلِ ۝ *Surely, Allah commands you to deliver trusts to those entitled to them, and that, when you judge between people, judge with justice. Surely, excellent is the exhortation Allah gives you. Surely, Allah is All-Hearing, All-Seeing.* (Al-Qur'ān: 4:58)	
8.	*Al-Effah*	Contentment, piety, ascetic Opposite qualities: Avarice, greed, bulimia	القناعة، الورع، الزهد صفات متنافية معه: الطمع، الجشع، الشره
		قُلْ لِلْمُؤْمِنِينَ يَغُضُّوا مِنْ أَبْصَارِهِمْ وَيَحْفَظُوا فُرُوجَهُمْ ۚ ذَٰلِكَ أَزْكَىٰ لَهُمْ ۗ إِنَّ اللَّهَ خَبِيرٌ بِمَا يَصْنَعُونَ 30 ۝ *Tell the believing men that they must lower their gazes and guard their private parts; it is more decent for them. Surely Allah is All-Aware of what they do.* (Al-Qur'ān: 24:30)	
9.	*Al-Wafah*	Trustworthiness, Keeping Covenants, Honesty, Sincerity Opposite qualities: Treachery, breach, betrayal, rejection, fraud, deficient measure	الأمانة، حفظ الذمم والعهود، الصدق، الإخلاص صفات متنافية معه: الغدر، النَّكث، الخيانة، الجحود، الغش، التطفيف
		وَأَوْفُوا بِعَهْدِ اللَّهِ إِذَا عَاهَدْتُمْ وَلَا تَنْقُضُوا الْأَيْمَانَ بَعْدَ تَوْكِيدِهَا وَقَدْ جَعَلْتُمُ اللَّهَ عَلَيْكُمْ كَفِيلًا ۚ إِنَّ اللَّهَ يَعْلَمُ مَا تَفْعَلُونَ91 ۝ *Fulfill the Covenant of Allah when you pledge, and do not break oaths after you swear them solemnly, while you have made Allah a witness over you. Surely, Allah knows all that you do.* (Al-Qur'ān: 16:91)	

(continued)

Table 2 (continued)

#	*Variable*	*Qualities (Translation)*	*Qualities (Arabic)*
10.	*Al-Samaha*	Facilitation, amnesty, generosity, altruism, good opinion about others Opposite qualities: Odious, agony, dispute, monopolization, mistrust	التيسير، العفو، السخاء، الإيثار، حسن الظن صفات متنافية معه: التعسير، الإعنات، المشاحة، الاستئثار، سوء الظن
	فَبِمَا رَحْمَةٍ مِنَ اللَّهِ لِنْتَ لَهُمْ وَلَوْ كُنْتَ فَظًّا غَلِيظَ الْقَلْبِ لَانْفَضُّوا مِنْ حَوْلِكَ فَاعْفُ عَنْهُمْ وَاسْتَغْفِرْ لَهُمْ وَشَاوِرْهُمْ فِي الْأَمْرِ فَإِذَا عَزَمْتَ فَتَوَكَّلْ عَلَى اللَّهِ إِنَّ اللَّهَ يُحِبُّ الْمُتَوَكِّلِينَ ○ *So (O Prophet) it is through mercy from Allah that you are gentle to them.* ***Had you been rough and hard-hearted****, they would have dispersed from* ***around you****. So,* ***pardon them****, and seek Forgiveness for them. Consult them in the matter and, once you have taken a decision, place your trust in Allah. Surely, Allah loves those who place their trust in Him.* (Al-Qur'ān: 3:159)		

Source Authors

which is singularly represented by gross domestic product (GDP). Also, GDP implicitly represents the philosophy of reason (enlightenment) and materialism.

The prayer of Prophet Ibrahim (as) also directs toward the importance of eternal actions (observation of Islamic rituals) which fulfills the commandments of Allah (*swt*), for gaining the worldly needs and wants. Even the worldly needs and wants are again tied up with the eternal welfare; *Our Lord, I have settled some of my children in a valley of no vegetation, close to Your sanctified House, so that, Our Lord, they may establish Ṣalāh. So, make hearts of people yearn towards them, and provide them with fruits, so that they may be grateful* (Al-Qur'ān: 14:37). Further on, Allah (*swt*) accepted His prayers and enlarged the circle of His blessings upon disbelievers, even though these blessings are minute and contain no reward in hereafter for them: *He (Allah) said, As for the one who disbelieves, I shall let him enjoy a little, then I shall drag him to the punishment of the Fire. How evil an end it is!* (Al-Qur'ān: 2:126).

In this context, the notion of growth and development with GDP as its target variable seems—not even in the smallest sense—compatible with *Hayat-e-Tayyaba*. Thus, we recommend developing *Hayat-e-Tayyaba* Index (HTI Index) to gauge the prosperity of *Ummah*.

6 Articulating and Measuring HTI

Religiosity and spirituality have started gaining footholds in academia. Apart from economics and finance, management sciences have taken a leap in formulating and measuring the impact of religion and spirituality on entrepreneurs, employees, and businesses. The prominent themes arising out of them are in the context of role of spirituality in developing entrepreneurial mind-set and workplace spirituality. Qureshi (2013) developed a theoretical model of "Entrepreneurship Plus" on the basis of Islamic spirituality. In this paper, he argues that Islamic spirituality "is instrumental in transforming the utilitarian, resource ownership focused and a fiercely competitive mindset into a mindset that seeks the pleasure of Allah (*swt*), has a belief in more from less (*Barakat*) and that of cooperation and service," thus impacting and enhancing the entrepreneurial process. Further on, the combined impact of Islamic spiritual orientation and the entrepreneurial process leads to *Nafs Mutmainna* (inner peace) and subsequently toward *Hayat-e-Tayyaba*. To empirically validate this theoretical model, a survey instrument (questionnaire) was designed containing constructs of Islamic spirituality and individual entrepreneurial orientation. The survey was conducted in six major cities of Pakistan—Karachi, Sukkur, Multan, Faisalabad, Islamabad, and Peshawar. Questionnaire was filled by 369 university-level students, belonging to various degree programs. All these students were participating in an entrepreneurship training workshop, which prepared them to participate in a business plan competition titled "INVENT - The Entrepreneurial Challenge," conducted by Institute of Business Administration, Karachi, in April 2013. Eleven different constructs were measured through this questionnaire, six of them were on Islamic spirituality (Qureshi 2013); two on spirituality or life outlook (Frey et al. 2005); and the rest of the three were on individual entrepreneurial orientation (Bolton and Lane 2012).

For articulating and empirically measuring HTI in this paper, we are utilizing the same data set. The constructs of Qureshi (2013) comprise of 29 questions on *Īmān* (Faith), *Ṣalāh* (Prayer), *Ilm & Zikr* (Knowledge & Remembrance), *ḥuqūq al-ʿibād* (The Rights of the People), *Ikhlāṣ & Iḥsān* (Sincerity & Excellence), *Dawah* (Invitation). And the constructs of Frey et al. (2005) comprise of 12 questions on self-efficacy and life scheme. The former construct covers the area of *Maqāṣid* al-Sharīʿah and the latter construct articulates life outlook; complete questionnaire is attached in the appendix. All the questions were asked on a scale of 1–5. All the questions are on micro-level, i.e., from an individual perspective. The *Maqāṣid* al-Sharīʿah questions were asked in quantitative way, were the answer have to be given within a range of Never, Few Times, Sometime, More Often, and Always. The answers were to be given by keeping in view the life spend in last seven months. For example, a question on prayer: "I pray all five prayers within their respective times" had to be answered within the given range by reflecting on the routine in the last seven months. Some other questions, e.g., "I recite the Holy Qur'ān – daily," have to be answered by keeping in view the daily routine over the past seven months. The life outlook questions were of more of qualitative type, which again contained questions from individual perspective, and had to be answered within a range of Strongly Agree, Disagree, Neutral, Agree, and Strongly Agree. For example, a question on life scheme: "There is a great void (emptiness) in my life at this time" had to be answered within the given range and after reflecting the feelings of the last seven months.

The questionnaire was printed and distributed among the workshop participants before the commencement of workshop, and was collected after the workshop ended. Key learnings from this whole exercise were[20]:

1. To keep the Islamic terminologies as simple as possible and translate it in local language. For example, word "Namaaz" would have been better and easy to grasp than "*Ṣalāh*"—in Pakistan context.
2. Develop a separate questionnaire for females or at least mark few questions specifically for females, as females have different obligations and method of offering. For example, males have to offer *ṣalāh* in *masjid* with *jamaat*; females have no such obligation.
3. Give the meaning or synonym or translation of difficult words in brackets.
4. Make specific and to the point questions. And take up only one context in a single question. Can develop more questions if the variable doesn't cover the essence. For example, question, "I precisely calculate my wealth for paying zakat and offering *qurbani*," now it contained two different things, *zakāh* and *qurbani* (*udhiyah*) and while viewing the context of Pakistan, more people are inclined toward *qurbani*. So it would have been better if two different questions were developed and asked.
5. Reverse questions are difficult to handle as it creates confusion among the participants and the results are distorted due to it. On the other hand, all positive questions make easy to fill—without reflecting—responses, which again don't give reliable results.
6. Avoid all type of questions which specify or target toward any *madhab*. Make the questions general, on the basis of *Maqāṣid* al-Sharīʿah.
7. A generalized section should be created for people of other religions to fill in. We faced Hindu and Christian participants during the survey. In order to not to hurt their feelings, we told them to fill the life view questions.

The collected data were compiled, cleaned, and organized for descriptive analysis. Below are the tables and discussion on the results of the survey. The tables are created gender-wise, city-wise, and overall.

[20]Few more are discussed in the analysis discussion.

All the results are out of a maximum score of 5. We have calculated the *Maqāṣid* al-Sharīʿah construct and life outlook construct separately, giving the average score of each construct and its sub-construct. Each construct and sub-construct has been given equal weightage. An overall combined average score converted into percentage is also given for easy reference and index creation (Tables 3, 4, 5, 6, 7, 8, 9, 10, 11, Figs. 1, 2, 3).

Out of 369 filled questionnaires, 275 were filled by males and 94 by females, with an average age of 23 and 21, respectively. Females showed slightly higher scores in micro-level *Maqāṣid* al-Sharīʿah than males.

Table 3 Gender-wise distribution: Male

Constructs	Maqāṣid *al-Sharīʿah*						*Life outlook*	
Sub-constructs	F	P	IZ	HI	IK	D	SE	LS
Average	3.644	3.731	3.204	3.842	3.829	3.427	3.479	3.806
Percentage (%)	72.88	74.62	64.09	76.84	76.59	68.53	69.58	76.11
No. of observations	268	266	268	272	271	255	252	253
Missing values	7	9	7	3	4	20	23	22
Total sub-average					72.26%	3.613	72.84%	3.642
Total average								3.627
Total percentage								72.55%
Average age	23.80							

Source Authors

Table 4 Gender-wise distribution: Female

Constructs	Maqāṣid *al-Sharīʿah*						*Life outlook*	
Sub-constructs	F	P	IZ	HI	IK	D	SE	LS
Average	3.962	3.750	3.283	3.699	3.891	3.339	3.659	3.858
Percentage (%)	79.23	75.00	65.66	73.98	77.83	66.79	73.18	77.16
No. of observations	94	94	94	94	94	89	88	88
Missing values	0	0	0	0	0	5	6	6
Total Sub-average					73.08%	3.654	75.18%	3.759
Total average								3.706
Total percentage								74.13%
Average age	21.45							

Source Authors

Table 5 City-wise distribution: Karachi

Constructs	Maqāṣid *al-Sharī'ah*						*Life outlook*	
Sub-constructs	F	P	IZ	HI	IK	D	SE	LS
Average	3.688	3.657	3.148	3.826	3.864	3.306	3.544	3.812
Percentage (%)	73.76	73.13	62.96	76.53	77.27	66.12	70.89	76.25
No. of observations	166	166	166	170	169	155	158	159
Missing values	6	6	6	2	3	15	14	13
Total sub-average					71.62%	3.581	73.56%	3.678
Total average								3.6295
Total percentage								72.59%
Average age	24.64							

Source Authors

Table 6 City-wise distribution: Sukkur

Constructs	Maqāṣid *al-Sharī'ah*						*Life outlook*	
Sub-constucts	F	P	IZ	HI	IK	D	SE	LS
Average	3.669	3.640	2.746	3.508	3.369	3.085	3.340	3.467
Percentage (%)	73.38	72.81	54.92	70.15	67.38	61.69	66.80	69.33
No. of observations	26	25	26	26	26	26	25	25
Missing values	0	1	0	0	0	0	1	1
Total sub-average					66.72%	3.336	66.72%	3.336
Total average								3.336
Total percentage								66.72%
Average age	21.55							

Source Authors

Table 7 City-wise distribution: Faisalabad

Constructs	Maqāṣid *al-Sharī'ah*						*Life outlook*	
Sub-constructs	F	P	IZ	HI	IK	D	SE	LS
Average	3.636	3.627	3.109	3.500	4.018	3.260	3.750	3.593
Percentage (%)	72.73	72.55	62.18	70.00	80.36	65.20	75.00	71.85
No. of observations	22	22	22	22	22	20	18	18
Missing values	0	0	0	0	0	2	4	4
Total sub-average					70.50%	3.525	73.42%	3.671
Total average								3.598
Total percentage								71.96%
Average age	20.15							

Source Authors

Table 8 City-wise distribution: Multan

Constructs	Maqāṣid *al-Sharī'ah*						*Life outlook*	
Sub-constructs	F	P	IZ	HI	IK	D	SE	LS
Average	3.938	3.570	3.169	3.713	3.763	3.285	3.616	4.040
Percentage (%)	78.75	71.41	63.38	74.25	75.25	65.70	72.32	80.81
No. of observations	32	32	32	32	32	33	33	33
Missing values	1	1	1	1	1	0	0	0
Total sub-average					71.46%	3.573	76.56%	3.828
Total average								3.701
Total percentage								74.01%
Average age	22.71							

Source Authors

Table 9 City-wise distribution: Islamabad

Constructs	Maqāṣid *al-Sharī'ah*						*Life outlook*	
Sub-constructs	F	P	IZ	HI	IK	D	SE	LS
Average	3.897	3.680	3.442	3.867	3.903	3.494	3.667	4.017
Percentage (%)	77.94	73.60	68.85	77.33	78.06	69.88	73.33	80.33
No. of observations	33	33	33	33	33	32	30	30
Missing values	0	0	0	0	0	1	3	3
Total sub-average					74.28%	3.714	76.84%	3.842
Total average								3.778
Total percentage								75.55%
Average age	24.91							

Source Authors

Table 10 City-wise distribution: Peshawar

Constructs	Maqāṣid *al-Sharī'ah*						*Life outlook*	
Sub-constucts	F	P	IZ	HI	IK	D	SE	LS
Average	3.701	3.965	3.494	3.947	3.920	3.756	3.399	3.829
Percentage (%)	74.02	79.31	69.88	78.94	78.41	75.13	67.98	76.58
No. of observations	83	82	83	83	83	78	76	76
Missing values	0	1	0	0	0	5	7	7
Total sub-average					75.94%	3.797	72.28%	3.614
Total average								3.706
Total percentage								74.11%
Average age	21.12							

Source Authors

Table 11 City-wise percentages in each sub-construct

	F (%)	*P (%)*	*IZ (%)*	*HI (%)*	*IK (%)*	*D (%)*	*SE (%)*	*LS (%)*
Karachi	73.76	73.13	62.96	76.53	77.27	66.12	70.89	76.25
Sukkur	73.38	72.81	54.92	70.15	67.38	61.69	66.80	69.33
Faisalabad	72.73	72.55	62.18	70.00	80.36	65.20	75.00	71.85
Multan	78.75	71.41	63.38	74.25	75.25	65.70	72.32	80.81
Islamabad	77.94	73.60	68.85	77.33	78.06	69.88	73.33	80.33
Peshawar	74.02	79.31	69.88	78.94	78.41	75.13	67.98	76.58

Source Authors
Yellow highlights show the highest cities in each sub-category, whereas the green ones show the second ranking

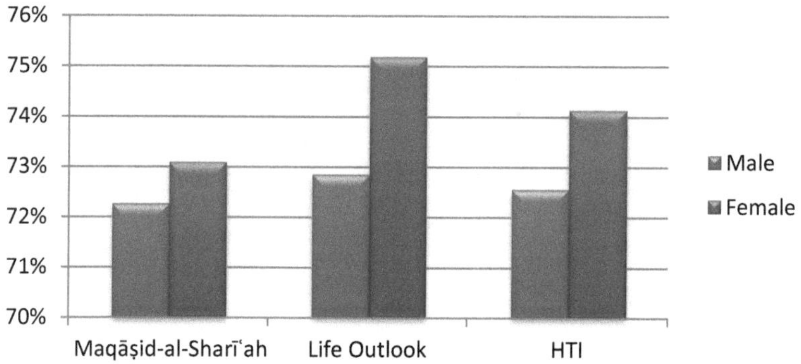

Fig. 1 Gender-wise distribution (*Source* Authors)

Similarly, the life outlook results showed higher scores for females. Overall, the *Hayat-e-Tayyaba* Index (HTI) for males is 72.55% and for females is 74.13%.

A number of respondents for Karachi, Sukkur, Faisalabad, Multan, Islamabad, and Peshawar were 172, 26, 22, 33, 33 and 83, respectively. Islamabad with 75.6% reported to be highest in HTI, followed by Peshawar 74.1% and Multan 74%. The average age of respondents from Islamabad had the highest average age among the sample; of 24.91 years, other demographic factors should also be studied. Peshawar reported 75.9%, the highest, in micro-level *Maqāṣid* al-Sharīʿah,

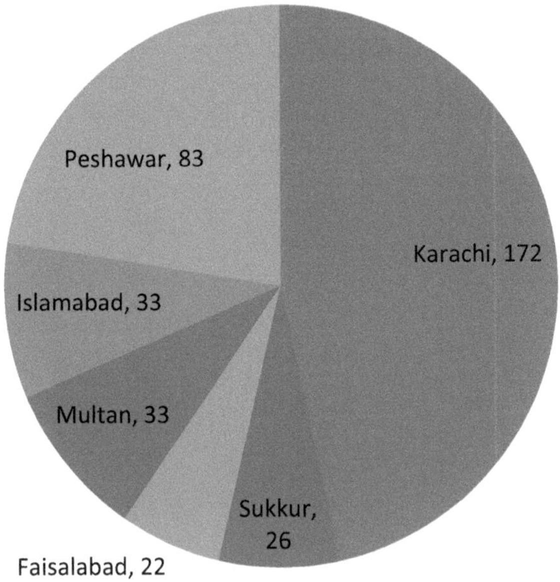

Fig. 2 City-wise number of respondents (*Source* Authors)

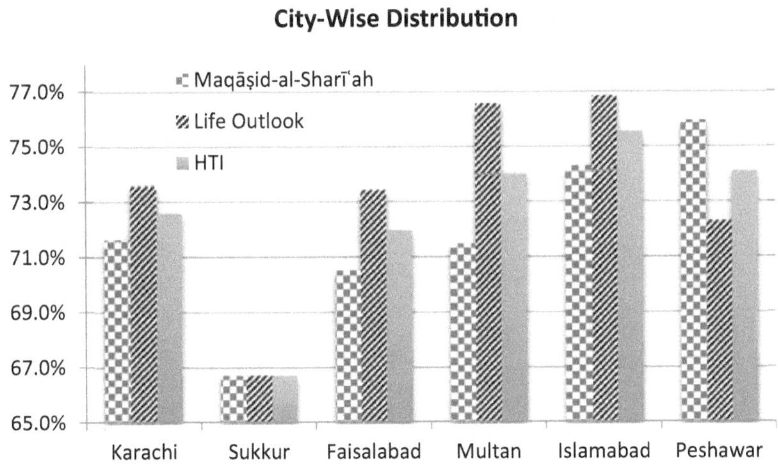

Fig. 3 City-wise distribution (*Source* Authors)

followed by Islamabad and Multan. Islamabad had the highest percentage of 76.8%, in life outlook.

These results are preliminary, indicating toward the possibility of designing and conducting HTI Index. The data size should have been much greater with representation from all levels of society and across Pakistan (Table 12, Fig. 4).

Table 12 Overall scenario: Pakistan

Constructs	Maqāṣid *al-Sharīʿah*						*Life outlook*	
Sub-constructs	F	P	IZ	HI	IK	D	SE	LS
Average	3.728	3.736	3.225	3.805	3.845	3.404	3.525	3.819
Percentage (%)	74.55	74.72	64.50	76.10	76.91	68.08	70.51	76.38
No. of observations	362	360	362	366	365	344	340	341
Missing values	7	9	7	3	4	25	29	28
Total sub-average					72.48%	3.624	75.18%	3.759
Total average								3.691
Total percentage								73.82%
Average age	23.22							

Source Authors

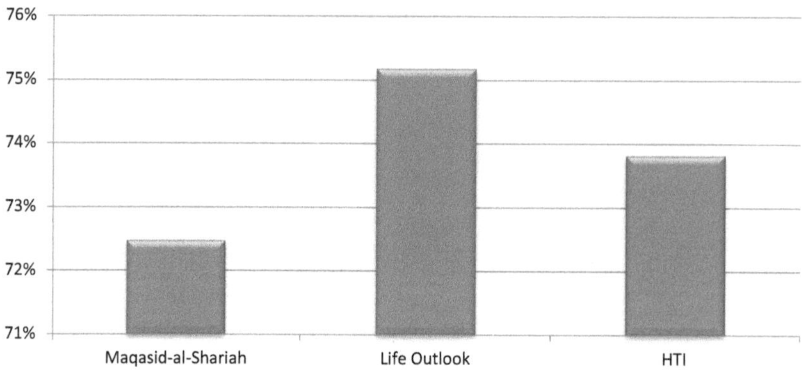

Fig. 4 Overall scenario: Pakistan (*Source* Authors)

The overall picture of Pakistan shows that the religiosity and spirituality are high. The individual-level *Maqāṣid* al-Sharīʿah is at 72.48%, whereas the life outlook is slightly higher at 75.18%, resulting in a HTI of 73.81%. People seem to feel satisfied and content with their life; still they have to deliver more on the Islamic rituals. Maybe, for the betterment of HTI we can assign some weightage to the constructs, rather than making them all at equal.

7 Conclusion

Our motive was to elaborate on the position of enlightened philosophers and their impact on the field of economics and society on the whole. We highlighted the fact that the field of economics is developed by explicitly rejecting the external constraints, i.e., existence of God, the importance of religion, life hereafter, rewards in heavens, and existence of hell. In contrast, the position of Islam as set by Allah (*swt*) and His Prophet Muhammad (*saaws*) in the Holy Qur'ān and Hadith was presented. The importance of *īmān* and *ākhirah* for the betterment of worldly life and life hereafter was presented. These aspects are to be taken as philosophical foundations for Islamic economics. It was discussed that the variables of conventional economics are in direct control of Allah (*swt*) and to gain positive increment in them and that also in an easy way needs a prior condition of *taqwá*—reduction in sins. Further on, we briefly discussed the role of *Maqāṣid* al-Sharīʿah and listed ten other variables, which, if combined, would give quantitative and qualitative dimensions to measure the real prosperity of individual, society, country, and *Ummah*, leading toward a more comprehensive measure then GDP—*Hayat-e-Tayyaba* Index (HTI). Here, HTI was articulated and measured through two broad constructs, representing *Maqāṣid* al-Sharīʿah from individual micro-level and life outlook. The data collected were represented gender-wise, city-wise, and overall country-wise, followed by discussion of HTI in all these contexts. Key learnings on questionnaire development and data collection methodology were also taken up. For further research and development, we need to elaborate the individual- and society-level variables for HTI—that also in light of above-discussed Islamic philosophy of economics so that accordingly, inwardly and outwardly, in both forms the mankind is not left out from the Islamic economic blessings.

Appendix

Survey Instrument: Questionnaire on Islamic Spirituality and Life View

#	*Item*
	Īmān—Faith
F1	I stay away from *ḥarām* acts in my work to avoid Allah's divine wrath
F2	I ask Allah to help me (*istikhara*) when I make important decisions in my life
F3	When confronted with problems I review my past actions for any sinful act
F4	I start my day with a *du'ā* to get support (*barakah*) of Allah (*swt*)
F5	If I am unsure of an act's permissibility, I still act upon it
	Ṣalāh—Prayer
P1	I pray all five prayers within their respective times
P2	I feel normal if I leave a *ṣalāh*
P3	When confronted with problems, I offer *ṣalāh* to seek help from Allah (*swt*)
P4	While outside I seriously look for *masjid* at *ṣalāh* time
	Ilm & Zikr—Knowledge and remembrance
IZ1	I spend sufficient time for seeking the knowledge of Islam—Daily
IZ2	I recite the Holy Qur'an—Daily
IZ3	I read and act upon at least one *Sunnah*—Daily
IZ4	I study *seerah* of our beloved Prophet (*saaws*)—Daily
IZ5	I make *zikr* of *kalima*, durood sharif and *istighfar*—Daily
	Ḥuqūq al-'ibād—The rights of the people
HI1	I spend some amount of my money in charity (*ṣadaqah*)
HI2	I break promises that I mak
HI3	I speak negative of others behind their back (backbiting)
HI4	I get angry on others easily for whatever mistake they make
HI5	I personally take care of my parents and grandparents
	Ikhlāṣ & Iḥsān—Sincerity and excellence
IK1	While doing any good action, my intention (*niyyah*) is to please Allah only
IK2	I precisely calculate my wealth for paying zakat and offering *qurbani*
IK3	I spend in charity in such a way that at least some people would know about it
IK4	I assist others in their work even though I don't gain any worldly benefit from it
IK5	I try not to misuse university (or office, market, hotels, airplane, etc.) resources freely available to me
	Dawah—Invitation
D1	I dedicate some time along with my family in order to learn Islamic teachings
D2	While going for *ṣalāh* I encourage my fellow Muslims to pray
D3	If an evil act is being done by someone, I do not consider it bad in my heart
D4	I dedicate some time for spreading the message of Islam to others because that is my responsibility
D5	I attend Islamic lectures (*bayanaat*)—Weekly

#	*Item*
	Self-efficacy
SE1	There is not much I can do to help myself
SE2	Often, there is no way I can complete what I have started
SE3	I can't begin to understand my problems
SE4	I am overwhelmed when I have personal difficulties and problems
SE5	I don't know how to begin to solve my problems
SE6	There is not much I can do to make a difference in my life
	Life scheme
LS1	I haven't found my life's purpose yet
LS2	I don't know who I am, where I came from, or where I am going
LS3	I have a lack of purpose in my life
LS4	In this world, I don't know where I fit in
LS5	I am far from understanding the meaning of life
LS6	There is a great void (emptiness) in my life at this time

References

Abdullah, H. *Sunnan Ibn Majah.*

Al-Jezairi. *Jamia Ul Usool Fi Aḥādīth Ar Rasool.* Maqtba Shamila.

Baghawi 1405 h. *Mishkat Al-Masabih.* Beruit, Lebonon: Mataba Al Islamia.

Bolton, D. L., & Lane, M. D. 2012. Individual Entrepreneurial Orientation: Development of a Measurement Instrument. *Education + Training, 54*(2–3), 219–233. https://doi.org/10.1108/00400911211210314.

Bukhari. *Sahih Bukhari.* Maqtab E Shamila.

Frey, B. B., Daaleman, T. P., & Peyton, V. 2005. Measuring a Dimension of Spirituality for Health Research. *Research on Aging, 27*(5), 556–577. https://doi.org/10.1177/0164027505277847.

Giddens, A. 2009. *Sociology.* Cambridge: Polity Press.

Gosepath, S. 2011. Equality. In E. N. Zalta (Ed.), *The Stanford Encyclopedia of Philosophy.* Spring 2011 Ed., Available from: http://Plato.Stanford.Edu/Archives/Spr2011/Entries/Equality.

Grondona, M. 2000. A Cutural Typology of Economic Development. In L. E. Harrison, & S. P. Huntington (Eds.), *Culture Matters: How Values Shape Human Progress.* New York: Basic Books.

Guyer, P. 1998 [2004]. Kant, Immanuel. In E. Craig (Ed.), *Routledge Encyclopedia of Philosophy.* London: Routledge. Available from: http://Www.Rep.Routledge.Com/Article/Db047.

Jones, M. S. 1996. *An Analysis and Critique of Immanuel Kant's "Critique of All Theology Based Upon Speculative Principles of Reason"* (Faculty Publications and Presentations, Paper 174). http://Digitalcommons.Liberty.Edu/Sor_Fac_Pubs/174.

Kant, I. 1993. *Opus Postumum*. Cambridge and New York: Cambridge University Press.

Kant, I. 2002. *Groundwork for the Metaphysics of Morals*. New Haven: Yale University Press.

Majlis Amne Mussessah Zaid bin Sultan Ale Nahiyan. 2012. *Muallama Zaid Lilqawaid al-Fiqhiya wa al-Usuliyah*. Mutahida Arab Imarat.

Montaner, C. A. 2000. Culture and the Behavior of Elites in Latin America. In L. E. Harrison & S. P. Huntington (Eds.), *Culture Matters: How Values Shape Human Progress*. New York: Basic Books.

Mueller, F. M. 1922. *Immanuel Kant's Critique of Pure Reason*. In *Commemoration of the Centenary of Its First Publication*. Translated into English (2nd Rev. ed.). New York: Macmillan. Available from: http://Oll.Libertyfund.Org/Simple.Php?Id=1442.

Nadvi, M. A. B. 2005. *Muashiyaat Ka Islami Falsafa*. Multan, Pakistan: Idara Talifaat Ashrafia.

Qureshi, M. S. 2013. *Entrepreneurship Plus: The Impact of Spiritual Orientation on Entrepreneurial Orientation, Market Orientation and the Entrepreneurial Process*. Paper Presented at the International Research Conference on Comtemporary Management Practices, Lahore School of Economics, Lahore, Pakistan.

Reisman, G. 1998. *Capitalism: A Treatise on Economics*. Ottawa, IL: Jameson Books.

Rice, H. 2013. Fatalism. In E. N. Zalta (Ed.), *The Stanford Encyclopedia of Philosophy*. Spring 2013 Ed., Available from: http://Plato.Stanford.Edu/Archives/Spr2013/Entries/Fatalism.

Rostow, W. W. 1961. *The Stages of Economic Growth* [S.L.]. Cambridge: Cambridge University Press.

Schönfeld, M. 2012. Kant's Philosophical Development. In E. N. Zalta (Ed.), *The Stanford Encyclopedia of Philosophy*. Winter 2012 Ed., Available from: http://Plato.Stanford.Edu/Archives/Win2012/Entries/Kant-Development.

Shatibi, Al. 1388. *Al-Muwafaqat Fi Usul Al-Sharia*. Khubar, Saudia Arabia: Dar-E-Ibn Affan.

Sterba, J. 1980. *Justice: Alternative Political Perspectives*. Belmont, CA: Wadsworth.

Thanvi, A. A. 2012. *Jaza Ul Amāl*. Karachi, Pakistan: Maqtaba Farooqia.

Tirmizi. *Jamia Al Tirmizi*. Maqtab E Shamila.

Williams, G. 2013. Kant's Account of Reason. In E. N. Zalta (Ed.), *The Stanford Encyclopedia of Philosophy*. Spring 2013 Ed., Available from: http://Plato.Stanford.Edu/Archives/Spr2013/Entries/Kant-Reason/.

CHAPTER 10

Islamic Inclusive Growth Index (i-IGI): Measurement and Determinants

Reza Ghazal and Muhamed Zulkhibri

1 Introduction

The concept of inclusive growth has been debated substantially by researchers and practitioners in domestic and international political circles. The concept has inspired the policies design and generated projects with impacted the views and the lives of many people in many countries. However, different interpretations of the concept of inclusive growth circulate in the literature. The concept is often used interchangeably with a suite of other terms, including 'broad-based growth,' 'shared growth,'

R. Ghazal · M. Zulkhibri (✉)
Islamic Research and Training Institute,
Islamic Development Bank, Jeddah, Saudi Arabia
e-mail: mzulkhibri@isdb.org

R. Ghazal
Business and Management Sciences Department,
University of Kurdistan-Hawler, Kurdistan, Iraq
e-mail: r.ghazal@ukh.ac

S. S. Ali (ed.), *Towards a Maqāṣid al-Sharīʿah Index of Socio-Economic Development*, Palgrave Studies in Islamic Banking, Finance, and Economics,
https://doi.org/10.1007/978-3-030-12793-0_10

and 'pro-poor growth.' By simple definition, inclusive growth focuses on both the pace and pattern of growth, economic growth which is a necessary and crucial condition for poverty reduction.

In Islam, development has dimensions of self and spiritual development, of the physical development, and of the development of society. The essential framework for individual and collective human progress are presented in the Qur'an and is, in turn, made operational by the traditions of the Prophet Muhammad (peace be upon him). The core principles of Islam place great emphasis on social justice, inclusion, and sharing of resources among the society, rich and poor. From Islamic development perspective, Chapra (2008) classifies at least five essential elements for developing a human development and well-being model from the theory of *Maqāṣid* al-Sharīʿah. Moreover, as classified by Imam Abu Hamid al-Ghazali, the discourse on the meaning of the term *Maqāṣid* al-Sharīʿah itself is focused more on the categories of the *Maqāṣid*.

In order to measure the progress of development, creation of composite indicators to measure countries development performance has recently attracted the attentions of many scholars, policy-makers, and institutions. Alternative measurement and concepts are being tested and increasingly used for policy-making at regional, national, and international levels. However, the construction of these indicators have met with considerable criticism at least in three dimensions: (i) the ability of the index to give a suitable measure of development due to the quality and limitation of raw data (Stiglitz et al. 2009); (ii) the technical limits of the index, the so-called weighting and aggregation problem (Mazumbar 2003); and (iii) the need to take into account more information and other variables and accounted for what really matters for the society, i.e., sustainability, environment, happiness, and religiosity (Nourry 2008).

The need for additional indicators to assess the economic and social progress has called for revisiting the worldview to take into consideration of a comprehensive approach to measure Islamic economics performance and social progress based on *Maqāṣid* al-Sharīʿah. Thus, the objective of the paper is to develop an Islamic Inclusive Growth Index (i-IGI), a composite index of growth inclusiveness based on Islamic principles for Muslim countries. It comprises of three sub-pillars to measure the countries' performance based on three building blocks of inclusiveness: (a) Islamic-adjusted economic growth incorporating *Maqāṣid* al-Sharīʿah's framework; (b) performance of poverty reduction; and (c) performance of the society inequality and social inclusion.

The paper is structured as follows. Section 2 provides brief concept of inclusive growth and *Maqāṣid* al-Sharīʿah. Section 3 provides the related literature review on the construction of economic and social index based on Islamic principles. Section 4 describes the methodology and data used for developing the index. Section 5 analyzes the results of the Inclusive Growth Index and Islamic Inclusive Growth Index and Sect. 6 finishes with the main conclusions.

2 Defining the Concept of Inclusive Growth and *Maqāṣid* al-Sharīʿah

2.1 Concept of Inclusive Growth

Over the past few years, inclusive growth has become a very popular topic among development practitioners. Despite broad use of the term, there seem to be different views on the issue of what may be called inclusive growth. Often, the concept of inclusive growth is identified with pro-poor growth, which differs from inclusive growth (Klasen 2010). The absolute definition of pro-poor growth suggests that what matters is the absolute rate at which the incomes of the poor are rising (Ravallion and Chen 2003; DFID 2004; Ianchovichina and Lundstrom 2009). Inclusive growth on the other hand, refers to the broader idea of a growth process that includes all segments of the society. It is about the extent to which economic growth creates opportunities for poor women and men through active participation in markets, communities, and states.

The Commission on Growth and Development (2008) notes that inclusiveness—a concept that encompasses equity, equality of opportunity, and protection in market and employment transitions—is an essential ingredient of any successful growth strategy. However, attempts to measure inclusive growth have remained limited. Traditionally, poverty (or inequality) and economic growth analyses have been done separately. Recent work indicates that there may not be a trade-off between equity and efficiency as suggested by Okun (1975) and 'that it would be a big mistake to separate analyses of growth and income distribution' (Berg and Ostry 2011).

Inclusive growth is important for very salient reasons: (i) ethical considerations of equity and fairness, growth must be shared and should be inclusive across different segments of populations and regions; (ii) growth with persisting inequalities within a country may endanger social peace and further weaken other disadvantaged and vulnerable sections of population—resulting in a waste of vast human capital that could otherwise be

Fig. 1 Policy pillars of inclusive growth (*Source* Adapted from Zhuang [2010])

used productively in creating economic outputs for sustainable growth; and (iii) continued inequalities in outcomes and access to opportunities in a country may result in civil unrest and violent backlash from people who are continually deprived, derailing a sustainable growth process.

The concept of inclusive growth follows three policy pillars supported by good institutions and governance (Zhuang 2010). As requirements to anchor inclusive growth strategy, the three pillars are aimed at high and sustained growth while ensuring that all members of the society benefit from growth: (i) High, efficient, and sustained growth to create productive jobs and economic opportunity; (ii) social inclusion ensures that all sections of the population, including those disadvantaged due to their individual circumstances, have equal opportunities; and (iii) social safety nets are required to protect the chronically poor and to mitigate the risks and vulnerabilities associated with transitory livelihood shocks.

Figure 1 depicts the three policy pillars of an inclusive growth strategy. In order to operationalize, the concept of inclusive growth, ADB (2011) proposes a framework of inclusive growth indicators. The proposed framework is not rigidly prescriptive to take into account gaps in the availability of timely and comparable statistics of good quality for a majority of the developing economies in the region. It ultimately attempts to help achieve the goal of reducing poverty and inequality (income and non-income) by measuring income and non-income outcomes and their distribution across population, as allowed by available data. The framework presents 35 quantifiable indicators to measure—outcomes and components of the three policy pillars of inclusive growth, as well as the components of good governance and strong institutions, which form the foundation of any inclusive growth strategy.[1]

2.2 *Concept of* Maqāṣid *al-Sharīʿah*

Muslim scholars have developed a theory known as *Maqāṣid* al-Sharīʿah (the objectives of the Sharīʿah). According to al-Raysuni (1992), the theory can be traced back as far as the third century after Hijrah (ninth century, A.D.). Most of the discussions in the past literature on *Maqāṣid* centered on its legal dimensions. The pioneering works emanated from scholars such as al-Shatibi (n.d.), al-Ghazali (1901), al-Juwayni (1979), Ibn Taymiyyah (al-Raysuni 1992), and Ibn 'Ashur (1998). The application of al-*Maqāṣid* in various disciplines including economics and finance has been gaining prominence in recent years. Among the leading economists, who have written on the subject are Chapra (1985, 2000), Siddiqi (2000), Ahmad (2000), Hasan (2004), Atiyah (2008), and Al-Najjar (2008).

The general objectives of Sharīʿah are commonly agreed by nearly all scholars of *al-Maqāṣid*, which are *Jalb al-Maṣāliḥ* (to promote virtues) and *Dafʿ al-Mafāṣid* (to remove harm) (Ibn 'Ashur 1998). Although there are some similarities in the principles (al-Raysuni 1992), some of these scholars differ in their classification of the specific objectives. *Maqāṣid* al-Sharīʿah provides a comprehensive framework that can be used to measure development. This framework is commonly represented by the three levels of *Maṣlaḥah* and the five universal values or essential elements (al-*Ḍarūriyāt* al-Khams).

[1] Income—Proportion of population living below the national poverty line; Proportion of population living below US$2 a day at 2005 PPP$; Ratio of income/consumption of the top 20% to bottom 20%. Non-income—Average years of total schooling (youth and adults); Prevalence of underweight children under-five years of age; Under-five mortality rate.

The *Maqāṣid* al-Sharīʿah is classified into five major categories according to Imam Al-Ghazali, a prominent and highly respected reformer in the eleventh century. He stated that the very objective of the Sharīʿah is to promote the well-being of the people, which lies in safeguarding of faith (*Dīn*), self (*Nafs*), intellect (*ʿaql*), posterity (*Nasl*), and wealth (*māl*). By promoting cooperation and mutual support within the family and society, it is also envisaged to spread the ethical values of compassion and guidance, establish justice, eliminate prejudice, and alleviate hardship. Hence, there is a general consensus that the primary objectives of the Sharīʿah (al-*Maqāṣid*) is to preserve the five essential elements, namely al-Dīn (religion), al-*Nafs* (life), al-*ʿaql* (intellect), *al-Nasl* (family institution), and al-*Māl* (wealth).

Muslim scholars in the past, notably al-Ghazali (1901), al-Shatibi (n.d.) and Ibn 'Ashur (1998), besides having discussed the five essential elements of al-*Maqāṣid*, they also discussed the levels of al-*Maqāṣid*, which termed as *maṣlaḥah*. The three levels of al-*Maqāṣid* are explained by earlier scholar in an ascending order as: *ḍarūriyāt* (Necessity), *ḥajiyāt* (Complement), and *taḥsiniyāt* (Embellishment). From a *Maqāṣid* perspective, the three levels of *maṣlaḥah* represent a growth path and stages of development. The first level, *ḍarūriyāt* represents the minimum level that every individual, institution, and nation must achieve. This level embodies the preservation of the five universal values or essential elements mentioned above. The second level, *ḥajiyāt*, provides avenues for the growth of the five elements, and the third level, *taḥsiniyāt*, represents the stage for their sustainability.

In recent years, the application of *Maqāṣid* al-Sharīʿah has varied across several disciplines. Many of the contemporary applications have been in the legal circle where *maṣlaḥah* has been used by Sharīʿah Advisory Councils of many Islamic banks as the basis for issuing fatwas. Although the parameters for the application of *maṣlaḥah* have been defined by several Sharīʿah bodies and academies (Bouheraoua 2008), these applications have hardly been extended beyond the fatwa sessions. On the other hands, in economics and finance, most literature on *Maqāṣid* al-Sharīʿah is essentially theoretical in nature, for example, Chapra (1985, 2008), Siddiqi (2000), Hasan (2004), and Ahmad (2000). Nevertheless, there are few studies that have tried to operationalize *Maqāṣid* al-Sharīʿah in the areas of economics and finance.

3 Related Literature on Measuring Islamic Economics and Social Progress

There have been numerous attempts to construct indicators or composite indices to measure economic welfare, sustainable development quality of life, and well-being. Among others are Human Development Index (HDI); the Quality of Life Index (QLI); the Happy Planet Index (HPI); Gross National Happiness (GHI); the Legatum Prosperity Index (LPI); the Multidimensional Poverty Index (MPI); Genuine Progress Indicator (GPI); and the Meaning of Life Index (MLI). HDI is a composite index widely used by international organizations to evaluate and rank countries in terms of three main indicators of economic and social welfare—income, health and education attainments.

In the Islamic literature, however, very few have attempted to integrate the religious aspect of development that reflects spiritual well-being, which has been recognized as an important component in the construction of the indices. Several indices have been developed a methodological framework, while others have constructed the indices as potential alternatives to the more commonly used indices based on conventional views of economic and social progress. However, there are few studies in the literature that develop Islamic indices: (i) the Ethics-Augmented Human Development Index (E-HDI) by Dar (2004); (ii) the Islamic Human Development Index (I-HDI) by Anto (2009); (iii) the Integrated Development Index (I-Dex) by Amin et al. (2013); and (iv) the Islamicity Index (I2) by Rehman and Askari (2010).

Dar (2004) proposes an ethics-augmented human development index (E-HDI) as a new indicator of socio-economic change and development. The E-HDI incorporates freedom, faith, environmental concerns, and the institution of family in the HDI and ranks countries of the world accordingly. The study constructs the E-HDI based on *Maqāṣid* al-Sharīʿah, and it conceptualizes social change and development for all countries. However, the ranking of countries in the study is based on the ordinal measure using the Borda Rule instead of on the actual values of E-HDI computed for all countries. Hence, there is a need to develop a comprehensive development index based on *Maqāṣid* al-Sharīʿah that can actually be computed for the ranking of countries' level of development.

Anto (2009) attempts to develop Islamic Human Development Index (I-HDI). The paper argues that the existing HDI is not fully compatible and sufficient in measuring human development from Islamic perspective. The index is comprised of Material Welfare Index (MWI) and Non-material Welfare Index (NWI), representing the five basic needs in *Maqāṣid* al-Sharīʿah. It also includes the Freedom Index and the Environment Index. The findings show that the rank composition between I-HDI and HDI is slightly different. A number of countries enjoy a better rank in I-HDI compared with HDI. On the other hand, several countries suffer a marked deterioration of rank. The high score group in I-HDI is still dominated mostly by Middle East Countries and the bottom line is still dominated by African Countries.

Rehman and Askari (2010) propose to measure the degree of religiosity of Islamic countries. It uses four sub-indices namely the Economic Islamicity Index (EI^2), the Legal and Governance Islamicity Index (LGI^2), the Human and Political Rights Islamicity Index (HPI^2), and the International Relations Islamicity Index (IRI^2) to measure government's adherence to Islamic principles in economics; legal integrity and governance environment; degree of civil and political rights; and relationship with the global community. The study shows that Islamic countries are not as Islamic, at least in the realm of economics, as one might expect; instead, it appears that the most developed countries tend to place higher on this Islamic Economic Index.

Amin et al. (2013) proposes to develop an integrated Islamic development framework and index based on and representing the *Maqāṣid* al-Sharīʿah or noble objectives of the Sharīʿah for OIC and non-OIC countries. The Integrated Development Framework based on *Maqāṣid* al-Sharīʿah has been developed based on the works by al-Ghazali and Abu Zaharah. Using content analysis, the operational definitions of each component of *Maqāṣid* al-Sharīʿah have been derived, and the dimensions identified based on the scope of the definitions. The elements have been selected for each dimension based on the relevant existing indicators. However, data availability still poses a major constraint in selecting more relevant indicators. Hence, the study does not proceed further to compute the actual index.

On the other hands, several studies attempt to incorporate the concept of *Maqāṣid* al-Sharīʿah approach into the field of Islamic finance. Dusuki (2007) and Hamdan (2014) attempt to relate *Maqāṣid* al-Sharīʿah to corporate social responsibility (CSR) and argue that the concept of CSR is not alien to Islam and any corporation that claims to follow Shariʿah-based principles should naturally practice CSR, as it enshrines Islam's true spirit. Similarly, Hameed et al. (2004) develop Islamicity Disclosure Index to measure and compare the performances of two Islamic banks. Mustafa et al. (2008) refine the research and develop a quantitative performance measure for Islamic banking from the theory of al-*Maqāṣid*. On the other hand, Larbani and Mohammed (2011) develops a decision making tool based on *Maqāṣid* al-Sharīʿah and their levels of *Maṣlaḥah* for the managers of firms to use in allocating their investible resources to vital sectors of the economy.

Bedoui (2012) proposes a framework to manage ethical (financial and non-financial) performances based on the concept of *Maqāṣid* al-Sharīʿah. The paper argues that considering the fact that business ethics is one of the most needed in the market nowadays, this framework is a solution for Islamic financial institutions and can be used for other organizations looking for ethical investments. The proposed framework is considered akin to a rating model to benchmark organizations based on the five *Maqāṣid* al-Sharīʿah. The graphical method used in the paper assigns a score 'the performance' to each axis in which represents one objective of the five dimensions of *Maqāṣid* al-Sharīʿah.

4 Data and Methodology

4.1 Data Descriptions

In this section, we provide the descriptions of the data used in constructing the Islamic Inclusive Growth Index (hereafter i-IGI) for the group of IsDB member countries, which the data is available. Table 1 presents the Gini index, poverty index, GDP growth, and ratio of non-interest income to total assets respectively (see Appendix 1 for details). These variables are used in constructing our indexes. According to Table 1, on inequality, Comoros is the most non-equal country among our sample countries with the Gini index at 64.3%, while Kazakhstan is the most equal country in terms of income distribution among its people with the Gini index at 29%.

In terms of poverty, Nigeria has the highest percentage of population under the poverty line at 68% followed by Mozambique at 59%, while Azerbaijan has the smallest percentage of population under poverty line at 0.4% followed by Albania at 0.6%. On economic growth, Azerbaijan has experienced the higher growth of 10% on average over 2007–2011, while Cote d'Ivoire experienced the lowest growth at 1.1%.

Table 1 Status of Muslim countries based on three pillars of inclusiveness (average 2007–2011)

	Poverty headcount ratio at \$1.25 a day (PPP) (% of population)	*GINI index*	*GDP growth (% annual)*	*Non-interest income as a ratio of total assets*
Albania	0.6	34.5	4.7	1.738
Azerbaijan	0.4	33.7	10.0	0.0001
Benin	47.3	38.6	3.7	N.A
Burkina Faso	44.6	39.8	4.9	2.968
Bangladesh	43.3	32.1	6.2	0.934
Cote d'Ivoire	23.8	41.5	1.1	N.A
Comoros	46.1	64.3	1.5	N.A
Djibouti	18.8	40.0	5.1	N.A
Egypt	1.7	30.8	5.2	1.437
Gabon	4.8	41.5	3.5	2.32
Guinea	43.3	39.4	2.5	N.A
Gambia	33.6	47.3	3.6	7.442
Guinea-Bissau	48.9	35.5	4.8	NA
Indonesia	20.3	35.9	5.9	2.371
Iran	1.5	38.3	4.0	N.A
Iraq	2.8	30.9	5.6	1.64
Jordan	0.1	34.6	5.2	0.912
Kazakhstan	0.1	29.8	5.6	0.423
Kyrgyz	5.3	35.4	5.1	N.A
Morocco	2.5	40.9	4.5	1.304
Maldives	1.5	37.4	6.6	11.32
Mali	50.4	33.0	4.5	N.A
Mozambique	59.6	45.7	7.0	5.102
Mauritania	23.4	40.5	2.6	4.169
Malaysia	0.0	46.1	4.4	0.956
Niger	43.6	34.6	4.5	4.675
Nigeria	68.0	48.8	6.9	3.343
Pakistan	21.0	30.0	2.8	1.516
Sudan	19.8	35.3	3.6	4.931
Senegal	29.6	40.3	3.5	0.672
Sierra Leone	51.7	35.4	5.6	N.A
Syria	1.7	35.8	4.9	0.498
Tajikistan	10.6	31.7	6.7	N.A
Tunisia	1.1	36.1	3.0	2.116
Turkey	0.8	39.2	3.7	1.855
Uganda	38.0	44.3	7.4	3.848
Yemen	17.5	37.7	1.6	1.353
Average	22.4	38.3	4.6	2.687

Note N.A stands for not available
Source World Bank Group Database; Bankscope

On non-interest income, more interestingly, Maldives has the highest non-interest income compared to total assets at 11.3%, while Azerbaijan has the least at less than 0.0001%.

4.2 *Methodology*

There have been some methodology suggested by different scholars and entities (i.e., ADB[2] and AfDB) on how to measure the inclusive index. However, most of the methodologies require significant numbers of data, which can explain why up to now no inclusive development index has numerically been calculated or presented. Having known these limitations on the data availability, we introduce an innovative simple inclusive index using the three most important components that can be understood from the definition of inclusiveness of growth.

According to the classical definition of inclusive development (or growth), a growth is called inclusive if all the society will benefit from that growth, especially the poor people. Alternatively, inclusiveness simply refers to the broader idea of a growth process that includes all segments of the society. In this context, the i-IGI is a summary measure of inclusive growth in Muslim countries. It intends to measure the average achievements in a country in three basic dimensions of inclusiveness: economic growth adjusted to incorporate Sharīʿah's aspect, country's performance on reducing proportion of population under poverty line, and reducing the inequality among the poor and rich. The i-IGI is the geometric mean of normalized indices measuring achievements in each dimension.

Using this definition as a starting point, our inclusive index comprises of three components: (i) GDP growth representing the growth component; (ii) inequality proxy by the Gini index to reflect the extent of inequality among the society; and (iii) the poverty index representing the proportion of population under the poverty line at $1.25 a day (measured at PPP). Another innovation that we did in the paper is to take into account of the Sharīʿah's role in the inclusiveness of the growth. Since the aims on reducing poverty and inequality are universal across the countries no matter whether the country is Muslim or not, we adjust only the growth part of the index to reflect the Islamic sense of growth by using the 'ratio of average non-interest income to total assets' as our growth-adjuster.

[2] See Appendix 2 for definition of indicators.

In order to control for the cyclical ups and downs in any of the components (especially for the 2007–2009 global financial crisis) used in constructing the index and therefore preventing the under-representativeness or over-representativeness of a specific year, we used an average of those indicators over 2007–2011 period. In addition, since an economy with more equality, lower poverty, and higher growth is the chief target and main objective of the countries, we need to transform the poverty and Gini indexes to be consistent comparatively. In this regard, we did two transformations on the poverty and inequality data to make them consistent and usable for the construction of the i-IGI. First, we inversed[3] them and second, we subtracted the indicators from 100, since they are reported as percentage. Using two ways of transformations can work also as a robustness check for the results. Figure 2 presents the flowchart in term of steps taken for the i-IGI construction.

In constructing the index, we also use two well-known but different methods: (i) MinMax method as suggested in HDI report and (ii) standardization method. Under the MinMax method, the first step is to create sub-indices for each dimension. Minimum and maximum values (known as goalposts) need to be set in order to transform the indicators into indices between 0 and 1. Because the geometric mean is used for aggregation, the maximum value does not affect the relative comparison (in percentage terms) between any two countries or periods of time (UN 2013). The maximum values are set to the actual observed maximum values of the indicators from the countries on a cross-section basis of 2007–2011 average.

The minimum values are set at 32 under the inverse transformation (and 0.015 under second transformation) for poverty headcount ratio at US$1.25 a day (PPP), at 35.7 (0.016 under second transformation) for both GINI index variables and at 1.1 for GDP growth (% annual). Progress is thus measured against minimum levels that a society needs to survive over time. Following HDI methodology and having defined the minimum and maximum values, the sub-indices are calculated as follows:

$$\text{Dimension Index} = \frac{\text{actual value} - \text{minimum value}}{\text{maximum value} - \text{minimum value}} \quad (1)$$

[3]Inversing means that we did the followings on poverty and Gini indexes: 1/Poverty ratio and 1/Gini Index. In the same way, subtracting from 100 means: 100-Poverty Index and 100-Gini Index.

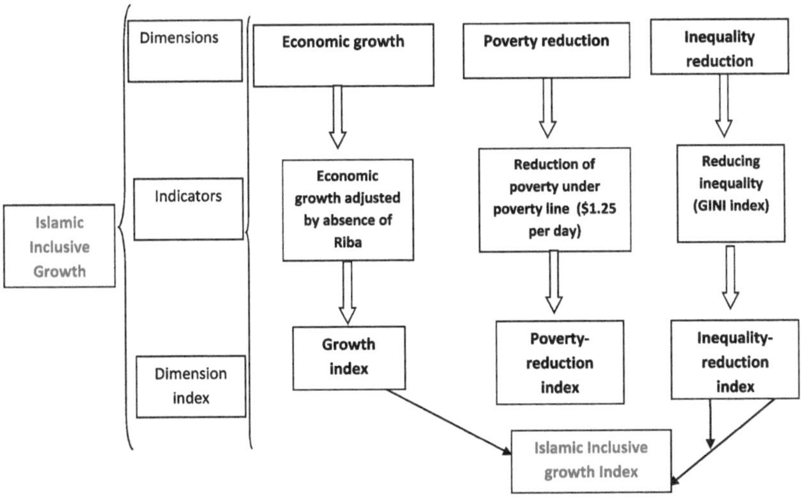

Fig. 2 Calculating the Islamic Inclusive Growth Index: A graphical flowcharts (*Source* Authors' own illustration based on HDI report)

For each dimension, Eq. 1 is applied to each of the subcomponents, then a geometric mean of the resulting indices is created. This is equivalent to applying Eq. 1 directly to the geometric mean of the subcomponents. Because each dimension index is a proxy for capabilities in the corresponding dimension, the transformation function from income to capabilities is likely to be concave (Anand and Sen 2000). The i-IGI is the geometric mean of the all dimension indices as follows:

$$\text{i-IGI} = \left(I_1^{1/3} * I_2^{1/3} * I_3^{1/3}\right) \tag{2}$$

where 3 represents the number of sub-indices, and I represents the sub-indexes. Equation 2 embodies imperfect substitutability across all i-IGI dimensions. It is thus addressed one of the most serious criticisms of the linear aggregation formula, which allowed for perfect substitution across dimensions. Some substitutability is inherent in the definition of any index that increases with the values of its components (UN 2013).

Under the standardization method the same methodology is applied except that instead of defining the goalposts (minimum and maximum values), each sub-index is standardized by the conventional standardization methodology. In other words, each sub-index is subtracted from the average of that sub-index for the whole group of countries and then it is divided by the standard deviation of the sub-index. In addition, under standardization method since some negative sub-indexes will be appeared, we had to shift the distribution of the sub-indexes merely to get positive numbers. It is worth mentioning that shifting the distribution will not affect the results.

5 Empirical Findings

Table 2 presents the rankings of Muslim countries in terms of inclusive growth and Islamic inclusive growth indices.[4] These rankings are based on both MinMax and standardization methods. In general, the findings are different from the findings of existing models in the literature (i.e., Rehman and Askari 2010; Anto 2009; Dar 2004), but pointed to the same conclusion that majority of the Muslim countries are not conforming to Islamic principles, at least in the realm of economic and development.

According to the rankings, over 2007–2011 Azerbaijan has ranked first on all inclusive growth indexes using various methodologies due to its strong performance on growth side during that period as well as very low proportion of population under the poverty line. However, when it comes to the Islamic version of the inclusive index (i.e., i-IGI), due to extremely low level of non-interest income of this country (compared to its assets), its place in ranking drops significantly to 26th, except for the case where MaxMin is built on second transformation.

The same result is also applied to Kazakhstan. Having high growth and low poverty have helped the country to rank 2nd in inclusive growth index, while drops to rank around 20th after taking into account the *Maqāṣid* al-Sharīʿah aspect of the index (Table 3). On the other extreme, Nigeria ranks 26 in terms of inclusive growth index due to its high levels of poverty and to some degree relatively high inequality, followed by Mozambique ranked at 25th.

In general, interestingly the Muslim countries in Sub-Saharan Africa improve in terms of ranking when it comes to i-IGI. The main reason can mainly due to low levels of bank assets. It can also be explained by the existence of some foreign-banks that have been established by Muslim countries especially from the Gulf region. There are some

[4]The values correspondent to the rankings are in Appendix 3.

Table 2 Ranking of inclusive growth and Islamic Inclusive Growth Index for Muslim countries

	IGMMT1	*i-IGMMT1*	*IGMMT2*	*i-IGMMT2*	*IGSTDT1*	*i-IGSTDT1*	*IGSTDT2*	*i-IGSTDT2*
Azerbaijan	1	26	1	4	1	26	1	26
Kazakhstan	2	20	2	1	2	19	2	20
Iraq	3	3	3	2	3	3	3	14
Maldives	4	1	4	26	4	1	4	8
Egypt	5	9	5	5	5	8	5	16
Jordan	6	14	6	3	6	14	6	10
Albania	7	7	7	6	7	7	7	1
Syria	8	22	8	8	8	22	8	6
Indonesia	9	4	9	11	9	4	9	11
Morocco	10	15	10	7	10	15	10	23
Turkey	11	13	11	9	11	13	11	2
Tunisia	12	11	12	10	12	10	12	21
Malaysia	13	19	13	12	13	20	13	17
Gabon	14	12	14	14	14	12	14	5
Sudan	15	2	15	13	15	2	15	3
Bangladesh	16	21	16	20	16	17	16	9
Pakistan	17	17	17	23	17	21	17	4
Uganda	18	6	18	15	18	6	18	22
Senegal	19	24	19	17	19	24	19	15
Niger	20	8	20	25	20	9	20	18
Mauritania	21	10	21	18	21	11	21	12
Burkina Faso	22	16	22	24	22	16	22	25
Yemen	23	23	23	21	23	23	23	19
Gambia	24	5	24	16	24	5	24	13
Mozambique	25	18	25	19	25	18	25	24
Nigeria	26	25	26	22	26	25	26	7

Note IGMMT1 refers to inclusive growth based on MaxMin method using the Transformation 1; IGSTDT1 refers to inclusive growth based on standardization method using Transformation 1; and i at the beginning refers to Islamic
Source Authors calculations

Table 3 Muslim countries' inclusive growth and Islamic Inclusive Growth Index

	IGMMT1	*IIGMMT1*	*IGMMT2*	*IIGMMT2*	*IGSTDT1*	*IIGSTDT1*	*IGSTDT2*	*IIGSTDT2*
Azerbaijan	0.883906	0.032563	0.531728	0.317032	4.500171	0.17	4.90429	0.18
Kazakhstan	0.775093	0.462134	0.52842	0.413207	3.944257	2.35	4.845404	2.89
Iraq	0.757441	0.708992	0.526939	0.405625	3.851285	3.60	4.420788	3.40
Maldives	0.747065	1.331496	0.404139	0.014889	3.786545	6.75	4.218708	3.95
Egypt	0.743269	0.665751	0.273043	0.260561	3.777822	3.38	4.207175	3.26
Jordan	0.72043	0.554571	0.220472	0.392948	3.654019	2.81	4.136592	3.71
Albania	0.700129	0.668124	0.218718	0.213332	3.548933	3.39	3.904797	6.96
Syria	0.693939	0.436824	0.213592	0.191316	3.514975	2.21	3.843655	4.07
Indonesia	0.66014	0.698728	0.193098	0.121552	3.339066	3.53	3.796912	3.62
Morocco	0.636389	0.551835	0.1916	0.195257	3.207496	2.78	3.671317	2.31
Turkey	0.62113	0.605834	0.184969	0.173138	3.131605	3.05	3.655002	4.85
Tunisia	0.610001	0.621644	0.153569	0.133165	3.078116	3.14	3.648479	2.85
Malaysia	0.594654	0.465	0.112041	0.117724	2.977073	2.33	3.494384	3.19
Gabon	0.583163	0.612742	0.087545	0.092663	2.931261	3.08	3.433033	4.27
Sudan	0.579714	0.783194	0.075114	0.10148	2.923944	3.95	3.373158	4.56
Bangladesh	0.566268	0.439334	0.072616	0.066211	2.854665	2.60	3.356973	3.83
Pakistan	0.565654	0.51576	0.069918	0.054245	2.848897	2.21	3.271225	4.47
Uganda	0.545345	0.678285	0.065712	0.081731	2.72432	3.39	3.220921	2.79
Senegal	0.504166	0.350539	0.060334	0.080072	2.526133	1.76	3.217799	3.28
Niger	0.502666	0.667111	0.059398	0.041298	2.519732	3.34	3.206684	3.13
Mauritania	0.489357	0.625129	0.058586	0.074841	2.448933	3.13	3.021254	3.59
Burkina Faso	0.477576	0.544749	0.057476	0.050457	2.383663	2.72	3.016212	2.10
Yemen	0.472443	0.414752	0.056927	0.064934	2.360995	2.07	2.956464	3.11
Gambia, The	0.443089	0.686622	0.052046	0.080653	2.196836	3.40	2.78145	3.55
Mozambique	0.36115	0.493471	0.051968	0.071008	1.743618	2.38	2.629709	2.31
Nigeria	0.196874	0.233664	0.046612	0.055322	0.682074	0.81	2.603899	4.04

Note IGMMT1 refers to inclusive growth based on MinMax method using the Transformation 1; IGSTDT1 refers to inclusive growth based on standardization method using Transformation 1
Source Authors calculations

countries, especially Tunisia and Turkey for which a consistent pattern of rankings is observed in such a way that their rankings are remained almost the same under both IGI and i-IGI rankings.

6 Conclusions

This paper is the first step toward establishing and constructing an Inclusive Index and Islamic Inclusive Index based on *Maqāṣid* al-Sharīʿah to gauge how Muslim countries perform on inclusive-related issues including economic growth, poverty, and inequality. Moreover, this framework is one of the solutions for Muslim countries to measure the overall performance based on the *Maqāṣid* al-Sharīʿah principles. In this study, different transformations and methods have been used to ensure the data requirement for inclusive index calculation is consistent and at the same time can be used as a robustness check for the overall results.

The overall observations are that despite the significant performance of Central Asian Muslim countries on various pillars of inclusiveness, their performances in terms of complying with the *Maqāṣid* al-Sharīʿah (specifically *riba*-free economy) are considerably low. On the other hand, low-growth Muslim countries in Sub-Saharan Africa have a promising performance based on the Sharīʿah-compliance aspect. The findings are different from the findings of existing models in the literature, but pointed to the same conclusion that Muslim countries are not conforming to Islamic principles, at least in the realm of economics.

For future research, the most vital step in constructing a more accurate and inclusive index to reflect the *Maqāṣid* al-Sharīʿah principle is to compile a more detail data covering most of the important indicators. Therefore, in order to complete the research on this issue, it is vital in the future research to provide an empirical assessment and discussion on the i-IGI's determinants for Muslim countries. This future research will also answer the usefulness of the new index (i-IGI) in explaining the variation of economic behavior in Muslim countries.

Appendix 1: Gini Index, Poverty Index, and GDP Growth

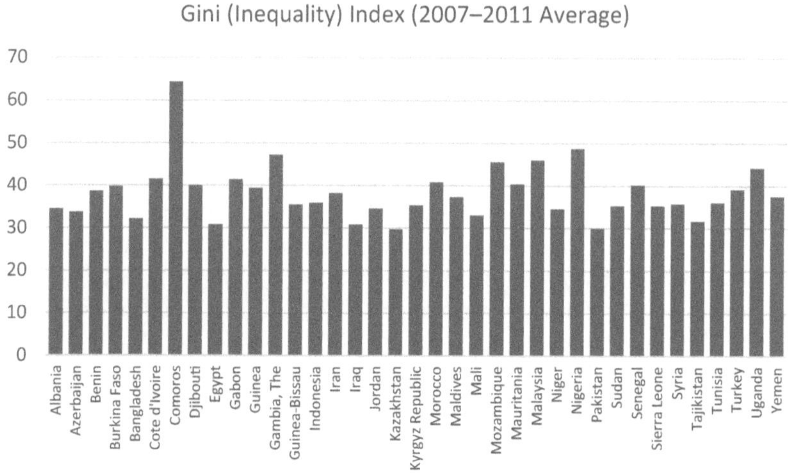

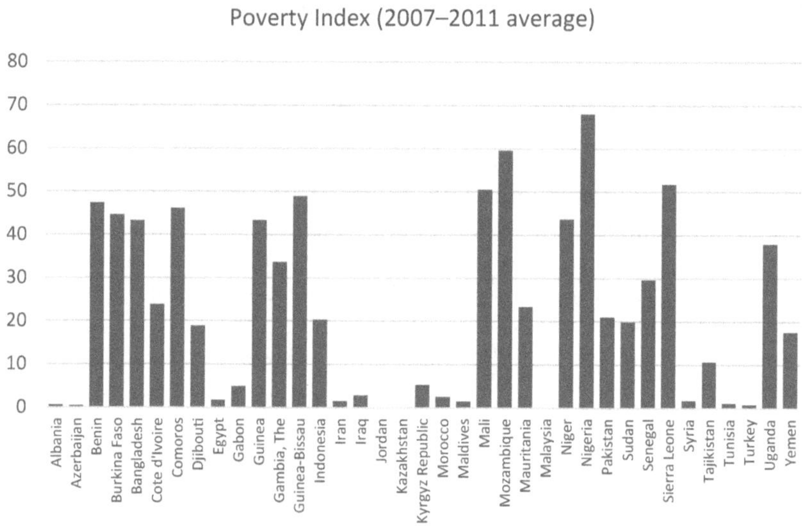

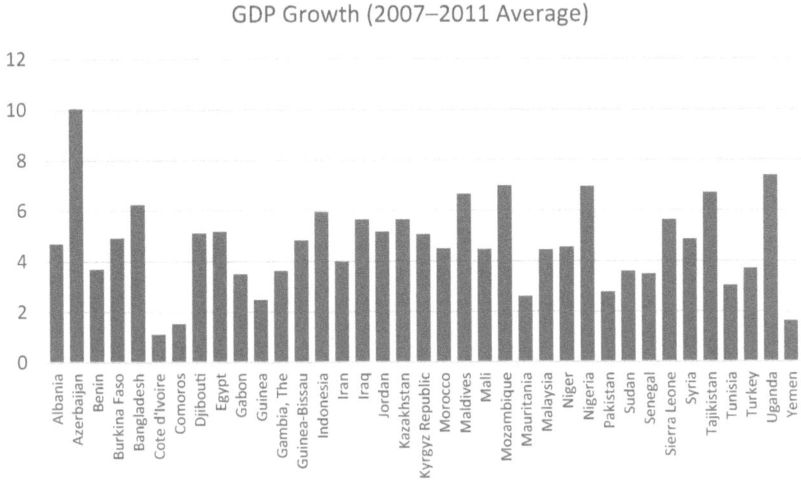

Appendix 2: Framework of Islamic Inclusive Growth Index: Pillars and Indicators

Dimensions	*Indicators*
1. *Income poverty and inequality*	
1.1. Income	1. Proportion of population living below the national poverty line
	2. Proportion of population living below $2 a day at 2005 PPP$
	3. Ratio of income or consumption of the top 20% to bottom 20%
1.2 Non-income	4. Average years of total schooling (youth and adults)
	5. Prevalence of underweight children under five years of age
	6. Under-five mortality rate
2. *Pillar 1: Growth and expansion of economic opportunities*	
2.1 Economic growth and employment	7. Growth rate of GDP per capita at PPP (constant 2005 PPP$)
	8. Growth rate of average per capita income/consumption 2005 PPP$ (lowest quintile, highest quintile, and total)
	9. Employment rate
	10. Elasticity of total employment to total GDP (employment elasticity)
	11. Number of own-account and contributing family workers per 100 wage and salaried workers
2.2 Key infrastructure endowments	12. Per capita consumption of electricity
	13. Percentage of paved roads
	14. Number of cellular phone subscriptions per 100 people
	15. Depositors with other depository corporations per 1000 adults

(continued)

(continued)

Dimensions	*Indicators*
3. *Pillar 2: Social inclusion to ensure equal access to economic opportunity*	
3.1 Access and inputs to education and health	16. School life expectancy (primary to tertiary) 17. Pupil-teacher ratio (primary) 18. Diphtheria, tetanus toxoid, and pertussis (DTP3) immunization coverage among 1-year-olds 19. Physicians, nurses, and midwives per 10,000 population 20. Government expenditure on education as percentage of total government expenditure 21. Government expenditure on health as a percentage of total government expenditure
3.2 Access to basic infrastructure utilities and services	22. Percentage of population with access to electricity 23. Share of population using solid fuels for cooking 24. Percentage of population using improved drinking water sources 25. Percentage of population using improved sanitation facilities
3.3. Gender equality and opportunity	26. Gender parity in primary, secondary, and tertiary education 27. Antenatal care coverage (at least one visit) 28. Gender parity in labor force participation 29. Percentage of seats held by women in national parliament
4. *Pillar 3: Social safety nets*	
4.1 Social safety nets	30. Social protection and labor rating 31. Social security expenditure on health as a percentage of government expenditure on health 32. Government expenditure on social security and welfare as a percentage of total government expenditure
5. *Pillar 4:* Maqāṣid *al-Sharī'ah principles*	
5.1 *Ḥifẓ al-Dīn*	33. Percentage of total expenditure in religious education 34. Overall ranking in corruption index
5.2 *Ḥifẓ al-'aql*	35. Primary enrollment rate 36. Secondary enrollment rate
5.3 *Ḥifẓ al-Nafs*	37. Universal Human Rights Index 38. Incidence of crime
5.4 *Ḥifẓ al- Māl*	39. International Property Rights Index
5.5 *Ḥifẓ al-Nasl*	40. Divorce rate
6. *Good governance and institutions*	
6.1 Good governance and institutions	33. Voice and accountability 34. Government effectiveness 35. Corruption Perceptions Index

Source Adapted from ADB (2011)

Appendix 3: IGI and i-IGI: MinMax and Standardization Methods

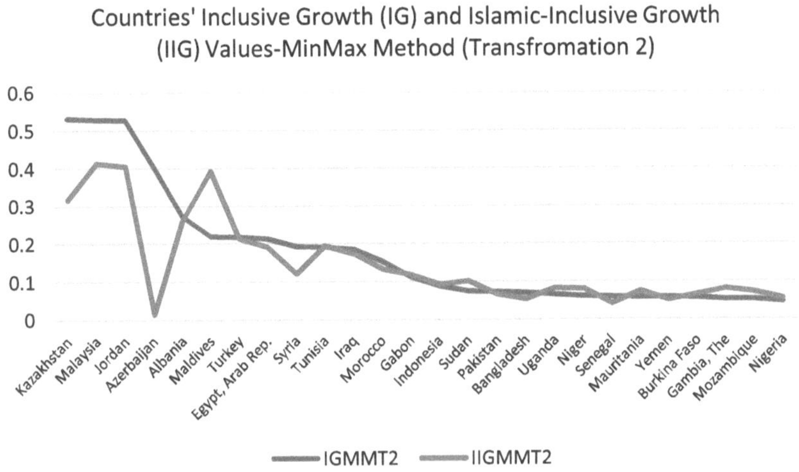

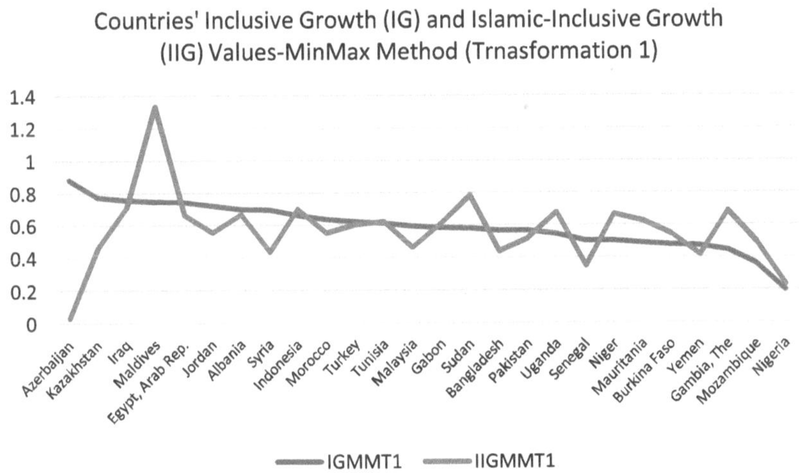

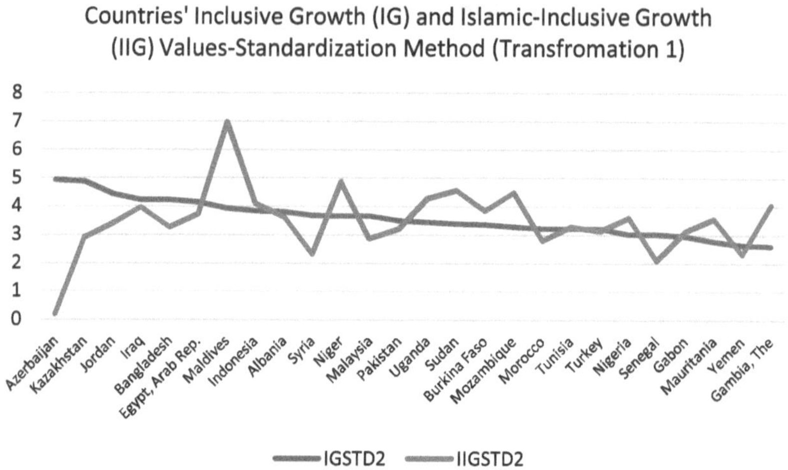
Countries' Inclusive Growth (IG) and Islamic-Inclusive Growth (IIG) Values-Standardization Method (Transfromation 1)
0
1
2
3
4
5
6
7
8
Azerbaijan
Kazakhstan
Jordan
Iraq
Bangladesh
Egypt, Arab Rep.
Maldives
Indonesia
Albania
Syria
Niger
Malaysia
Pakistan
Uganda
Sudan
Burkina Faso
Mozambique
Morocco
Tunisia
Turkey
Nigeria
Senegal
Gabon
Mauritania
Yemen
Gambia, The
IGSTD2
IIGSTD2

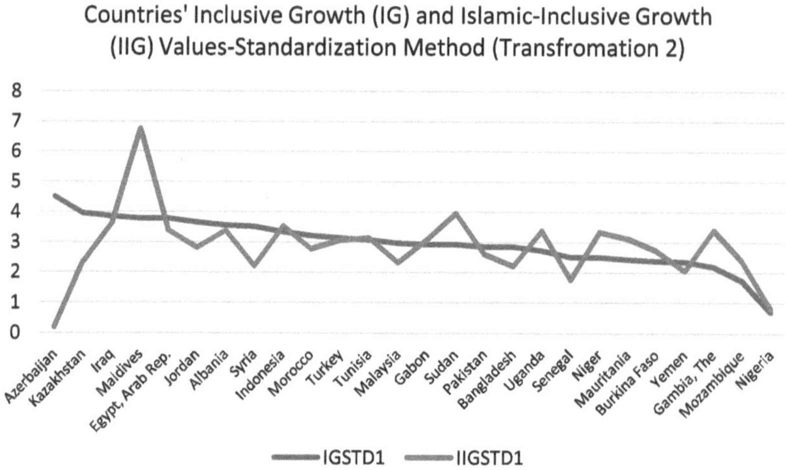
Countries' Inclusive Growth (IG) and Islamic-Inclusive Growth (IIG) Values-Standardization Method (Transfromation 2)
0
1
2
3
4
5
6
7
8
Azerbaijan
Kazakhstan
Iraq
Maldives
Egypt, Arab Rep.
Jordan
Albania
Syria
Indonesia
Morocco
Turkey
Tunisia
Malaysia
Gabon
Sudan
Pakistan
Bangladesh
Uganda
Senegal
Niger
Mauritania
Burkina Faso
Yemen
Gambia, The
Mozambique
Nigeria
IGSTD1
IIGSTD1

References

ADB. (2011). *Key indicators for Asia and the Pacific 2011: Framework of inclusive growth indicators* (Special supplement). Manila: Asian Development Bank.

Ahmad, K. (2000). Islamic finance and banking: The challenge and prospects. *Review of Islamic Economics* 9, 57–82.

Al-Ghazali, A. H. (1901). *Al-mustasfa min ʿilm al-usul* (1st Ed.). Cairo, Egypt: Al-Matba'ah al-Amiriyyah.

Al-Jawziyyah, I. Q. (n.d.). *I'lam al-muwaqi'in*, ed. Taha 'Abd al-Rauf. Beirut: Dar al-Jil.

Al-Juwayni, A. (1979). *Al-burhan fi usul al-fiqh*, ed. Abdul Azim al-Dib. Cairo: Dar al-Ansar.

Al-Najjar, U. A. (2008). Maqāṣid *al-Sharīʿah bi ab'adin jadidah*. Beirut: Dar al-Gharb al-Islami.

Al-Raysuni, A. (1992). *Al-Nazariyah al- Maqasid ʿInda al-Imam al-Shatibi* (2nd Ed.). Riyadh: Al-Dar al-'Alamiyyah lil Kitab al-Islami.

Al Sari, A. M. (n.d.). Basic human needs the Islamic theory. Unpublished thesis.

Amin, R. M., Yusof, S. M., Haneef, M. A., Muhammad, M. O., and Oziev, G. (2013). *The integrated development index (i-dex): A new comprehensive approach to measuring human development*. 9th International Conference on Islamic Economics and Finance, 9–10 September.

Anand, S., and Sen, A. (2000). The income component of the human development index. *Journal of Human Development* 1(1), 83–106.

Anto, M. H. (2009). Introducing an Islamic human development index (I-HDI) to measure development in OIC countries. *Islamic Economic Studies* 19(2), 69–95.

Atiyah, G. E. (2008). Nahw taf'eel *Maqāṣid* al-Sharīʿah (Towards revitalizing al-*Maqāṣid*). International Institute of Islamic Thought, Herndon, VA, USA.

Bedoui, M. H. (2012). *Shariʿa-based ethical performance measurement framework* (CEFN Working Paper). University of Paris.

Berg, A., and Ostry, J. D. (2011). *Inequality and unsustainable growth: Two sides of the same coin?* (IMF Staff Discussion Note 11/08). Washington: International Monetary Fund.

Bouheraoua, S. (2008). Dhawabit al-Ta'amul Ma'a Mabadi al-Malaah Wa al-Dharurah Fi al-Mu'amalat Al-Maliyyah al-Mu'asirah. International Sharīʿah Scholars Dialogue. Hilton Hotel. Kuala Lumpur, 23–24 December.

Chapra, M. U. (1985). *Towards a just monetary system*. Leicester: The Islamic Foundation.

Chapra, M. U. (2000). *The future of economics: An Islamic perspective*. Leicester: The Islamic Foundation.

Chapra, M. U. (2008). *The Islamic vision of development in the light of* Maqāṣid *al-Sharīʿah.* Jeddah: Islamic Research and Training Institute, Islamic Development Bank.

Commission on Growth and Development. (2008). *The growth report: Strategies for sustained growth and inclusive development.* Washington, DC: World Bank.

Dar, H. A. (2004). On making human development more humane. *International Journal of Social Economics* 31(11/12), 1071–1088.

DFID. (2004). *What is pro-poor growth and why do we need to know?* (Pro-Poor Growth Briefing Note 1). London, UK: Department for International Development.

Dusuki, A. W., and Irwani, N. (2007). *Maqāṣid* al-Sharīʿah, significance and corporate social reponsibility. *The American Journal of Islamic Social Sciences* 24(1), 25–45.

Hamdan, M. (2014). Corporate social responsibility of Islamic banks in Brunei Darussalam. In *Corporate social responsibility in Asia CSR, sustainability, ethics and governance*, ed. K. C. P. Low et al., 85–107. Cham: Springer.

Hameed, S., Pramano, S., Bakhtiar, A., and Bahrom, N. (2004). *Alternative performance measures for Islamic banks.* 2nd International Conference on Administrative Sciences. King Fahd University of Petroleum and Minerals, Saudi Arabia, 19–21 April.

Hasan, Z. (2004). Measuring the efficiency of Islamic banks: Criteria, methods and social priorities. *Review of Islamic Economics* 8(2), 5–30.

Ianchovichina, E., and Lundstrom, S. (2009). *Inclusive growth analytics framework and application* (Policy Research Working Paper 4851). Washington, DC: World Bank.

Ibn ʿAshur, M. al-Tahir. (1998). Maqāṣid *al-Sharīʿah al-Islamiyyah*, ed. Muhammad al-Tahir al-Misawi. Kuala Lumpur: al-Basa'ir.

Klasen, S. (2010). *Measuring and monitoring inclusive growth: Multiple definitions, open questions, and some constructive proposals* (ADB Sustainable Development Working Paper Series No. 12). Manila: ADB.

Larbani, M., and Mohammed, M. O. (2011). Decision making tools for resource allocation based on Maqid Al- Sharah. *Islamic Economic Studies* 19(2), 51–68.

Mazumbar, K. (2003). A new approach to human development index. *Review of Social Economy* 61(4), 535–549.

Mustafa, O. M, Razak, D., and Fauziah M. T. (2008). *The performance of Islamic banking based on the Maqid framework.* IIUM International Accounting Conference (INTAC IV). PutraJaya Marroitt, 25 June.

Nourry, M. (2008). Measuring sustainable development: Some empirical evidence for France from eight alternative indicators. *Ecological Economics* 67(3), 441–456.

Okun, A. M. (1975). *Equality and efficiency: The big trade-off.* Washington, DC: Brookings Institution.

Ravallion, M., and Chen, S. (2003). Measuring pro-poor growth. *Economics Letters* 78, 93–99.

Rehman, S. S., and Askari, H. (2010). How Islamic are Islamic countries? *Global Economy Journal* 10(2), 1–29.

Siddiqi, M. N. (2000). Islamic banks: Concept, precept and prospects. *Review of Islamic Economics* 9, 21–35.

Stiglitz, J., Sen, A., and Fitoussi, J. P. (2009). *Report by the commission on the measurement of economic performance and social progress.* International Commission on Measurement of Economic Performance and Social Progress, Paris.

The World Bank Group, database at https://data.worldbank.org/.

UN. (2013). *2013 Human development report: The rise of the south: Human progress in a diverse world.* New York: United Nations Development Programme.

Zhuang, J., ed. (2010). *Poverty, inequality, and inclusive growth in Asia: Measurement, policy issues, and country studies.* Manila: Asian Development Bank.

CHAPTER 11

Paradigmatic and Conceptual Framework for Islamic HDI

Necati Aydin

1 Introduction

UN Human Development Index (HDI) emerged as a response to the shortcoming of using income per capita as a proxy for development (Seth 2009; Srinivasan 1994a, b; Sagar and Najam 1998; Ogwang 1994). It was developed based on the notion of human capabilities as outlined by Nobel Laureate Amartya Sen (1984). The current version of the index is composed of three dimensions: economic, educational, and health. Development in economic dimension is measured through income per capita, while educational dimension is assessed through two

This conceptual paper was empirically tested for ten Muslim countries in another paper by the author. That study measured Islamic HDI for those countries and compared with their score of conventional HDI. The rankings in the Islamic HDI for all Muslim countries except two differed from those in the conventional HDI (Aydin 2017).

N. Aydin (✉)
Department of Finance, College of Business,
Alfaisal University, Riyadh, Saudi Arabia

S. S. Ali (ed.), *Towards a Maqāṣid al-Sharīʿah Index of Socio-Economic Development*, Palgrave Studies in Islamic Banking, Finance, and Economics,
https://doi.org/10.1007/978-3-030-12793-0_11

variables (mean years of schooling and expected years of schooling). Health dimension is captured through the life expectancy at birth proxy. The idea behind chosen dimensions is simple, but powerful: Human beings will unleash their potential once they have good financial means, and great health and educational services (Dasgupta and Weale 1992; Desai 1993; Herrero et al. 2010; Murray 1993).

Even though HDI index seems value-neutral (Despotis 2005; Ivanova et al. 1999; Noorbakhsh 1998a, b), indeed, it reflects values of the Western secular paradigm in which it was formulated (Lind 2004). According to the secular paradigm, human life beyond death is just a myth. Ontologically speaking, the secular paradigm is materialist. It does not recognize any reality beyond material world. It even denies existence of God. Thus, human mind is the only guide to define reality and purpose in life. Epistemologically speaking, there is no absolute truth. Everything is ultimately relative and subjective as argued by post-modernists. Likewise, secular anthropology does not accept human nature with God-given ability toward good and bad. Rather, it sees human nature as tabula rasa (blank slate) which can be nurtured. Therefore, within the secular paradigm, human development is defined strictly from a worldly perspective. There is no need to work toward spiritual and moral development with the assumption that there will be afterlife. Given the fact that ultimate goals (*maqāṣid*) of secular and Islamic worldviews differ substantially (Chapra 2008), their perspectives of human development have to differ as well. Indeed, this paper is an attempt to present such differences and provide a theoretical and conceptual framework for a comprehensive HDI based on *Maqāṣid*-i Sharīʿah.

2 From *Maqāṣid-I* Qur'ān to *Maqāṣid-I Insān*

The current HDI is not proper measure of human development from an Islamic perspective mainly due to the paradigmatic differences. The index is developed based on a secular paradigm with its ontological, epistemological, anthropological, and teleological perspectives. As human life is limited to this world, human development is strictly defined within one-dimensional life. Thus, its economic model, the free market capitalism, gives no room for the hereafter. It is a worldly project. It offers worldly paradise through free market system. It does not accept any reality beyond the material one. Therefore, it has its strict view of human nature. It attempts to reduce human experience to biochemical reactions. On the other hand, Islamic economics relies on a Quranic paradigm. We call it *tawhīdī* paradigm due to the importance of Tawhid in the Islamic worldview. Indeed, Tawhid is the essential message of the Qur'ān and the defining worldview of Islam. The *Tawhīdī* paradigm takes both this world and the hereafter as a reality while setting goals for people. Thus, Islamic economics has to function within the *Tawhīdī* paradigm with its ontology, epistemology, anthropology, and teleology.

As outlined in the chart below, we link the *Tawhīdī* paradigm to the *Maqāṣid-i* Qur'ān (Qur'ānic goals). Then, we define Islamic economics with its distinguishing axioms, goals, theories, policies based on the *Tawhīdī* paradigm. Finally, we define human developmental goal as becoming perfect human (al-*insān al-kameel*) through *taqwá* (abstaining from what is forbidden) and *amal-i saleeh* (implementing whatever is ordained or recommended).

The *Maqāṣid-i* Qur'ān is defined based on the writings of Said Nursi. He defines the four essential goals of Qur'ān as follows: divine unity (*al-tawḥīd*), prophethood (*al-nubūwwah*), the resurrection of the dead (*al-ḥashr*), and justice (*al-adālah*) (Nursi 1996a). Tawhid means the oneness of God with His works, names and adjectives. Indeed, if we have to define a single goal for the Qur'ān, that would be Tawhid. It is the base for other goals as well. Prophets were sent to help us seeing the *Tawhīdī* ontology, anthropology, and teleology through *Tawhīdī* epistemology. Prophets have been sent since the first person to convey message from God to humanity informing them about their Divine mission and setting best example on how to fulfill such mission. *Al-hashr* is eternal life in which people will be rewarded or punished according to their deeds in this life. Finally, *adālah* is to be just in our relations with each other and with God. In other words, *adālah* is to give everyone their rights whatever they might be. In Nursi's view, worship is part of *adālah* because it is paying the rights of God (Fig. 1).

In short, the paradigmatic differences between Islamic and capitalist economics have dire consequences when comes to HDI. Particularly, the two systems differ significantly in terms of their understanding of human goals (*maqāṣid*) and human nature. Before suggesting a new HDI, we want to redefine Islamic economics and *maqāṣid-i* Sharī'ah after outlining key components of the *Tawhīdī* paradigm.

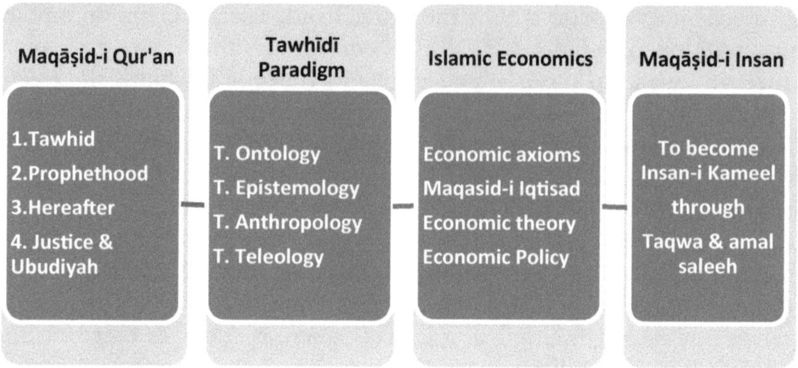

Fig. 1 Linking the *Tawhīdī* paradigm to the *Maqāṣid-i* Qur'ān (Qur'ānic goals) (*Source* Author's own)

3 The *Tawhīdī* Paradigm and Islamic Economics

Is there objective reality? What is this? Is there objective truth? What is the purpose of life? Is there universal characteristics of human nature? Answers to those questions in Islam are central around the concept of Tawhid, the existence of one God. According to the *Tawhīdī* paradigm, God is not the product of human imagination; He is necessary existence behind the existence of everything. The knowledge about God is the highest objective truth verified by both revealed books and the book of the universe. Human is not a random product of evolutionary process, he is God's greatest project. Islam is not a marginal religion dealing with dealing spiritual life alone. It is a religion providing guidance and well-being for both this life and the hereafter. Therefore, the word *falāh* (real well-being) and its derivatives have been used in the Quran many times. In the five time daily azan (call to prayer), people are also invited to *falāh*. Islam aims to achieve its goal through its value-based and God-centered moral and spiritual worldview (Aydin 2013, 1–34).

3.1 *Tawhīdī Ontology*

Ontologically speaking, God is real and the source of reality. He is the necessary existence while everything else is contingent. We know about His existence through his words and works. For that matter, knowing God is different than believing in the existence of God. While the latter is a form of belief in the existence of God, the former is much more than belief in God. It is to getting to know God. In this context, belief is a means which "connects man to the All-Glorious Maker." In other words, belief is not acceptance, "it is a relation" (Nursi 1996a, *The Words*, 23rd Word, p. 319). It connects human to God. In contrast, "unbelief severs the relation," it leaves human alone in the universe. Nursi follows Islamic tradition not talking about the nature of God because it is beyond the comprehension of human mind in this world. However, Nursi details essential quality (*shu'unat*), attributes (*sifaat*), and names (*isim*) of God who is one, eternal, necessary existent, self-sufficient, all-good, all-knowing, all-powerful, all-wise, most-merciful, most-kind, etc. Nursi argues that the reality of everything in the universes is the Divine names. The names come from the Divine attributes and the Divine attributes come from the Divine quality (*shu'unat*).

3.2 *Tawhīdī Epistemology*

For the *Tawhīdī* paradigm, objective truth does exist. God is Truth and source of Truth. While the secular paradigm relies on the light of human mind alone in its ontological and epistemological worldviews, the *Tawhīdī* paradigm relies on both reason and revelation. Islam does not ask people to shut down their minds and blindly follow the Divine revelation. Indeed, it is important to note that the very first message from God to the Prophet Muhammed (pbuh) (and humanity) was not "believe!" or "worship!". It was "*iqra* (read!)." In other words, the prophet (and humanity) was not asked to accept the ontological reality regarding God. He was first asked to pursue epistemological reality through using reading.

From an Islamic point of view, it can be said that God makes Himself known to humanity through His words and works. If we listen to the Divine Revelations and read His works in the universe, we will know His attributes. We should begin our reading from the self because the knowledge of the self will help us to know God. Once we understand that we are absolutely impotent and needy, we will realize that nature could not produce anything on her own. Everything from an atom to galactic systems is the works of God and under His control at every moment. He is not the god of gaps. He is the God of everything at every moment according to the Quran. Therefore, becoming a believer is nothing more than the recognition of and participation to the universal submission.

In this regard, belief is not a blind acceptance; it is an affirmation and bearing witness (*shahādah*) to the manifestation of God.

3.3 *Tawhīdī Anthropology*

From the Islamic perspective, knowing self is even more important, as the Prophet says, "he who knows himself knows his Lord." In other words, knowing self is the key to know God. However, as Gazhali points out, knowing self is not an easy job. Human nature is composed of complex characteristics. It contains animal character in terms of eating, drinking, sleeping, and reproducing. It contains beast character like harming others for his benefits. It contains Satanic and angelic characters. Each of these potential characters is developed through certain nutrition: "Each one of these qualities has its own distinct food that nourishes it, sustains and promotes it's growth, resulting in the promotion of goodness and the approved behavior" (Ghazzali and Winter 1997, p. 2). In other words, human conveys propensity to become animal, Satan, and angel. Animals are of two kinds, good and bad ones. If a person only pursues animal desires, he would be like a good animal. If he pursues his interests at the cost of others, he will become like beast. The goal is to become like angels "to behold the glory of Allah" and to be "freed from immoral sensual pleasures and arrogant anger on your fellow men" (Ghazzali and Winter 1997, p. 4). Every person has a potential to become like animal, beast, Satan, or angel.

Inspired largely by the writings of some Muslim scholars such as Al-Ghazali and Nursi, I developed a new theory of human nature: "A Grand Theory of Human Nature (GTHN)," using the palace and resident metaphors that follow (Aydin 2012). If we compare the human body to a luxury recreational vehicle (RV), the following elements of human nature would be the companions on this vehicle: *King, Judge, Wazir, Elephant, Showman, Dog, and, Driver*. The *King* is the spiritual heart that is the source of love and inspirational knowledge. The *Judge* is the conscience that is the source of positive feelings after performing "good things" and negative feelings experienced after doing "bad things." The *Wazir (prime minister)* is the mind. The *Elephant* is the animal spirit, which is the source of animalistic desires. The *Showman* is the self-centric ego that pursues power and possession to show its importance to others. The *Dog* is an inner drive for protection of personal belongings with potential to oppress others for their possessions.

The *Driver* is the deciding self (free will) that drives that the vehicle under the influence of the residents.

From the perspective of the *Tawhīdī* anthropology, we cannot talk about our needs and desires with a singular voice. They are originated from six different sources. Our authentic happiness depends on how fulfill the needs and desires of the key elements of our nature. We are just rational being using sensual data and making categorical reasoning. We are also driven by key internal faculty with conflicting desires. From the Islamic perspective, we could not reach happiness by pursuing the interests of animal spirit and self-centric ego. Rather, we should give priority to our spiritual, intellectual, and moral needs. We should learn the ways to control our animal and egoistic desires.

3.4 *Tawhīdī Teleology*

From the Islamic point of view, as everything in the universe is created for certain purposes, human being is also created for certain purposes. The main purpose of human is not to boost the self, turning him to an inner god. The purpose is also not to serve the animal spirit, as becoming his slave. Rather, the purpose is to understand our nature embedded with infinite impotence and poverty and act accordingly. It is to disclose our almost infinite potential by relying on the Divine power and mercy through understanding our true nature. In other words, the purpose is to excel spiritually, intellectually, and morally and be "*insān-i kamil*" (perfect human) by disclosing our human potentiality as much as we can.

The Qur'ān clearly states the purpose behind the creation of human beings: "I have not created the jinn and humankind but to (know and) worship Me (exclusively)" (The Quran, 51:56). As described by Ghazali, the transcendental achievement would be possible through God-centric life: "The purpose of life is to reach the '*martaba*' the status of *tawhid* (oneness of Allah), understand it, inculcate it in his being to follow His dictates to reach the pedestal of the *akhlaqe alaia* (the grandeur of conduct). It would mean a singular achievement of transcending from the *bashari'at*' (being a human being: fallible) to the '*maqame haqiqat*' i.e. the position of verity and the truth sublime" (Ghazzali and Winter 1997, p. 747). From the Qur`anic perspective, human being is a (perhaps the) major project of God. The Islamic worldview is built upon this project.

In short, from the *Tawhīdī* teleology, the purpose of life is to pursue God's pleasure by fulfilling our mission as desired and designed rather than pursuing self-pleasure. However, from the Islamic perspective, well-being in this life and in the hereafter will be realized as by-product of God's pleasure.

3.5 *Redefining Islamic Economics*

Islamic economics has been a key subject matter among diverse pool of Muslim scholars such as commentators of the Quran, jurists, historians, and social, political, and moral philosophers. In a recent paper, we define Islamic economics based on the *Tawhīdī* paradigm, particularly its ontological, epistemological, and teleological differences from the materialist worldviews as follows: "Islamic economics foresees an economic system based on the Islamic worldview aiming to realize spiritual, moral, intellectual, social, and material well-beings of individuals in this life and the hereafter through allocation and distribution of scarce resources in a morally guided market system" (Aydin 2013, 1–34). Thus, the answers to the core questions could be as follows: What to produce? Produce goods and services which help human beings to excel spiritually, intellectually, morally, and socially. What to produce? Produce the basic goods and services for everyone, but others for those who could afford. Accumulate spiritual, moral, and social capital in addition to physical and financial capital. How to produce? Produce through efficient and fair market mechanism. Likewise, Islamic financial instruments should be based on the *Tawhīdī* paradigm. Their Sharīʿah compatibility should not be defined only according to *ribā*, haram, gambling, and speculation. Rather, they should be assessed based on their ultimate outcome in terms of their contribution to human moral, intellectual, and spiritual excellence.

4 *Maqāṣid-i Insān* in Islamic Vs. Capitalist Economics

We think that the distinctive feature of Islamic economics should come from its *Tawhīdī* paradigm which sets very different *maqāṣid* (ultimate goals) for people in compare to the secular paradigm. As Aydin argues in a paper,[1] the capitalist economic system which relies on the secular

[1]Aydin, Necati (2014): "Luxury Consumption and Role of IBF in the GCC," The paper will be published in an edited book on Islamic Economics and Finance in GCC by Gerlach Press.

paradigm encourages works for living, wealth and knowledge as means to the intermediate ends which are power (control), pleasure (satisfaction), and praise (show). Therefore, the system promotes the functional and positional goods and services to satisfy animal desires and ego. The ultimate goal or final end is considered to be happiness through consumption. Even knowledge is a means for either wealth or ego-satisfying positions. Scientific and technological advancement are not for understanding truth or virtue, they are for power and pleasure. Therefore, paradoxically, despite remarkable scientific, technological, and economic advancement, we have not seen a significant change in the subjective well-being. Rather, we see the dark sides of decadent civilization with the rise of suicide, homicide, ecocide (killing of environment), and suicide (killing of human soul).

Indeed, we can argue Islamic civilization differs significantly from the secular Western civilization. If the latter is "mall-centered," the former is "mosque-centered" civilization. If the latter is "fun-centered," the former is "*fadhillah* (virtue) centered" civilization. If the latter heads toward "Hollywood," the former heads toward "Holy Makkah." Therefore, Islamic economic system has to different than free market capitalism.

In the Islamic (moral) economic system which relies on the *Tawhīdī* paradigm, it is not only permissible but worship to work for living, wealth, and knowledge. However, unlike capitalist system, they are not means for power and pleasure; they are means for truth and virtue. In other words, the pursuant of wealth is for performing virtuous actions while the pursuant of knowledge to learn virtue and truth. In the following hadith, the Prophet (pbuh) clearly states that wealth and knowledge are just means: "*Envy is permitted only in two cases: A man whom Allah gives wealth, and he disposes of it rightfully, and a man to whom Allah gives knowledge which he applies and teaches it*" [Al-Bukhari and Muslim]. The ultimate goal is not happiness, but excellence or perfection as a human being. It is to be real human being who is portrayed in the Qur'ān as being potentially superior to all creatures including angels. Therefore, the ultimate goal is to realize God's human project as described in the Quran by raising *insān-i* kamil (perfected human). Happiness is the by-product of such accomplishment.

Muslim scholars discuss Islam as a comprehensive guidance toward human perfection. Thus, the purpose of Islamic law (*Maqāṣid-i* Sharīʿah) is to help human in fulfilling his Divine mission. Indeed, the Qur'ān makes it clear that the universe in general and human in particular were not created for nothing: "*And We did not create the heavens and earth and that between them in play*" (44: verse 38). "*Then did you think that We created you uselessly and that to Us you would not be returned?*" (23: verse 115). Rather, the Qur'ān conveys the conversation between God and angels on the creation of human as a vicegerent on earth: "*Behold, thy Lord said to the angels: 'I will create a vicegerenton earth'*" (2:30). Thus, from the Qur'ānic perspective, human has been given great potentials to fulfill his mission of khalīfah (vicegerent) over other creatures: "*And We have certainly honored the children of Adam and carried them on the land and sea and provided for them of the good things and preferred them over much of what We have created, with [definite] preference*" (17: 70).

The Qur'ān states that human beings are created in the best form (*ahsan-i taqwim*): "Surely, we have created human of the best stature, as the perfect pattern of creation" (Q. 95:5). This refers to the potential in human beings. Indeed, the Qur'ān clearly indicates that human beings are potentially superior to all creatures, even angels. Therefore, when Adam was created the angels were asked to "prostrate before Adam!" The superiority of Adam was not coming from wealth, pleasure, fame, etc. It was coming from his ability to learn the names of God in a comprehensive manner. According to Nursi, the names "are the realities and sources" of sciences and creation.[2] Thus, the ultimate purpose of life for humans is to excel in virtuous and sincere deeds in order to fulfill his mission of vicegerent and earn God's pleasure.

Indeed, one can argue that Islam is not but a comprehensive guide to raise *insān-i kamil.* Therefore, Nursi describes Islam as a "supreme humanity."[3] In other words, the ultimate goal of Islam is to raise "supreme humanity" or *insān-i kamil.* The success of human project depends the use of great potential:

> From the Islamic point of view, as everything in the universe is created for certain purposes, human being is also created for certain purposes. The main purpose of human is not to boost the self, turning him to an inner god. The purpose is also not to serve the elephant, as becoming his slave. Rather, the purpose is to understand our nature embedded with infinite

[2] Ibid., 270.

[3] Ibid., 356.

impotence and poverty, and act accordingly. It is to disclose our almost infinite potential by relying on the Divine power and mercy through understanding our true nature.

With his unmatched ability to both good and bad, human can be the best and the worse of the creation as stated by Nursi:

> Since man has been created on the most excellent of patterns and has been given most comprehensive abilities, he has been cast into an arena of trial and examination in which he may rise or fall to stations, ranks, and degrees from the lowest of the low to the highest of the high, from the earth to the Divine Throne, and from minute particles to the sun. He has been sent to this world as a miracle of Divine Power, the result of creation, and a wonder of Divine art before whom have been opened two roads leading either to infinite ascent or infinite descent.[4]

Scholars generally agree with Ghazali that the following shall be assured by the Sharī'ah in helping human to fulfill his mission: "*The very objective of the Sharī'ah is to promote the well-being of the people, which lies in safeguarding their faith (Dīn), their self (Nafs), their intellect ('Aql), their posterity (Nasl), and their wealth (Māl). Whatever ensures the safeguard of these five serves public interest and is desirable, and whatever hurts them is against public interest and its removal is desirable.*" It is clear that the goal is not individual hedonic utility maximization. Thus, societal development shall include spiritual, moral, intellectual, and social dimensions.

In short, the ultimate purpose in human development is to excel spiritually, intellectually, socially, and morally and become *insān-i kamil* (perfect human) through use his great potentiality. The current discussion of *maqāṣid* within the context of Islamic finance is largely limited to the means rather than the final end. However, even if the means are in line with the Sharī'ah, the final end might not be. Therefore, the actual focus should on the final end. Likewise, any measure of human development should also focus on the ultimate *maqāṣid-i* Sharī'ah rather than conflicting worldly outcome. However, we think it is better to reformulate the aforementioned *maqāṣid* based on the *Tawhīdī* anthropology as suggested below.

[4]Nursi, *The Words*, 341.

5 Defining Human Nature Within the *Tawhīdī* Anthropology

Tawhīdī anthropology is substantially different than secular anthropology which denies the spiritual dimension of human nature. In other words, *Tawhīdī* and secular paradigms have different views on what human is and what he should be. Therefore, the measurement of human development has to be different. Since the purpose of HDI is to measure human development, we have to start with the understanding of human nature whether it is given by God or nurtured by society.

What does the human self consist of? As stated before, Aydin came up with seven key elements of human nature. According to his theory, three of these elements have a positive quality namely, *Spiritual Heart, Human Conscience, Mind, while other three has a negative quality namely, Animal spirit, Self-Centric ego, and Oppressive ego, finally the seventh element is Free Will or the deciding self.*

First element of human nature is the King or the "spiritual heart". While the King has the unlimited capacity for love, compassion, and inspiration, one needs to uncover his needs and desires and to fulfill them unleash his power. From an Islamic perspective, as well argued by Nursi, the King finds true satisfaction only with the knowledge, submission, and love of God. "When you give it (love) to its true owner, you will be able to love everything without distress in His name and as His mirrors" (Nursi, *The Words*, 24th Word, p. 368). Although there are two other characteristics of the spiritual heart, which are compassion and inspiration, we want to concentrate the scope on the love only. Of course, love pre-requisites knowledge. As Nursi argues, if one knows God with His love-worthy attributes and names, he will give all of his love to Him. After all, the reality of everything, from *Tawhīdī* ontology point of views, is nothing but the names of God. Thus, as the Qur'ān clearly states, human hearth can only be satisfied with the remembrance (which means knowledge and love) of God: "Those who believe, and whose hearts find their rest in the remembrance of God - for, verily, in the remembrance of God [human's] hearts do find their rest" (The Qur'ān, 13:28).

In the second element of human nature is the Judge who is a metaphor to describe the "*Human Conscience*". Human conscience is the inner judge who decides what is right and what is wrong. God created the entire human with this inner judge, so that this inner judge causes the feel of guilty for committing a wrong behavior while causes the feel of inner peace when doing some good behavior.

The third element of human nature is the "*Mind*" or metaphorically, *Wazir (the Prime Minister)* who is supposed to work under the command of the King. Aydin (2012) describes the mind as the intellect, logic, and memory which serves the spiritual heart. The mind has a great innate passion to learn and pursue truth. As stated by Aydin "The mind is created with ability to wonder and learn about the truth of everything. Therefore, it is thirsty for knowledge and meaning. It asks questions and enjoys learning their answers."

The fourth element of human nature is the "*Animal Spirit*". Aydin uses elephant as a metaphor referring to the innate animal spirit which has the capacity for sensual experience through using the five senses. He desires many things such as food, drink, sleep, and sex. Animal spirit has been presented in the Islamic literature as the bad self "*Nafs Ammara.*" It simply implies the extent to which the human is living only to satisfy his own sensual desires. From an Islamic perspective, animal spirit is given certain pleasure for motivating him toward the desired destination. The King and Wazir are riding the animal spirit rather than being his servant. For that matter, the control of animal spirit is very important. Indeed, one can argue that one of the essential purposes of moral values in Islam is to restrain animal spirit within the control of the King and the Wazir.

The fifth element of human nature is the "*Self-Centric Ego*". Aydin (2012) resembles it to showman in his metaphorical RV example stating that *the Showman* "is motivated by acts that acquire recognition, identity, fame, etc. and frequently compares his own possessions with those of others." However, in Nursi's terms, those humans who seek the fame and recognition by possessions will and up to be slaves not masters.

The "*Oppressive Ego*" or what is metaphorically described by the "dog" is the sixth element of the human nature. Aydın (2012) describes it as "an inner drive for protection of personal belongings with potential to oppress others for their possessions." Therefore, he argues that the dog has to be bounded by the moral and religious frame to prevent from oppressing others for his own interest. The dog is equivalent of the power of anger (kuvvai-ghadabeyah). As states by Nursi, from an Islamic perspective, the middle way of the power of anger is the courage which prevents this power to take any of the bad extremes of oppression or the cowardice (Nursi 1996b, *the Rays*, 15th Ray, First Station, p. 587).

Seventh element of human nature is the "*Deciding Self*," the free will. It can be seen as the driver of the human RV. According to Aydin (2012), deciding self is the main source of self-awareness and works as a channel for interacting with the external environment. In other words, it is the ability to choose and make decisions in life. The freedom is to select among options presented in daily decisions. This is an ultimate power to make a decision. It also sets basis for accountability. According to the self-determination theory (SDT), the degree to which any of the needs for *autonomy, competence*, and *relatedness* is unsupported within a social context will have robust harmful ramifications on wellness in that setting.

Looking carefully to these seven elements of human nature, we can notice that the every human has a positive side in terms of his (Spiritual Heart, Conscience, and Mind) as well as a negative side in terms of (Animal desires, self-centric ego, and Anger). If he holds the free will to full-control his own life by controlling his own self. If he makes his choices to maximizing the positive while minimizing the negative aspects, he will be able to progress as a good human indeed a developed one. However, since negative elements of human nature are not constrained, people can commit injustice in their relationship with others. They need the Divine guidance to keep their bad sides under control by a moderate way of life. The Qur'ān and Sunnah aims to implant good character among people to prevent transgression. That is way the Qur'ān presents the Prophet (pbuh) as a best example and praises his excellent character: "You are surely of a sublime character, and do act by a sublime pattern of conduct" (Q. 68:4).

In short, we cannot measure human development unless we understand human nature and ideal human character. According to the *Tawhīdī* anthropology, human has great potential both toward good and evil. Indeed, he can descend to the lowest of low or ascend to the highest of high. The ultimate purpose of Sharī'ah is to help human toward his excellence.

6 Measuring Human Development Based on the *Tawhīdī* Paradigm

We think measuring human development has to start with understanding of human nature and human goals within the *Tawhīdī* paradigm. As stated before, the ultimate goal for human is to reach his perfection (becoming *insān-i kamil*). That is possible through flourishing the positive elements of human nature while controlling the negative elements. Thus, we can argue that Islamic HDI should be based on the comprehensive understanding of human nature as outlined above. We think that Islamic HDI is the function of controlling the negative side of human nature while unleashing its positive sides. Thus, from an Islamic perspective, human is supposed to develop toward perfected human (*insān-i kamel*) among all creatures fulfilling his mission of khalifa on the earth. While the standard HDI has focused mainly on Health, Education, and Income (Foster et al. 2005; Hicks 1997), we see that the Islamic world view of the human development should be more comprehensive than the usual view. This is because Islam in its nature as a religion has always concerned by integrating the whole aspects of life aiming at living a good fruitful life or what is called "*Al-Hayat Al-Tayyeba.*" Pursuing the pleasure of God in all behaviors will guide his choices for achieving his ultimate purpose in life. In the *Tawhīdī* teleology, Aydin states that "*the purpose of our life is to excel spiritually, intellectually, and morally and be "insān-i kamil (perfect human)" by disclosing our human potentiality as much as we can.*"

We can link the five traditionally accepted *maqāṣid-i* Sharīʿah to the key elements of human nature within the *Tawhīdī* anthropology. This will allow us to base human development to human nature. It will place *Maqāṣid-i* Sharīʿah within the *Tawhīdī* paradigm. In other words, once we raise *insān-i* kameel, the *maqāṣid* of protecting faith, self, intellect, offspring, and wealth will be accomplished. Indeed, with engaging in good deeds (*amal-i saleeh*) and abstaining from bad deeds (*taqwá*), one will flourish his spiritual, moral, and intellectual sides while controlling his animal spirit, ego, and anger. This will lead to provision for conscience, intellect, and heart while protection against the aggression of animal spirit, ego, and anger. Since society is made of individuals, through perfecting individuals, we will create a better society. We will mostly prevent injustice in human relations.

7 Variables for an Islamic HDI[5]

Although some Islamic countries are achieving a good pace of development according to the existing HDI index, we argue that this is not an indication that they are doing well in terms of helping people to make progress toward *insān-i kamil.* In this section, we will present proxy

[5]This part is based on a working paper on measuring Islamic HDI by Dr. Necati Aydin and Mostafa Kamel (doctorate student at King Saud University at the time of workshop).

variables to index human development in terms of progress in the seven dimensions of human nature. We will keep the existing three variables because they overlap with some of elements of human nature as defined by the *Tawhīdī* anthropology. We will suggest several new variables to full account for human development both in terms of restraining negative elements and fostering the positive elements of human nature. The ultimate goal is to combine these data into one index, rank countries according to their score, and observe if there is any difference between the UNDP's HDI and the new proposed Islamic HDI.

7.1 The Proxy Variable for the Spiritual Heart (the King)

As discussed before when individual gives his love to the most worthy one who is God, he can be truly satisfied. Then, he can love everything else as mirrors to the names of God. This will be part of God's love too. In such case, love will be source of pure joy without real pain. Thus, such a person will be able to love everything without distress. Loving friend, brother, or even couple in the name of the God without any consideration of waiting any kind of payback benefits is purest level of the appreciation. This non-materialistic need cannot be satisfied by accumulating income. We think person with sincere spiritual life could accomplish such satisfaction. We will use the answer to the questions on spirituality from the world value survey to measure how each society fulfills the need of spiritual heart. The world value survey interviews random samples representing most of the world's people asking them to their view in a number of different subjects which contribute to a better understanding of what people all over the world believe and want out of life. We will use the response to the following questions by each nation: Do you believe in God? How often do you pray? How you rank the importance of God in your life? Do you believe in hell? In what will you trust if there is a conflict between science and religions? Aggregating the answer for those questions will reflect the extent to which societies enjoy a spiritual heart.

7.2 The Proxy Variable for the Mind (the Wazir)

We will use the two education variables in the current HDI. However, we think it is also important to measure the quality of education. Particularly, the age of Information, we think the access to and quality of higher education is very important in the development of science and technology. There are several competing proxy variables which could account for the quality of education in general and in higher education in particular. We prefer to use the index of academic publishing because of the fact that the most qualified universities are distinguished by their first-tier academic publishing while is a good proxy for patenting as well.

7.3 The Proxy Variable for the Human Conscience (the Judge)

Conscience is the inner judge that enables human to distinguish right and wrong. It makes him to feel guilty when conducting anything considered bad or unjust. Absence of conscience has played an important role in the spread of corruption in the world. Basically, corruption behaviors such as receiving and giving bribes or using connections to gain advantage over others or making money can't be practiced unless there is a complete absence of conscience. For that reason, for the conscience, we propose using the Corruption Perception Index (CPI) published by transparency international to rank countries according to the spread of corruption in it. The CPI measures perception of corruption by business people opinions surveys or performance assessments analysts due to the difficulty of measuring absolute levels of corruption. 2012 CPI draws on 13 different surveys and assessments from 12 different institutions such as African Development Bank, World Bank, Freedom House, the Bertelsmann Foundation, the Economist Intelligence Unit, Global Insight, International Institute for Management Development, Political and Economic Risk Consultancy, Political Risk Services, the World Economic Forum, and the world justice project. For a country to appear in the CPI, it must be assessed by at least three sources.

7.4 The Proxy Variable for the Animal Spirit (the Elephant)

Animal spirit (*nafs ammarah*) seeks satisfaction mainly through sensual pleasures such as eating, drinking, and sexual pleasure. From an Islamic perspective, the animal desires can be only satisfied through moderate lifestyles within the permissible realm. Sinful pursuant of sensual pleasure is impediment toward human perfection. For the sake of simplicity and data availability, we will use tracking of Google search for the words such as sex and porn for each country while measuring IHDI. We acknowledge that rating the entertaining TV channels or the circulation of certain newspapers and magazines could be used as a proxy variable for the animal spirit.

7.5 *The Proxy Variable for the Self-Centric Ego (the Showman)*

Self-centric ego is well-known with its association with luxury consumption behavior. People have the innate desire to seek praise through show off through possessions of goods, positions, or skills. Since in consumer culture, the love to show off and feeling proud mostly practiced through the tendency to own luxurious items such as cars, furniture, and watches, we propose using the luxury consumption Luxury Goods Worldwide Market Study by Bain and Company to trace the luxury consumption among countries.[6]

7.6 *The Proxy Variable for the Oppressive Ego (the Dog)*

Practicing the oppressive ego most probably leads to serious ramifications. One of these harmful consequences is crimes with its different types. Somehow crimes always are the results of attempting to impose control over others possessions. While protecting self-possessions against strangers is not criminalized in any legal system, trying to obtain or control other's belongings in any ways is surely considered crime. To this end, we propose to use Intentional Homicides per 100,000 People Crime Index published by the United Nations Development Program as a proxy variable for the oppressive ego to see to what extent people are developed to restraint their oppressive ego.

7.7 *The Proxy Variable for the Free will (the Driver)*

Finally, the freedom of choice is important for human being in fulfilling his role as the khalifa of God on the earth. In Chapra terms, "Freedom is indispensable for the development of the human personality. Without it he/she may lack the initiative and drive that are necessary for creativity and innovation and, consequently, for human development and well-being." It is important to note that freedom in Islamic sense is substantially different than freedom in secular worldview. For that matter, freedom is not doing whatever you want to do as long as it does not

[6]Hofstede Ranking Individualistic versus collectivistic cultures: http://geert-hofstede.com/dimensions.html; http://www.clearlycultural.com/geert-hofstede-cultural-dimensions/individualism/.

harm others. Rather, freedom is doing whatever you want to do as long as it is not harmful to yourself and others. Pursuing the desire of animal spirit is not considered freedom. It is a form of slavery. Thus, the more we gain our freedom from other individuals and inner negative residents, the more we will act freely to progress toward perfection. Having said that, we think freedom by laws are crucial for righteous people to fully flourish their positive dimensions. Therefore, for the free will, we will use to use the index of ***"Freedom in the World"*** which is a yearly survey and report by Freedom House that attempts to measure the degree of democracy and political freedom in every nation.

References

Aydin, Necati. (2012). "Grand Theory of Human Nature and Happiness." *Humanomics*, Vol. 28, No. 1, pp. 42–63.

Aydin, Necati. (2013). "Redefining Islamic Economics as a New Economic Paradigm." *Islamic Economic Studies*, Vol. 21, No. 1, pp. 1–34.

Aydin, Necati. (2017). "Islamic vs Conventional Human Development Index: Empirical Evidence from Ten Muslim Countries." *International Journal of Social Economics*, Vol. 44, No. 12, pp. 1562–1583. Available at https://doi.org/10.1108/IJSE-03-2016-0091.

Chapra, M. Umer. (2008). The Islamic Vision of Development in the Light of the Maqāsid Al-Sharī'ah, Islamic Development Bank, Jeddah.

Dasgupta, P., and Weale, M. (1992). "On Measuring the Quality of Life." *World Development*, Vol. 20, No. 1, pp. 119–131.

Desai, M. (1993). "Income and Alternative Measures of Well-Being." In *Monitoring Social Progress in the 1990s*, ed. D. G. Westendorff and D. Ghai. United Nations Research Institute for Social Development. Avebury: Aldershot.

Despotis, D. K. (2005). "A Reassessment of the Human Development Index via Data Envelopment Analysis." *Journal of the Operational Research Society*, Vol. 56, No. 8, pp. 969–980.

Foster, J. E., Lopez-Calva, L., and Szekely, M. (2005). "Measuring the Distribution of Human Development: Methodology and an Application to Mexico." *Journal of Human Development*, Vol. 6, No. 1, p. 529.

Ghazzali, and Winter, T. J. (1997). *Al-Ghazali on Disciplining the Soul: Kitab Riyadat Al-Nafs; & on Breaking the Two Desires: Kitab Kasr Al-Shahwatayn: Books XXII and XXIII of the Revival of the Religious Sciences: Ihya Ulum Al-Din*. Cambridge: Islamic Texts Society.

Herrero, C., Martinez, R., and Villar, A. (2010). "Multidimensional Social Evaluation: An Application to the Measurement of Human Development." *Review of Income and Wealth*, Vol. 56, No. 3, pp. 483–497.

Hicks, D. A. (1997). "The Inequality-Adjusted Human Development Index: A Constructive Proposal." *World Development*, Vol. 25, No. 8, pp. 1283–1298.

Ivanova, I., Arcelus, F. J., and Srinivasan, G. (1999). "An Assessment of the Measurement Properties of the Human Development Index." *Social Indicators Research*, Vol. 46, pp. 157–179.

Lind, N. C. (2004). "Values Reflected in the Human Development Index." *Social Indicators Research*, Vol. 66, No. 3, pp. 283–293.

Murray, J. L. (1993). "Development Data Constraints and the Human Development Index." In *Monitoring Social Progress in the 1990s*, ed. D. G. Westerndorff and D. Ghai, pp. 40–64.

Noorbakhsh, F. (1998a). "A Modified Human Development Index." *World Development*, Vol. 26, No. 3, pp. 517–528.

Noorbakhsh, F. (1998b). "The Human Development Index: Some Technical Issues and Alternative Indices." *Journal of International Development*, vol. 10, pp. 589–605.

Nursi, Said. (1996a). *The Words*. Trans. Sukran Vahide. Sozler Publications.

Nursi, Said. (1996b). *The Rays*. Trans. Sukran Vahide. Sozler Publications.

Ogwang, T. (1994). "The Choice of Principle Variables for Computing the Human Development Index." *World Development*, Vol. 22, No. 12, pp. 2011–2014.

Sagar, A., and Najam, A. (1998). "The Human Development Index: A Critical Review." *Ecological Economics*, Vol. 25, pp. 249–264.

Sen, A. (1984). *Resources, Values and Development*. Oxford: Basil Blackwell.

Seth, S. (2009). "Inequality, Interactions, and Human Development." *Journal of Human Development and Capabilities*, Vol. 10, pp. 375–396.

Srinivasan, T. N. (1994a). "Human Development: A New Paradigm or Reinvention of the Wheel?" *The American Economic Review*, Vol. 84, No. 2, pp. 238–243.

Srinivasan, T. N. (1994b). "Data Base for Development Analysis: An Overview." *Journal of Development Economics*, Vol. 44, pp. 3–27.

CHAPTER 12

A Structural Model for Human Development, Does *Maqāṣid* al-Sharīʿah Matter!

Mehdi Mili

1 Introduction

To establish good social relations in society, human always needs moral principles that define the limits of his moral and ethical responsibilities in the society. These principles are always related to the importance of religion in the country. Generally, Islamic countries have not experienced this problem because *Islamic* Sharīʿah is based on a comprehensive system of morality and can therefore treat all ethical issues in the society of a canonical point of view. It is also flexible enough and adapts perfectly to new situations.

Ethical principles of Islam constitute the basic foundation for human development. Ethic is not a separate discipline in Islam. It is part of the

M. Mili (✉)
University of Bahrain, College of Business Administration,
Zallaq, Bahrain

S. S. Ali (ed.), *Towards a Maqāṣid al-Sharīʿah Index of Socio-Economic Development*, Palgrave Studies in Islamic Banking, Finance, and Economics,
https://doi.org/10.1007/978-3-030-12793-0_12

law itself. Muslims scholars tried in the past to rely on theories and ethical principles when ethical issues arise. Following Al-Ghazali (1901) and Al Fasi (1380H), ethical theory of Islam is based on five objectives for *Maqāṣid* al-Sharī'ah: preservation of religion (*al-Dīn*), life (*al-Nafs*), intellect (*al-'Aql*), progeny (*al-Nasl*), and wealth (*al-Māl*). These objectives of Sharī'ah defend ethical principles in society and are likely to affect human well-being in the world. Several researchers (Chapra [2008], Al-Najjar [2008], Crane [2009], …) defend this thesis, but the majority did not attempt to quantify the impact of *Maqāṣid* al-Sharī'ah on human development. This paper contributes to the literature by proposing an empirical approach for testing the impact of *Maqāṣid* al-Sharī'ah on the human development index.

Unlike the secular market paradigm, human well-being in Islam does not depend essentially on the maximization of wealth and consumption. It requires a balanced satisfaction of both material and spiritual needs of the human personality. The spiritual need is not satisfied only by the fives pillars of Islam, it requires individuals to shape theirs behavior in accordance with the Sharī'ah (Islam teachings), which is designed to enable the realization of *Maqāṣid* al-Sharī'ah namely socioeconomic justice and well-being of all God's creatures. Neglect the spiritual needs or physical needs impede the realization of true well-being and exacerbate the symptoms of anomie, such as frustration, crime, alcoholism, drug addiction, divorce, mental illness, and suicide, revealing all a lack of inner life satisfaction of individuals.

Human development is known as an economic, social, cultural, and political process for continuous improvement of the welfare of all individuals on the basis of their active and meaningful participation in development and equitable sharing of the wealth generated. It is based on the satisfaction of basic human needs on an ongoing basis to ensure safety and social stability. In the Qur'ān, this concept results in reconstruction and reform in the ground. *Al araaf* -56 "Do no mischief on the earth, after it hath been set in order, but call on Him with fear and longing (in your hearts): for the Mercy of Allah is (always) near to those who do good."

The extrapolation of the texts of the Qur'ān and the *Sunna* and the legal provisions of worship and transactions show that human development is a legitimate target which must be established in the nation by their various brackets. So, everyone according to his responsibility and influence must reach this objective. Ibn 'Ashur (1998) suggests that

Maqāṣid al-Sharīʿah in their three levels (the essentials [*ḍarūriyāt*], the complementary [*ḥajiyāt*], and the embellishments [*taḥsiniyāt*]) contribute to the development of human life in all its aspects (social, religious, economic, and other aspects). He claims that Islam provides a comprehensive approach for reform that starts with the reform of people which lead to the development of the society eventually leading to the goodness of the world.

Despite this emphasis on morality, Islam does not recognize distinction between the material and the spiritual. All social, economic, educational, and any type of human efforts have spiritual character fully compliant with Islamic values. If a person is working hard to ensure his own welfare, the welfare of his family and his society, it is as spiritual as the act of prayer as long as the physical effort is guided by moral values and it does not remove him from the fulfillment of his social and spiritual obligations.

Thus, the ideal behavior within this paradigm is not synonymous with selflessness; it simply means the pursuit of self-interest within the constraints of social interest from all claims to scarce resources through the filter of moral values. These values are an inseparable part of the Sharīʿah and have been sent to all people at different periods in history, by a succession of prophets of God. Therefore, according to Islam, there is a continuity and similarity in the value system of all revealed religions to the extent that the message has not been lost or distorted through the centuries.

This paradigm assumes that individual behavior orients morality in an appropriate socioeconomic and political environment and contributes to the realization of socioeconomic justice and general human well-being, as the paradigm of market economy requires that the behavior in a competitive market must defend the social interest.

However, while the traditional economy presupposes the predominance of self-interested behavior in all individuals, Islam does not assume the predominance of ideal behavior. It adopts the realistic position that some people act in purely ideal manner and some behave in purely self-interested manner; however, the behavior of most people tends to be somewhere between these two extremes.

Given that the ideal behavior is held to be more favorable to the goal of human well-being, Islam tries to bring individual behavior as close as possible to the ideal. It tries to create an enabling environment through social structure based on moral values and an effective system of motivation relying both on economic and social reform.

This environment can be created by an adequate public education, the creation of an effective framework of safeguards and by improving the existing socioeconomic, legal, and political institutions. Doing the five pillars of Islam is necessary, but not sufficient, to create this environment. They tend to make individuals and groups aware of their social obligations and motivate them to stand by the moral principles and values even if they go against their short-term interests. *Maqāṣids* al-Sharīʿah' aim to idealize human behavior in order to develop the society in accordance with ultimate principles that preserve the well-being of mankind.

The aim of this paper is to show the impact of objectives *Maqāṣid* al-Sharīʿah' on human development. We adopt the objectives of *Maqāṣid* al-Sharīʿah according to the five principles advanced by Al-Ghazali.

The writings of *Imam Al-Ghazali* (1091) identify the *Maqāṣid* al-Sharīʿah in preserving fives requirements (*called al-usool al-khamsah*). These principles are not the only ones but the principal *Maqāṣids* al-Sharīʿah. Our approach aims to propose a PLS-Path model to measure well-being in light of *Maqāṣid* al-Sharīʿah. It considers the interrelationship that may exist between the fives principles of *Maqāṣid* al-Sharīʿah.

The rest of the paper is organized as follow. Section 2 presents the literature review concerning the impact of *Maqāṣid* al-Sharīʿah on human well-being. It exposes also our empirical approach. Section 3 presents a detailed interpretation of the results. Section 4 concludes.

2 Impact of *Maqāṣid* al-Sharīʿah on Human Well-Being

Reference works on *Maqāṣid* al-Sharīʿah arising from some scholars of Islam such as Al-Ghazali (1901), Al-Shatibi (2004), Ibn 'Ashur (1998), and Ibn Taymiyyah (Al-Raysuni 1992) focused on the legal dimensions to determine *Maqāṣid* al-Sharīʿah. Recently, several researchers have attempted to test the impact of a proper application of these *maqāṣid* on the human environment in all its aspects.

Chapra (2008) proposed a theoretical framework that addresses human development from a narrow perspective of *Maqāṣid* al-Sharīʿah. His work seems a philosophical progress that lacks quantitative effort to support its findings. Other researchers have tried to develop human development indexes that incorporate religious principles. Dar (2004) developed the ethics-augmented human development index (HDI-E). He integrated for the first time explicitly ethical dimension through the incorporation of faith, freedom, and the environmental aspect in human development index.

Anto (2009) suggests that human development in Islamic perspective must be based on *Maqāṣid* al-Sharīʿah and developed an index of human development based on the principles of Islam. He improved his index by including the right to freedom and the protection of the environment.

Unlike these works, our objective is not the creation of a new index for human development. But, we seek to test the impact of these *Maqāṣid* on human development. The five objectives of *Maqāṣid* al-Sharīʿah that we consider in our study were developed in the twelfth century by the scholar Al-Ghazali (d. 1111) in his work *on fiqh* titled *Al Mustsafa*. It was then subsequently enhanced by Ibn Taymiyyah (d. 1328) and Abu Ishaq Al-Shatibi (d. 1388).

To test the impact of each objective of *Maqāṣid* al-Sharīʿah on human well-being, we apply a consistent econometric approach partial least square-path (PLS-Path) that allows us to estimate complex causal relationship between latent variables measured themselves by manifest variables (observed variables). Our empirical approach considers the objectives of *Maqāṣid* al-Sharīʿah as latent unobservable variables that affect human development in each country. Each of the five objectives of *Maqāṣid* al-Sharīʿah will be measured by a number of manifest observable variables. We consider the following causal model (Fig. 1):

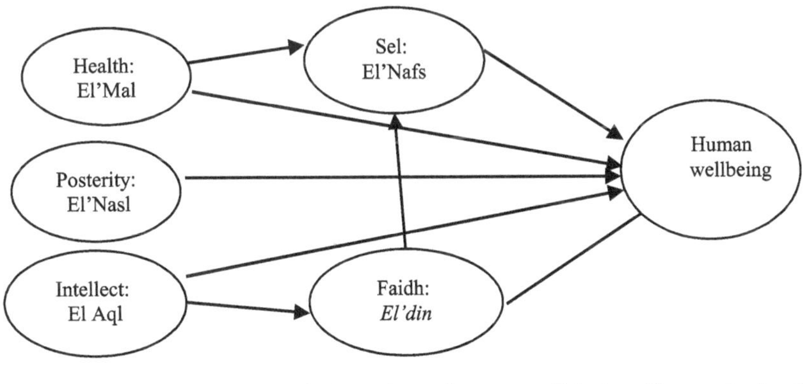

Fig. 1 Impact of *Maqāṣid* al-Sharīʿah on human well-being (*Source* Author's own)

We collect cross-sectional data on 30 Islamic countries relating to the year 2011. For each country, a set of 15 indices are collected from different sources (see Table 1). If the information for a measurement variable is not available on 2011, we select that of the previous year. The

Table 1 Dimensions of components of *Maqāṣid* al-Sharī'ah

Latent variables	*Measurement indicators*	*Data sources*
Ḥifẓ al-Nafs	Health Care Index	Poverty http://www.numbeo.com/health-care/rankings_by_country.jsp
	Human Rights Index	http://www.ohchr.org/EN/HRBodies/Pages/UniversalHumanRightsIndexDatabase.aspx
	Crime Index	http://www.numbeo.com/crime/rankings_by_country.jsp
	Poverty gap	http://data.worldbank.org/topic/
Ḥifẓ al-Dīn	Percentage of total expenditure in religious education	Ministry of Education/Ministry of Finance of respective country
	Government Favoritism of Religion Index	http://www.thearda.com/internationaldata/index.asp
	Government Regulation of Religion Index	http://www.thearda.com/internationaldata/index.asp
Ḥifẓ al-'Aql	Primary enrollment rate	http://stats.uis.unesco.org/unesco/TableViewer/document.aspx?ReportId=143&IF_Language=eng
	Secondary enrollment rate	http://stats.uis.unesco.org/unesco/TableViewer/document.aspx?ReportId=143&IF_Language=eng
	Public spending on education, total (% of GDP)	http://data.worldbank.org/indicator/SE.XPD.TOTL.GD.ZS/countries?display=default
Ḥifẓ al-Māl	International Property Rights Index	http://www.internationalpropertyrightsindex.org/about
	Inclusive Wealth Index	http://www.unep.org/pdf/IWR_2012.pdf
Ḥifẓ al-Nasl	Divorce rate	UN; Euromonitor
	Child mortality rates	Mortality rate, under-5 (per 1000 live births)
Human wellbeing	Human Development Index	https://data.undp.org/dataset/Human-Development-Index-HDI-value/

Source Author's own

correction of missing data was used only for a few variables since this problem does not arise in the case of the human development index.

Table 1 reports the measurement indicators associated with each latent variable as well as sources of the data. The first objective of *Maqāṣid* al-Sharī'ah is *Ḥifẓ al-Nafs* which means the preservation of life and health. This objective will be measured by four indicators that measure the effort expended by each country to protect lives and alleviate the poverty of his peoples.

To ensure the protection of human life, it must first be a human life that comes into existence, then this life can be preserved and survive. So, it is necessary to prohibit the assassination, to heal every disease and provide enough food. These are the means to achieve the objective of *Ḥifẓ al-Nafs*. We assume that *Ḥifẓ al-Nafs* involves reducing the crime rate in the country and the preservation of human rights. We propose the following indicators for *Ḥifẓ al-Nafs*: the health care index, poverty gap which measures the intensity of poverty in the country, human rights index, and the crime index.

The healthcare index reflects the overall quality of the healthcare system, healthcare professionals, equipment, staff, doctors, cost, etc.

Poverty gap index is defined as the average poverty gap in the population as a proportion of poverty threshold. *Crime index* is an estimation of overall level of crime in each country.

The second component of *Maqāṣid* al-Sharī'ah is *Ḥifẓ al-Dīn* which means the preservation of religion. We measure this component by the effort of the state to spend on the education of religion and to promote religion in society and to implement rigorous regulation of religion. We consider the following three measurements indicators: percentage of total expenditure in religious education, government favoritism of religion index and the government regulation of religion index.

The component *Ḥifẓ al-'Aql* includes the right to education and freedom of opinion. The role of government in *Ḥifẓ al-'Aql* can be conjugated by spending on education. The following indicators are considered for this objective: primary enrollment rate, secondary enrollment rate, and total public spending on education (% of GDP).

Ḥifẓ al-Māl implies good government practices in the allocation of resources in the country. It also includes the protection of property and wealth of individuals and the prohibition of stealing. The first measurement used for *Ḥifẓ al-Māl* is the international property rights index which measures the intellectual and physical property. The second factor is the inclusive wealth index that captures the value of resources depleted by human activities in the assessment of economic growth.

The last objective is *Ḥifẓ al-Nasl* which can be measured by the size of the divorce rate in the country and the government's ability to reduce the rate of child mortality.

In this paper, we use a structural approach to test the impact of *Maqāṣid* al-Sharīʿah on human well-being index. PLS is a structured equation modeling technique that can analyze structural equation models (SEMs) involving multiple-item constructs, with direct and indirect paths. This approach is a method of analysis to study the impact of a number of blocks of variables on the same individuals (Tenehaus 1998). The PLS-Path regression is a powerful approach for analyzing models because of the minimal demands on measurement scales, sample size, and residual distributions. The emphasis of PLS is on predicting the responses as well as on understanding the underlying relationship between variables.

Generally, groups of variable have some particular features such as high correlations. This leads to a problem of multicollinearity and makes it difficult predictive modeling using classical regression methods, hence, the use of structural equation models of latent variable.

In our research, we consider six groups of variables, each of which is determined by i manifest variables: *Let* X_{ij} be the vector of i manifest variables of the latent variable j. Each group variable is observable expression of a latent variable ξ_j whose average is denoted m_j.

A hierarchical classification of manifest variables is first performed to obtain blocks of variables representing the latent variables in the model to estimate. The causal relationships between these blocks are made with partial correlations.

Then, the external model is specified with the reflective mode to the extent that manifest variables were chosen so that they reflect the dimension to which they refer.

The estimation procedure consists of two types of estimates of latent variables and the estimation of structural equations.

– The Estimation of Latent Variables

Latent variables ξ_j are estimated in two ways: the y_j estimated from the manifest variables X_{ji} and internal estimate z_j derived from external estimates y_i of ξ_i related to ξ_j.

It is, therefore, an iterative algorithm, comprising the following steps: First, we estimate the latent variables based on the external model (each latent variable is estimated based on manifest variables of the block)

$$y_j = \sum_{h=1}^{p_j} w_{jh} x_{jh}$$

where the coefficient w_{jh} represents the external weight.

Then, we estimate latent variables based on the internal model (each latent variable is estimated based on other latent variables that are related).

$$z_j = \sum_{y_i \to y_j} e_{ji} y_i$$

where e_{ji} is the internal weight which is defined by choosing a schematic structural calculation.

In the following step, we establish a relationship between the two types of estimates for determining the external final weight: $w_{ij} = \text{cov}(X_{ij}, z_j)$.

We repeat these three steps until convergence in the estimates of the latent variable.

– The Estimation of Structural Equation

Once scores (external final estimate) are obtained, we estimate the coefficient of internal model using multiple regression classics (MCO) or PLS. Indeed, the structural equations are estimated by replacing each latent variable by external estimate.

In this study, the relationship of the PLS algorithm is estimated using the PLS regression instead of OLS regression. Indeed, for two blocks of variables X and Y, the OLS regression explains the variable Y at the expense of variable X. It can produce aberrant signs and insignificant coefficients. Contrary, PLS regression explains both Y and X. It solves the problem of multicollinearity with the construction of major components.

Table 2 Homogeneity and unidimensionality of MVs blocks

Latent variables	*Dimensions*	*Cronbach's alpha*	*D.&G.'s Rho (ACP)*	*Critical value*	*Eigenvalues*
Ḥifẓ al-Nafs	4	0.043	0.890	0.888	2.685
					0.844
					0.637
					0.099
Ḥifẓ al-Dīn	3	0.067	0.993	0.774	1.605
					0.943
					0.731
Ḥifẓ al-ʿAql	3		0.917	0.829	1.811
					0.714
					0.403
Ḥifẓ al-Māl	2	0.059	0.844	1.311	2.529
					0.979
Ḥifẓ al-Nasl	2		0.730	0.749	1.319
					0.932
Human wellbeing	1	0.106	0.857	1.135	1.477

Source Author's own

3 Results and Interpretation

We perform PLS-PM analysis involving only reflective indicators for the inner estimation. Since each reflective block represents only one latent construct, it needs to be one dimensional. This is why a preliminary exploratory analysis for verifying the composite reliability of blocks is required. Two different measures are available to test block one dimensionality in PLS-PM framework: Dillon-Goldstein's rho and Cronbach's alpha. According to Chin (1998), Dillon-Goldstein's rho is considered a better indicator than Cronbach's alpha as it is based on the results from the model rather than on the correlations observed between the manifest variables in the dataset. Following Werts et al. (1974), a block is considered homogeneous if this index is greater than 0.7.

The results of composite reliability test are resumed in Table 2. Since the Dillon-Goldstein's rho index is always greater than 0.7, we can deduce that all six blocks of manifest variables can be considered one dimensional. In addition, all blocks are unidimensional because only the first eigenvalue for each block is greater than one. Therefore, the reflective model is appropriate.

Table 3 Intercorrelations of the latent variables for first-order constructs

	Ḥifẓ al-Nafs	*Ḥifẓ al-Dīn*	*Ḥifẓ al-ʿAql*	*Ḥifẓ al-Māl*	*Ḥifẓ al-Nasl*	*Human wellbeing*
Ḥifẓ al-Nafs	**0.851**					
Ḥifẓ al-Dīn	0.629	**0.635**				
Ḥifẓ al-ʿAql	0.121	0.420	**0.738**			
Ḥifẓ al-Māl	0.034	0.502	0.689	**0.743**		
Ḥifẓ al-Nasl	0.182	0.258	0.375	0.632	**0.788**	
Human wellbeing	0.474	0.471	0.512	0.453	0.627	**0.720**

Notes The bold diagonal figures are the square root of the average variance extracted; the off-diagonal figures are the correlations of the latent constructs
Source Author's own

To test differently the discriminant validity of the model, we can compare the square root of the average variance extracted (AVE) for each construct with the correlation between each construct and other constructs in the model. Measurement variables are considered to have adequate discriminant validity if the square root of the AVE for each variable is greater than the correlation between the construct and any other measures in the model. As shown in Table 3, all constructs in the estimated model also fulfill this condition of discriminant validity.

After confirming the composite reliability, we can examine the relationship between each manifest variable and its own latent variable. In Table 4, we present the weights of the relationships between each manifest variable and its own latent variable, together with the standardized loadings. On the same table, we report also average communality index that measures the ability of each latent variable to explain its own manifest variables. Since this index is higher than 0.5 for most blocs, we can conclude that, globally, latent variables are powerful at explaining their own manifest variables.

The latent variable *Ḥifẓ al-Māl* expresses a slightly small value than 0.5. This can return to the ignorance of other measure variables that can better characterize the level of *Ḥifẓ al-Māl* in each country. A low value in a loading factor suggests that the indicator has little relation to the associated construct variable. All indicators of a block of variables must reflect the same construct.

Table 4 Normalized outer weights and average communalities

Variable latent	*Manifest variables*	*Loadings*	*Normalized outer weights*	*Average communality*
Ḥifẓ al-Nafs	Health Care Index	1.042**	0.905	
	Human Rights Index	1.377	0.026	
	Crime Index	−0.010*	0.055	
	Poverty gap	−1.954*	0.153	0.541
Ḥifẓ al-Dīn	Government Regulation of Religion Index,	4.427**	0.833	
	Percentage of total expenditure in religious education	2.982*	0.166	
	Government Favoritism of Religion Index	0.077	0.103	0.628
Ḥifẓ al-ʿAql	Primary enrollment rate	4.981**	0.715	
	Secondary enrollment rate	2.354*	0.103	
	Public spending on education, total (% of GDP)	1.785**	0.037	0.587
Ḥifẓ al-Māl	International Property Rights Index	3.258**	0.477	
	Inclusive wealth index	1.249*	0.051	0.321
Ḥifẓ al-Nasl	Divorce rate	−4.767**	8.370	
	Child mortality rates	−1.371*	0.131	0.591
Human wellbeing	Human Development Index	2.184**	0.136	0.570

***, **, * denote significance at the 1%, 5% and 10% levels, respectively
Source Author's own

The normalized weight measures the impact of the corresponding manifest variable in computing the latent variable score as an index and the standardized loadings.

Ḥifẓ al-nafas seems positively and significantly affected by the healthcare index and non-significantly affected by the human rights index. However, crime index and poverty gap have negative and significant impact on *Ḥifẓ al-Nafs* in each country. Healthcare index is the most important measure that characterizes *Ḥifẓ al-Nafs* since it expresses the higher normalized outer weight. The table shows that *Ḥifẓ al-Dīn* depends significantly on government regulation of religion index and the percentage of total expenditure in religious education, while the government favoritism of religion index has no significant effect on *Ḥifẓ al-Dīn*. This can be explained by the nature of our sample of countries that may

Table 5 Goodness of Fit Index for the hole model

	GoF	*GoF (Bootstrap)*	*Inner bound (95%)*	*Outer bound (95%)*
Absolute	0.483	0.492	0.469	0.598
Relative	0.842	0.844	0.791	0.869
Outer model	0.834	0.869	0.848	0.894
Inner model	0.831	0.837	0.818	0.863

Source Author's own

have the same support for the implementation of the practices of Islam in their societies.

Regarding *Ḥifẓ al-ʿAql*, it appears significantly and positively affected by the three variables of measures considered. Primary enrollment rate seems the most important factor that ensures *Ḥifẓ al-ʿAql* in the country. Divorce rate has more significant impact on *Ḥifẓ al-Nasl* than child mortality rate. Finally, the human development index developed by United Nations appears to be significantly representing the human well-being.

Table 5 shows that the goodness of fit index[1] for both the structural and measurement models is satisfactory with an absolute GoF value of 0.483 and an equal contribution of measurement model in constructing it. The relative GoF is very high. So are inner and outer models GoF.

After checking the reliability and validity of the relationship between manifest and latent variables, we present in the following the results of the estimation of the impact of latent variables (objectives *Maqāṣid* al-Sharīʿah) on the human development index. Since the PLS approach is distribution free, the nonparametric bootstrap procedure is used to estimate the t-statistics and the significance levels for the structural path coefficients (Chin 1998). The results of structural model are summarized in Fig. 2. In our PLS model, we test also whether *Ḥifẓ al-Dīn* has an impact on *Ḥifẓ al-Nafs*.

The regression coefficients and associated *t-values* are shown on the links (arrows) between exogenous and endogenous latent variables. Except *Ḥifẓ al-Māl*, all constructs variables in the model have positive

[1]A global criterion of goodness of fit (GoF) can be given (Espisito 2008) by the geometric mean of the average communality and the average R^2: $\mathrm{GoF} = \sqrt{(\text{average communality}) \times (\text{average } R^2)}$.

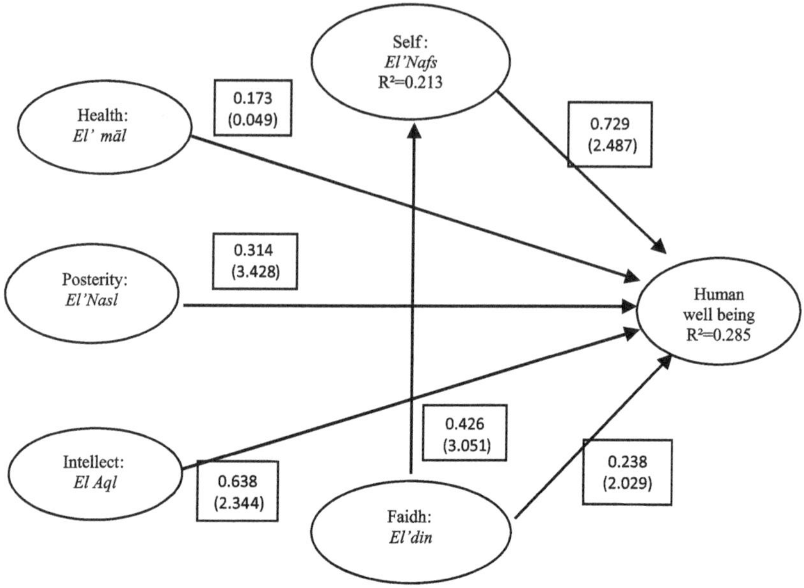

Fig. 2 Results of PLS estimation for the theoretical model (*Source* Author's own)

and significant effects on human well-being. This confirms that *Maqāṣid* al-Sharīʿah are likely to contribute to the development of human life in its economic and social aspects. The results show that the proposed model for human well-being has an R^2 of 0.285. Additionally, the R^2 for the outcome constructs of *Ḥifẓ al-Nafs* is 0.213.

Ḥifẓ al-Nafs and *Ḥifẓ al-ʿAql* seem to be the two main objectives of *Maqāṣid* al-Sharīʿah that most affect human development in Islamic countries since they express high coefficients of 0.729 and 0.638, respectively. The effort deployed by the government to preserve ownership of individuals (*Ḥifẓ al-Māl*) has no significant effect on the human development index. We suggest that this index should be better studied in future work since this indicator may reflect the stability of the security conditions in the country which has undoubtedly an impact on the quality of life in the country.

Ḥifẓ al-Dīn also appears significant but have relatively lower impact on human development. We argue that the effect of *Ḥifẓ al-Dīn* is exercised on the human development index indirectly through its impact on *Ḥifẓ al-Nafs*. Indeed, *Ḥifẓ al-Dīn* has a positive and significant impact

Table 6 Impact and contribution of exogenous latent variables on the endogenous human well-being

	Ḥifẓ al-Nafs	*Ḥifẓ al-Dīn*	*Ḥifẓ al-'Aql*	*Ḥifẓ al-Māl*	*Ḥifẓ al-Nasl*
Correlation	0.254	0.024	0.170	0.043	0.043
Path coefficient	0.729	0.238	0.638	0.173	0.314
t-statistic	2.487	2.029	2.344	0.049	3.428
Contribution to R^2 (%)	43.093	15.942	26.501	2.584	11.88

Source Author's own

on *Ḥifẓ al-Nafs* with a coefficient of 0.426 and, in fact, strengthen the principles of Islam in the society through promoting of religious teachings or by establishing a regulatory framework able to maintain religious principles as a basis for the individual must necessarily have an effect on reducing indexes of crime or human rights. This will have an impact on *Ḥifẓ al-Nafs* globally.

Let's study the results of the structural model estimates. Table 6 shows the correlation and regression path coefficients linking each exogenous latent variable to human well-being. The interpretation of this table should be done in conjunction with Table 3 which presents the loading factors. We can conclude that all path coefficient estimates of the structural model are significant except *Ḥifẓ al-Māl* which appears insignificant.

The results show that *Ḥifẓ al-Nafs* has the major contribution to R^2 (43.093%). The contribution of *Ḥifẓ al-Māl* to R^2 is the lower one. *Ḥifẓ al-'Aql* contributes higher than *Ḥifẓ al-Dīn* to R^2 explaining human development. Table 7 shows that all latent variables explain 28.7% of human well-being development.

They found that *Ḥifẓ al-Nafs is* the major objective of *Maqāṣid* al-Sharī'ah affecting the human well-being can be justified by the teaching of both the Qur'ān and *Essouna*. The Prophet *Mohammed* said,

Table 7 Goodness of Fit Index for the structural model

R^2	R^2 *(Bootstrap)*	*Ecart-type*	*Inner bound (95%)*	*Outer bound (95%)*
0.287	0.296	0.053	0.257	0.298

Source Author's own

"I will be an enemy of who kill a person with whom we have a deal." He also said: "One who kills a person, non-Muslim under the protection of the State, shall not smell the fragrance of Paradise" (Narrated by Bukhari). *Ḥifẓ al-Nafs* values also the efforts of those who work for the safeguarding of life, we know that according to the Qur'ān that whoever kills an innocent soul, it is as if he killed all mankind, and that who saves one soul, it is as if he saved the whole humanity. *Ḥifẓ al-Nafs* is also explained by the reduction of crime rate in Islamic countries. The Prophet Mohamed did not pray the dead (*Janazah*) on a suicidal, it was just to highlight the seriousness of suicide. Only the companions of the Prophet prayed on him and asked Allah to forgive him. The prophet is justified in saying: "I do not pray on his body, so that Muslims do not commit suicide." Suicide is an act of weakness, depression and despair, the one who commits suicide a great sin but can receive forgiveness and mercy of God.

4 Conclusion

This study develops an empirical approach to test the real impact of *Maqāṣid* al-Sharīʿah on the human well-being index. Our work is based on the five objectives advanced by Al-Ghazali (1111). For each objective, we selected a number of measurement indicators based specially on existing data. Our results show that *Ḥifẓ al-Nafs is* the major objective of *Maqāṣid* al-Sharīʿah affecting the human well-being, while *Ḥifẓ al-Māl* has no significant effect on the human development index. Limitation of our study to the fives principles proposed by Al-Ghazali can be considered as a limitation to this work.

Taqi al-*Dīn* Ibn Taymiyyah (d. 728/1328) was the first researcher to add new principles of *maqāṣid*, such as contract enforcement, preservation of kinship, honoring the rights of his relatives, the love of God, sincerity, loyalty, and moral purity. Thus, Ibn Taymiyyah revised the scope of the *maqāṣid* from an open list of values, and its approach is generally accepted by contemporary scholars, including Ahmad Al-Raysuni (2006).

In a very illustrious research, Ibn 'Ashur (1945/2006) provides some explicit aspects of *Maqāṣid* al-Sharīʿah that lead to human development, namely promoting the welfare (*Jalb al-masalih*) and avoiding the evils (*Dar al-mafāṣid*).

Bibliography

Al-Ghazali, Abu Hamid. (1901). *Al-mustasfa min ʿilm al-usul* (1st Ed.). Cairo, Egypt: Al-Matba'ah al-Amiriyyah.

Al-Najjar, U. Abd al-Majid. (2008). *Maqāṣid* al-Sharīʿah *bi ab'adin jadidah.* Beirut: Dar al-Gharb al-Islami.

Al-Raysuni, A. (1992). *Al-Nazariyah al- Maqasid ʿInda al-Imam al-Shatibi* (2nd Ed.). Riyadh: Al-Dar al-Alamiyyah lil Kitab al-Islami.

Al-Raysuni, Ahmad. (2006). *Imam Al-Shatibi's Theory of the Higher Objectives and Intents of Islamic Law.* Herndon, VA: International Institute of Islamic Thought.

Al-Shatibi, Abu Ishaq. (2004). *Al-muwafaqat fi usul* al-Sharīʿah. Beirut: Dar al-Kutub al-ʻIlmiyah.

Anto, M. H. (2009). Introducing an Islamic Human Development index (I-HDI) to Measure Development in OIC Countries. *Islamic Economic Studies* 19(2), pp. 69–95.

Chapra, M. U. (2008). *The Islamic Vision of Development in the Light of Maqāṣid* al-Sharīʿah. Jeddah: Islamic Research and Training Institute, Islamic Development Bank. http://www.irti.org/.../IDBDevelopments/.../The%20Islamic%20Vision%20of%20Development%207.pdf.

Chin, W. W. (1998). The Partial Least Squares Approach to Structural Equation Modeling. In G. A. Marcoulides (ed.), *Modern Methods for Business Research* (pp. 295–336). Mahwah, NJ: Lawrence Erlbaum Associates.

Crane, R. D. (2009). *Maqāṣid* al-Sharīʿah: A Strategy to Rehabilitate Religion in America. Eightieth Birthday Celebration Lecture, International Institute of Islamic Thought. Herndon, VA, USA.

Dar, Humayon A. (2004). On Making Human Development More Humane. *International Journal of Social Economics* 31(11/12), pp. 1071–1088.

Esposito Vinzi, V. (2008). *The Contribution of PLS Regression to PLS Path Modelling: Formative Measurement Model and Causality Network in the Structural Model.* In Joint Statistical Meetings (JSM), American Statistical Association, Denver, CO, USA, August 7th.

Hasan, Zubair. (2004). Measuring the Efficiency of Islamic Banks: Criteria, Methods and Social Priorities. *Review of Islamic Economics* 8(2), pp. 5–30.

Hassan, K., and Mahlknecht, M. (2011). *Islamic Capital Markets: Products and Strategies.* West Sussex: John Wiley.

Ibn ʻAshur, Muhammad al-Tahir. (1998). *Maqāṣid* al-Sharīʿah *al-Islamiyyah*, ed. Muhammad al-Tahir al-Misawi. Kuala Lumpur: al-Basa'ir.

Ibn ʻAshur, Muhammad al-Tahir. (2006). *Treatise on Maqāṣid* al-Sharīʿah. Herndon, VA: International Institute of Islamic Thought.

Taqî al-D-m ibn Taymiyyah, *Majmû' Fatâwâ Shaykh al-Islâm Ibn Taymiyyah*, comp., ʻAbd al-Rahmân ibn Qâsim (Beirut: Muassasat al-Risâlah, 1398 AH), 32: 134.

Tenehaus, M. (1998). *La Régression PLS: Théorie et Pratique*. Paris: Editons Technip.

Werts, C. E., Linn, R. L., and Jöreskog, K. G. (1974). Intraclass Reliability Estimates: Testing Structural Assumptions. *Educational and Psychological Measurement* 34(1), pp. 25–33.

CHAPTER 13

Assessing Socio-Economic Development Based on *Maqāṣid* al-Sharīʿah Principles: Normative Frameworks, Methods and Pilot Implementation in Indonesia

Rahmatina Kasri and Habib Ahmed

1 Introduction

Maqāṣid is presumably one of today's most important intellectual means and methodologies for Islamic studies, particularly in Islamic jurisprudence (Auda 2008). Outside this area, however, it is rarely discussed in contemporary Islamic scholarships. This is presumably related to the difficulties in translating the concept into workable developmental models and policies (Kasri 2012). As such, even though there have

R. Kasri (✉)
Faculty of Economics and Business, Universitas Indonesia,
Jakarta, Indonesia
e-mail: rahmatina@ui.ac.id

H. Ahmed
Durham University Business School, Durham, UK
e-mail: habib.ahmed@durham.ac.uk

S. S. Ali (ed.), *Towards a Maqāṣid al-Sharīʿah Index of Socio-Economic Development*, Palgrave Studies in Islamic Banking, Finance, and Economics,
https://doi.org/10.1007/978-3-030-12793-0_13

been persistent calls to expand and implement the concepts of *Maqāṣid* al-Sharīʿah to economic and development studies particularly considering underdevelopment and poverty persistently exist in most of the contemporary Muslim countries (Al-Sufi 2013; Chapra 2008; Mirakhor and Askari 2010), the concept is rarely applied in such studies.

With this perspective, the paper discusses the basic concepts of *Maqāṣid* al-Sharīʿah as the foundation to translate them into appropriate development models and policies. Based on the similarity and significance of works in developing the *Maqāṣid* principles, it is argued that human well-being/poverty is one of the central themes in the historical deliberations and should be the same when using it to frame policies to resolve development challenges in current Muslim world. Considering that increasing well-being and reducing poverty are also the main development objectives, it subsequently develops a general framework to assess socio-economic development status of Muslim countries in the light of *Maqāṣid*. It also provides a workable example to show how this framework can be implemented in evaluating the well-being changes of Muslims in Indonesia.

Following this introduction, the paper is structured as follow. Section 2 discusses the basic concepts related to *Maqāṣid* al-Sharīʿah while Sect. 3 reviews the concepts of poverty/well-being. Based on the literature review, a general framework for assessing the socio-economic development of Muslim societies is developed in Sect. 4. A simple, linear and decomposable multidimensional *Maqāṣid* al-Sharīʿah-based poverty index is also briefly discussed. In Sect. 5, the index is subsequently applied to a case study which evaluates the welfare changes amongst the recipients of *zakāh* in Indonesia. Primary data collected through a survey conducted in 2011 covering 685 households living in nine cities of Greater Jakarta Metropolitan area in Indonesia are used to carry out this exercise. The final section concludes the study and notes some remarks for future research.

2 *Maqāṣid* al-Sharīʿah and Human Well-Being/Poverty

2.1 *Basic Concepts and Classifications of* Maqāṣid *al-Sharīʿah*

The term '*Maqsid*' (plural: *Maqāṣid*) literally means a purpose, intent, objective, principle, goal or end. *Maqāṣid* al-Sharīʿah could therefore be literally defined as the objectives, purposes, intents, ends or principles behind the Islamic law or Islamic rulings (Ashur 2006) or the higher objectives of the lawgiver (Al-Raysuni 2005). Some scholars also refer *Maqāṣid* al-Sharīʿah as 'people's interests' (*masalih*; singular *maṣlaḥah*)'.[1] These interpretations are slightly wider than the literal meaning and reflect the 'interest for humanity' in the meaning of *Maqāṣid* al-Sharīʿah (Auda 2008).

Maqāṣid al-Sharīʿah is normally classified according to the levels of *maṣlaḥah*, beginning with the essentials (*ḍarūriyāt*), the needs (*ḥajiyāt*) and the luxuries (*taḥsiniyāt*). The essentials or primary interest can be defined as things which are vital to human survival and well-being, such that their 'destruction' will jeopardize a normal order of life in society.[2] The needs or complementary interest (*ḥajiyāt*) can be seen as benefits which seek to remove severity and hardship that do not pose serious threats for the survival of normal life.[3] Meanwhile, the luxuries or embellishment (*taḥsiniyāt*) can be regarded as things that seek to attain

[1] For example, Imam al-Juwayni uses the term al-*maqāṣid* and public interest (*al-masāliḥ al-ammah*) interchangeably (Auda 2008). Imam al-Ghazali places *maqāṣid* under what he called as 'unrestricted interests (*al-masāliḥ al-mursalah*)', which is agreed by his followers al-Razi and al-Amidi (Al-Raysuni 2005). Meanwhile, al-Qarafi links *maṣlaḥah* and *maqāṣid* through a fundamental principle in which 'a purpose (*maqsid*) is not valid unless it leads to the fulfillment of some good (*maṣlaḥah*) or the avoidance of some mischief (*mafsadah*)' (Auda 2008: 20).

[2] It is often classified into what preserves one's faith, soul, wealth, mind and offspring. In relation to this, adultery, alcohol or wine-drinking and intoxicants are banned in Islam as they pose threats to the protection and well-being of family (offspring) and the integrity of human intellect (soul and mind), respectively. Islam also bans thefts, monopoly, hoarding of wealth (*rikaz), riba* and *gharar* transactions to protect the human wealth. The preservation of faith is also a necessity for human life, albeit probably more in the afterlife sense because Islam perceives life as a 'comprehensive' journey in the world and the hereafter (Kamali 2008).

[3] With respect to ritual worship (*ibāḥah*), for example, *shariah* has granted many concessions (*rukhas*) such as shortening of prayers and opening of fast for the sick and traveller in order to make things easier for Muslims. In daily 'worldly' life (*muamalah*), examples of this need are marriage, trade and means of transportation. Although Islam encourages and regulates these activities, the lack of any of these needs is not a matter of life and death especially on an individual basis. However, if the shortage becomes widespread and jeopardizes people's life, they could be considered as necessities and thus move from the level of complementary interests to the level of necessities.

refinement and perfection in the conduct of people at all level of achievement (Kamali 2008).[4]

Recently, following some critics regarding the 'inability' of the *Maqāṣid* approach to cope with complexities of time and solve current problems of the *ummah*, dimensions of the 'classical' *Maqāṣid* have been extended into various aspects (freedom, human rights, etc.) and particular scopes (based on rulings, scope of people, etc.) (Auda 2008). The 'new' *Maqāṣid*, however, have some similarities and differences with the classical perspective particularly in relation to human well-being/poverty as will be discussed in the next section.

2.2 Maqāṣid *Principles and Human Well-Being/Poverty*

The historical development of *Maqāṣid* principles can be generally classified into three milestones (Kasri 2012), as illustrated in Fig. 1. First, the early *Maqāṣid* period developed by jurists during the first four Islamic centuries (1–4 AH). In this period, works on *Maqāṣid* were dominated by attempts to survey and find '*wisdoms-behind-rulings*' from the scripture and not directly to the well-being objectives. Despite that, most of the wisdom discussed was closely related to the important aspect of human well-being.[5] Second, the major *Maqāṣid* period lasted from the fifth to the eight of Islamic century (5–8 AH). This is the 'golden' period where Islamic scholars devoted their time and attention to develop appropriate juristic methods and subsequently construct fundamentals of the *Maqāṣid* principles in which human well-being/poverty

[4]This is reflected in the use of, among others, perfume, jewellery, stylish clothing, beautiful homes and sporty cars. These things are important and perfecting human life, although in lower priorities than the essentials and the needs. They also serve as further signs and proofs for God's endless mercy and generosity towards human life.

[5]For example, al-Tarmidzi al-Hakim wrote *Kitab al-Salah wa Maqāṣiduna* (the Book of Prayers and Their Purposes) in which the wisdom and spiritual 'secrets' behind each of the prayers rituals (such as 'confirming humbleness' as the *maqsid* or purpose behind glorifying God's with every move during prayers (*takbeer*) or 'focusing on one's prayers' as the *maqsid* behind facing the direction of the *Ka'bah)* are discussed. Abu Zayd al-Balkhi wrote a book dedicated to *maṣlaḥah* called *Masalih al-Abdan wa al-Anfus* (Benefits for Bodies and Souls). This book explains how Islamic practices and rulings contribute to human's health, physically and mentally, which are important aspects of human well-being. Another example is a more comprehensive volume of 335 chapters written by al-Qummi, which 'rationalize' believing in God, Prophets, heavens as well as the wisdoms behind prayers, fasting, pilgrimage, charity, and other moral obligations (Al-Raysuni 2005; Auda 2008).

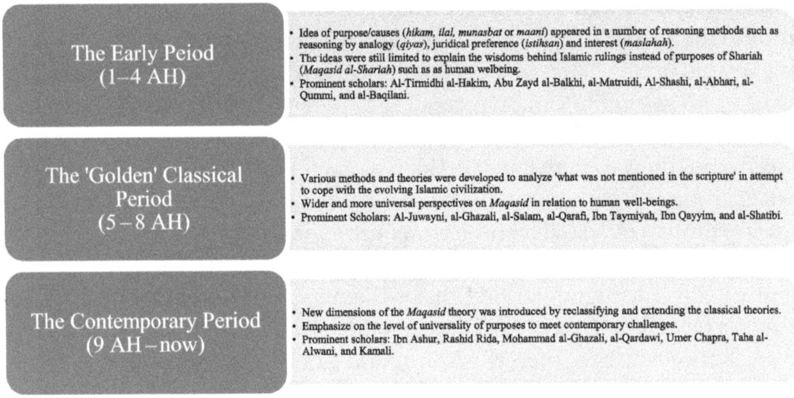

Fig. 1 Three developmental milestones of *Maqāṣid* principles (*Source* Kasri [2012])

became the focus.[6] Finally, the contemporary period (from 9AH to now, but especially from thirteenth Islamic century onwards) could be defined as a period marked by extensions of the 'classical' principles of *Maqāṣid* based on the complexities of time and the need to reform the current Islamic world. Reform in the economic and development dimensions were amongst the most important reforms during the period.[7]

Based on the similarity and significance of works in developing the *Maqāṣid* principles, it is argued that human well-being/poverty is a central theme in the historical deliberations of *Maqāṣid*. This is particularly

[6]Imam al-Juwayni was probably the first scholar who introduces a theory of 'levels of necessity' which later inspired his followers to develop the *maqāṣid* principles (Auda 2008). However, the most influential works on *maqāṣid* during this period are probably the works developed by al-Ghazali with his 'order of necessities', al-Shatibi and his postulate '*Maqāṣid* as fundamentals' and Ibn Taimiyyah and Ibn-Qayyim who calls for 'what *shariah* is all about' (Al-Raysuni 2005). Some of the relevant works/citations will be mentioned later in this section.

[7]Ibn Ashur, for instance, emphasized purposes dealing with the 'nation' (*ummah*) instead of those dealing with individuals. Rashid Rida included 'reform' and 'women's rights' in his theory of *maqāṣid*. Al-Qardhawi embraced the need 'to preserve true faith, maintain human dignity/rights and build a more cooperative world' (Auda 2008). More recently, Chapra emphasized that the ultimate objective of all Islamic teaching is to be a blessing for mankind, which could only be fulfilled by promoting the real well-being (*falāḥ*) of all people on earth (Chapra 2008).

reflected in the writings and conceptualizations of *Maqāṣid* al-Sharīʿah during the classical and contemporary period. Al-Ghazali, for instance, formulated that, 'The objective of the *Shariah* is *to promote the well-being of all mankind* [emphasize added], which lies in safeguarding their faith (*dīn*), their human self (*nafs*), their intellect (*ʿaql*), their posterity (*nasl*) and their wealth (*māl*)' (in Chapra 2000: 118). Ibn Taymiyyah believed that 'Islamic law came to *realize and enhance human well-being* [emphasize added], and to minimize and neutralize sources of harm and corruption...' (in Al-Raysuni 2005: 28:34). Ibn Qayyim, the student of Ibn Taymiyyah, added that, 'Islamic law is all about wisdom and *achieving people's welfare* [emphasize added] in this life and the afterlife. It is all about justice, mercy, wisdom and good' (in Auda 2008: 20–21). Meanwhile, Al-Shatibi specifically wrote *Kitab al-Maqāṣid* which essentially suggest that the fundamentals of Islamic jurisprudence are definitive in nature and founded on the law's universals (objectives) included in the essentials (*ḍarūriyāt*), exigencies (*ḥajiyāt*) and embellishments (*tahsiniyah*). Furthermore, based on an inductive method rooted in the Qur'ān, he contended that the essential objectives can be observed in five dimensions namely religion (*dīn*), human life (*nafs*), progeny (*nasl*), material wealth (*māl*) and human reason (*ʿaql*) (in Al-Raysuni 2005: 28).

It is also notable that most of the scholars have recommended relatively similar methods to achieve the objectives namely through opening access (promotion) of human well-being and protection/prevention of the things that could harm achievement of the objectives. Al-Ghazali suggested that, 'Whatever ensures the safeguard of these five [objectives], serves public interest and is desirable' (in Chapra 2000: 118). Al-Izz ibn Abd al-Salam argued that Islamic law basically consists of two interests, namely either interests that prevent what would cause harms or achieve what would bring benefits (in Al-Raysuni 2005: 30–32). Similarly, al-Qarafi wrote about 'opening the means to achieving good ends' which could be interpreted as opening access to realize human well-being (in Auda 2008: 20). Meanwhile, al-Shatibi contended that Islamic law is aimed to preserve the essential interests by preserving their existence and protecting them from annihilation (in Al-Raysuni 2005: 107–109).

While the human well-being goal is also acknowledged by contemporary scholars, in the past few decades attention has been given to other purposes such as freedom and justice which is strongly relevant in the context of Islamic revivalism (Auda 2008). Nevertheless, in today's context where poverty and underdevelopment are the main development challenges faced by most Muslim nations,[8] promoting the real well-being and reducing poverty can be considered as one of the important goals. Indeed, it is mentioned that the ultimate objective of all Islamic teaching is to be a blessing for all mankind, which could only be fulfilled by promoting the real well-being (*falāḥ*) of all people on earth (Chapra 2008: 1–3). Thus, increasing human well-being or reducing poverty is arguably a central higher purpose of *Maqāṣid* al-Sharīʿah according to the contemporary scholars.

Somewhat unsurprisingly, the central theme of *Maqāṣid* (i.e. increasing human well-being or reducing poverty) has also become the main development objective since the past few decades (Iqbal 2002; Mirakhor and Askari 2010; World Bank 1990).[9] This is presumably due to the fact that developing world, including the Muslim countries, has persistent poverty and even getting poorer over time (Chen and Ravallion 2008; Iqbal 2002; Obaidullah 2008) albeit various attempts have been done to alleviate poverty since the 1990s (Booth and Mosley 2003).

Before proceeding to the next section, it is worth noting that effective poverty alleviation policies may not be feasible without clear concepts of poverty/well-being that can be consistently measured (Sirageldin 2000; World Bank 2001). Thus, it is important to clearly understand the conceptualizations of poverty/well-being prior to developing appropriate framework to measure it based on new perspectives such as the *Maqāṣid* principles. These are the main focus of the next sections.

3 Review of Conventional Concepts of Poverty/Well-Being

In contemporary poverty/well-being studies, there are two major approaches to the definitions and measurements of poverty. The first approach is the narrow approach to poverty, which considers poverty simply in material/monetary terms. Under this approach, poverty is

[8]More than half a billion of the world's poor is Muslim and lives under abject poverty with incomes below US$2 a day (Obaidullah 2008). Most of them have very limited access to education and health-care facilitates as well as lived with poor housing and poor sanitation facilities (Ahmed 2004).

[9]In this study, the terms, increasing well-being and reducing poverty, are used interchangeably and sometimes simultaneously as they basically have similar essence.

typically measured by comparing individuals' income/consumption with some defined thresholds (poverty line) below which they are considered to be poor. With this approach, aggregate poverty index such as the headcount index and the poverty severity index are widely used to represent the poverty conditions (Ravallion 1994). The second broader approach goes beyond the traditional monetary measure and includes possession of specific types of consumption goods/services such as shelter, health care and education as the basic needs. This approach implies that a household without access to the basic entitlements indeed lives in poverty (Haughton and Khandker 2009; Townsend 1985; Yunus 2007). The Human Development Index (HDI) is often seen as a representative measure of poverty under this approach (Anand and Sen 1997).

More recently, discussion within the second approach has been extended into the capability approach. Pioneered by the works of Nobel Laureate Amartya Sen, it is argued that poverty/well-being comes from the capability to function in society. Specifically, poverty arises when people lack key capabilities which leave them with 'deficiencies' and inadequate resources to exist in a society (see, for instance, Anand and Sen 1997; Sen 1993, 2005). Such deficiencies include, amongst others, low incomes, low education, poor health, insecurity, low self-confidence, a sense of powerlessness and the absence of rights such as freedom of speech (Robeyns 2005). Furthermore, poverty is seen as deprivation of capabilities and lack of multiple freedoms that people value or have reasons to value (Alkire 2007). Viewed in this way, capability poverty is a multidimensional phenomenon that largely depends on people's norms and values. Under this approach, the Multidimensional Poverty Index (MPI) launched by the United Nation in 2010 is generally seen as a representative measure of multidimensional poverty (Alkire and Deneulin 2009).

Following the conceptualizations above, Fig. 2 illustrates three main steps typically taken to measure poverty and compares the approaches commonly used in the current conventional poverty studies. Although this framework is generally applied in measuring the monetary poverty (Alkire and Foster 2007), it is increasingly being utilized to develop the multidimensional poverty measures under the capability approach (Comim and Qizilbash 2008). However, as multidimensional poverty is a relatively new concept in economic and poverty studies, the framework is not strictly applied in the discipline (Alkire and Foster 2011;

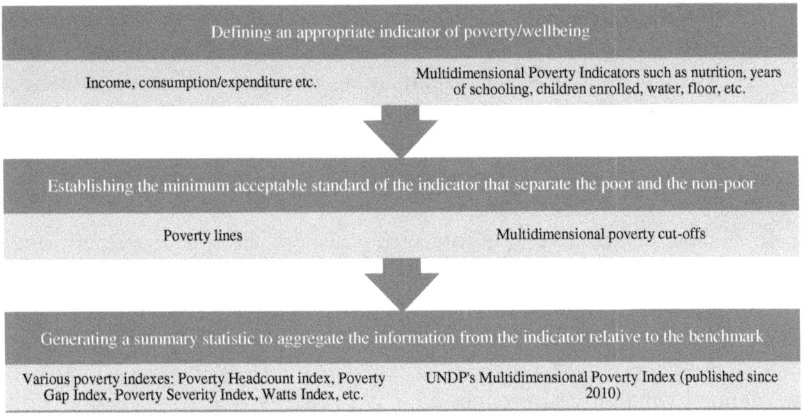

Fig. 2 Major steps in measuring poverty (*Source* Author's summary from various sources)

Ravallion 2011) and a number of other issues need to be considered in assessing poverty across the multiple dimensions.[10]

In defining the appropriate indicator of poverty under the first perspective, the choice is normally between income and consumption/ expenditure.[11] Each indicator has strengths and weaknesses.[12] Therefore, the choice of an appropriate welfare indicator must eventually be adjusted to the research objectives (Haughton and Khandker 2009).

[10]According to Alkire (2007), there are a number of important issues which require consideration to assess poverty across the multiple dimensions. The issues include (i) how to choose the domains or dimensions; (ii) how to choose relevant indicators for the domains and related capabilities; (iii) how to model the interaction among indicators and among dimensions; (iv) how to set relative weights for each dimension and indicator; (v) how to aggregate or compare across individuals or groups; (vi) how to aggregate across dimensions or, alternatively, to perform rankings and comparisons; and (vii) how to incorporate freedom and agency into multidimensional capability poverty measures. Discussions on these issues are still ongoing until now.

[11]There are a number of other indicators such as calories consumed per person per day, food consumption as a fraction of total expenditure, nutritional status and observer assessment. However, they are rarely used in calculating (monetary) poverty.

[12]Given the limited number of income sources, it is normally easier to measure income than consumption. Nevertheless, it is also likely to be underreported. In contrast, while some expenditure is not incurred regularly, expenditure as a whole is usually easier to recall and less understated than income (Haughton and Khandker 2009).

As for the multidimensional poverty, theoretically there are unlimited options for the poverty/well-being dimensions and indicators (Alkire 2002). As such, the choices of the most appropriate indicators have been a subject of ongoing debate amongst the proponents. It is notable, however, that taking account of people's norms/values is considered as an appropriate method in selecting the dimensions and indicators of poverty/well-being (Alkire 2007).[13]

In policy perspective, an interesting aspect of the aforementioned debate is the 'limits' to the number of dimensions and indicators used for constructing the multidimensional poverty index. On the one hand, some scholars—including Amartya Sen, the pioneer of the capability approach—believe that there is no 'fixed list' of capabilities to go with the general capability approach. This is primarily due to the impossibility of compiling a list that could be used for every purpose and that is unaffected by the importance of different capabilities. As a result, the capabilities should be selected in the light of the values of the referent population and the purpose of the study (Sen 2004).[14] However, other scholars, such as philosopher Martha Nussbaum (2003), argue that such a condition has created problems for policy makers trying to focus their attention on fighting poverty. She also contended that the specification of one 'list' of domains or central capabilities is necessary to ensure that the content of the capability approach carries a critical force and therefore the possibility of the 'wrong' freedoms being prioritized and expanded could be minimized.[15]

[13]It is noted by Alkire (2007: 7) that in the practical applications of the capability approach and related multidimensional [poverty] approaches, the methods of identifying capabilities or poverty dimensions are surprisingly straightforward. Most researchers draw implicitly on five selection methods, either alone or in combination, based on (i) existing data/convention, (ii) assumption of what people do/should value, (iii) public 'consensus', (iv) ongoing deliberative participatory processes, and (v) empirical evidence from multidisciplinary studies regarding people's values.

[14]Despite that, Sen (2004: 80) said that 'I have nothing against the listing of capabilities but must stand up against a grand mausoleum to one fixed and final list of capabilities'.

[15]Nussbaum (2003: 33) strongly argued that 'capabilities can help us to construct a normative conception of social justice...only if we specify a definite set of capabilities as the most important ones to protect. Sen's "perspective of freedom" is too vague. Some freedoms limit others; some freedoms are important, some trivial, some good, and some positively bad. Before the approach can offer a valuable normative gender perspective, we must make commitments about the substance'.

Despite the ongoing debate, literature generally suggests that there are a number of indicators commonly used in empirical studies related to multidimensional poverty (see Appendix 1). The indicators are drawn not only from poverty/well-being studies, but also from sociology, anthropology, psychology/psychometric, philosophy, culture/behaviour as well as the quality of life and happiness studies. Some notable dimensions and indicators frequently used in the studies are indicators related to life and/or health (food, nutrition, housing, clothing, access to healthcare services, water, sanitation, etc.), education (literacy, basic education, years of schooling, children enrolled, etc.), economic aspects (work/employment, working conditions, economic security, etc.), religion/spiritual aspects (transcendence-creativity, transcendence peace with God, morality, religious observance, etc.) and other social/family indicators (marriage, children, peace, harmony, participation in/attachment to local community, personal liberty and freedom, etc.).

Furthermore, in establishing a poverty standard, a poverty line is commonly used as a benchmark. In monetary poverty analysis, a poverty line could be technically defined as the level of income/expenditure needed for an individual/household to escape poverty.[16] Thus, it could be considered the minimum income/expenditure required for meeting the basic needs (Ravallion 1998).[17] With respect to multidimensional poverty analysis, there are two general approaches to determine the poverty threshold. One approach is to use a particular (yet somewhat ad hoc) poverty cut-off point based on researcher's judgement, while another approach is to directly ask the poor whether they are deprived in a particular dimension of well-being or not.

Under the multidimensional poverty analysis, the first approach is used by Mack and Lansley (1985) who identified people as poor if they were poor in three or more out of 26 deprivations. It is also utilized in UNICEF's Child Poverty Report 2003, as mentioned by Gordon et al. (2003), in which a child is called deprived if he/she

[16]A poverty line is usually (and officially) defined for an individual. However, since poverty studies are mostly conducted on the household level, the common approach is to construct one per capita line for all individuals and adjust the line with household composition or size. This implies that a household poverty line could be generated by multiplying the per capita line with the household size. For further discussion, see Ravallion (1998).

[17]The current literature also recognizes the so-called subjective poverty line constructed by directly asking people about their poverty line. In practice, the self-rated measure is often used as a complement to the more traditional 'objective' poverty lines.

suffers in two or more dimensions of poverty. Quite recently, a more general (yet somewhat normative) 'dual cut-off' method of identification has been introduced and employed in the construction of the UNDP's Multidimensional Poverty Index (Alkire and Foster 2011). With this approach, a person is defined as poor if he/she is deprived in two to six out of 10 of the MPI's indicators (UNDP 2010).[18] The second approach, which directly asks the poor about their poverty/well-being status, is mostly used in psychological/psychometric happiness and behavioural studies. Examples of such studies are the studies on identification of multidimensional poverty in Germany (Van Praag and Ferrer-i-Carbonell 2008) and Luxemburg (Fusco and Dickes 2008).

Once the poverty/welfare measure and the poverty benchmark are determined, aggregate poverty measures can be constructed. Under this approach, the aggregate statistics include poverty indexes such as Poverty Headcount Index, Poverty Gap index, Poverty Severity Index and Watt Index.[19] As for multidimensional poverty, there have been recent attempts to aggregate various dimensions of poverty into a single composite index called the Multidimensional Poverty Index.[20] Developed from the 'counting' method initially proposed by Atkinson (2003) and Bourguignon and Chakravarty (2003), the MPI is basically the product of the multidimensional poverty headcount (the proportion of people who are multidimensionally poor) and the average number of deprivations each multidimensionally poor household experienced (the intensity of their poverty) in three dimensions and 10 indicators with equal weights (Fig. 3).

[18]In a recent publication, Alkire and Foster, who developed the Multidimensional Poverty Index, admit that 'The choice of *k* could therefore be a ***normative one*** [emphasis added], with *k* reflecting the minimum deprivation count required to be considered poor in a specific context under consideration' (Alkire and Foster 2011: 483).

[19]For more discussion on the index, see Haughton and Khandker (2009).

[20]Some studies consider the Human Development Index (HDI) and the Human Poverty Index (HPI) introduced by the United Nations Development Program (UNDP) in 1990 and 1997, respectively, as multidimensional poverty indices. However, when the indices were launched, they were never meant to represent the multidimensional poverty concept. Rather, HDI is 'a composite index that takes into account three types of deprivations', which is closer to the broad approach to poverty. Meanwhile, HPI is a composite index based on several parameters known to influence human capabilities. Only recently have the indices been 're-categorized' as multidimensional poverty indices. Despite that, as emphasized in the UNDP's 2010 Human Development Report, HPI has recently been replaced by the Multidimensional Poverty Index (UNDP 2010: 95).

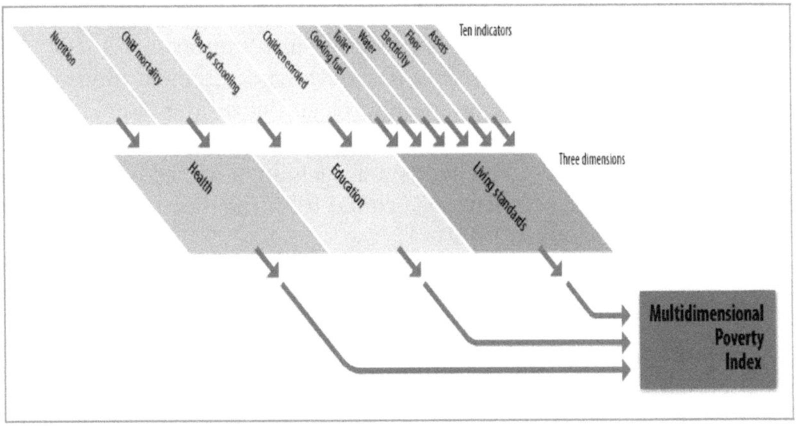

Fig. 3 The Multidimensional Poverty Index (*Source* Alkire and Santos [2010], in UNDP [2010: 96])

More recently, however, it has been pointed out that a single aggregate index is not appropriate and can never be a sufficient statistic of poverty under the multidimensional nature of the approach. Indeed, it is suggested that a credible set of multiple indices such as 'health poverty' or 'education poverty' be developed rather than a single-composite multidimensional poverty index (Ravallion 2011). Given the ongoing debates, it is anticipated that the method(s) for aggregating the multidimensional poverty measure will continue to be refined in the future (Alkire et al. 2011).

In addition to the issues above, some other issues might need to be considered prior to assessing multidimensional poverty/well-being. An important issue is modelling the interaction between dimensions and indicators of the poverty/well-being measure. The choices range from linear relationship to non-linear relationships[21] and require rigorous examinations prior to model the measure (Alkire 2007). Another issue is setting the relative weight for each dimension and indicator. While most studies and current indices (such as HDI and MPI) use equal weight for

[21]Examples of the nonlinear relationships are the equations representing the poverty severity index and the Watts index. For a detailed discussion of the index, see Haughton and Khandker (2009).

each dimension and indicator (Atkinson 2003),[22] it is possible to utilize unequal weight provided that appropriate justifications are made.[23] If cross-country comparison becomes one of the measurement objectives, it is necessary to think about the method to aggregate the individuals and subsequently compare or perform the rankings of the index/measures generated (Alkire 2007). Finally, data availability also needs to be taken into account if global comparison is aimed from the measurement results (Haughton and Khandker 2009).

4 General Framework for Developing a *Maqāṣid* al-Sharīʿah-Based Multidimensional Poverty Measure

Following discussion in the previous sections, at least three stages are needed to construct a *Maqāṣid*-based multidimensional poverty/well-being measure. The stages are (i) defining poverty/well-being indicators (i.e. choosing the dimensions and indicators) suitable with the *Maqāṣid* perspective, (ii) defining the relevant poverty/well-being threshold, and (iii) constructing an appropriate *Maqāṣid*-based multidimensional poverty/well-being measures.

In the first stage, it is argued that the *Maqāṣid* principles—particularly those advocated by al-Ghazali and al-Shatibi—provide relevant guidance in selecting the appropriate poverty/well-being dimensions. To recall, the classical scholars have recommended the safeguarding of five main dimensions of human well-being, including faith (*dīn*), human self (*nafs*), intellect (*'aql*), posterity (*nasl*) and wealth (*māl*) as the main objective of *shariah*. In contemporary time, the dimensions could be interpreted into religious/spiritual, health, education, family/social and economic dimensions.

The Ghazalian/Shatibian maxim is considered as an appropriate framework to examine multidimensional aspects of human well-being for at least two main reasons, including (i) its relevance to current situation in the Muslim world where poverty and backwardness persistently exist most notably in the past few centuries and (ii) its approach which

[22]See also Technical Note 4 in Human Development Report 2010 (UNDP 2010) and Alkire and Foster (2011).

[23]For example, economic dimension of HDI might have a higher weight that education dimension if there are strong reasons (such as gaining more importance worldwide due to economic recovery) to do so.

limits the poverty/well-being dimensions into five dimensions such that policy makers could focus their attention and resources to the aspects.[24] Furthermore, from a technical perspective, it is notable that a measurement is easier when it involves relatively limited number of concepts. In this respect, despite its limitations, human well-being as measured by the five levels of necessities is relatively easier to measure than those described under an unlimited or open-ended list of human well-being indicators as prescribed by other scholars particularly Ibn Taymiyyah and Ibn Qayyim.[25] In a more practical context, it is also more useful to be able to say useful things of what happening and thereby contribute to or at least inspire policy making with the useful empirical findings[26] while keeping 'alternative' discourses alive.

It is also contended that the *Maqāṣid* principles left the most suitable operational indicators for the Muslim society to determine according to the current conditions and norms/customs (*'urf*) of the people. In Islamic studies literature, this 'method' has been practised not only by the classical scholars but also by the Prophet (pbuh) and the companions (Mattson 2003). However, it is notable that the *Maqāṣid* principles suggest that human well-being could be achieved through opening access (promotion) and protection of the essentials from potential harms such that people have abilities to exist in society and ultimately have a meaningful life and achieve *falāḥ*. This implies that access and ability should be the focus of the indicators. Based on this consideration, suitable indicators could be selected from a bunch of indicators presented in the earlier table. Examples of such indicators are also presented in Table 1.

[24]This is similar to the perspective of Nussbaum who contended that the specification of one 'list' of domains or central capabilities is necessary to ensure that the content of the capability approach carries a critical force and therefore the possibility of the 'wrong' freedoms being prioritized and expanded could be minimized.

[25]This is similar with the position of Amartya Sen in the debate of operationalizing the capability approach.

[26]In relation to this, in an article on the revolutions that occur within economics, a prominent British economics John Hicks acknowledges that economists' need for a focus. 'In order that we should be able to say useful things about what is happening, before it is too late, we must select, even select quite violently. We must concentrate our attention, and hope that we have concentrated it in the right place. We must work, if we are to work effectively, in some sort of blinkers' (1983: 4; quoted from Alkire 2007: 115–116).

Table 1 Examples of operational indicators for a *Maqāṣid*-based multidimensional poverty measure

Dimension	*Element (Operational Indicator)*
Health: Access and ability to meet basic needs and become (physically) healthy	1. Consumption 2. Access to health care 3. Awareness of health 4. Frequency of sickness
Education: Ability to access education and be knowledgeable	5. Access to school 6. School attendance 7. Basic knowledge from schooling 8. Academic/school achievement
Economy: Access and ability to earn income and sustain a living	9. Skill 10. Employability 11. Income 12. Purchasing power 13. Savings
Faith: Access and ability to know and practise one's religion	14. Prayers and fasting 15. Islamic/Qur'anic studies 16. Charity (*ṣadaqah*) 17. *Hajj* (great pilgrimage)
Social: Access and ability to manage a family that is Islamic and well-functioning in society	18. Better future for family 19. Harmony 20. Un-Islamic or anti-social activities 21. Participation in community activities

Source Authors' own

In the second stage, an 'Islamic' poverty threshold needs to set up to determine a measure that can distinguish the poor from the non-poor. In this respect, as discussed earlier, current literature on multidimensional poverty suggests that the threshold could be either determined based on researcher's judgement or determined based on people's perception (i.e. by directly asking the poor whether they are deprived in a particular dimension of well-being or not). However, it seems that up to now there is no strong consensus regarding the most suitable multidimensional poverty threshold including the methods to generate it. Indeed, the choice of the threshold is relatively normative and usually determined by the objectives of the study. As such, bearing the purpose of constructing the Islamic poverty measure, a *Maqāṣid*-based multidimensional poverty could adopt one of the strategies above in setting a poverty line.[27]

In the final stage, *Maqāṣid*-based multidimensional poverty measures can be constructed once the dimensions/indicators and poverty/well-being threshold are selected. However, as mentioned in the previous section, currently there seems to be no widely acceptable measure of multidimensional poverty/well-being. Indeed, debates are still ongoing on whether to use a single-composite multidimensional poverty index (such as the MPI) or multiple composite poverty indices (such as health poverty index or education poverty index). While both methods have their strengths and weaknesses, it appears that the most suitable method for aggregating such measure is determined by the purpose of constructing such index.[28]

Moreover, in relation to the technical model, it is argued that a simple linear model with equal weight amongst the dimensions/indicators is preferable than the others. This is particularly due to its simplicity and easy methods of calculation. This has proven to be the case with the widely used poverty headcount index, poverty gap index and poverty severity index in the literature of monetary poverty.[29] As such, an aggregate single-composite linear model of *Maqāṣid*-based multidimensional poverty index is proposed. Such a general model could be generally formulated as follow.

[27] It is realized that some Muslim scholars have discussed the minimum living sustenance in the context of eligibility to pay and receive *zakāh*. Specifically, *zakāh* must be paid if the assets reach a certain amount of *zakatable* assets, usually in excess of the basic needs of those subject to paying *zakāh*, known as *nisab*. This minimum amount is usually calculated in terms of money. For example, based on the Hadith narrated by Abu Mas'ud, al-Thauri suggested that the minimum income required for satisfying the basic necessities of eating and living for a day and a night is around fifty *dirhams* of money (in al-Qardawi 2000). Therefore, it is more suitable in assessing monetary based measure of poverty instead of the multidimensional measure.

[28] On the one hand, proponents of MPI argue that a single-composite index is powerful in directing attention of policy makers regarding poverty conditions of nations (see, for instance, Alkire and Santos 2010). However, others argue that it is a single-composite index cannot give sufficient information for policy makers to direct their resources and solve the dimensional poverty problems (see, for instance, Ravallion 2011). Thus, each party seems to have solid arguments to defend their positions in which the purpose of constructing the index becomes their main concern.

[29] For more discussion on the index and their advantages, see Haughton and Khandker (2009).

$$\text{MSMPI} = \frac{1}{n}\sum_{i=1}^{n} H + \text{Ed} + R + \text{Ec} + S \tag{1}$$

In which MSMPI is *Maqāṣid* al-Sharīʿah Multidimensional Poverty Index; n is the weight for each dimension/indicator, which is assumed to be equal for each dimension and indicator (i.e. $n = 1/5$)[30]; H, Ed, R, Ec and S are the weighted average value/score of poverty/well-being in health, education, religious/spiritual, economic and social dimensions, respectively.[31] Note that the model could be static (i.e. only measure well-being condition in one time period) or dynamic (i.e. measure well-being conditions in two periods or the changes in the conditions) depending on the purposes of study and data availability.

With a similar method, a set of multiple linear indices could be constructed for each of the poverty/well-being dimension.

$$H = \frac{1}{n}\sum_{i=1}^{n} X_i \tag{2}$$

In which H is *Maqāṣid*-based poverty index in health dimension, which is derived from an equally weighted score of the indicators ($X_{i,}$ i = 1…n) constructing the index. This general formula could be used to generate a multiple set of poverty/well-being index in other dimensions (i.e. Ed, R, Ec and S). As such, the aggregate-composite index (from Eq. 1) is basically decomposable into five composite indices for each dimension of poverty/well-being. Furthermore, it is possible to do other decomposition (by group of people, location, etc.) provided that the subgroups data is available.[32]

[30] Equal weight was given to each indicator/dimension since there is no strong justification to prioritize one variable above the others. This method has been adopted in many studies, resulting in the Human Development Index and other similar development indices (Anand and Sen 1997; Anto 2009; Dar and Otiti 2002).

[31] The value/score could be generated either from researcher's judgment or people's perceptions discussed earlier.

[32] For example, if socio-demographic profiles of respondents (age, gender, education, occupation, income group, etc.) are available, the index could be decomposed according to those characteristics.

5 Implementation of MSMPI in Indonesia

5.1 *Data and Methods*

To provide an illustration for the implementation of the *Maqāṣid*-based multidimensional poverty index, this study uses information collected from a survey of 685 households receiving *zakāh* assistance in nine cities[33] of the Greater Jakarta Metropolitan area of Indonesia in 2011. The group is selected mainly because they are all Muslims households, mostly poor and have received *zakāh* assistance for around a year such that it is possible to analyze their poverty/well-being changes after receiving the assistance by using the *Maqāṣid* framework. Furthermore, the Greater Jakarta area was selected to enable a more focused and rigorous analysis. The primary data were collected in 2011 by utilizing the clustered random sampling method which enabled collection of 685 valid (sampling) responses from 5605 population.[34]

A questionnaire-based survey (interview-administered questionnaire) sought information on socio-demographic profiles[35] and perceptions regarding the changes in the households' poverty/well-being conditions after (with) receiving *zakāh* assistance.[36] Using the framework discussed above, the poverty/well-being changes are analysed in five dimensions

[33]The cities include Jakarta Utara (North Jakarta), Jakarta Timur (East Jakarta) Jakarta Pusat (Central Jakarta), Jakarta Barat (West Jakarta), Jakarta Selatan (South Jakarta), Depok, Tangerang, Bogor and Bekasi.

[34]With the clustered random sampling method, the primary data are collected randomly (i.e. based on a table of random sampling) and sequentially according to the households' city of residence. The list of *zakāh* recipients was obtained from seven large Indonesian *zakāh* organizations willing to participate in this study. There were around 5605 households receiving *zakāh* assistance in Greater Jakarta in 2011. From the list, around 700 of the households are randomly selected by using the sampling method. However, only around 685 of the data (questionnaires) were valid for further analysis. Despite that, analysis with 685 samples should be enough because literature suggests that to achieve 99% confidence level and 5% margin error only around 600 samples are needed (Bartlett et al. 2001).

[35]The main information asked includes socio-demographic profile of head of household (age, gender, marital status, education and occupation) and household size.

[36]Ideally, two-round of survey (i.e. before and after) must be conducted to collect the data with an experimental study design. However, due to time and budget constraint, it was decided to conduct one survey asking conditions in two period of time. This method has been implemented by, among others, Jehle (1994) and Beik (2010) to measure the changes in poverty amongst *zakāh* recipients in Pakistan and Indonesia.

(i.e. health, education, religion, economic and social) suggested by the Ghazalian/Shatibian *Maqāṣid* principles covering 21 indicators developed from the existing literature (see again Table 2). The indicators used in the economic dimension, for instance, are mostly adopted from Allardt (1993) and Rahman and Ahmad (2010) with the focus to access

Table 2 Profile of respondents (Zakāh recipients)

Variable	*Frequency*	*Percent*	*Cumulative Percent*
Age			
15–45	433	63.21	63.21
46–64	226	32.99	96.2
>64	26	3.8	100
Total	685	100	
Gender			
Female	499	72.85	72.85
Male	186	27.15	100
Total	685	100	
Marital status			
Single parent	257	37.52	37.52
Married	428	62.48	100
Total	685	100	
Highest education			
Not going to school	97	14.16	14.16
Elementary school	199	29.05	43.21
Junior high school	158	23.07	66.28
Senior high school	213	31.09	97.37
College/University	18	2.63	100
Total	685	100	
Occupation			
Not working	328	47.88	47.88
Informal sector labour	91	13.28	61.17
Trader/small businessman	194	28.32	89.49
Employee	60	8.76	98.25
Others	12	1.75	100
Total	685	100	
Types of Zakāh assistance			
Economic	183	26.72	26.72
Education	298	43.5	70.22
Health care	51	7.45	77.66
Social	153	22.34	100
Total	685	100	

Source Authors' own

and ability to earn income and sustain a living for the family. Meanwhile, the social indicators are taken from studies such as those by Ahmed (2002) and Narayan et al. (2000).

Furthermore, to measure the perception, an itemized rating[37] on the scale of 1–6 was utilized.[38] Score 1–3 reflect negative changes (extremely worse, worse and slightly worse), meanwhile score 4–6 reflect positive changes (slightly better, better and extremely better). As such, any scores above 4 suggest that respondents experience well-being improvement or poverty reduction. This implies that the score of 4 is the cut-off point for the multidimensional poverty measure.

Once the data were obtained, this study constructed a single-composite *Maqāṣid*-based multidimensional poverty index for each of the poverty dimension (see Eq. 2). As recommended in literature, the multiple set of index is viewed as the most appropriate representation of the multidimensional nature of poverty (Ravallion 2011). However, it also calculated an aggregate measure for all well-being/poverty dimensions (see Eq. 1) which is suggested as useful for focusing the attention of policy makers regarding the importance of the findings (Alkire et al. 2011). The results are presented in the next section.

5.2 Main Findings and Discussions

Generally speaking, descriptive statistics of the respondents reveal that most of the poor households receiving *zakāh* assistance in Greater Jakarta Indonesia were those led by someone relatively young, female, married, uneducated and mostly not working (see Table 2). Additionally, the household size was relatively large with an average number of 5.1 members. These results are hardly surprising since the profiles are the typical characteristics of poor people in Indonesia (Alisjahbana and Yusuf 2003).

Further results suggest that most of the households received some sort of education assistance (43.5%) from the *zakāh* organizations. The assistance is usually provided for the children in the household and given in terms of scholarships (for tuition fee), school supplies and

[37]An itemized rating is a rating of a subject matter (degrees change, etc.) in which numerical scales with various points (usually between 3 and 10 point scales, as needed) are provided for each item so that the respondents can choose the appropriate number suitable for their conditions.

[38]An even-numbered rating (scale of 1–6) is used to avoid neutral and biased answers.

Table 3 Results of the *Maqāṣid*-based Multidimensional Poverty Index

Dimension of Poverty/Well-being	*Obs.*	*MSMPI*	*Std Dev.*	*Min.*	*Max.*
Health	677	4.20	0.73	2	6
Education	581	4.55	0.79	2	6
Religion	297	4.06	0.74	2	6
Economic	466	3.65	0.76	1.4	6
Social	90	4.16	0.67	2.75	6
Average		*4.12*			

Source Authors' own

other school-related expenditure. Additionally, economic assistance and social assistance were received by around 26.7 and 22.3% of respondents, respectively. The economic assistance is given in many forms including working capital (cash and non-cash/in-kind) assistance. Meanwhile, health-care assistance was received by only around 7.45% of the households.

The estimated *Maqāṣid* al-Sharīʿah Multidimensional Poverty Index (MSMPI) is reported in Table 3. In aggregate level, the estimated index has a score of 4.12. Since the value is higher than four, it can be concluded that the well-being of the households has slightly increased after receiving *zakāh* assistance. In other words, the households' poverty has decreased due to the contributions of *zakāh* institution. However, the aggregate-composite index cannot tell which dimensions actually have the poverty reduction impacts of *zakāh*. As such, the table also reports the decompositions of the aggregate index.

It is shown that the households have enjoyed slightly higher well-being (or slightly lower poverty) in four out of five well-being/poverty dimensions as the MSMPI scores are all above the cut-off points of four. The highest welfare enhancement is found with respect to education dimension (score 4.20), followed by health dimension (score 4.20) and social dimension (score 4.16). Meanwhile, the smallest poverty reduction is found in relation to economic dimension (score 3.65).

Further examination for each of the well-being dimensions is summarized in Table 4. It is apparent from the table that the highest well-being improvement was experienced in the educational dimension. On average, around 87.34% of the respondents mentioned that the household's well-being in terms of children's school attendance, literacy, school achievement and access to school had increased significantly after the receipt of support from the *zakāh* institutions. Amongst the indicators, the most positive changes were felt in relation to school attendance and literacy (i.e. ability to read and do mathematical calculations), which seem to be particularly related to the educational assistance provided by the institution.

In contrast, the smallest poverty reduction impact was felt in the economic dimension. Only 53.92%, or slightly more than half, of the households expressed positive changes in well-being. Specifically, purchasing power and savings were found to be the measures in which most of the households had reported deterioration in their daily lives, as indicated by the large proportions of negative changes. However, in terms of skills, employability and income, improvements were actually more prevalent. It is therefore suggested that, although the households have experienced improvement in their economic resources (i.e. the first three indicators), for some reasons the positive changes could not be translated into higher economic outcomes (i.e. purchasing power and savings).

Overall, the findings suggest that *zakāh* institutions have successfully reduced the poverty condition of the household receiving *zakāh* assistance in Greater Jakarta Indonesia from 2010 to 2011. The largest poverty reduction is felt in education dimension, while the smallest reduction is experienced in economic dimensions. This result is an expected result from the institution of *zakāh*, which add empirical evidence regarding the positive contribution of *zakāh* institution in reducing poverty in Muslim countries. Additionally, in the context of this study, it provides a workable example on how *Maqāṣid* al-Sharīʿah principles could be implemented in measuring socio-economic policy results in Muslim societies.

From policy perspective, the findings have at least three implications. Generally speaking, first, negative changes (i.e. higher poverty) in each indicator provide a 'clue' for the government and relevant institutions regarding the area that needs their supports. Similarly, positive changes indicate that policies in the areas are relatively successful in increasing the recipients' welfare. Second, *zakāh* institutions have provided valuable contributions that increased education well-being of the recipients. Accordingly, government needs to learn and perhaps collaborate with the Islamic social institution to further improve the model. Third, it is evident that the poor's economic outcomes (i.e. purchasing power and savings) did not change significantly although their economic resources

Table 4 Specific changes in multidimensional poverty measure

Poverty measure/ indicator	*N*	*Negative changes (not-improved/poorer)*		*Positive changes (improved/less poor)*	
		Frequency	*Percentage*	*Frequency*	*Percentage*
Health dimension					
Food consumption	684	166	24.27	518	75.73
Access to health service	677	183	27.03	494	72.97
Health awareness	684	102	14.91	582	85.09
Quality of health	683	138	20.2	545	79.8
Average			21.60		78.40
Education dimension					
School access	599	89	14.86	510	85.14
School attendance	597	63	10.55	534	89.45
Literacy	585	70	11.97	515	88.03
School achievement	595	79	13.28	516	86.72
Average			12.67		87.34
Religious/spiritual dimension					
Praying and fasting	682	52	7.62	630	92.38
Islamic/Qur'anic study	674	127	18.84	547	81.16
Charity	672	171	25.45	501	74.55
Hajj	299	208	69.57	91	30.43
Average			30.37		69.63
Economic dimension					
Skill	663	210	31.67	453	68.33
Employability	660	263	39.85	397	60.15
Income	684	253	36.99	431	63.01
Purchasing power	559	363	64.94	196	35.06
Savings	562	320	56.94	242	43.06
Average			46.08		53.92
Social dimension					
Future	663	111	16.74	552	83.26
Harmony	681	67	9.84	614	90.16
Anti-social behaviour	94	36	38.3	58	61.7
Community activity	672	127	18.9	545	81.1
Average			20.95		79.06

Source Authors' own

(skills, employability and income) have increased. This implies that the current economic system might not in favour of the poor. All these implications should be of concern by the government and other relevant institutions.

6 Concluding Remarks

Despite calls to expand and implement the concept of *Maqāṣid* al-Sharīʿah to frame policies aimed to resolve current development challenges in Muslim world, it has been rarely utilized by Muslim scholars. This paper, therefore, attempts to translate the *Maqāṣid* principles and proposes a general framework to assess the socio-economic development of Muslim societies based on the principles. It also provides a workable example on how the *Maqāṣid* al-Sharīʿah principles could be implemented in assessing socio-economic policy results in Muslim societies.

Despite the attempts, it is realized that the general framework provided could be improved in many ways. The current study focuses on the translation of the *Maqāṣid* principles in choosing dimensions/indicators for constructing a simple linear multidimensional poverty index based on the Islamic perspective. It did not focus, however, on the technicalities to generate alternative forms of models or test the model specifications/properties that could best reflect the multidimensional poverty/well-being in Islamic countries. Cross-country comparison is also another issue not addressed in this paper, since it is focused on comparing the poverty/well-being changes in one group of people over time. These are some of the areas of research that could be investigated in further studies to further advance research on contemporary applications of *Maqāṣid*.

Appendix 1: Multidimensional Poverty/Well-Being Indicators

No.	*Dimensions/Indicators*	*References*
1	Nutrition, shelter, health, mortality rate, education, political freedom, economic facilities, social opportunities, transparency guarantees, security	Sen (1993, 1996, 1999)
2	Life; bodily health; bodily integrity; senses, imagination and thought; emotions; practical reason (education); affiliation; other species; play; control over one's environment	Nussbaum (2003)
3	Relatedness, transcendence-creativity, rootedness, sense of identity and individuality, the need for a frame of orientation and devotion	Fromm (1955)
4	Input-output (nutrition, water, air); climate balance with nature (clothing, shelter); health; community; symbolic interaction and reflection (education)	Galtung (1980)

No.	*Dimensions/Indicators*	*References*
5	Life; knowledge (understanding and education); meaningful work and play; friendship and other valued kinds of human relationships; authentic self-direction; transcendence 'peace with God' or some non-theistic but more-than-human source of meaning and value	Finnis (1980)
6	Nutritional food/water, protective housing, work, physical environment, healthcare, security in childhood, significant primary relationships (marriage), physical security, economic security, safe birth control/childbearing, basic education	Doyal and Gough (1991)
7	Having economic resources, housing, employment, working conditions, health, education; attachments/contacts with local community, family and friends, associations, colleagues, etc.; self-determination, leisure-time (social) activities, meaningful work and opportunities to enjoy nature	Allardt (1993)
8	Longevity, infant/child mortality, preventable morbidity, literacy, nourishment, personal liberty and freedom	Anand and Sen (1994)
9	Health/nutrition/sanitation/rest/shelter/security; literacy/basic intellectual and physical capacities; positive freedom or autonomy; negative freedom or liberty; understanding or knowledge; participation in social life	Qizilbash (1996)
10	Material well-being (having enough food, assets and work); bodily well-being (being and appearing well, health, physical environment); social well-being (being able to care for, bring up, marry and settle children, peace, harmony, good relations in the family/community); security (a physically safe and secure environment, lawfulness and access to justice, confidence in the future); psychological well-being (peace of mind, happiness, harmony, spiritual life and religious observance, freedom of choice and action)	Narayan et al. (2000)
11	Morality, food, family, friendship, material resources, intelligence, romantic, relationship, physical appearance, self, income, housing, social life	Biswas-Diener and Diener (2001)
12	Health (nutrition/food, child mortality); education (years of schooling, children enrolled); Living standard (cooking fuel, toilet, water, electricity, floor and assets).	Alkire and Santos, in UNDP (2010)

Source Author's summary from the listed references

References

Ahmed, H. (2002). Financing Micro Enterprises: An Analytical Study of Islamic Microfinance Institutions. *Islamic Economic Studies, 9*(2), 27–64.

Ahmed, H. (2004). *The Role of Zakah and Awqaf in Poverty Alleviation*. Jeddah: Islamic Research and Training Institute, Islamic Development Bank.

Al-Raysuni, A. (2005). *Imam al-Shatibi's Theory of the Higher Objectives and Intents of Islamic Law*. London: International Institute of Islamic Thought.

Al-Sufi, T. H. (2013). *Maqāṣid* al-Sharīʿah *as a Framework for Poverty Alleviation*. Paper presented at the International Conference on Poverty Alleviation and Islamic Economics & Finance: Current Issues and Future Prospects, Durham University, UK.

Alisjahbana, A., & Yusuf, A. A. (2003). *Poverty Dynamics in Indonesia: Panel Data Evidence* (Padjadjaran University Working Paper).

Alkire, S. (2002). Dimensions of Human Development. *World Development, 30*(2), 181–205.

Alkire, S. (2007). Choosing Dimensions: The Capability Approach and Multidimensional Poverty. In N. Kakwani & J. Silber (Eds.), *The Many Dimensions of Poverty*. New York: Palgrave Macmillan.

Alkire, S., & Deneulin, S. (2009). *An Introduction to the Human Development and Capability Approach*. London: Earthscan.

Alkire, S., & Foster, J. (2007). *Counting and Multidimensional Poverty Measures* (Oxford Poverty and Human Development Initiative Working Paper). Oxford: Oxford Poverty and Human Development Initiative.

Alkire, S., & Foster, J. (2011). Counting and Multidimensional Poverty Measurement. *Journal of Public Economics, 95*(7), 476–487.

Alkire, S., Foster, J., & Santos, M. (2011). Where Did Identification Go? *Journal of Economic Inequality, 9*(3), 501–505.

Alkire, S., & Santos, M. (2010). *Acute Multidimensional Poverty: A New Index for Developing Countries*. Human Development Research Paper 11. UNDP–HDRO, New York.

Allardt, E. (1993). Having, Loving, Being: An Alternative to the Swedish Model of Welfare Research. In M. C. Nussbaum & A. Sen (Eds.), *The Quality of Life* (pp. 88–95). Oxford: Clarendon Press.

Anand, S., & Sen, A. (1994). *Sustainable Human Development: Concepts and Priorities*. New York: United Nation Development Program.

Anand, S., & Sen, A. (1997). *Concepts of Human Development and Poverty: A Multidimensional Perspective*. New York: United Nation Development Program.

Anto, M. (2009). Introducing an Islamic Human Development Index (I-HDI) to Measure Development in OIC Countries. *Islamic Economic Studies, 19*(2), 69.

Ashur, I. (2006). *Treatise on Maqāṣid* al-Sharīʿah. London: International Institute of Islamic Thought.

Atkinson, A. B. (2003). Multidimensional Deprivation: Contrasting Social Welfare and Counting Approaches. *The Journal of Economic Inequality, 1*(1), 51–65.

Auda, J. (2008). *Maqāṣid* al-Sharīʿah*: A Beginner's Guide*. London: International Institute of Islamic Thought.

Bartlett, J. E., Kotrlik, J. W., & Higgins, C. (2001). Organizational Research: Determining Appropriate Sample Size in Survey Research. *Information Technology, Learning, and Performance Journal, 19*(1).

Beik, I. (2010). *Economic Role of Zakat in Reducing Poverty and Income Inequality in the Province of Dki Jakarta, Indonesia: Case Study of the Government Board of Zakat and Dompet Dhuafa Republika*. Unpublished PhD Thesis, International Islamic University of Malaysia.

Biswas-Diener, R., & Diener, E. (2001). Making the Best of a Bad Situation: Satisfaction in the Slums of Calcutta. *Social Indicators Research, 55*(3), 329–352.

Booth, A., & Mosley, P. (2003). *The New Poverty Strategies: What Have They Achieved? What Have We Learned?* New York: Palgrave Macmillan.

Bourguignon, F., & Chakravarty, S. R. (2003). The Measurement of Multidimensional Poverty. *Journal of Economic Inequality, 1*(1), 25–49.

Chapra, M. (2000). *The Future of Economics: An Islamic Perspective*. Leicester: Islamic Foundation.

Chapra, M. U. (2008). *The Islamic Vision of Development in the Light of Maqāṣid* al-Sharīʿah. Jeddah: Islamic Research and Training Institute, Islamic Development Bank.

Chen, S., & Ravallion, M. (2008). *The Developing World Is Poorer Than We Thought, but No Less Successful in the Fight Against Poverty*. Washington: World Bank.

Comim, F., & Qizilbash, M. (2008). *The Capability Approach: Concepts, Measures and Applications*. Cambridge: Cambridge University Press.

Dar, H. A., & Otiti, S. F. (2002). *Construction of an Ethics-Augmented Human Development Index with a Particular Reference to the OIC Member Countries* (Working Paper). Loughborough: Loughborough University.

Doyal, L., & Gough, I. (1991). *A Theory of Human Needs*. New York: Guilford Press.

Finnis, J. (1980). *Natural Law and Natural Rights*. Oxford: Oxford University Press.

Fromm, E. (1955). *The Sane Society*. New York: Rinehart and Winston.

Fusco, A., & Dickes, P. (2008). The Rasch Model and Multidimensional Poverty Measurement. In N. Kakwani & J. Silber (Eds.), *Quantitative Approaches to Multidimensional Poverty Measurement* (pp. 49–62). New York: Palgrave Macmillan.

Galtung, J. (1980). *The True Worlds: A Transnational Perspective*. New York: Free Press.
Gordon, D., Nandy, S., Pantazis, C., Pemberton, S., & Townsend, P. (2003). *The Distribution of Child Poverty in the Developing World*. Bristol: Centre for International Poverty Research.
Haughton, J., & Khandker, S. R. (2009). *Handbook on Poverty and Inequality*. Washington: World Bank.
Iqbal, M. (2002). *Islamic Economic Institutions and the Elimination of Poverty*. Leicester: Islamic Foundation.
Jehle, G. (1994). Zakat and Inequality: Some Evidence from Pakistan. *Review of Income and Wealth, 40*(2), 205–216.
Kamali, M. (2008). *Maqāṣid* al-Sharīʿah *Made Simple*. Herndon: International Institute of Islamic Thought.
Kasri, R. A. (2012). *Can Financial and Social Performance of Zakāh Institution Be Assessed by Using the Maqāṣid* al-Sharīʿah *Approach*? Paper presented at the 5th Kyoto-Durham International Workshop in Islamic Economics and Finance "New Horizons in Islamic Economics: Critical Perspectives on the Financial and Social Performance of Islamic Finance", Kyoto, Japan.
Mack, J., & Lansley, S. (1985). *Poor Britain*. Crows Nest, NSW: G. Allen & Unwin.
Mattson, I. (2003). Status-Based Definitions of Need in Early Islamic Zakat and Maintenance Laws. In M. Bonner, M. Ener, & A. Singer (Eds.), *Poverty and Charity in the Middle Eastern Context* (pp. 31–52). Albany: State University of New York Press.
Mirakhor, A., & Askari, H. (2010). *Islam and the Path to Human and Economic Development*. New York: Palgrave Macmillan.
Narayan, D., Chambers, R., Shah, M. K., & Petesch, P. (2000). *Voices of the Poor: Crying Out for Change*. Washington: World Bank.
Nussbaum, M. C. (2003). Capabilities as Fundamental Entitlements: Sen and Social Justice. *Feminist Economics, 9*(2–3), 33–59.
Obaidullah, M. (2008). *Role of Microfinance in Poverty Alleviation: Lessons from Experiences in Selected IDB Member Countries*. Jeddah: Islamic Research and Training Institute, Islamic Development Bank.
Qizilbash, M. (1996). Ethical Development. *World Development, 24*(7), 1209–1221.
Rahman, M., & Ahmad, F. (2010). Impact of Microfinance of IBBL on the Rural Poor's Livelihood in Bangladesh: An Empirical Study. *International Journal of Islamic and Middle Eastern Finance and Management, 3*(2), 168–190.
Ravallion, M. (1994). Measuring Social Welfare with and Without Poverty Lines. *The American Economic Review, 84*(2), 359–364.
Ravallion, M. (1998). *Poverty Lines in Theory and Practice*. Washington: World Bank.

Ravallion, M. (2011). On Multidimensional Indices of Poverty. *Journal of Economic Inequality, 9*, 235–248.

Robeyns, I. (2005). The Capability Approach: A Theoretical Survey. *Journal of Human Development, 6*(1), 93–117.

Sen, A. (1993). Capability and Well-Being. In A. Sen & M. Nussbaum (Eds.), *The Quality of Life*. Clarendon: Oxford University Press.

Sen, A. (1996). On the Foundations of Welfare Economics: Utility, Capability and Practical Reason. In F. Farina, F. Hahn, & S. Vannucci (Eds.), *Ethics, Rationality and Economic Behavior*. Oxford: Clarendon Press.

Sen, A. (1999). *Development as Freedom*. Oxford: Oxford University Press.

Sen, A. (2004). Capabilities, Lists, and Public Reason: Continuing the Conversation. *Feminist Economics, 10*(3), 77–80.

Sen, A. (2005). Human Rights and Capabilities. *Journal of Human Development and Capabilities, 6*(2), 151–166.

Sirageldin, I. (2000). Elimination of Poverty: Challenges and Islamic Strategies. *Islamic Economic Studies, 8*(1), 1–16.

Townsend, P. (1985). A Sociological Approach to the Measurement of Poverty—A Rejoinder to Professor Amartya Sen. *Oxford Economic Papers, 37*(4), 659–668.

UNDP. (2010). *The Real Wealth of Nations: Pathways to Human Development Series*. New York: United Nations Development Program.

Van Praag, B. M. S., & Ferrer-i-Carbonell, A. (2008). A Multi-dimensional Approach to Subjective Poverty. In N. Kakwani & J. Silber (Eds.), *Quantitative Approaches to Multidimensional Poverty Measurement* (pp. 135–154). New York: Palgrave Macmillan.

World Bank. (1990). *World Development Report 1990: Poverty*. Washington: World Bank.

World Bank. (2001). *World Development Report 2000/2001: Attacking Poverty*. Washington: World Bank.

Yunus, M. (2007). *Creating a World Without Poverty: Social Business and the Future of Capitalism*. New York: Public Affairs.

CHAPTER 14

Non-Monetary Poverty Measurement in Malaysia: A *Maqāṣid al*-Sharīʿah Approach

Mohamed Saladin Abdul Rasool and Ariffin Mohd Salleh

1 Introduction

Islamic institutions in Malaysia play a variety of socio-economic roles such as poverty alleviation. To perform this role, these institutions face a major task in identifying the poverty group. Most of these institutions measure and operationalize poverty from the monetary perspective using variables such as income, expenditure or consumption. According to Yusuf Al-Qardawi (1980), self-sufficiency for an individual is defined as the availability of basic food, drink, shelter and other needs considered as basic by the society in which he or she lives and belongs to. In addition, Al Sabai explains that the minimum living standard is inclusive of having family, housing and transportation (Monzer 1982). Failure to attain these stipulated needs qualifies an individual to be poor. Poverty is not only complex and multidimensional in nature, but it goes beyond the

M. S. A. Rasool (✉) · A. M. Salleh
Universiti Teknologi MARA, Shah Alam, Malaysia
e-mail: saladin@melaka.uitm.edu.my

S. S. Ali (ed.), *Towards a Maqāṣid al-Sharīʿah Index of Socio-Economic Development*, Palgrave Studies in Islamic Banking, Finance, and Economics,
https://doi.org/10.1007/978-3-030-12793-0_14

notion of income and encompasses social, economic and political deprivations (Shirazi and Amin 2009).

The main objective of the paper is to present a non-monetary poverty measurement from an Islamic perspective. The proposed Islamic Poverty Indicator (IPI) consists of *maqāṣid-al* Sharīʿah (objective of the religion) dimensions, namely religion, knowledge, physical self, offspring and wealth. The IPI, formulated using the weighted index method, is expected to exemplify poverty from a multidimensional perspective. This paper is organized as follows. The next section outlines the literature review whereas the methodology undertaken in this study is deliberated in Sect. 3. Section 4 presents the findings of the study. Finally, the conclusion and recommendations of the study were highlighted in the final section.

2 Literature Review

Presently, *zakāt* institutions in Malaysia use the monetary method to conceptualize poverty. The Poverty Line Income (PLI) and Had al Kifayah (HAK) methods are commonly utilized to determine the poor. However, researchers have argued that the current monetary approach is unable to reflect the multidimensional nature of poverty. Due to these reasons, policy makers and researchers in developed nations have opted for other approaches such as capability and social exclusion approaches which are multidimensional in nature that includes non-monetary indicators as mentioned by researchers such as Sen (1977, 1987, 1992), Nasbaum (1997, 2003), Laderchi (2000), Laderchi et al. (2003), Wagle (2005, 2008, 2009), Alkire and Foster (2007, 2010), and Ravallion (1998, 2012). The UNDP developed the Human Poverty Index (HPI) and Human Development Index (HDI) through the studies by Sen and recently introduced the Multidimensional Poverty Index (MPI) developed by Alkire and Santos (2010). The HPI measured poverty from three dimensions, namely the mortality rate (short life), knowledge and the overall standard of living (access to private and public resources). Similarly, health, education and standard of living have been included in the MPI using ten indicators. It is obvious that MPI has been extended from the HPI with the addition of new indicators although the dimensions were quite similar.

Nolan and Whelan (2010, 2012) highlighted that non-monetary indicators together with monetary data would be able to improve the measurement and understanding of poverty especially in rich countries. Employing the MPI, Awan et al. (2011, 2012) measured poverty in Pakistan by using the data of Pakistan Social and Living Standard Measurement Survey 2005–2006. The study used nine dimensions such as electricity, asset, water, sanitation, housing, education, expenditures, land and empowerment. Results indicate that the majority of Pakistan's households are deprived in five dimensions: empowerment, land, housing, sanitation and asset. In another study, Shirvanian and Bakhshoodeh (2012) found out that education and housing are vital dimensions that should be addressed by policy makers in Iran to combat poverty. Alternatively, Ali and Ahmad (2013) asserted that health care and education are critical aspects of poverty alleviation based on their multidimensional poverty study in Punjab, Pakistan.

In Malaysia, studies on multidimensional poverty were embarked by Mohd Harun et al. (2007, 2009) who focused his study on Malaysian natives. Specific dimensions that contributed to the high poverty incidence of natives were found to be social and economic exclusions such as education facilities, health care and infrastructure were highlighted. Another study by Che Mat et al. (2012) was undertaken in Baling, a district in Kedah, a state in northern Malaysia. Education, health, the standard of living and wealth were chosen to represent the dimensions of poverty. These researchers used five different thresholds to identify the poor group, thus yielding the poverty rates which were all much higher compared to the conventional PLI method.

Although multidimensional poverty has now been researched widely in the mainstream economy, studies have been lacking in the Islamic world except for studies by Islamic Relief (2008) and Rasool et al. (2011, 2012). These authors suggest the five principles of *maqāṣid al*-Sharīʿah principles as the dimensions of the poverty measurement, namely religion, physical self, knowledge, offspring and wealth.

3 Methodology

The dimensions in the IPI would be based on human needs (*maqāṣid al*-Sharīʿah) principles according to Islam as mentioned by JAWHAR (2007) and Rosbi and Sanep (2010). The proposed IPI would be based on the MPI developed by Alkire and Santos (2010). The main difference between the proposed IPI and the MPI developed by Alkire is the weightage in IPI is not equal in accordance with the *maqāṣid al*-Sharīʿah principles as suggested by Al-Ghazalli who pioneered these principles (Kamali 2009). According to Al-Ghazalli, the objective of the Sharīʿah or *maqāṣid al*-Sharīʿah is to promote well-being of all mankind which lies in safeguarding their religion, physical self, knowledge, offspring and wealth and is in a hierarchy. Another scholar, Shatibi concurs with these five objectives of Sharīʿah and their hierarchical sequence. Although the majority of scholars do agree with the five dimensions of *maqāṣid al*-Sharīʿah proposed by Al-Ghazalli and endorsed by Shatibi, there are scholars who argued on the hierarchical sequence proposed by these two scholars (Salleh and Rasool 2013). Thus, in the present study expert opinion was chosen to determine whether the hierarchy of the dimensions in the Malaysian settings at the present time is similar to the ideas of Al-Ghazalli and Shatibi. Although expert opinion could lead to biasness, this problem was reduced by choosing a panel of expert with vast experience in the field of poverty. In addition, the selected experts have various backgrounds such as Islamic economics, Islamic studies, development economics and Islamic development.

The overall process of the IPI formulation consists of three steps. Firstly, the consensus of scholars who are experts and experienced in the practice of *zakāt* was sought in deciding the dimensions and each of their indicators with the assumption that all indicators in a particular dimension are equally weighted. These selected dimensions and indicators were then sent to selected experts to examine its face validity. Secondly, weightage of each of the dimensions was calculated based on the rankings given by the scholars. The function of the weightage is to reflect the importance of each of the dimensions in the index. Thirdly, IPI computation and interpretation together with threshold determination were carried out. The overall expert review was undertaken through face-to-face interview involving a few rounds.

The non-monetary poverty measurement, the Islamic Poverty Indicator (IPI) , was formulated in accordance with *maqāṣid al*-Sharīʿah principles, incorporating the methods by Alkire and Santos (2010). The formula for IPI is as below:

$$\text{IPI}w = (W_1\text{PS} + W_2\text{WE} + W_3\text{OS} + W_4\text{KN} + W_5\text{RE}) \times 100\% \quad (1)$$

where

PS—physical self, WE—wealth, OS—offspring, KN—knowledge, RE—religiosity

and

W_1, W_2, … W_5—weightage.

4 Empirical Results

4.1 Dimensions, Weightages and Indicators

All the experts agree with the five dimensions of *maqāṣid al*-Sharīʻah principles. The non-monetary measurement, IPI, is shown by the following equation, with the weightage of each dimension derived from the rankings determined by expert review as shown by Table 1:

$$\mathrm{IPI} = (0.252\,\mathrm{PS} + 0.129\,\mathrm{WE} + 0.138\,\mathrm{OS} + 0.186\mathrm{KN} + 0.295\,\mathrm{RE}) \times 100\% \tag{2}$$

The equation shows that 29.5% of poverty is contributed by spiritual factors, followed by 25.2% physical self, 12.9% wealth, 18.6% knowledge and 13.8% offspring. Thus, the spiritual dimension is with the highest weightage, about 30%. On the other hand, wealth is the lowest weightage dimension contributing almost 13% to the incidence of poverty. Hence, this result shows that experts in the present study have identified that all the dimensions as relevant and significant in the Malaysian context and are in accordance with the hierarchical sequence as proposed by Al-Ghazalli and Shatibi. Next, indicators agreed by more than 75% of the experts were used as the main criteria to decide the final list of variables to be included in the IPI. Initially, a number of indicators were listed based on various sources such as Waggle (2005, 2008, 2009), JAWHAR (2007), Islamic Relief (2008), Alkire and Santos (2010), Alkire and Foster (2012), Awan et al. (2011, 2012), and Che Mat et al. (2012). The final indicators in the study were derived through expert review where thirteen indicators from five dimensions were identified (Table 2). Firstly, religiosity is considered as an important dimension of human needs. It is inclusive of religious knowledge, religious obligation, contribution and mosque activities. Secondly, physical self are needs in daily life such as health care and quality of dwelling or living place. Thirdly, knowledge or mind development is essential in developing the intellectual level and skills of individuals. It is inclusive of education level and skills. Fourthly, family or offspring is an important element of human needs. Finally, wealth accumulation such as savings or investments and ability to generate income or revenue from economic activities complete the formulation of the IPI.

Table 1 Results of weightage determination of dimensions

Dimension	*Rank by experts*														*Mean*	*Wi*
	×*1*	×*2*	×*3*	×*4*	×*5*	×*6*	×*7*	×*8*	×*9*	×*10*	×*11*	×*12*	×*13*	×*14*		
Religiosity	1	1	1	1	1	1	1	1	1	2	1	1	1	1	4.429	0.295
Physical self	2	2	2	1	2	1	1	1	2	1	1	2	2	4	3.786	0.252
Wealth	4	4	4	1	5	2	2	1	5	5	1	4	5	5	1.929	0.129
Knowledge	3	3	3	1	3	3	2	1	3	4	1	3	3	3	2.786	0.186
Offspring	5	5	5	1	4	4	2	1	4	3	1	5	4	2	2.071	0.137

Dimension	*Value assigned*														*Mean*	*Wi*
	×*1*	×*2*	×*3*	×*4*	×*5*	×*6*	×*7*	×*8*	×*9*	×*10*	×*11*	×*12*	×*13*	×*14*		
Religiosity	5	5	5	3	5	4.5	4.5	3	5	4	3	5	5	5	4.429	0.295
Physical self	4	4	4	3	4	4.5	4.5	3	4	5	3	4	4	2	3.786	0.252
Wealth	2	2	2	3	1	3	2	3	1	1	3	2	1	1	1.929	0.129
Knowledge	3	3	3	3	3	2	2	3	3	2	3	3	3	3	2.786	0.186
Offspring	1	1	1	3	2	1	2	3	2	3	3	1	2	4	2.071	0.137

Source Authors' own

4.2 *Weightage of Indicators and Cut-Offs*

After determining the indicators to be included in the IPI, the weightage of each indicator was calculated to determine the contribution of each indicator. The total relative weightage of the thirteen indicators would be 100, exemplifying if a household is deprived of all the thirteen indicators, meaning a household is completely deprived of means to perform daily activities to lead a decent living. The relative weightage of each indicator is obtained by dividing the weightage of each dimension with the number of indicators in each dimension as shown in Table 2.

The next step is to decide the cut-off point or the threshold at two levels, one at the indicator level and the other at the index level. At the indicator level, deprivation of a particular indicator could be interpreted as a threshold. For example, if a household do not have basic religious knowledge, then this inadequacy of religious knowledge is the threshold

Table 2 Indicators, weightage and threshold

Variables	*Relative weight (%)*	*Deprived if...*
Religiosity		
Religious knowledge	7.4	Household head has no basic religious knowledge
Religious obligations	7.4	Not performing of religious obligation
Contribution	7.4	No contribution to close family members
Mosque activities	7.4	No attendance at mosque programmes
Physical self		
Dwelling	12.6	Dwelling is deteriorating
Health and not disabled	12.6	Household member with serious disease and disabled
Wealth		
Employment type	4.3	Household head without permanent job
House ownership	4.3	Household does not own house (land)
Savings and investment	4.3	Household head or members without savings and investment
Knowledge		
Education level	9.3	Household head did not attend secondary school
Skills	9.3	Household head without any skills
Offspring		
No. of children	6.9	Household without children
Attend schooling	6.9	Any children did not attend school

Source Authors' own

Table 3 Threshold (*cut-off*) of IPIs

Islamic Poverty Index (IPI)	Cut-off *for poor (K1)*	Cut-off *for destitute (K2)*
IPI1	40	70
IPI2	45	75
IPI3	50	80

Source Authors' own

of religious knowledge. At the index level, if the total score of total weightage of indicators (TWI) is more than the threshold value, denoted by K which would be determined by the researcher, then the household would be defined as poor. From an Islamic point of view, an individual or household is defined as poor if the household needs acquired is less than the total need whereas destitute is a situation where the household is unable to sustain even 50% or half of the needs. From a monetary point of view, this cut-off point is easily identified based on the PLI or HAK method. However, from the non-monetary perspective, it is difficult to quantify the 50% or 100% level of needs. Alkire and Santos (2010) used K=30% in their study with the assumptions that a deprivation of 30% is sufficient to classify the household as poor. This value was obtained from a rigorous exercise of applying different K values to the index formulation. For this study, 3 cut-off points or thresholds are selected. Each cut-off consists of K1 that represents poverty line, whereas K2 represents destitute threshold. Thus, the three IPIs are constructed based on the cut-off points as shown in Table 3.

4.3 Poverty Determination Across Different Thresholds

For IPI1, the cut-off or threshold is decided based on K1 (TWI)=40% and K2=70%. For IPI2, the cut-off or threshold is decided based on K1 (TWI)=45% and K2=75%. For IPI2, the cut-off or threshold is decided based on K1 (TWI)=50% and K2=80%. Table 4 presents the various possible situations of deprivations and the status of poor based on the score of TWI calculated. For instance, in situation 1, the household is deprived of all indicators in the two dimensions with the smallest weightage, namely offspring and knowledge; then the household is not poor according to all the IPI1, IPI2 and IPI3 because the calculated TWI is less than the cut-off point or threshold of the three IPIs which are 40 (IPI1), 45(IPI2) and 50 (IPI3):

Table 4 Determination of poor and destitute

Situation	*Deprived indicators*[a]					*TWI*	*IPI1*	*IPI2*	*IPI3*
	R	*PS*	*K*	*OS*	*W*		*K1 = 40, K2 = 70*	*K1 = 45, K2 = 75*	*K1 = 50, K2 = 80*
1	0	0	0	2	3	26.7	Not poor	Not poor	Not poor
2	0	0	2	2	3	45.3	Poor	Poor	Not poor
3	0	1	2	2	3	57.9	Poor	Poor	Poor
4	0	2	2	2	3	70.5	Destitute	Poor	Poor
5	4	2	0	0	0	54.8	Poor	Poor	Poor
6	4	2	1	0	0	64.0	Poor	Poor	Poor
7	4	2	2	0	0	63.3	Poor	Poor	Poor
8	3	2	2	2	0	79.8	Destitute	Destitute	Poor
9	3	2	2	2	1	84.1	Destitute	Destitute	Destitute

Source Authors' own
[a] *Note* R—religiosity, PS—physical self, K—knowledge, OS—offspring, W—wealth

$$\text{TWI} = 4.3 + 4.3 + 4.3 + 6.9 + 6.9 = 26.7$$

On the other hand, if the household is deprived of all the indicators in the two dimensions with the biggest weightage, namely physical self and religiosity as shown by situation 5, then the household is poor according to all the three IPI, IPI2 and IPI3 because,

$$\begin{aligned}\text{Total weightage of indicators (TWI)} &= 12.6 + 12.6 + 7.4 + 7.4 + 7.4 + 7.4\\ &= 54.8 \text{ (more than 40, 45 and 50)}\end{aligned}$$

The situations depicted in Table 4 are hypothetical as the real situation would be a mixture of deprivations of various dimensions. Hence, there would be a lot of combination of deprivations giving different degree of deprivations. As a summary, it could be deduced that the severity of poverty depends on the number of deprived indicators and the weightage of each of the indicators. In general the more number of deprived indicators and the higher the relative weightage, the more deprived multidimensionally is the situation. The main issue in the context of IPI is determining the appropriate threshold as the multidimensional measurement or IPI is a non-monetary indicator (unmeasurable physically). Thus, it is subjective to select whether 40, 45, 50% or other suitable K value as it would have a strong impact on the selected poverty group. If the K is too high, the deprived group would be smaller compared to a lower value of K as it needs a bigger number of indicators to be deprived.

Hence, researchers need to come up with suitable K values with appropriate justifications.

5 Conclusion and Recommendation

The IPI proposed in the study is an initial attempt using *maqāṣid al*-Sharīʿah principles in developing a non-monetary multidimensional poverty measurement. The present paper proposes a multidimensional perspective of poverty measurement in the context of *zakāt* institutions utilizing weighted index as a tool of measurement. Although there are limitations of using index such as summarizing too much and communicating less, this method proposes a multidimensional perspective of measuring poverty. The paper introduced the IPI as a non-monetary poverty measurement incorporating the five *maqāṣid al*-Sharīʿah principles, namely religiosity, physical self, knowledge, offspring and wealth which were weighted hierarchically parallel with the ideas of Al-Ghazalli and Shatibi. These findings show the relevancy and significance of *maqāṣid al*-Sharīʿah in the present economic and social environment. Thus, the formulation of the IPI would have an impact on Islamic institutions as it gives a new perspective of measuring poverty from a micro-perspective. Hence, the IPI is envisaged to reflect the multidimensional phenomenon of poverty in a more holistic way. Thus, it is strongly recommended that a comprehensive study to further develop the IPI is carried out. Comparison with monetary poverty measurement is vital to see the differences between these methods. This would enhance the poverty measurement from an Islamic perspective as it comprises of non-monetary dimensions that would complement the existing monetary poverty measurements.

References

Ali, S., and Ahmad, N. (2013). "Human Capital and Poverty in Pakistan: Evidence from the Punjab Province." *European Journal of Science and Public Policy, 11*, 36–41.

Alkire, S., and Foster, J. (2007). "Counting and Multidimensional Poverty." *Journal of Public Economic, 95*(7), 476–487.

Alkire, S., and Foster, J. (2012). "Counting and Multidimensional Poverty Measurement." *Journal of Public Economics, 95*(7–8), 476–478.

Alkire, S., and Santos, M. E. (2010). *Acute Multidimensional Poverty: A New Index For Developing Countries.* OPHI Working Paper 38, Oxford University Press, Oxford.

Awan, M. Sarwar, Waqas, Muhammad, and Aslam, M. A. (2011). "Multidimensional Poverty in Pakistan: Case of Punjab." *Journal of Economics and Behavioral Studies, 2*(8), 133–144.

Awan, M. Sarwar, Waqas, Muhammad, and Aslam, M. A. (2012). *Multidimensional Measurement of Poverty in Pakistan.* MPRA Paper No. 41532.

Che Mat, S. H., Hakim, R., and Jumali, S. N. (2012). "Indeks kemiskinan pelbagai dimensi sebagai alternatif pengukuran kemiskinan: Kajian kes di daerah Baling, Kedah." *Jurnal Ekonomi Malaysia, 46*(1), 3–12.

Harun, M. F., and Abdullah, A. F. (2007). *Kemiskinan Mengikut Teori Konvensional Dan Perspektif Islam.* UPENA.

Harun, M. F., and Aini, I. N. (2009). *Pembangunan Masyarakat Orang Asli Dilema Kemiskinan Dan Terpinggir.* UPENA.

Islamic Relief Worldwide. (2008). *Definitions of Poverty.* Birmingham, UK.

JAWHAR. (2007). *Manual Pengurusan Zakat.* Jabatan Perdana Menteri Malaysia.

Kamali, M. H. (2009). *Maqasid Made Simple.* The International Institute of Islamic Institute (IIIT).

Laderchi, C. R. (2000). *The Monetary Approach to Poverty: A Survey of Concept and Methods.* QEH Paper Series 58.

Laderchi, C. R., Ruhi, S., and Steward, F. (2003). *Does It Matter That We Don't Agree on The Definition of Poverty.* QEH Paper Series 17.

Monzer, K. (1982). "Taxation in an Islamic Economy," in *Fiscal Policy and Resource Allocation in Islam,* edited by Ziauddin Ahmad et al., International Centre for Research in Islamic Economics, King Abdul Aziz University, Jeddah.

Nolan, B., and Whelan, C. (2010). "Using Non-Monetary Deprivation Indicators to Analyse Poverty and Social Exclusions: Lesson from Europe?" *Journal of Policy Analysis and Management Spring, 29*(2), 305–325.

Nolan, B., and Whelan, C. (2012). "Using Non-Monetary Deprivation Indicators to Analyze European Poverty and Social Exclusion," in *Counting the Poor: New Thinking About European Poverty Measures and Lessons for United States,* edited by J. D. Besharov and A. K. Couch, Oxford University Press, Oxford.

Nussbaum, M. (1997). *Capabilities and Human Rights.* Fordham Law Review.

Nussbaum, M. (2003). "Capabilities as Fundamental Entitlements: Sen and Social Justice." *Feminist Economics, 9*(2–3), 33–59.

Rasool, M. S. A., Harun, M. F., Mohd, S. A. M., and Idris, N. (2011). "Poverty Measurement in Malaysian *Zakat* Institutions: A Theoretical Survey." *Jurnal Ekonomi Malaysia, 45,* 123–129.

Rasool, M. S. A., Salleh, A. F., and Harun, M. F. M. (2012). "Poverty Measurement by Islamic Institutions." *World Academy of Science, Engineering and Technology, 6*(5), 813–815.

Ravallion, M. (1998). *Poverty Lines in Theory and Practice*. LMS Working Paper 133, The World Bank.

Ravallion, M. (2012). *Poor or Just Feeling Poor. On Using Subjective Data in Measuring Poor.* Policy Research Working Paper 5968, The World Bank.

Rosbi, A. R., and Sanep, A. (2010). *Pengukuran keberkesanan agiham zakat: Perspektif maqasid al-syariah.* Proceedings of Seventh International Conference The Tawhidi Epistemologi: *Zakat* and Waqf Fund. 6th–7th January. Institut Islam Hadhari, UKM Bangi, Malaysia.

Salleh, A. F., and Rasool, M. S. A. (2013). "An Alternative Measure of Well-being from Sharīʿah Principles," in *Islamic Philanthropy for Ummah Excellence,* edited by N. Mohamad, et al. Institut Kajian *Zakat* Malaysia, Universiti Teknologi MARA.

Sen, A. K. (1977). *Development as Freedom (DAF)*. Oxford University Press, Oxford.

Sen, A. K. (1987). "The Standard of Living: Lives and Capabilities," in *The Standard of Living*, edited by G. Hawthorn, The Tanner Lectures (Clare Hall), Cambridge.

Sen, A. K. (1992). *Inequality Reexamined*. Harvard University Press, Cambridge, MA.

Shirazi, N. S., and Amin, M. F. (2009). "Poverty Elimination Through Potential *Zakat* Collection in OIC Countries: Revisited." *The Pakistan Development Review, 48*(4), 739–754.

Shirvanian, A., and Bakhshoodeh, M. (2012). "'Investigating poverty in Rural Iran': The Multidimensional Poverty Approach." *Agricultural Sciences 3* (5), 640–650.

Wagle, U. (2005). "Multidimensional Poverty Measurement with Economic Well-Being, Capability and Social Inclusion: A Case from Katmandu, Nepal." *Journal of Human Development, 6*(3), 301–328.

Wagle, U. (2008). "Mutidimensional Poverty: An Alternative Measurement Approach for the United States?" *Social Science Research, 37*(2), 559–580.

Wagle, U. (2009). "Capability Deprivation and Income Poverty in the United States, 1994 and 2004: The Measurement Outcomes and Demographic Profiles." *Social Indicators Research, 94*(3), 509–533.

Yusuf al-Qardawi. (1980). "*Fiqh al-zakah.*" Translated by Monzer Kahf, Scientific Publishing Centre, King Abdul Aziz University, Jeddah.

CHAPTER 15

Theory and an Application of Maqāṣid al-Sharīʿah-Based Measurement Index for Socio-Economic Development: Index Method and Prototype Index

Salman Syed Ali and Hamid Hasan

1 Introduction

Debate on how to measure development and progress of societies has never ended. Different normative theories have been proposed and many more measures or indices have been devised (Stanton 2007). These range from simple measure such as GDP per capita to more complex Human Development Index (HDI). Some of these indices

S. S. Ali (✉)
Islamic Research and Training Institute,
Islamic Development Bank, Jeddah, Saudi Arabia
e-mail: ssyedali@isdb.org

H. Hasan
King Faisal University, Hufuf, Saudi Arabia

IIIE, International Islamic University, Islamabad, Pakistan

S. S. Ali (ed.), *Towards a Maqāṣid al-Sharīʿah Index of Socio-Economic Development*, Palgrave Studies in Islamic Banking, Finance, and Economics,
https://doi.org/10.1007/978-3-030-12793-0_15

measured progress and development through the degree of reduction in income poverty. Some went further and tried to measure growth in social opportunities and distribution of those opportunities within low-income groups so as to measure inclusiveness of growth (e.g. Ali and Son 2007). Some went even further and attempted to measure capabilities deprivation and the extent to which these deprivations can be reduced (e.g. Alkire and Foster 2011). Going further, some have focused on freedom deprivation to measure reduction in multidimensional poverty.

However, all these measures involve value judgement. Without a sound moral underpinning, they remain ad hoc because moral values cannot be created from empirical observations only. Revealed knowledge provided by revealed religion can provide the purpose of life and moral values that can underpin the purpose and scope of measurement of well-being and development.

This paper begins with rationalization of why and what to measure (Sect. 2). It then provides an axiomatic approach (Sect. 3), and an application with data to measure Maqāṣid al-Sharī'ah-based development (Sect. 4) with some conclusions and thoughts on further possibilities.

2 Theoretical Framework

Islam, which is continuation and completion of the monotheistic religions, provides a law of dos and don'ts called Sharī'ah. Scholars who examined Sharī'ah rules observed that essentially all dos and don'ts that are in Sharī'ah are for protection and continuity of human society. They found that these rules are there for protection of five aspects or dimensions:

1. Protection of self (or life);
2. Protection of faith;
3. Protection of wealth;
4. Protection of intellect; and
5. Protection of progeny.

Protections mentioned here are not for one-time protection. They are also not restricted to protection against degradation from the existing level of each dimension (say the dimension of life) [in whatever way it is measured], but they are also about enhancement and improvement. In *fiqh* terminology, it is about *daf al-mafasid* (removal of degrading factors and constraints) *jalb al masaleh* (attainment and enhancement of benefits) (for a disucssion in the context of economics see, Siddiqui 2009). Thus for example, protection of self (or life) can include protection against:

- Attack on life (by others or self-inflicted),
- Violent crimes,
- Injury (by others or self-inflicted or due to exogenous factors),
- Loss of dignity and honour,
- Disease,
- Unhealthy living conditions,
- Hunger,
- Poverty,
- Fear and Insecurity of life, etc.

From the enhancement aspect it can include:

- Health,
- Quality of life, Feeling of contentment,
- Moderation in consumption,
- Healthy habits, etc.

This opens up the question of minimum protection and then also enhancement of the dimension and likelihood of its sustainability at the achieved level. All these aspects are desirable. Since Sharī'ah provides some basic protections, therefore anything that strengthens and enhances those protections is also desirable.

2.1 Objectives of Islam vs Objectives of Sharī'ah

The objective or purpose of Islam is to guide human beings to make them successful, individually and collectively in al-Akhirah (long run) and in this world (short run). It is also to save them from the great failure or the ultimate great loss.

The purposes of all prophets to mankind had been: (i) to recite them ayat of Allah, (ii) cleanse impurities of all kinds from humans and enhance them, (iii) teach them the book, (iv) provide them wisdom, and (v) teach them that they did not know.[1]

Since the book (Sharī'ah) deals with legal issues (the critical dos and don'ts), therefore its purpose is to provide protection of some basic elements: self, faith, wealth, intellect, and progeny. So that (a) the life continues and (b) it becomes easy to qualify the test and (c) the opportunity of testing remains until the dooms day (*yaoum al-qiyamah*).

Whereas, *hikmah* (wisdom) is more general it expands to moral values, enhancement of collective life, and understanding of the basics of Sharī'ah. It pertains to development, refinements, and enhancements of success in this world and in al-Akhirah by guiding us to best ways for putting Sharī'ah into practice. It pertains to how we can act in our collective life based on our common understanding of Sharī'ah while taking into consideration each other's psychology and our own position in this universe. The Quranic reference to Luqman's wisdom points to our above understanding and explanation.

Tazkiyah on the other hand pertains more to individual souls, cleansing them of impurities (physical, mental, and spiritual) that provides enhancement and growth of individual character. It can be collective only in the sense of aggregating over individuals.

Measurement of society's development for success in this world and chances of success of average individual in al-Akhirah will require methods to measure these three major aspects (*tazkiyah*, book and *hikmah*). The progress in attainment of the objectives of Sharī'ah provides the basic minimum for humans. The progress in *hikmah* attainment provides measurement of collective outcome. The progress in *tazkiyah* attainment provides measurement focused at individualistic level that is in hearts and hidden.

[1] Prophet Ibrahim's supplication to Allah mentioned in Quran (2:129) was for raising a prophet from among them who shall recite to them Allah's ayat and teach them His book and wisdom, and purify them. Allah accepted this supplication and sent His Prophet Muhammad (*sallalah-o-alaihi-wassallam*) but gave His own hierarchy of these four demands/tasks/requirements from the Prophet. Allah moved the fourth task to be the second and added a fifth task as well. Quran (2:151) mentions that Allah has sent among you a prophet from among you who recites to you Allah's ayat, purifies you and teaches you the Book and wisdom and teaches you that which you did not know.

2.2 On the Measurement of Socio-Economic Development

We cannot measure *tazkiyah* (and *taqwah*) of others, and we are not required to do this evaluation.[2] So, this aspect has to be dropped from our measurement. The nature of *tazkiyah* (and *taqwah*) is such that it determines the outcome of the test that Allah has created in this world for humans. This test is in longevity of life as well as in short life; it is in plenty as well as in dearth of wealth; it is in having offspring as well as infertility; it is also in having high intellect as well as in low intellect; and in high state of *iman* and low state of *iman*. Therefore, again we cannot conclude that the *tazkiyah* is increasing or decreasing with wealth, life, progeny, or intellect. Hence the socio-economic progress indicator we are after will abstract away from this aspect.

In this context, one can understand the meaning of the authentic hadith. The Prophet (peace and blessings of Allah be upon him) said: "How wonderful is the situation of the believer, for all his affairs are good. If something good happens to him, he gives thanks for it and that is good for him; if something bad happens to him, he bears it with patience, and that is good for him. This does not apply to anyone but the believer" (Narrated by Muslim, No. 2999).[3]

Suhaib (R.A.) reported that Allah's Messenger (ﷺ) said: strange are the ways of a believer for there is good in every affair of his and this is not the case with anyone else except in the case of a believer for if he has an occasion to feel delight, he thanks (God), thus there is a good for him in it, and if he gets into trouble and shows resignation (and endures it patiently), there is a good for him in it.[4]

حَدَّثَنَا هَدَّابُ بْنُ خَالِدٍ الأَزْدِيُّ، وَشَيْبَانُ بْنُ فَرُّوخَ، جَمِيعًا عَنْ سُلَيْمَانَ بْنِ الْمُغِيرَةِ، - وَاللَّفْظُ لِشَيْبَانَ - حَدَّثَنَا سُلَيْمَانُ، حَدَّثَنَا ثَابِتٌ، عَنْ عَبْدِ الرَّحْمَنِ بْنِ أَبِي لَيْلَى، عَنْ صُهَيْبٍ، قَالَ قَالَ رَسُولُ اللَّهِ صلى الله عليه وسلم " عَجَبًا لأَمْرِ الْمُؤْمِنِ إِنَّ أَمْرَهُ كُلَّهُ خَيْرٌ وَلَيْسَ ذَاكَ لأَحَدٍ إِلاَّ لِلْمُؤْمِنِ إِنْ أَصَابَتْهُ سَرَّاءُ شَكَرَ فَكَانَ خَيْرًا لَهُ وَإِنْ أَصَابَتْهُ ضَرَّاءُ صَبَرَ فَكَانَ خَيْرًا لَهُ ".[5]

[2] One can do self-evaluation of own *iman* and *taqwa* but not of others in any real sense.

[3] http://hadithcheck.blogspot.com/2010/11/sahih-how-wonderful-is-affair-of.html.

[4] http://sunnah.com/urn/271380.

[5] Reference: Sahih Muslim 2999.
In-book reference: Book 55, Hadith 82.
USC-MSA web (English) reference: Book 42, Hadith 7138.

However, among the tests too much or too little of a good thing pose sever test of humans as compared to having moderate amounts of good things that are sufficient. If someone is given plenty of wealth than others then if such people are spending their wealth on themselves, their family and on others as charity then this would be beneficial for them as well as beneficial for the society. We would say the society is progressing.

Simultaneous to the above message of *indeterminacy*, it is also clear from Islam's message that Allah does not want people to put themselves in undue hardships neither in acts of worship (*ibādah*) nor in their mutual dealings (*muamalāt*); He does not recommend inviting tests and difficulties on themselves. Allah would like to provide ease over difficulty and would like his slaves also to choose in similar way. Thus, there is a clear preference for ease and lightness over difficulties and burden. Due to this, health is preferable over disease (though there can be test in both situations), sufficiency over poverty, open available time over shortage of time, happiness over misery, etc.

2.3 Narrowing the Focus of Measurement

Since the objectives of laws are to provide a minimum level of protection, it is relatively easier to measure and compare progress towards achievement of that minimum than measuring and comparing progress across societies through variables that do not have an upper bound. With minimum level attainment approach, we can measure whether or not these protections are universally available to everyone in the existing and the future population. If these protections are not available to all, then the progress in this direction can be measured by finding the proportion of the existing population who do not fall in the deprived group. Or 1 minus the proportion of population to whom those protections are not available. In this method of measurement, the target/goal becomes well-defined and the gap between the present position and the target provides a measure of society's progress. Therefore, we intend to focus on the "book" part and gauge the progress in terms of attainment of minimum threshold for each *maqsad* (objective) of Sharī'ah. While t*azkiyah* and *hikmah* (which respectively come before and after the "book" in the hierarchy) will be captured indirectly, as the attainment of the legal objectives at a larger population level is not possible without progress in these other two aspects.

In the section below, we provide an axiomatic approach with an application to measure Maqāṣid al-Sharī'ah-based development. In this example, we have used only the opinion surveys, however, it need not be restricted to such. Objective and verifiable economic and social data can also be combined.

3 Axioms and Index

3.1 *Practical Aspects of Measurement*

The moral backslide along with human sufferings and socio-economic decline in most of the Muslim countries, and in developing countries in general pose serious policy challenges for these countries in the context of human welfare. The safeguarding of faith, life, intellect, posterity, and property—the Maqāṣid al-Sharī'ah (MS)—has been considered as a pivotal to enhancing human welfare by eminent classical Muslim scholars like al-Ghazali and al-Shatiabi. Relatively more recently, Chapra (2008), among others, emphasizes the use of MS in socio-economic development of Muslim world. There has been a need to build an information base on MS to assist policy makers in realizing these goals (Maqāṣid) which not only cover social and economic dimensions, like human development, but also include values, morality, family, and faith and thus provide an encompassing framework for development in Muslim countries. The paper aims to contribute to this effort by developing a framework by deriving axioms from Qura'n and Sunnah related to each objective of Sharī'ah and then construct a Maqāṣid al-Sharī'ah (MS) index following Alkire and Santos (2010) and Alkire and Foster (2011) dual cut-off multidimensional counting approach. The paper selects a counting approach vis-à-vis a welfare approach since the former is an application tool whereas latter is a theoretical framework (see Atkinson 2003, for comparison between these two approaches). Among the counting approaches, the paper chooses Alkire-Foster (AF) approach due to its axiomatic properties and empirical content. Since no survey questionnaire is specifically designed for measuring MS, the MS are quantified by grouping the survey questions in World Values Survey (WVS) that seem to relate to each dimension of MS. The advantage of using WVS dataset is that it is available in public domain for most of the countries and hence provides a common dataset for a cross-country comparison. The questionnaire used is checked for conformity with the MS axioms.

As noted above, the multidimensionality of human welfare has long been recognized by Muslim scholars and much earlier then Amartya Sen. However, Sen (1985, 2000) and Haq (1995) make it popular and usable by developing HDI. The parsimony and multidimensionality have made HDI a very good indicator for evaluating human development across the world. Inspired by this experience, many scholars have attempted to extend HDI in MS direction (see, e.g., Dar 2004; Anto 2009; Rehman and Askari 2010; Amin et al. 2013). Although these indices facilitate a cross-country comparison and help policy makers to set goals, yet they do not provide details or decomposition at regional or at household/individual levels within each country. Such details could be useful for effective policy implementation at grass root level and could also be applied for project appraisal, and for evaluation of sectoral or institutional performance. At the same time, it could be aggregated to show an overall picture. The present paper is a first attempt in this direction.

3.2 Axioms for Maqāṣid al-Sharī'ah Measurement

The objectives of Sharī'ah could be achieved in the highest degree only when Sharī'ah is implemented in true letter and spirit. The section illustrates the desirable properties of an MS index with a key objective to attain justice in a society. These desirable properties are mentioned as axioms. In general, higher values of MS index are desirable but for the MS deprivation index the lower values are appropriate.

These axioms are derived from the Sharī'ah (Qur'an and Hadith). One of these *ahadith* is about the questions to be asked from every person by Allah on the Day of Judgement. These questions are related to life, youth, earning and spending wealth, and knowledge, which can be linked to four of the five Maqāṣid al-Sharī'ah: preservation of life, preservation of posterity, preservation of property, and preservation of intellect respectively whereas the fifth—preservation of faith—encompasses all five questions: *The prophet Muhammad (S.A.W.) said: "The son of Adam will not pass away from Allah until he is asked about five things: how he lived his life, and how he utilized his youth, with what means did he earn his wealth, how did he spend his wealth, and what did he do with his knowledge"* (Sahih hadith reported by Imam Al-Tirmithi).

Because of the importance of these five dimensions for this world and the world hereafter, we list some of the axioms for each MS dimensions to guide us in developing or selecting appropriate indicators for MS:

1. **Wealth Protection Axioms**:
   1.1 Transfer: MS index should increase whenever *Zakāt and Sadaqat* are transferred from an individual above the poverty line to an individual below the poverty line.
   1.2 Intergenerational Transfer: MS index should increase whenever inheritance amount is transferred according to Sharī'ah to all heirs.
   1.3 Exchange: MS index should decrease whenever money is borrowed/lent on interest (*Ribā*).
   1.4 Spending: if spending increases in *Israf* or *Tabzeer*, then MS index should decrease in value. In case of moderation (*Iqtisād*) in spending in *Ḥalaal* and *Mubaaḥ* goods and services, then MS index should increase in value.
   1.5 Earning: If *ḥalaal* earning increases, then MS index should increase and if earning through *ḥaraam* means (like gambling, hoarding, less-than full measurement *tatfeef*, *ribā*, etc.) increases, then MS index should decrease.
   1.6 Accumulation: if wealth accumulates with regular payment of *Zakāt and Sadaqat*, then MS index should increase, and if wealth accumulates without any payment of *Zakāt*, then MS index should decrease.
   1.7 Risk: if risk of loss of wealth increases, then MS index should decrease.
   1.8 Fairness: if there is fair access to earning, then MS index should increase.

2. **Life Protection Axioms**:
   2.1 Security: MS index should increase when life security increases.
   2.2 Health: MS index should increase if there is an access to health facilities.
   2.3 Time use and leisure activities: MS index should increase if time is better utilized in Sharī'ah compliant activities.
   2.4 Physical fitness: MS index should increase for easy and affordable access to sports and fitness facilities.

3. **Intellect Protection Axioms**:
   3.1 Fairness: MS index should increase if there is fair access to learning for all.
   3.2 Harmfulness: MS index should decrease if there is an easy access to activities harmful for intellect.

   3.3 Practice: MS index should increase if religious knowledge is turned into practice.
   3.4 Education: MS index should increase with the level of education.
   3.5 Research: MS index should increase for useful and applied research.

4. **Faith Protection Axioms**:
   4.1 Prayers: MS index should increase for easy access to Masjid for daily prayers.
   4.2 Umrah/Hajj: MS index should increase with affordability for performing Umrah/Hajj.
   4.3 Fasting: MS index should increase for convenience in fasting during *Ramadhan*.
   4.4 Zakāt: MS index should increase for easy access to zakāt collection/payment.
   4.5 Religious education: MS index should increase with easy access to quality Islamic education.
   4.6 Time spent: MS index should increase for time spent on religious education and programmes or time spent in Masjid.
   4.7 *Ghuloo*: MS index should decrease for exceeding what is required.

5. **Posterity Protection Axioms**:
   5.1 Marriage: MS index should increase for easy and affordable access to marriage.
   5.2 Family life: MS index should increase for happy family life.
   5.3 Solidarity: MS index should increase if children spending time with their parents and grand parents.
   5.4 Immorality: MS index should decrease for access to immoral activities.
   5.5 Mortality: MS index should decrease for child mortality in family.
   5.6 Home: MS index should increase for mother staying at home for upbringing children.
   5.7 Time spent: MS index should increase if children spent time in Sharī'ah compliant activities.
   5.8 Respect: MS index should increase for respect of parents.
   5.9 Religious practice for kids: MS index should increase if children memorizing part or whole Qur'an and going to Masjid.

3.3 Data and Methodology

3.3.1 Data

The most important aspect of developing MS index is to have indicators fully represent MS dimensions. Ideally, indicators related to MS should be developed from a questionnaire that satisfies above axioms. But practically such questionnaire is not available at the moment, and we need to search for proxies that do the job. The survey data that is available on public domain and that provides somewhat relevant information is WVS data. It has many survey rounds, and each round has slightly different questionnaire. The latest survey for 2010–2012 has not yet completed, but it has more relevant questions than the questions asked in the available survey data for 2005–2008 and for earlier years.

The present study uses survey data for 2005–2008 for Pakistan to illustrate the application of methodology used in this study. It analyses the survey questions for 2010–2012 and 2005–2008 for consistency with MS axioms.

In Table 1 shows the grouping of survey questions for each MS dimension such that the association between indicators within each dimension is theoretically strong. We list the variables related to a dimension given in the latest WVS. Table 2 gives MS dimensions with indicators for WVS 2010–2012. A comparison of these two tables shows that WVS 2010–2012 is more close to the axioms:

3.3.2 Methodology

The AF methodology proposes a family of multidimensional measures by extending the unidimensional Foster-Greer-Thorbeke (FGT) poverty measures. Among these measures, the adjusted headcount index (M_0) is an appropriate choice where survey responses are ordinal in nature. The calculation of M_0 in a sequence of 12 steps is given in Alkire and Foster (2007) whereas in terms of mathematical notations and structure, it is given in Alkire and Foster (2011). In what follows, we summarize 12 steps to calculate M_0:

Step-1: Choose unit of analysis
Step-2: Choose dimensions
Step-3: Choose indicators
Step-4: Set poverty lines (first cut-off)

Table 1 Maqāṣid al-Sharīʿah dimensions and their indicators in WVS 2010–2012

Dimension	*Variable*	*Indicator hint (see full question in the survey)*
Fatih	V145	Attendance in religious services
	V146	Frequency in prayer
	V147	Religious, non-religious or atheist person
	V148	Belief in God
Life	V55	Freedom of choice in life
	V177	Preferred not to go out at night
	V179	Victim of crime last year
	V180	Immediate family victim of crime last year
	V183	A war involving my country
	V184	A terrorist attack
	V185	A civil war
	V188	Gone without enough food to eat
	V189	Felt unsafe from crime in your home
Intellect	V182	Not being able to give my children a good education
	V248	Highest level of education
	V172	Alcohol consumption in streets
	V175	Drug sale in streets
Posterity	V203	Homosexuality: justifiable
	V203A	Prostitution
	V204	Abortion
	V205	Divorce
	V206	Sex before marriage
	V209	Parents beating children
Property	V59	Satisfaction with financial situation
	V171	Occurrence of robberies
	V181	Worry about losing job or not finding a job
	V239	Which income group you belong to

Source Authors' own

Step-5: Apply poverty lines
Step-6: Count the deprivations for each person
Step-7: Set the second cut-off
Step-8: Apply second cut-off (k) to obtain the set of poor persons and censor all nonpoor data
Step-9: Calculate the headcount (H)

$H = q/n$ where q is the number of people who are multidimensionally poor, and n is the total population

Step-10: Calculate the average poverty gap (A)

Table 2 Maqāṣid al-Sharīʿah dimensions and their indicators in WVS 2005–2008

MS dimension	*WVS 2005–2008*	*Survey questions hints*
	Variable ref.	
Faith		
faith1	a006	Importance in life: religion
faith2	f028	How often you attend religious services
Life		
life1	a009	State of health
life2	a170	Satisfaction with your life
Intellect		
intellect1	d071	Traits in women: women educated
intellect2	f124	Justifiable: drinking alcohol
intellect3	x025	Highest education level attained
Posterity		
post1	a001	Importance in life: family
post2	d019	A woman has to have children to be fulfilled
post3	f118	Justifiable: homosexuality
post4	f119	Prostitution
post5	f120	Abortion
post6	f121	Divorce
Property		
prop1	c006	Satisfaction with financial situation of household
prop2	x047	Scales of income
prop3	x047r	Income level

Source Authors' own

$A = \frac{\sum_1^q c}{q}$ where c is deprivation score of multidimensionally poor and is obtained by adding the deprivation score in each dimension. If a poor person is deprived in three dimensions, then his score is obtained as follows: $c = c_1 + c_2 + c_3$.

Step-11: Calculate the adjusted headcount (M_0)

$$M_0 = H \cdot A$$

Step-12: Decompose by group and breakdown by dimension

$$\text{Contrib}_j = \frac{\sum_1^q c_j/n}{M_0}$$

It shows contribution of dimension j to multidimensional poverty.

The range of each dimension is computed by summing up the minimum and maximum values of its indicators, measured on Likert scales, and its cut-off value or deprivation threshold using general perception in an Islamic society. The summation of indicator values is justified for dimensional unity and reduces random measurement error in each indicator.

Following the methodology given above, we develop a distribution matrix that shows values of each dimension received by each individual. Then we count the number of persons falling below cut-off in each dimension and represent it by a deprivation matrix and add deprivations count in all dimensions by a vector of deprivation count assuming equal weights.

We apply second cut-off to number of dimensions to check how many individuals are considered poor given the number of dimensions. Initially, we assume that any person deprived in more than two dimensions ($k=2$) is considered poor in Maqāṣid al-Sharī'ah (MS). Applying the second cut-off generates censored deprivation matrix and censored vector of deprivation count.

Using FGT poverty measures in multidimensions, we compute MS shortfall headcount index (H), MS shortfall intensity index (A), and MS shortfall headcount adjusted index (M_0). The contribution of each dimension in overall MS shortfall is also computed. All of these indices help policy makers to concentrate on areas of improvement in terms of formulation and effective implementation of economic, social, and public policies in these areas.

4 Application

4.1 Application: A Case of Pakistan

The latest WVS has many questions related to MS, as noted above, but it has not been completed yet (at the time of writing). Therefore, the study uses WVS 2005–2008 for Pakistan with a sample size of 2000 individuals to illustrate the application of AF methodology. The WVS 2005–2008 has many questions not directly related to each dimension of MS. Given the limitation, this survey provides a proxy for each dimension. Nevertheless, the study illustrates how the counting approach could be applied using a survey data.

The following table shows grouping of indicators according to their closeness with a dimension using individual as a unit of analysis.

Table 3 shows MS dimensions and their minimum and maximum values. The poverty line or first cut-off is determined according to the common belief of an Islamic society.

Table 3 Maqāṣid al-Sharīʿah dimensions and their indicators with deprivation cut-offs

	WVS 2005–2008			*Deprivation*
MS dimension with deprivation criterion	*Variable ref.*	*Min value*	*Max value*	*Cut-off point*
Faith				
faith1	a006	1	4	3
faith2	f028	1	6	4
		2	10	7
Anyone having score below 7 considered poor in faith dimension				
Life				
life1	a009	1	4	2
life2	a170	1	9	5
		2	13	7
Anyone having score below 7 considered poor in life dimension				
Intellect				
intellect1	d071	1	5	3
intellect2	f124	1	9	7
intellect3	x025	1	8	5
		3	22	**15**
Anyone having score below 15 considered poor in intellect dimension				
Posterity				
post1	a001	1	4	3
post2	d019	0	1	1
post3	f118	1	4	4
post4	f119	1	8	8
post5	f120	1	10	8
post6	f121	1	9	6
		5	36	**30**
Anyone having score below 30 considered poor in posterity dimension				
Property				
prop1	c006	1	9	5
prop2	x047	1	10	5
prop3	x047r	1	3	2
		3	22	**12**
Anyone having score below 12 considered poor in property dimension				

Source Authors' own

4.2 Results and Discussion

Following the AF methodology, the headcount index (H) is 39% which indicates incidence of poverty in the sense of falling short from a desirable level in Maqāṣid Sharī'ah. In the present example, it means 39% of the sample population is poor in more than two dimensions. The intensity of poverty is calculated by average deprivation (A) which turns out to be 31%. That means the average poor person is deprived in 31% of the dimensions. The M_0 which shows multidimensional poverty in MS in the present context is calculated by multiplying H and A, that is, the headcount (H) is adjusted for intensity (A). Surprisingly, it is as low as 12% since intensity is low as compared to incidence of poverty. In Table 4 shows contribution of each dimension in overall poverty M_0 (Fig. 1).

The lowest contribution in M_0 is posterity, whereas the highest contribution in M_0 is property. That is, protection of material wealth is below the minimum desired threshold and it is contributing about 50% for keeping people below the multidimensional MS-based poverty. While the lowest contributor to the overall shortfall in achieving Maqāṣid al-Sharī'ah-based progress is from posterity protection dimension. Based on this analysis, an immediate policy direction for Pakistan is to focus attention on improving the safety and security of wealth of the poor and weak and improving the law and order situation.

In this example, we have worked only with a lower bound (a minimum), being above it is desirable for the society. However, there are situations where excesses are also bad and in contravention of the objectives of Sharī'ah. The counting approach can be modified to take care of both limits. In case of consumption, for example, the number of people below a threshold level of consumption indicates a shortfall from the socially desired level using Maqāṣid al-Sharī'ah perspective. Similarly, number of people involved in excessive consumption (*israf*) from

Table 4 Shows contribution of each dimension to overall shortfall/deprivation/poverty (M_0)

Dimension	*Contribution (%)*
Fatih	9.40
Life	16.67
Intellect	19.60
Posterity	4.20
Property	50.00
Overall	100

Source Authors' own

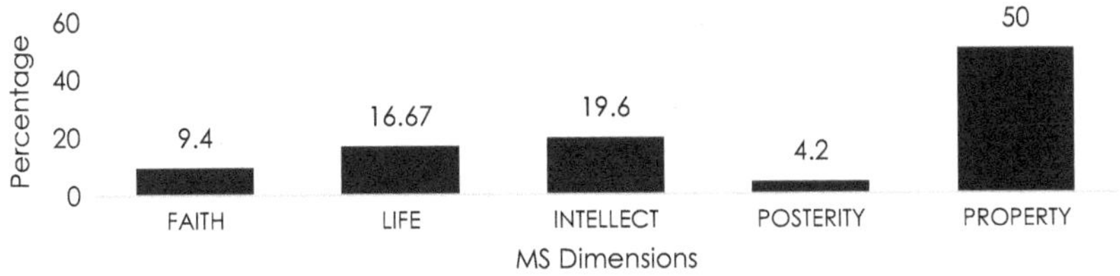

Fig. 1 Contribution of MS dimensions to multidimensional poverty M_0 in Pakistan (*Source* Authors' own)

the norm (e.g. becoming obese) or when there exists sever poverty are also not desirable. A confirming set or compliant set between these two extremes can be created and its members counted to create a development indicator.

4.3 Comparison with Other Estimates

Comparing the multidimensional poverty using Maqāṣid al-Sharī'ah-based Index (MS Index) with the MPI measure calculated for Pakistan by the OPHI and UNDP, we find that Pakistan fared better in MS-based Index M_0, as well as in the incidence (H) and average intensity (A) of poverty. Though, strictly speaking, the two measures are not comparable due to differences in their definition of dimensions, deprivation threshold cut-offs, and the survey data. The MS-based approach used more dimensions and higher thresholds for deprivation cut-off than the OPHI-UNDP index, yet the poverty numbers are lower. This indicates better socio-economic conditions in the Maqāṣid al-Sharī'ah dimensions.

Comparing the MS-based poverty with the usual income poverty, we can say that there are more poor people in terms of MS-based poverty in Pakistan ($H = 39\%$) than income-poor who fall behind $1.25 a day (22.6%) (Table 5).

These differences are easy to visualize in the following two figures. We also note that in general, a Maqāṣid al-Sharī'ah-based Index can be different from an income-based index or the other multidimensional indexes. However, in the present case, the difference is also because of the nature of data. We have used a combination of opinion and facts survey as opposed to only facts survey that are generally used in the other measures (Figs. 2 and 3).

Table 5 Comparison of MS-based poverty index with other poverty indexes

Calculation method	*Survey*	*Year*	*Multidimensional Poverty Index (MPI = H × A)*	*Incidence of poverty (H) (%)*	*Average intensity across the poor (A) (%)*
MS based I	WVS	2008	0.12	39.0	31.0
OPHI and UNDP	DHS	2007	0.264[a]	49.4[a]	53.4[a]
Percentage of income poor ($1.25 a day)	HIES	2006		22.6[b]	
Percentage of income poor ($2.00 a day)	HIES	2006		61.0[b]	
Percentage of poor (national poverty line)	HIES	2006		22.3[b]	

Notes
[a]OPHI (2011). Country Briefing: Multidimensional Poverty Index (MPI) at a Glance
[b]The World Bank (2011). "World Development Indicators." Washington, DC
Source Authors' own

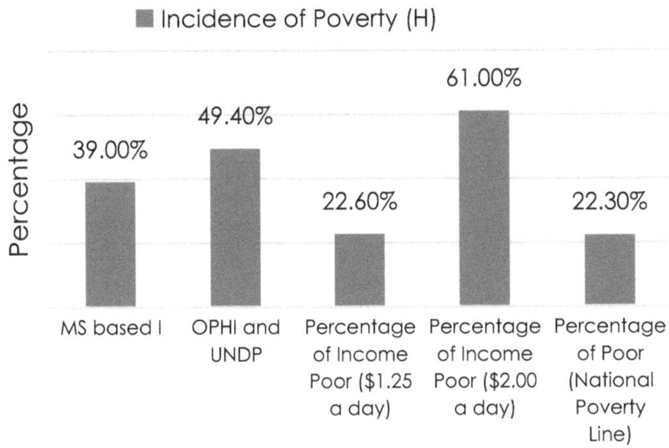

Fig. 2 Comparison of poverty using different measures

Fig. 3 Comparison of multidimensional poverty

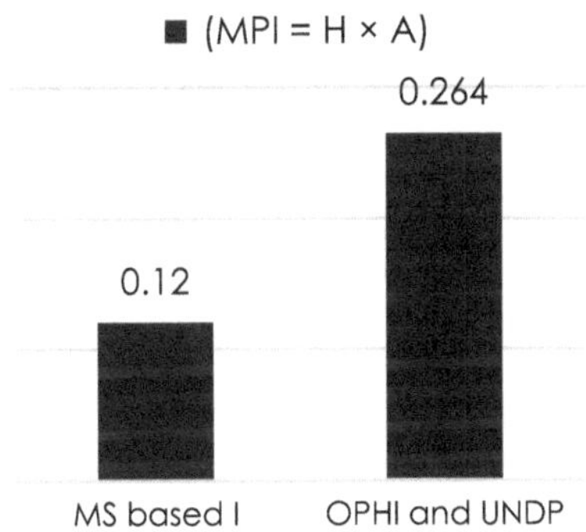

References

Ali, Ifzal, and Son, Hyun Hwa. (2007). Measuring Inclusive Growth. *Asian Development Review*, 24(1), pp. 11–31.

Alkire, S., and Foster, J. (2007, revised in 2008). Counting and multidimensional poverty measurement. OPHI Working Paper 7, University of Oxford.

Alkire, Sabina, and Foster, James. (2011). Counting and Multidimensional Poverty Measurement. *Journal of Public Economics*, 95(7), pp. 476–487. https://doi.org/10.1016/j.jpubeco.2010.11.006.

Alkire, S., and Santos, M. E. (2010). 'Acute Multidimensional Poverty: A New Index for Developing Countries'. OPHI Working Paper 38, Oxford University; also published as Human Development Research Paper 2010/11.

Amin, Ruzita Mohd, Abdullah Yusof, Selamah, Haneef, Mohamed Aslam, Mohammed, Mustafa Omar, and Oziev, Gapur. (2013). 'The Integrated Development Index (I-Dex): A New Comprehensive Approach to Measuring Human Development', Paper presented at 9th International Conference on Islamic Economics and Finance: Growth, Equity and Stability: An Islamic Perspective. Istanbul, Turkey. 9-10 September 2013. Published as Chapter 13 in: *Islamic Economic: Theory, Policy and Social Justice*, H. A. El-Karanshawy et al. (Editors), Bloomsbury Qatar Foundation, 2015, pp. 159–172.

Anto, M. H. (2009). Introducing an Islamic Human Development Index (I-HDI) to Measure Development in OIC Countries. *Islamic Economic Studies*, 19(2), pp. 69–95.

Atkinson, A. B. (2003). Multidimensional Deprivation: Contrasting Social Welfare and Counting Approaches. *The Journal of Economic Inequality*, 1(1), pp. 51–65. https://doi.org/10.1023/A:1023903525276.

Chapra, M. Umer. (2008). The Islamic Vision of Development in the Light of Maqāsid al-Sharī'ah. (Research Paper). Jeddah: Islamic Research and Training Institute (IRTI).

Dar, Humayon A. (2004). On Making Human Development More Humane. *International Journal of Social Economics*, 31(11/12), pp. 1071–1088.

Haq, Mahbub ul. (1995). *Reflections on Human Development*. Oxford University Press, Delhi.

Muslim, Sahi Muslim. Available at http://sunnah.com/urn/271380 and http://hadithcheck.blogspot.com.

OPHI. (2011). Country Briefing: Multidimensional Poverty Index (MPI) at a Glance.

Rehman, S. S., and Askari, H. (2010). How Islamic Are Islamic Countries? *Global Economy Journal*, 10(2), pp. 1–29.

Sen, Amartya. (1985). *Commodities and Capabilities*, North Holland, Amsterdam.

Sen, Amartya. (2000). A Decade of Human Development. *Journal of Human Development*, 1(1), pp. 17–23.

Siddiqui, Muhammad Nejatullah. (2009). Maqasid-e-Shariat (in Urdu) [Objectives of the Sharī'ah], Markazi Maktabah-e-Islami, New Delhi.

Stanton, Elizabeth A. (2007). *The Human Development Index: A History*. Political Economy Research Institute, University of Massachusetts-Amherst Working Paper No. 127, February. Available at http://scholarworks.umass.edu/cgi/viewcontent.cgi?article=1101&context=peri_workingpapers.

World Bank. (2011). "World Development Indicators." Washington, DC. http://en.wikipedia.org/wiki/Multidimensional_Poverty_Index.

Index

S. S. Ali (ed.), *Towards a Maqāṣid al-Sharīʿah Index of Socio-Economic Development*, Palgrave Studies in Islamic Banking, Finance, and Economics,
https://doi.org/10.1007/978-3-030-12793-0

Kolibri 360 GmbH
Ferdinand-Jühlke-Straße 7
99095 Erfurt, Deutschland
produktsicherheit@kolibri360.de